Tariff Wars and the Politics

of Jacksonian America

New Perspectives on Jacksonian History
Mark Cheathem, Cumberland University,
and Beth Salerno, Saint Anselm College, series editors

This series examines the period from 1812 to 1861, spanning the decades when Andrew Jackson was a significant figure both in life and in memory. The chronological definition of the series recognizes the importance of the War of 1812 in elevating Jackson to national recognition and his continued importance, even after his death in 1845, to United States politics and society in the years leading up to the Civil War. But while Jackson gives one name to this period, alternative titles of early republic, antebellum, and age of association make clear how political, economic, sectional, and organizational movements intersected to shape this critical era. The editors are particularly interested in books that address the democratization of the United States, broadly defined, and the many groups that jockeyed for power and influence in that process.

Editorial Advisory Board
John Belohlavek, University of South Florida
Andrew K. Frank, Florida State University
Lorri Glover, Saint Louis University
Ronald A. Johnson, Texas State University
Stephen A. Mihm, University of Georgia
Kirsten E. Wood, Florida International University

Tariff Wars and the Politics of Jacksonian America

William K. Bolt

Vanderbilt University Press

NASHVILLE

This book is printed on acid-free paper.
Manufactured in the United States of America

Library of Congress Cataloging-in-Publication Data on file
LC control number 2016015316
LC classification number E381 .B68 2016
Dewey class number 320.973/09034—dc23
LC record available at *lccn.loc.gov/2016015316*

ISBN 978-0-8265-2136-1 (hardcover)
ISBN 978-0-8265-2137-8 (paperback)
ISBN 978-0-8265-2138-5 (ebook)

To William F. Bolt
and
Martin C. Miller

Contents

Illustrations

Tables

Preface

T HE AVERAGE AMERICAN today probably thinks very little about tariffs. During the Jacksonian period, however, the tariff served as a divisive political issue in the decades prior to the Civil War. Generally speaking, those Americans living in the more heavily populated and developed northeastern and mid-Atlantic states supported a high tariff that allowed a national domestic marketplace to develop, while those residing in the more geographically dispersed southern and western states favored a low tariff because they often found it more feasible to import goods from overseas than to ship them in from their neighbors to the north.

Political debates over the tax on imports did not just center on its economic consequences, however. Those were significant, of course, as the tariff, along with federal land sales, was one of the two main revenue streams for the United States government. What Bolt demonstrates is that economics, while important, was not at the heart of southern whites' fear of the tariff. Their concern was the government's power to enforce the tariff and to use the revenue generated as it saw fit. Would the government use tariff revenue to force industrialization and modernization? Would it find a way to take tariff revenue and put it toward the emancipation and colonization of enslaved African Americans? These questions were important ones to southern white enslavers, whose economic, political, and social culture depended upon cash crops and enslaved labor.

Beyond this critical argument is another one: the tariff symbolized what it meant to be an American. A low tariff could produce a reliance on imported goods, which hindered the full flourishing of an American national identity. Those who desired a low tariff were often seen as clinging to a European past and culture that flew in the face of the United States' very independence. On the other hand, a high tariff represented a commitment to a domestic marketplace of production and consumption. The trade-off, however, was that a burgeoning domestic marketplace required industrialization and urbanization. Both of these developments possessed perceived drawbacks: crime, disease, homelessness, and, perhaps most importantly, a lack of economic, personal, and political independence. In sum, at the heart of the tariff debate was the tension that existed between the Hamiltonian vision of a modern, industrial United States capable of competing in the global economy and the Jeffersonian vision of a yeoman republic comprised of independent farmers.

The Jacksonian-era tariff continues to hold an important place in twenty-first-century debates. Internet forums are replete with arguments that the Civil War was fought over the perceived inequality of national tariff policy that punished white southerners for pursuing cash-crop agriculture on the backs of enslaved people. At the heart of that argument, even if its proponents fail to acknowledge it, is the reality that their concern is not historical but political: what can the federal government tell Americans to do with their property and income? In the Jacksonian period, the issue was enslaved African Americans who were held as economic investments; today, the issues range from guns to income taxes. Understanding the Jacksonian-era tariff, therefore, helps us better comprehend concerns about federal power and opposition to it, both then and now.

Mark Cheathem
Cumberland University

Acknowledgments

S O MANY PEOPLE HAVE ASSISTED, encouraged, and supported me in the years that it has taken to complete this work. I am honored to acknowledge their efforts.

Richard Ellis, at the University at Buffalo, first introduced me to the politics of the age of Jackson. His encyclopedic mind always had an answer to whatever question I would pose. I have incorporated his anecdotes and stories into several of my own courses. I am grateful that he took an interest in a young and inexperienced historian and that he shared his knowledge of antebellum politics. When I first began examining the tariff, he provided numerous ideas to explore and investigate. I regret that he did not live to see this work completed.

Dan Feller graciously read and suggested avenues for pursuit for every chapter. His gentle critiques and sharp analysis have improved this work. Dan and his staff at the Papers of Andrew Jackson, Tom Coens and Laura Eve Moss, also provided me with Jackson documents whenever the need arose.

Mark Cheathem also read the entire manuscript, caught several errors, and offered excellent advice to make the book more engaging to a wider audience. Whenever I needed an answer to a question regarding the Age of Jackson, he responded immediately. My editor at Vanderbilt University Press, Eli Bortz, trimmed a lot of fat and eliminated most of the fluff from my prose. Were it not for his edits one can only guess how long this final product might have been.

Some of the friends I made while in Knoxville, Tennessee, continued to aid me in my work on the tariff. Paul Bergeron read the later chapters of the manuscript. He offered insights into the complicated nature of antebellum Tennessee politics. Always an editor, he helped to tighten several chapters too. Aaron Crawford took time out of his busy schedule to comment on numerous chapters as well. He provided documents that he had uncovered while conducting his own research on antebellum Virginia. Wayne Cutler, who allowed me to serve as an assistant editor at the James K. Polk Project, was always willing to discuss Polk and political economy before the Civil War. He allowed me to have access to all the files that the Polk Project had uncovered on Polk and his part in American politics.

My colleagues at Francis Marion University have supported me in various ways. A generous summer research stipend allowed me to put the finishing touches on the manuscript. Some chapters were read as part of the Humanities and Social Sciences Symposium. The comments that I received from my colleagues in disciplines other than history are greatly appreciated. Damon Scott helped me design the tables that analyze the roll call votes in this work. John Britton, Jacquie Campbell, and Scott Kaufman examined different chapters and offered comments. Chris Kennedy, my department chair, arranged my schedule so that I could complete the task at hand. He allowed me to teach an upper-division course on Jacksonian democracy, where I was able to test out some of my ideas. Elena Eskridge-Kosmach, Mary Louise Nagata, and Louis Venters offered advice on getting a manuscript published and also gently pushed me to submit the manuscript to a publisher. Last, the history majors at Francis Marion University have encouraged me to finish this work. They have asked about the work as it has progressed, and they have also assisted me by explaining various biblical references in congressional speeches whenever I asked them.

Many librarians have gone to great lengths to assist me. Tammy Ivins and Steve Sims at the James Rogers Library at Francis Marion University each procured an incredible amount of microfilm for me. Lucas Clawson provided copies of letters from the Hagley Museum and Library. Graham Duncan did the same with letters from the South Caroliniana Library.

My family has been a great source of aid during the entire process. My wife, Megan, demonstrated incredible patience and took on extra burdens so I could devote more time to finishing this task. My four-year-old daughter, Delaney, helped convince me to finish the manuscript once and for all by telling her friends that the Abominable Snowman from Rudolph "was abominable, like one of Daddy's tariffs." Erin Lawrimore, my sister-in-law, opened her home to me when I needed to return to the research triangle of North Carolina to examine some sources that I had missed during my earlier research trips. My parents, in the great city of Buffalo, New York, never stopped encouraging me. No matter how bleak things looked, their optimism and willingness to help got me through some tough stretches. Finally, my love of history was instilled in me by my two grandfathers. At family functions, I usually gravitated to whatever section of the room they were in. I enjoyed listening to them discuss their time in the army, the old neighborhoods, and crooked politicians. When I began studying history they both urged me on and offered generous financial assistance. To their memories I dedicate this book.

Although I have lived in Dixie for close to fifteen years, I have still retained my Yankee stubbornness. I have incorporated almost all the recommendations of my friends and colleagues in this endeavor, but I have kept a few areas unaltered. Any mistakes are entirely my own.

Tariff Wars and the Politics

of Jacksonian America

Introduction

TWO DIFFERENT METHODS for raising the sum necessary for the support of the Government are open to its national legislators—the one by direct taxation, and the other by a tariff on importations," Schuyler Colfax of Indiana announced in 1857. "No one here, amid all the revenue propositions which have been made or suggested, proposes the first."[1] Three years later, Garnett B. Adrain of New Jersey echoed Colfax's comment. "There are but two ways of raising the necessary revenue for the support of the national government, either by direct taxation, or by means of a tariff," he noted. "The first method, that of direct taxation, has comparatively but few advocates, and will not likely ever become adopted in this country."[2] Colfax, Adrain, and probably every American politician who has held office has realized that direct taxes are not popular. Before the Civil War, the American people did not have to worry about a federal tax collector coming to their door. The reason why was the tariff. The federal government typically obtained close to 90 percent of its revenue from customs receipts.[3]

Even though the tariff provided the federal government with such a large portion of its income, historians have neglected its study. Perhaps the perceived complexity of the tariff has scared historians. "Questions on political economy are certainly among the most complicated of any within the scope of the human mind," Thomas Jefferson opined in 1821. But not all agreed with Jefferson's assessment. For the Americans who lived throughout the 1820s, 1830s, and 1840s, the tariff was constantly before them. Most sessions of Congress saw debates to change the tariff. Editors reprinted congressional debates on the tariff and habitually commented on tariff proposals. The American people frequently sent petitions to Congress urging members either to increase or lower the tariff. Congressmen groused that their tables "groaned" under the weight of these petitions. "This subject, fellow citizens, has been so complicated by discussion, that, for many of you, it may seem abstruse," Lauchlin Bethune declared in 1831. "There is not, however, any mystery in it. Its practical operation depends on the simplest laws of trade; all duties, whether import or export, direct or indirect, are burthens upon the labor and produce of the country." Constant and repeated discussions of a tariff perhaps made it esoteric for many Americans of the nineteenth century, but these tariff debates, oftentimes instigated by the people and not their elected officials, brought more and more Americans into the political process.[4]

Table 1. Effects of the tariff on the American economy

Year	Customs	Value of imports	Average rate	Total revenue	% from tariff
1816	$36,307,000	$147,103,000	24.7	$47,678,000	76.2
1817	$26,283,000	$99,250,000	26.5	$33,099,000	79.4
1818	$17,176,000	$121,750,000	14.1	$21,585,000	79.6
1819	$20,284,000	$87,125,000	23.2	$24,603,000	82.5
1820	$15,006,000	$74,450,000	20.2	$17,881,000	83.9
1821	$13,004,000	$52,503,000	24.8	$14,573,000	89.2
1822	$17,590,000	$75,942,000	23.2	$20,232,000	86.9
1823	$19,088,000	$68,531,000	27.7	$20,541,000	92.9
1824	$17,878,000	$67,985,000	26.2	$19,381,000	92.2
1825	$20,009,000	$85,393,000	23.4	$21,841,000	91.6
1826	$23,341,000	$72,407,000	32.2	$25,260,000	92.4
1827	$19,712,000	$67,629,000	29.2	$22,966,000	85.8
1828	$23,206,000	$76,181,000	30.5	$24,764,000	93.7
1829	$22,682,000	$62,687,000	36.2	$24,828,000	91.4
1830	$21,922,000	$58,131,000	37.7	$24,844,000	88.2
1831	$24,224,000	$89,785,000	27.0	$28,527,000	84.9
1832	$28,465,000	$86,780,000	32.8	$31,866,000	89.3
1833	$29,033,000	$75,670,000	38.4	$33,948,000	85.5
1834	$16,215,000	$58,123,000	27.9	$21,792,000	74.4
1835	$19,391,000	$71,955,000	27.0	$35,430,000	54.7
1836	$23,410,000	$97,924,000	23.9	$50,827,000	46.1
1837	$11,619,000	$71,739,000	16.2	$24,954,000	46.6
1838	$16,159,000	$52,837,000	30.6	$26,303,000	61.4
1839	$23,138,000	$85,690,000	27.0	$31,483,000	73.5
1840	$13,500,000	$49,946,000	27.0	$19,480,000	69.3
1841	$14,487,000	$61,927,000	23.4	$16,860,000	85.9
1842	$18,188,000	$69,535,000	26.2	$19,976,000	91.1
1843	$7,047,000	$29,179,000	24.2	$8,303,000	84.9
1844	$26,184,000	$83,668,000	31.3	$29,321,000	89.3
1845	$27,528,000	$95,107,000	28.9	$29,970,000	91.9
1846	$26,713,000	$96,224,000	27.8	$29,700,000	89.9
1847	$23,748,000	$104,773,000	22.7	$26,496,000	89.6
1848	$31,757,000	$132,283,000	24.0	$35,736,000	88.9
1849	$28,347,000	$125,480,000	22.6	$31,208,000	90.8
1850	$39,669,000	$155,428,000	25.5	$43,603,000	91.0

Continued on next page

Table 1. Continued

Year	Customs	Value of imports	Average rate	Total revenue	% from tariff
1851	$49,018,000	$191,118,000	25.6	$52,559,000	93.3
1852	$47,339,000	$183,253,000	25.8	$49,847,000	95.0
1853	$58,932,000	$236,595,000	24.7	$61,587,000	94.8
1854	$64,224,000	$271,277,000	23.7	$73,800,000	87.0
1855	$53,026,000	$236,595,000	22.4	$65,351,000	81.1
1856	$64,023,000	$257,684,000	24.9	$74,057,000	86.5
1857	$63,876,000	$294,161,000	21.7	$68,965,000	92.6
1858	$41,790,000	$202,293,000	20.7	$46,655,000	89.6
1859	$49,566,000	$259,047,000	19.1	$53,486,000	92.7
1860	$53,188,000	$279,872,000	19.0	$56,065,000	94.9

Sources: *Merchants' Magazine and Commercial Review*, May 1860, 578;
Historical Statistics of the United States, 712.

Rancorous debates regarding the tariff occurred during the Age of Jackson. After the Senate ratified the Treaty of Ghent in 1815, the infant American manufacturing establishments believed that they needed protection from European manufacturers. Congress responded with the mildly protective tariff of 1816. This measure passed by large margins in both houses of Congress. Few realized the repercussions that this legislation would have in the next thirty years, however. When manufacturers tried to increase duties in 1820 with the Baldwin tariff, the House passed it, but the Senate tabled it. Four years later, Congress raised import duties and did so again in 1828. The 1828 tariff, dubbed the "tariff of abominations" by southerners, nearly precipitated a civil war when the state of South Carolina nullified it and the subsequent tariff of 1832. At the urging of President Andrew Jackson, Congress averted bloodshed by passing a last-minute compromise tariff that lowered rates over ten years. This compromise tariff of 1833 remained in effect for nearly ten years. But with the sharpest and final cuts about to be implemented, which would have reduced the rate on all imported goods to 20 percent, Congress enacted new tariff legislation in 1842. This tariff reinstituted highly protective rates on foreign imports. Southerners cried foul over higher rates because they believed that they gave northern manufacturers a monopoly, which then allowed these manufacturers to charge higher prices for their goods. Although advocates of a high tariff had won a major victory in 1842, this victory lasted for only four years. The tariff of 1846, typically dubbed the Walker tariff, lowered most duties and commenced an era of tariffs for revenue purposes only. Congress would not enact another protective tariff until it passed the Morrill tariff in 1861.

This book attempts to show why the tariff was an important part of the national narrative in the antebellum period. The debates in Congress over the tariff were acrimonious, and many of these bills passed by less than five votes. Vice presidents had to break tie votes, and, on a few occasions, the Speaker of the House voted to break or cause a tie vote. Manufacturers argued that they could survive and prosper only if the federal government offered them protection. Many sectors of society rejected the notions of the manufacturers. Farmers and workingmen regarded the tariff as an instrument that granted the class of American manufacturers an unfair monopoly. Why did the federal government cater to one sector of society and not others, they demanded? Shippers believed that tariffs hindered trade and drove off their business. Strict constructionists considered any tariff not designed for revenue to be unconstitutional. All foes of the tariff maintained that it inflated prices.

The tariff was not a "wedge" issue that politicians manipulated for their own electoral success. The American people believed that their economic success and even their individual liberties depended on a protective tariff or a low tariff. The American public, and not elected officials, drove the tariff debates, and this fact, accompanied by the passion surrounding the debates in Congress, the close votes, the menace of special interests, the fear that the tariff fostered monopolies, the talk of the tariff causing a severing of the union, and the fact that the great men of the antebellum period all participated in the debates, makes the antebellum tariff a compelling story that needs to be integrated into the narrative of the Age of Jackson.

The tariff helped to spread democracy throughout America in the antebellum period. Because of the tariff and its sister issues of internal improvements, banking, and public lands, more and more Americans became involved in the political process. They began urging their elected leaders either to raise or lower the tariff. "Our government rests in public opinion," Abraham Lincoln declared in 1856; "whoever can change public opinion, can change the government."[5] Elections, both presidential and congressional, had participation rates eclipsing 80 percent in the antebellum era, and one of the issues that galvanized the people and sent them to the polls was the tariff. American citizens, whether they were protectionists or free traders, sent scores of petitions to Congress beseeching Congress to grant their prayers. Many towns offered resolutions praising or criticizing the actions of congressmen who took part in the tariff debate. Protectionists and antiprotectionists both conducted mass meetings designed to draw the attention of the public to their position. The political parties quickly seized on the idea of holding conventions of their own, as did abolitionists, commercial interests, and temperance advocates. The democratic aspect of the tariff is revealed by the fact that northern districts sent men to Congress with an understanding that they had to secure as much protection as possible for an interest that sustained the livelihood of the families in their districts. If a representative failed to secure protection, then his prospects for reelection faded. Voting the wrong way on a tariff could destroy the political prospects of ambitious men. Since the tariff helped to spread democracy, this work fits into a major trend in the historiography of the Age of Jackson that has emerged in the past decade.[6]

The spreading of democracy caused by the tariff evoked bitter sectional controversy among Americans. Northerners claimed that they needed a tariff to protect their industries and also their wages. Southerners alleged that the tariff forced them to buy goods at increased prices. Having lost the argument against the tariff on its merits, in the 1820s, southerners began to argue that the Constitution did not allow Congress to enact a protective tariff. Mathew Carey, a leading advocate of the protective tariff, wrote in 1823 that southerners threatened disunion to defeat tariff bills. "Whether they are serious or use it by way of bravado, it ought to be repelled with indignation, as turbulent and seditious," he declared. "The subject is to the last degree delicate—and ought to be cautiously forborne even in jest. It is playing with edge tools." Whether by design or by accident, the controversy involved in every tariff bill helped widen the breach between the North and the South. The tariff did not cause the Civil War, but it increased tensions between northerners and southerners in the decades before the War of the Rebellion began.[7]

Although historians have neglected the tariff, it was discussed and debated by many Americans before the Civil War. The first major debate in Congress after the ratification of the Constitution surrounded the tariff of 1789. Madison lamented the difficulty in crafting a tariff that catered to so many diverse interests. "It has unluckily happened in a variety of instances that compromises between local views have been made at the expense of the general interest," James Madison informed Tench Coxe. "This is an evil not to be altogether avoided."[8] The debate on the tariff of 1789 began in early April. The final bill did not reach George Washington's desk until July. Washington, who wanted it known that he wore a suit made of American cloth to his inaugural, signed the tariff of 1789 into law on the nation's thirteenth birthday. The preamble to this bill provided: "Whereas it is necessary for the support of government, the discharge of the debts of the United States, and the encouragement and protection of manufactures, that duties be laid on goods, wares, and merchandise imported." Since Madison authored and Washington approved an act with "protection of manufactures" in the preamble, later defenders of the constitutional power of Congress to levy a protective tariff often pointed to the tariff of 1789 as an act that provided them with a sufficient precedent.[9]

The tariff of 1789 provided the new nation with much-needed revenue. However, this tariff became law before Alexander Hamilton became secretary of the treasury. Later critics of the protective system who referred to it as the "Hamiltonian" system and to Hamilton as the father of it were only partially correct. Hamilton transmitted to Congress his *Report on Manufactures* two years later. Before the Civil War, high-tariff supporters drew many of their arguments from this report. While Hamilton supported tariffs, he preferred the federal government to issue bounties to American manufactures. A bounty acted as a subsidy to a manufacturer. American manufacturers who received these bounties used them to offset foreign tariffs. The British ministry supported British manufacturers through bounties, and Hamilton wanted the federal government to do the same for American manufacturers. Much like Madison, he viewed tariffs as transitory and lasting for only a short duration. Hamilton wanted the federal government to lay duties on foreign manufactures. He then wanted the government apply the proceeds from those duties to American manufactures in the form of bounties. This process had the dual effect of depriving foreign manufactures of a market and providing American manufactures with the tools necessary to compete in foreign markets. Hamilton's agrarian opponents, led by Secretary of State Thomas Jefferson, disapproved of his vision for the new nation. They particularly disliked how Hamilton pointed to the general welfare clause to sustain the constitutionality of his proposed program. The questions pertaining to the constitutionality of a protective tariff received no attention during Hamilton's lifetime, but after 1824, every congressional tariff debate included constitutional arguments.[10]

The Democratic-Republicans, or the party of Jefferson, had opposed all of Hamilton's financial plans during the 1790s, while they were out of power. Once in power, however, they refrained from dismantling the Hamiltonian system. "We can pay off his [Hamilton's] debt in 15 years," Jefferson wrote in 1802. "But we can never get rid of his financial system. It mortifies me to be strengthening principles which I deem radically vicious, but this vice is entailed on us by the first error."[11] Jefferson's supporters repealed all of Hamilton's direct taxes. This left the tariff and the sale of western lands as the major sources of income for the government. Jefferson's party might have accomplished their goal of paying off the debt, but then the War of 1812 erupted. In order to increase revenue, Republicans in Congress passed the tariff of 1812. This tariff doubled the assigned duties on goods imported into the United States. The average rate now became 33 percent.[12]

On April 5, 1814, while the war still raged, Samuel D. Ingham of Pennsylvania offered a resolution in the House. "Resolved, That the Secretary of the Treasury be directed to report to Congress, at their next session, a general tariff of duties, conformably to the existing situation of the general and local interests of the United States." Ingham, who is probably best known for being chased out of Washington City at gunpoint by John H. Eaton in 1831 thanks to his role in a sex scandal that became known as the Eaton Affair, perhaps had the best claim to starting the debate on the tariff in the Age of Jackson. Democracy would soon begin to flourish throughout the land. But Ingham's seemingly harmless proposal spawned a controversy that inadvertently placed the nation on a path that would end in the early morning hours of Charleston Harbor in April 1861.[13]

1

"The new system which out Hamiltons Alexander Hamilton"

DURING THE WAR OF 1812, British general Phineas Rial pondered his fate while he sat in an American prison in Berkshire, New York. As he stared out from his cell, he saw a woolens factory. One of his guards noticed how the general seemed fascinated with this factory. He began teasing the officer, but the sharp-witted Rial turned the tables on his jailor. "You may as well stop where you are, and save your money," Rial announced. "For depend upon it, we will destroy all your manufactories as soon as peace takes place." The young American, no doubt puzzled by this statement, resolved that he would not be outdone by an officer whom American forces had captured at the Battle of Lundy's Lane. "Not by fire, I trust?" he snapped. "No," responded the captive, "but a *few millions sterling, more or less, will be no object to our government, to root up your manufactures in the bud.*"[1]

The story of Rial mocking his captor, which appeared in 1817, is more than likely apocryphal. However, it reveals the apprehensions that Americans felt when they stared out onto the Atlantic Ocean and saw the puffy white sails of British mariners arriving at American ports. These ships no longer carried British soldiers to menace the American people. Instead, their cargo holds contained British manufactured goods. Americans now feared that British manufacturers would "dump" their products in American ports in an effort to destroy American manufacturers. The British might suffer a short-term loss by doing this; but by killing their competitors, they would gain control of the marketplace and could recoup their losses quickly. The cheap price of labor in Great Britain and the accessibility to raw materials from Britain's colonial empire allowed the British to transport and sell their goods in America at a profit in spite of shipping and insurance costs. To even the playing field between American and British manufacturers, American entrepreneurs began calling for a new tariff. Congress responded with the tariff of 1816. This tariff offered protection to American industries. More importantly, the tariff of 1816 and its successor tariffs helped to spread democracy in America. Many Americans took an active interest in the tariff and began agitating for either higher tariffs or lower ones. Nobody recognized it at first, but the tariff helped to unleash a tidal wave of democracy that would reach a crescendo with Andrew Jackson's elevation to the presidency in 1828.[2]

The War of 1812 represented a break from precedent for the United States. A younger generation of Americans who had not participated in the Revolution had begun to exert their influence over public policy. This younger group of leaders initiated a cultural, political, and economic revolution in America. Nationalism inspired them. They began appropriating funds for roads, turnpikes, bridges, canals, army bases, coastal fortifications, and other public works at the state and federal levels. Younger politicians embraced the march of a market-oriented economy. Their policies sought to expand this market revolution. By appropriating funds toward internal improvements, which would lower shipping costs and open new markets in the West, American entrepreneurs had more reasons to invest their capital into manufacturing.[3]

While most Americans cheered the ratification of the Treaty of Ghent in 1815, which ended the War of 1812, some Americans sensed potential trouble. Right after Congress declared war against Great Britain in 1812, it had passed a revenue bill known as the tariff act of 1812. This legislation stipulated that one year after the United States and Great Britain ended hostilities, it would no longer be in force. As a result, the moment the Senate approved the Treaty of Ghent, a one-year countdown commenced until the duties on imported goods entering the United States would be repealed and the country would revert to the prewar duties. If the nation went back to the prewar duties, the result would be catastrophic, or so some claimed, for Americans who made their living through the manufacturing of such goods as textiles, spirits, rope, sugar, and iron.[4]

Shrewd congressmen anticipated the pending problems. From 1801 through 1811, the federal government received $148 million in revenue, $134 million of which came from customs receipts. In most years, the federal government obtained close to 90 percent of its annual revenue from customs receipts. If imported goods landed at American ports with very low or no duties whatsoever, the nation would have to resort to direct taxation to sustain itself. The Republican Party, which had controlled Congress and the presidency since 1801 and which had come to power on the pledge that the party would repeal all direct taxes, did not want to go back on its promise to the American people and levy internal taxes during a time of peace. Just eight days after the final ratification of the Treaty of Ghent, John W. Eppes, chairman of the House Committee on Ways and Means, offered a motion asking "that the Secretary of the Treasury be directed to report at the next session a general tariff of duties proposed to be imposed upon imported goods, wares, and merchandise." The entire House quickly concurred with the Virginian's motion.[5]

When the second session of the Fourteenth Congress commenced in the charred capital city at the end of 1815, President James Madison reminded the members that the national debt had climbed to $127 million. The reduction of the public debt became the primary concern of most congressmen. In his next-to-last annual message to Congress, Madison recommended to Congress that it adjust the tariff. When Congress selected the branches of industry entitled to "public patronage," those sectors of the economy that relieved the nation from foreign dependence should be given preference.[6]

Petitions seeking assistance for certain interests had begun arriving in Washington even before Madison discussed the tariff. Most of these had been sent by manufacturers. One newspaper editor observed: "Many of the members [of Congress]

seem still to have a hankering after the flesh pots of Old England and notwithstanding the experience of the late war, do not appear to understand the connections
which exists between the prosperity of our own manufactures, and the prosperity,
real independence, and liberties of this country."[7] Whereas this editor perceived
patriotism and the further march of democracy in these petitions, George Washington Logan detected avarice. "The love of honest fame, predominant during the
revolutionary war, is changed into cupidity, disinterestedness into selfishness-and
the public good is sacrificed to personal views of ambition," Logan wrote to Thomas
Jefferson.[8]

Americans asking their government to assist their economic interests ran counter to the principles of the Revolution. Republican orthodoxy dictated that Americans should be self-sacrificing and disinterested citizens. Having the government
bestow favors on a manufacturing interest ran against the ideals of the Revolution.
Those Americans not interested in manufacturing viewed the asking of favors as
the ultimate betrayal of republican ideals because it resembled the practices of
Great Britain. Those who placed their own interests or personal gain above the
community or nation allowed for corruption and despotism. Balancing the conflicting interests of capitalism and republicanism dogged the generation of Americans who lacked firsthand knowledge of the sacrifices made by their revolutionary
forefathers.[9]

The Old Republicans, a faction of the Republican Party comprising southern
politicians who advocated rigid economy and retrenchment in expenses, found
themselves on the defensive at the end of 1815 and in the beginning of 1816. It
looked as if the rest of the nation had moved forward while these ideologues remained trapped in the past. Madison called for a protective tariff, and former
president Thomas Jefferson announced his support for manufacturing. "We must
now place the manufacturer by the side of the agriculturalist," Jefferson mused.[10]
Newspapers throughout the country reprinted Jefferson's letter. Although Jefferson
never countenanced a protective tariff, his endorsement of manufacturing perhaps
swayed some wavering members of his party to support the pending tariff. On February 5, 1816, with little debate, Congress extended the war tariff until June 30.[11]

Eight days later, Secretary of the Treasury Alexander Dallas communicated his
report on a proposed tariff to the House of Representatives. "The present policy of
the government is directed to protect, and not to create manufactures," Dallas proclaimed.[12] This sentence crystallizes Dallas's conception of how a tariff should function. He did not want to use the legislative power of Congress to create a manufacturing establishment, but he sought to use the powers given to the House and
Senate to assist those that already existed. He recommended three classes of duties
for goods imported into the United States. The first class included manufactured
items that had an extended history of being produced within the United States.
Cabinets, cannons, carriages, iron castings, leather bridles, muskets, paper, and
window glass fell into this category. Dallas believed that a prohibitory duty could
be laid on these items since Americans produced enough of them to meet current
demand. For the second class, Dallas included goods that had only recently begun
to be produced in the United States. The secretary hoped that with "proper cultiva-

tion," these goods could soon meet the demand of Americans. Axes, beer, coarse cottons, woolens, metal buttons, nails, shovels, and spades fell into the second class. Dallas placed products that Americans did not manufacture at all in the third class. These goods, such as luxury items, would have a tariff rate designed to produce revenue only. Dallas reasoned that his tariff would bring in $17 million of revenue annually.[13]

Dallas's report revealed that the Republican Party had carved out a new position. As the minority party in the 1790s, the Republicans had warned about the dangers of replicating the British model of government-sponsored manufacturers. Now in power, many Republicans urged an increased role for the government over the economy. This trend had begun during the war and would continue now that it had concluded. Dallas tried to chart a middle course that might appeal to all members of the Republican coalition. His proposal sought to "protect" American manufacturers from the established British ones. This protection would also allow the government to reduce its debt. Dallas's critics might fear the potential effects of protectionism, but he would not go as far as economic nationalists such as Hezekiah Niles and Mathew Carey, who championed prohibition of all foreign manufactured goods.[14]

Even though it carried the full weight and approval of the administration, Dallas's report competed with the petitions of Americans for the attention of the House. Cotton manufacturers submitted the largest number of petitions seeking relief. If the House used the requests of the people rather than Dallas's report to structure the tariff bill, it could have been interpreted as the will of the people triumphing over the views of a Washington leader. Conversely, if the House rejected the petitions and framed the tariff based on Dallas's report, it could have been argued that politicians had turned their backs on the people. The House split the difference and referred the petitions to the Committee of Commerce and Manufactures and sent Dallas's report to the Committee on Ways and Means.

On the same day as Dallas's report arrived in Congress, Thomas Newton of Virginia, the chairman of the Committee of Commerce and Manufactures, presented a report warning about the problems of state-sponsored manufacturing. "Different sections of the nation will," Newton began, "according to their position, the climate, the population, the habits of the people, and the nature of the soil, strike into that line of industry which is best adapted to their interest and the good of the whole." Newton warned against enacting legislation that would force certain Americans into pursuits that their soil and geography would not sustain. Although he did not reference Adam Smith, Newton had endorsed Smith's invisible-hand principle. Nothing came of Newton's report, however.[15]

Almost one month after Newton presented the report of the Committee of Commerce and Manufactures, William Lowndes, the chairman of the Committee on Ways and Means, offered a new tariff proposal. Born in the lowcountry of South Carolina in 1782, Lowndes endured poor health throughout his entire life. In 1810, he won election to the House of Representatives. Arriving in the capital city in 1811, Lowndes found lodgings in the "War Mess" that included George M. Bibb, John C. Calhoun, Henry Clay, Felix Grundy, and Langdon Cheves. Along with his messmates, Lowndes helped to secure a declaration of war against Great Britain in the summer of 1812. By the time he drafted his tariff bill in 1816, he had risen to the upper echelons of the Republican Party. When Lowndes made known his intention to speak in the House, all recognized that his words carried the approval of the administration.[16]

Lowndes's bill emerged after thorough research and investigation. In addition to manufacturers, the South Carolinian conferred with merchants, navigators, and farmers. He sought their input on the effects of the tariff on their branches of industry. While crafting the bill, and then later during the debate, Lowndes listened to the suggestions that fellow congressmen offered him, including his political enemies. Lowndes appeared willing to accept the suggestions of his fellow House members. He discussed the duties that should be levied on cotton goods with Massachusetts Federalist Timothy Pickering. The New Englander advised Lowndes that high duties hurt the shipping interests of his region: if fewer imports arrived in America, then New England mariners would lose a large portion of their business. The South Carolinian's bill used Dallas's plan as a model, but it included numerous alterations. The majority of the changes that Lowndes made lowered the duties proposed by Dallas. These reductions made the tariff less protective than Dallas wished. Lowndes wanted protection, but not if it threatened the main source of revenue for the nation.[17]

Only nine days after Lowndes presented his bill, Speaker Henry Clay offered an amendment to it. A Virginian by birth, Clay left the Old Dominion for the blue-grass of Kentucky in 1797 to advance his law career. He rose quickly in Kentucky politics, so much so that in 1806, the state legislature elected him to be one of the state's senators, even though he had not yet turned thirty. Clay disliked the slow pace of business in the Senate and craved a change. In 1811 he entered the House, where his Republican colleagues elected him Speaker on the very first ballot. Witty, confident, intelligent, comfortable around ladies, and no stranger to the field of honor, Clay won the respect of House Republicans. Dubbed the "Star of the West," he enjoyed the Washington nightlife and gambled frequently.[18]

To determine how far the House intended to go toward protecting domestic manufactures, Clay proposed to increase the duty on imported cottons from 25 to 33 percent. Samuel Smith, a Republican from Baltimore with ties to the merchant community in that city, opposed Clay's motion, along with Lowndes. The House defeated it by a vote of fifty-one to forty-three. This rejection did not represent an auspicious beginning for the members who wanted the tariff to be highly protective. Undeterred, Clay made a motion to change the duty to 30 percent, instead of 25. This gambit by the Speaker changed the nature of the debate.[19]

Samuel Ingham of Pennsylvania spoke next. Ingham declared that the primary purpose of a tariff was protection. Congress had already passed bills to augment the revenue, he announced. Ingham claimed that Americans had invested over one hundred million dollars in manufacturing in the past decade. These investments provided employment for thousands of Americans. A protective tariff would protect these workers, but it would also assist the manufacturer, the farmer, and the navigator. Because of this, Ingham considered the tariff a "great principle of national policy," since it sought to "perpetuate the security, the peace, and especially the independence of the nation." According to Ingham, Congress had a duty to promote the prosperity and happiness of its people, and the tariff performed that duty. When Ingham concluded his remarks, the House voted to accept Clay's amendment by seven votes.[20]

Patriotism and state pride now took over the debate. Bolling Robertson of Louisiana moved to lower the duties on certain imported wines. Samuel Smith of Maryland wanted to maintain the duties on Spanish and Portuguese wines. Since Spain and Portugal levied a high duty on American flour, Smith believed that Congress should retaliate by levying high duties on exports from those countries. Kentucky's Benjamin Hardin spoke against the motion and then told Robertson, "If Louisianans could not obtain wine, they could obtain an abundant supply of whiskey from Kentucky in lieu of it." Robertson retorted by saying that he considered his constituents to be a "sober people," and he wanted cheap wines "to save them [Louisianans] from the whiskey offered by the gentlemen by Kentucky." Warming to the task, Robertson concluded by saying, "The liquid fire of alcohol would, in so warm a climate, be poison to them, and its use be more pernicious than arsenic." With tempers flaring, Clay stepped down from the Speaker's chair to prevent the two congressmen from challenging each other to a duel over alcohol. Clay expressed remorse that "his friend from Louisiana had declared war against the whiskey of the west, and regretted, if such was the fact, that the taste of the people of Louisiana was so bad as to prefer bad claret to good whiskey." Following Clay's address, the House rejected Robertson's motion.[21]

On April 4, John Randolph began a lengthy tirade against the bill. Randolph had been a prominent floor leader when Jefferson served as president, but his eccentricities prompted the Republican leadership to strip him of his power. In the wake of the war, Randolph became the most vocal opponent of the increase of federal powers, but few Republicans heeded his warnings. Benjamin Ruggles, an Ohio representative, told a Buckeye editor about a twelve-hour speech Randolph had given. In that lengthy address, Randolph spoke favorably of no person except "George Washington and himself," and he had discussed every topic "from the creation of the world to the present time." In 1816, Randolph sat in the House in isolation and influenced few pieces of legislation. Most observers recognized that he could erupt at any moment, however.[22]

When Randolph concluded his speech, he made a motion for the indefinite postponement of the tariff bill. He rescinded the motion with the understanding that he would be able to present it later. Ingham recognized the shrewdness of this tactic. Randolph had a penchant for delivering lengthy speeches in his high-pitched voice, during which many members left the chamber. If Randolph suspended his speech and made his motion after enough of the tariff's supporters had fled the House in disgust, the bill might be lost. To prevent this, Ingham walked into an adjoining committee room where he found his friend John C. Calhoun of South Carolina working on legislation to create a new national bank. The Pennsylvanian asked Calhoun to come into the House chamber and speak on the pending tariff. Ingham figured that Calhoun's appearance would offer comfort to members and that it would reaffirm the administration's support for the measure under debate. Calhoun responded that he had no notes and had not prepared to speak on the tariff. At this juncture, Ingham baited Calhoun by telling him that his nemesis Randolph had commenced another of his incoherent tirades. Few Republicans liked confronting the caustic Virginian, yet Calhoun apparently enjoyed debating Randolph.[23]

The Calhoun who entered the House chamber that April day should not be confused with the Calhoun seen in the daguerreotypes of the 1840s. Born in upcountry South Carolina in 1782 and educated in Connecticut under Federalists, Calhoun passed the bar in South Carolina but found the law not to his liking, so he entered politics. In the South Carolina legislature, he assisted in the "Compromise of 1808," which soothed tensions between the upcountry and lowcountry regions of the Palmetto State. When he entered Congress in 1811, Calhoun performed the role of majority leader or majority whip to Speaker Clay, even though that title had not yet come into existence. By 1816, Calhoun still remained far from the "cast-iron man" that Harriet Martineau would describe decades later.[24] His nationalism knew no bounds. "We see every where a nationality of feeling," he told the House in his first speech of that year. "We hear sentiments from every part of the House in favor of union, and against sectional spirit. What had produced this change? The glory acquired by the late war, and the prosperity which had followed it."[25] Calhoun refused to view political economy in 1816 in zero-sum terms like other mercantilists. All America would gain from the tariff. However, Calhoun lacked the clairvoyance to anticipate the effects that the war would have on the powers of the federal government.

In his unprepared speech, Calhoun spoke in favor of the tariff, because it provided for the "security of the country." Like most others in Congress, Calhoun viewed the Treaty of Ghent as a temporary truce and not as a final settlement between Great Britain and the United States. Future wars between the United States and Great Britain, Calhoun predicted, would be "long and bloody."[26] Tobacco and cotton farmers would be hurt the most in these wars because of the cessation of the coasting trade. A protective tariff might diminish the advantages of the British navy because Americans soldiers would not be dependent on foreigners for weapons. Calhoun saw the tariff as just one measure to allow the United States to defeat the British in the next war. The South Carolinian wanted Congress to undertake a program of internal improvements, which would allow for a more rapid transfer of goods, military supplies, and troops throughout the union. This tariff, Calhoun declared, did not seek to force manufacturing onto the people but rather encouraged more capital to be invested into cotton and woolen manufacturing. Although Calhoun typically used logic and force of reason to end his speeches, in this instance, he resorted to a bit of oratory by concluding: "the *liberty* and the *union* of this country were inseparably united."[27] For Calhoun, the tariff in 1816 would bring the country together and alleviate sectional tensions, producing a stronger union that would secure the blessings of liberty for all Americans.

For the remaining years of his life, Calhoun tried to explain his support for the tariff in 1816, because he publicly opposed the protective policy beginning in the early 1830s. In the tariff debates of the 1830s, Calhoun's opponents reminded him of his position in 1816. A campaign biography published in 1843 (perhaps written by Calhoun himself) confirmed that Calhoun gave his speech on the tariff with no preparation. *The Life of John C. Calhoun* suggested that the tariff of 1816 did not contain protectionist principles because the industries often associated with protection, such as iron, did not exist in 1816. Calhoun would not be the last politician to parse logic and "spin" a vote on a tariff bill.[28]

As the House prepared to vote on the tariff, Randolph delivered a three-hour speech against the bill. He sensed "a strange and mysterious connection between this measure and one [the bill to charter a new national bank] which had just passed, and was now beyond the control of this House." The House passed Calhoun's bank bill on March 14 by nine votes, and Randolph seemed to be warning his colleagues about the resurgence of the Hamiltonian system. He informed his friends back in Virginia that he planned on "making a desperate stand against the new system which out Hamiltons Alexander Hamilton."[29] Few heeded his warning. After Randolph's address, Clay called for the yeas and nays. The House approved the tariff of 1816 by a vote of eighty-eight to fifty-four.[30]

House Republicans supported the tariff by a margin of two to one. Of the thirty-two Republicans who opposed the tariff of 1816, twenty-six of them represented the southern states of Georgia, Louisiana, North Carolina, South Carolina, Tennessee, and Virginia. Republicans from these states also provided the tariff of 1816 with seventeen votes of approval. No future protective tariff would receive as much support from the South as this one. Most Republicans did not share Randolph's fears about the reappearance of the Hamiltonian system.[31]

Why did southerners support this tariff but oppose every other protective tariff? It appears that some southerners, such as Calhoun, saw this tariff as temporary. The duties on cottons and woolens would be reduced in June 1819 to 20 percent. Other southerners endorsed the tariff in 1816 since they believed that manufacturing might develop in the South. Unlike New England manufacturers, southerners would not have to pay high transportation costs since cotton would not have to travel as far to the looms. The dream of manufacturing cotton clothes never materialized in the South. With most of their funds invested in land and slaves, southerners had little capital remaining to invest in their own mills. A series of failed canal projects and a decline in the price of cotton after the tariff of 1816 went into operation dashed the hopes of the South replicating the example of New England.[32]

Southerners may have supported the tariff in 1816 because increased revenue would allow the government to repeal the remaining direct taxes that had been levied during the War of 1812. Jeffersonian dogma held that taxes led to corruption and consolidation by the federal government. While some southerners disliked manufacturing and believed that it tarnished the morals of society, it represented a lesser evil compared to continued taxation. Both taxation and manufacturing reminded southerners of the Hamiltonian financial system, but the former seemed to be the greater evil. If the federal government continued imposing direct taxes, then

Table 1.1. House vote, 1816

	Republicans		Federalists		Total	
	For	Against	For	Against	For	Against
New England	1	0	16	10	17	10
Middle	36	5	8	5	44	10
South	17	26	0	7	17	33
West	10	1	0	0	10	1
Total	64	32	24	22	88	54

Source: *House Journal*, 14th Cong., 1st Sess., 8 April 1816, 610–12.

Note: In this table and all the subsequent ones, the New England states are Connecticut, Maine, Massachusetts, New Hampshire, Rhode Island, and Vermont. The middle states are Delaware, Maryland, New Jersey, New York, and Pennsylvania. The southern states are Alabama, Arkansas, Florida, Georgia, Louisiana, Mississippi, North Carolina, South Carolina, Tennessee, Texas, and Virginia. The western states are California, Illinois, Indiana, Iowa, Kentucky, Michigan, Missouri, Ohio, Oregon, and Wisconsin.

the northern majority might attack slavery. For many Republicans, then, increased duties on foreign imports would allow the nation to pay off the debt more rapidly, remove taxes on the people, and decrease the threat of excessive federal power.

Suggestions that Congress passed the tariff of 1816 to aid New England textile manufactures are misguided. They stem from the fact that future tariffs were passed for the benefit of that region. In 1816, the New England states of Connecticut, Massachusetts, New Hampshire, Rhode Island, and Vermont provided the tariff with seventeen favorable votes and ten unfavorable votes. However, fourteen New England representatives abstained from voting on the tariff. This could indicate that they could not make up their mind or that they were afraid of casting a vote that would be deemed unpopular by the people back home. No other region had as many abstentions as New England on the final vote. But in 1816, cotton manufacturing competed with the shipping industry to be the dominant sector of the New England economy. During the House debate, Francis Cabot Lowell arrived in Washington to lobby on behalf of the tariff. Lowell had emerged as the leader of the Boston Manufacturing Company, which led the nation in the production of cotton fabrics. He urged Daniel Webster to include a high duty on cotton cloths. Webster appeased Lowell by including a duty of 30 percent for a two-year period and then a 25 percent duty for two more years, which would then be reduced to 20 percent. The moderate duty of 30 percent and the quick reductions proposed by Webster suggest that New England cotton manufacturers, like southerners, viewed protection as temporary.[33]

The Federalists found themselves divided over the tariff in 1816. The tariff could help the emerging cotton manufacturers in New England, but it could also injure those who earned their livelihood through the shipping industry. Confronting the tariff as an economic issue was problematic, but it was also a difficult political issue for the Federalists. The tariff, along with the national bank, had been a core principle for the Federalists in the 1790s. The Republicans had already stolen the national bank as an issue and made it their own and seemed to be doing the same thing with the tariff. One Federalist in Maryland offered a toast that charged Republicans with hypocrisy: "Federalism, the rock of safety; Democracy has been obliged to desert experimental measures, and adopt the same principles which they reviled and impeached in others."[34]

The difficulties that Federalists faced are revealed by the votes in the House on the tariff. Twenty-four Federalists voted for the tariff, while twenty-two opposed it. All the Federalists who voted for the bill represented districts above the Mason-Dixon Line. While some of their southern Republican adversaries envisioned a more dynamic and cosmopolitan society for their region or voted for the tariff out of patriotism, all the southern Federalists perceived the possible dangers to their region in the form of the tariff. Whether these Federalists had linked the tariff and slavery cannot be discerned from the available sources. However, four years later, many southerners, regardless of their political affiliations, would unite these two issues.[35]

When the votes of the southern Republicans and southern Federalists are combined, it suggests that support for the tariff in the South may not have been as widespread as is thought. The states of Georgia, Louisiana, North Carolina, South Carolina, Tennessee, and Virginia provided this tariff with seventeen votes of approval and thirty-three negative votes. Thus, 34 percent of southerners voted for this measure, which is high compared to later protective tariffs. But a large majority of southern congressmen opposed a protective tariff.[36]

As a result of the approaching adjournment, the Senate had little time to deal with the tariff bill. The precedent of the House passing a tariff bill late in the session and forcing the Senate to rush its debate on the bill would be repeated on most tariff bills in the future. On April 17, Robert Goodloe Harper of Maryland made a motion for the postponement of the bill until after August 1. If successful, this maneuver would kill it. The Senate rejected Harper's move by a vote of twenty-seven to three. Two days later, on the motion to send the bill to a third reading, the tariff received the votes of twenty-five members. Only seven voted against it. Four of the negative votes came from Federalists. The three Republican senators who voted against the measure came from North Carolina and Virginia. The next day, the upper chamber approved the bill without a recorded vote, and Madison signed it into law. "You will see," Madison wrote to William Eustis, "that a very important provision has been made for fostering our manufactures. This will have the double effect of enlarging our revenue for a time, and, by lessening our future importations, aid in rescuing our commerce from that unfavorable balance which embarrasses all our monied institutions and financial operations."[37]

Because of the divisions within each party, Daniel Webster sensed that the tariff would cause a political realignment. The New Hampshire representative believed that the possibility existed for a new political party centered on the manufacturing interest to emerge. This could occur since both parties contained supporters and opponents of the protective tariff. A new political alignment aiding manufacturers would not be sectional because support for manufacturing had followers in every region of the country in 1816. Webster's premonition about the formation of a party composed entirely of high tariff-supporters proved to be misguided. Friends of American manufacturing made their way into all the political parties in the antebellum period.[38]

The tariff of 1816 went into operation on July 1 of that year. Its authors believed that it would set average duties at a rate of 25 percent, and the average rate was just under 25 percent. The impending tariff legislation, however, prompted Europeans to send their goods to America in hope of evading the increase of duties. In 1816, $147 million of foreign goods arrived in America. US customs officials collected thirty-six million dollars' worth of duties. In 1817, the first full year of the tariff, ninety-nine million dollars' worth of foreign goods landed in America, and customs collectors took in twenty-six million dollars' worth of taxes. In 1816 and in 1817, the average rate stood close to 25 percent. But in 1818, $122 million of foreign goods arrived at American ports. The United States collected only seventeen million dollars from these goods. This dropped the average rate to 14 percent. After Congress increased the rates on iron, aluminum, and wines, the average rate jumped to 23 percent in 1819 and then fell to 20 percent in 1820.[39]

The minimum principle on cotton fabrics made cotton manufactures the big winner of this tariff. This principle evoked little discussion in 1816, but it caused acrimony in the years ahead. Under the minimum principle, imported cotton goods that cost less than twenty-five cents per square yard were assessed a duty as if they were worth twenty-five cents. The minimum principle added more teeth and protection to the tariff. If foreign manufacturers made improvements or cut labor costs that reduced the total price of their good, the minimum principle offered American manufacturers another line of defense. The minimum principle would be incorporated into most succeeding tariffs. As a result of the minimum principle, cotton manufacturing increased exponentially with the tariff of 1816. Before 1816, American consumption of cotton stood at around eleven million pounds annually. By 1827, Americans used over thirty-four million pounds of cotton each year. Iron manufacturers also won under the tariff of 1816. Most forms of iron now paid a specific duty. Iron bars and bolts had their duties doubled under the new tariff.[40]

Many members of Congress viewed the tariff as a means to provide encouragement to American manufacturing establishments, and this tariff, though mildly protective when compared to the tariffs that followed it in the 1820s, should be considered a protective tariff. Randolph recognized this when he claimed that the tariff "out Hamiltons Alexander Hamilton." The minimum principle made it protective. Furthermore, its authors and supporters envisioned it as a protective tariff and not just a revenue measure. However, its authors and supporters considered the 1816 tariff as a temporary piece of legislation. The framers of this tariff did not expect protectionism to become permanent. Most of its supporters, particularly those in New England and in the South, expected that after only a few years, with the debt lowered and American manufacturers able to compete against outside competition, Congress would lower or remove most tariff barriers.[41]

Assessing the overall success of any tariff is problematic. The tariff of 1816 brought in between seventeen and twenty-six million dollars' worth of customs duties annually. When the tariff of 1816 went into operation, the national debt stood at $127 million. On January 1, 1824, it had fallen to $99 million. This reduction took place while the nation endured the Panic of 1819. In this respect, the tariff of 1816 would have to be regarded as a successful piece of legislation. It could also be seen as a triumph because it endured longer than the average antebellum tariff. The tariff of 1816 would remain the law of the land until 1824.[42]

After the conclusion of the first session of the Fourteenth Congress, Republicans congratulated themselves on their achievements. "Perhaps there has been no session since '93 which has shown so little of party spirit as the one just ended," the *Richmond Enquirer* declared. "The Republicans reposed upon their laurels; their opponents retired from the contest in despair. . . . The session began, and might have ended in perfect harmony, but for Mr. John Randolph who takes a delight in blowing the trumpet of discord. His influence, however, is nearly gone forever."[43] In this session, in addition to passing a protective tariff, Republicans chartered a new national bank, strengthened the national defense, and took steps toward creating a federally sponsored program of internal improvements. Republicans also felt confident that their candidate would win the presidency that fall. The congressional caucus nominated James Monroe over William H. Crawford for the presidency. Although some Republicans urged Crawford to challenge the caucus decision in the general election, the Georgian refused. In the fall, Republicans closed ranks around Monroe as he won an easy victory over Federalist Rufus King.[44]

Inspired by the tariff and the writings of economic nationalists like Niles and Carey, supporters of American manufacturing established the American Society for the Encouragement of American Manufactures on December 31, 1816. Similar societies at the state and local level quickly joined this organization in its calls to make the tariff of 1816 permanent and to prohibit the importation of cotton fabrics. These societies worked together to keep the tariff issue before the American people. Goaded by these societies, Americans began transferring their capital into manufacturing. When Americans charged supporters of these societies and domestic manufacturing with abandoning republican principles, the members pointed to the rolls of the American Society for the Encouragement of American Manufactures, which included John Adams, Thomas Jefferson, James Madison, and Daniel Tompkins. If these men did not consider the support of manufacturing a violation of republican principles, then how could any other American? When Americans grumbled over the tariff and the decision of Congress to offer assistance to American manufacturers, proponents of manufacturing then reminded them of George Washington's support of the tariff of 1789. By shielding themselves behind the names of the Founding Fathers, American manufacturers positioned themselves to parry any future attacks against their industry.[45]

When members of the Fourteenth Congress informed their constituents of what had occurred in Washington City, several reminded them of the tariff. However, most of the congressmen who discussed the tariff with their constituents did not approve it. Lewis Williams of North Carolina told voters that he viewed the tariff as a departure from the principles enunciated by the Founding Fathers. Congress used the tariff to push Americans into "pursuits" that did not suit them. At the core of Williams's argument was the fact that protective tariffs coerced Americans to leave their farms and move into urban areas to work in manufacturing centers. This policy made little sense to Williams because America contained "extensive tracts of uncultivated land." Increased duties, Williams feared, led to a loss in revenue from imports. Thus, Americans would have to suffer direct taxation to make up for lost revenue. Taxation would unleash untold evils that might threaten the republic. Williams contended that the increased duties did not assist the spinning and weaving now being undertaken in the southern states. "It is the great companies and individuals of immense wealth, which require such an advantage over the laborer in the field, as to ask him to tax himself to keep them in operation," Williams wrote.[46] In nearby Tennessee, Isaac Thomas reiterated much of what Williams had penned. Thomas argued that the tariff created an "aristocratical interest" in America. The high duties, which bordered on being prohibitory, placed "the country at the mercy of a horde of Yankee capitalists, who never fail to fleece all with whom they have any dealings." Thomas ended his section on the tariff with another sectional thrust at the North. "Agriculture is no longer cherished as the great fountain from which the wealth and independence of the nation flows; but is subsidized for the support of Yankee weavers."[47] Thomas's use of "Yankee capitalists" invoked both a sectional and a class-based argument against the tariff.

A few other Americans commented on the tariff of 1816. For instance, an editor in Annapolis, Maryland, disliked the new tariff because he thought that higher prices would be passed on to consumers. "By this tariff," he argued, "thousands and tens of thousands of dollars are drawn from the people in a way they do not perceive."[48] A Kentuckian voiced his approval of the tariff at a Fourth of July celebration: "Domestic manufactures—Important to our independence as a nation-they were ably supported by our representative in Congress."[49] An anonymous pamphlet writer in New York disliked the tariff because of its complexity, which might force customs collectors to make mistakes when applying the duties. But this tariff, according to this writer, catered to the rich because it imposed high duties on goods that the lower classes regarded as necessities.[50]

The main reason many Americans failed to notice the tariff resulted from one of the final actions of the Fourteenth Congress. Just before Congress adjourned, and with little debate, members voted themselves a pay raise. Instead of a per diem rate, congressmen approved a salary of fifteen hundred dollars per session. "All the great measures of the session are very popular. I hear not one objection to the bank, Tariff, or taxes," Calhoun informed Alexander Dallas from his home, "though the measures of Congress at the last session are so generally popular, yet, I expect great changes in this part of the Union at the coming election. The compensation bill is much objected to."[51]

When the members of the Fourteenth Congress returned to their homes, they learned that the public disapproved of the Compensation Act. Speaker Clay faced a difficult reelection challenge against John Pope as a result of his endorsement of the compensation measure. Clay admitted his mistake, begged forgiveness, repented his sin of supporting the Compensation Act, and secured his seat only after vowing to work for its repeal. Calhoun defended his vote and defeated three challengers. Well-known members such as Webster and Randolph declined to seek another term in the House because of the furor over their votes. Few congressmen escaped the carnage brought on by the unpopularity of the compensation bill, however. Nearly two-thirds of the Fourteenth Congress lost their seats. Republicans and Federalists, northerners and southerners—all suffered at the polls. The wrath of the voters made no distinction between parties or sections. Even those who voted against the compensation bill suffered defeats. The Republican leadership survived intact, but many of their backbench supporters succumbed to the outrage of the electorate. These new congressmen would enter Congress committed to a policy of retrenchment.[52]

The American economy commenced a brief boom period after 1816. The number of banks increased from fewer than two hundred fifty in 1816 to almost four hundred in 1818. Credit became readily available to many Americans, and they used this to construct internal improvements and purchase western lands. Banks and bank notes appeared not only in urban areas but also in most rural regions. Paper money and credit allowed for foreign goods to enter the nation at an increased rate. In 1816, the balance of trade against the United States stood at just under seventy million dollars. The next year it fell to just under fourteen million dollars. In 1818, however, it climbed to almost thirty-three million dollars. The continual imbalance of trade against America meant that more and more specie left American ports for Europe. With no wars being waged in Europe and bountiful European harvests, European nations no longer needed American goods. The Corn Laws of Great Britain prohibited the importation of foreign grain products. Shrewd western farmers evaded the Corn Laws by exporting their grain from Canada, but the laws had their desired effect—American farmers could not ship their grain to the workers in Great Britain. Cotton, which fetched a price of thirty-three cents a pound in 1816, dropped to fourteen cents a pound in 1819. The peace in Europe, the poor balance of trade, the enactment of the Corn Laws, and a series of reckless banking practices in the United States all combined to produce an economic downturn beginning in 1818 that reached a crescendo in 1819. The Panic of 1819 demonstrated to Americans that the slowing of the economy along seaboard regions now affected inland regions. The American economy had become unified and then suffered as a result of this unification.[53]

The panic hit the southern and western states the hardest. Hemp manufacturers in Lexington, Kentucky, and Cincinnati, Ohio, became unable to pay their laborers, and, as a result, over a thousand laborers wandered the streets of the western cities. The new national bank had lavished credit to westerners after its creation. When the bank called in its loans and refused any extensions, westerners vented their anger against it. "Kentucky has never witnessed such a period of commercial distress and embarrassment," observed an Ohioan in Cincinnati.[54] A Kentucky editor described the dire predicament of westerners. "We have seen in the short space of about four years, the entire capital, vested in home manufactures, amounting to upwards of two hundred millions of dollars, sacrificed by the imprudence of the national government, in permitting our country to be overrun with British goods."[55] In Alabama, Charles Tait, a former senator from Georgia, wrote to Georgia representative Thomas W. Cobb, "I can only say that we are in no condition to pay taxes. We are all in debt."[56]

Americans placed the blame for the panic at the feet of numerous programs and institutions. Many pointed to the low duties established by the tariff of 1816. This tariff, they charged, still allowed the British to land goods in America and make a profit. The imbalance of trade, supporters of a tariff alleged, drained the country of its specie reserves, which in turn depressed real estate values and resulted in poverty for Americans involved in any aspect of manufacturing. An upward revision of the tariff would put a stop to this practice, they argued. The effects of the panic could be alleviated if Americans adopted a strict economy and, as a group of residents in Newcastle County, Delaware, affirmed, by *the encouragement of a market at home, by fostering and protecting domestic manufactures.*"[57]

In a Thanksgiving sermon delivered in 1819, Lyman Beecher discussed the panic with his Presbyterian congregation in Connecticut. Using biblical citations and references, Beecher urged Americans to be more frugal and to work harder. Beecher's address embodied many of the same principles at which proponents of the "American System" would soon begin pointing. Beecher viewed agriculture, commerce, and manufactures as being interconnected. "They are all parts of one whole, and so mutually dependent on each other, that if one prospers, they all prosper, and if one suffers they all suffer, and if not immediately, yet inevitably, in the course of events," he announced. Beecher discussed how internal improvements shortened the distance to markets, increased the volume of goods, and augmented the value of surplus goods. While he praised farmers and merchants, Beecher pointed to manufacturers as a class that needed government assistance. "If there ever was a subject which demanded governmental wisdom to prevent the evils of individual discretion, amounting to national calamity," Beecher averred, "it would seem to be that of limiting the national consumption of foreign manufactures, by fostering our own, thus preventing the adverse balance of trade, and securing the steady presence of a circulating medium, adequate to the exigencies of national enterprise." Urged on by Beecher and others, manufacturers prepared to ask Congress for more assistance.[58]

When Congress convened in December 1819, most expected the tariff to be a source of debate as a result of the panic. In his third annual message, President Monroe acknowledged the financial troubles of the nation early in his address. "The pecuniary embarrassments which have so deeply affected the commercial interests of the nation have been no less adverse to our manufacturing establishments in several sections of the Union," he told Congress. The president then added, "It is deemed of great importance to give encouragement to our domestic manufactures. In what manner the evils which have been adverted to may be remedied, and how far it may be practicable in other respects to afford to them further encouragement, paying due regard to the other great interests of the Union, is submitted to the wisdom of Congress."[59] Monroe did not give a full endorsement to the protective policy, but by suggesting that manufacturers receive "encouragement," and only cryptically referencing the other interests of commerce and agriculture, he seemed to be urging Congress to offer more protection to manufacturers. Yet, in spite of the necessity of tariff reform brought on by the panic, the tariff had to wait because furor over the Missouri territory consumed the attention of Congress and the nation.

2

"Whatever the people will, at any particular moment, must be done"

O N A FALL DAY LATE IN 1819 in Braintree, Massachusetts, John Adams sat down and resumed his correspondence with Thomas Jefferson, his sometime friend and sometime enemy. "Congress are about to assemble and the Clouds look Black and thick, Assembling from all points, threatening thunder and lightning," Adams noted. "The Spanish Treaty, the Missouri Slavery, the encouragement of Manufactures by protecting duties or absolute prohibitions, the project of a bankrupt act, the plague of Banks, perhaps even the Monument for Washington, and above all the bustle of Caucuses for the approaching election."[1] When Jefferson received Adams's letter, he dismissed most of his friend's worries. "The banks, bankrupt law, manufactures, Spanish treaty are nothing," the Virginian chided. "These are occurrences which like waves in a storm will pass under the ship." But Jefferson, much more than Adams, feared the danger that Missouri's application for admission into the union as a state posed to the safety of the nation. "From the battle of Bunker's hill to the treaty of Paris we never had so ominous a question," he declared.[2]

Three weeks after Jefferson responded to Adams, Adams's son, Secretary of State John Quincy Adams, retired to his bedroom and, as on most nights, poured his vitriol and thoughts into his diary. Unbeknownst to the younger Adams, when he recorded his ideas for January 2, 1820, he repeated the fears that his father had raised to Jefferson shortly before. "There are several subjects upon which the public mind in this country is taking a turn which alarms me greatly for the continuation of this Union," the younger Adams confided to his diary. He then listed the potential causes that might disrupt the union: "the bank; the currency; the internal improvement question; the extension or repression of slavery; the conflicting ambition of the great states of New York and Virginia, and the workings of individual ambition, mingling with all these controversial topics." Adams avoided listing the "encouragement of manufactures" in his diary. Six days later, after a conversation with President James Monroe, he reiterated the problems confronting the United States. This time he included "the depression of manufactures" along with the other issues.[3] The nation, not yet a half century old, entered a perilous time. With so many forces threatening to cause trouble and perhaps even tear the union apart, John Adams, his son, Jefferson, and others pondered ways to guide the nation through an unexpected maelstrom.[4]

Because of the Panic of 1819, every economic interest clamored for relief, but American manufacturers acted with much more energy than farmers, merchants, and shippers. Northern manufacturers petitioned Congress to increase duties on manufactured items imported from abroad and sent their advocates to Washington to lobby on their behalf. Mathew Carey flooded Washington City with copies of *Addresses of the Philadelphia Society for the Promotion of National Industry*. This document challenged the free-trade doctrines of Adams Smith. According to Carey, free trade deprived the nation of specie and resulted in poverty. All the great and wealthy nations of the world, Carey contended, had achieved their greatness through the restrictive system. Farmers, merchants, and navigators denounced the propaganda of manufacturers. The supporters of protection were labeled as "greedy capitalists" and proponents of a "moneyed aristocracy." William Plumer, a retired politician from New Hampshire, added, "the zeal and talents and industry of the manufacturers in their application to Congress and their addresses to the people, induces many to think that the public voice is almost unanimously in their favor; but this is *not the fact*." According to Plumer, all the memorials, speeches, and petitions from manufacturers had overinflated their actual numbers.[5]

The emergence of the slavery issue prevented the national legislature from focusing on a tariff in early 1820. In 1816, the tariff remained a stand-alone issue. In 1820, it became interwoven with the peculiar institution when Missouri sought admission into the union. Some northern congressmen, incensed at the power that southerners exerted in national politics and fearful that another slave state would only augment that influence, opposed Missouri's admission into the union. Southerners worried about the precedent that would be set if Congress placed restrictions on a state's entrance into the union. Talk of disunion and civil war became common.[6]

As members of Congress argued over Missouri at the end of 1819 and the beginning of 1820, a resident of the capital city penned a letter to a friend in Charleston, South Carolina. To this writer, northerners had attacked the southern way of life. Once the northerners in Congress disposed of the Missouri question, the unidentified writer continued, it would continue the attack with the tariff, which favored only the North and injured the South. "As measures of this kind will very materially affect our foreign commerce, and the prices of produce, they will necessarily be opposed by the Southern States," he lamented. "But as the Western States will join with the North in supporting them, they will in all probability pass."[7] Southerners now sensed that the tariff might be injurious to their economic livelihood. More importantly, southerners saw threats to their way of life from sources beyond of their control. To meet this attack, southerners along the coast abandoned their homes and sought their fortunes in the fertile lands of the Southwest. By the end of the decade, planters in South Carolina and Georgia charged that the fields of Alabama, Mississippi, and Louisiana yielded two times more cotton than the lands along the Atlantic Ocean. Although only a trickle in the 1820s, the immigrants arriving in the United States bypassed the South and landed in northern ports and migrated to the Midwest. Northern states acquired more representatives, while Virginia, the Carolinas, and Georgia failed to keep pace. A final concern for southerners came from the fact that Monroe had failed to anoint a presidential successor. Secretary of State John Quincy Adams occupied the post regarded by many as the stepping-stone to the presidency. If Adams opposed slavery like others in the North, this could lead to a more direct assault against the institution in a few more years. When southern members of Congress viewed the political landscape in 1820, they saw possible threats in every direction.[8]

The extended Missouri debate signaled that Congress would have little time available to debate other matters. At the end of January, Speaker of the House Henry Clay bemoaned that Missouri continued to command the attention of Congress. His frustration centered on the prolonged debate over Missouri taking time away from the tariff, which he favored. Some congressmen, however, may have welcomed this extended delay over Missouri as a means of obstructing pending legislation that they opposed.[9]

In an attempt to hasten the business of the session, the Senate united the separate bills admitting Maine and Missouri as states into a single bill on February 16. Senator Jesse B. Thomas proposed that slavery not be allowed in future states residing north of 36° 30". Though a compromise measure, this package pleased few Americans. "Let Maine go to the Devil," Charles Hammond exclaimed to John C. Wright. "This is in my mind a great question and fraught with important consequences. A new state of parties must grow out of it."[10] William A. Trimble, an Ohio senator, informed his brother: "The Senate is I believe, determined not to admit Maine unless Missouri is admitted without restriction. The Southern people are much excited. They have pursued a course which I was not prepared to expect and which I think is not calculated to produce to them a favorable result on the present question nor a favorable effect on the future deliberations of Congress. The dissolution of the Union has been openly threatened."[11] The Senate approved the measure, and then Clay cajoled enough northerners to support it in the House. By a vote of ninety to eighty-seven, the House passed the Senate bill for the admission of Missouri with the provision barring slavery excluded. For the moment, the nation avoided a crisis. But would the northern attacks on southern society during the admission of Missouri prompt southerners to extract a measure of revenge on legislation that the North considered vital, as Trimble suggested? Even though the South had emerged victorious, it had been a costly, and in some respects, embarrassing victory because southerners had to defend an institution that had been abandoned or was in the process of being terminated in the rest of the nation.[12]

Immediately after news of the compromise reached Charles Tait in Alabama, he informed Senator John Williams Walker that the people of his home region considered the compromise "entirely satisfactory." Tait then admitted that the North could expect few favors from the South in the future. "The sword has been drawn and the scabbard thrown away," Tait noted.[13] Rufus King of New York perhaps captured these bitter feelings best when he confirmed to Massachusetts Federalist Christopher Gore, "the slave question at present is matter of memory only; but very deep and resentful impressions have been made among the slave States, and towards individuals their feelings are not likely to wear away."[14]

Many northerners agreed with King's assessment. The South, they maintained, would seek revenge on the North as a result of the attacks on slavery. That region may have gotten Missouri admitted as a slave state, but the federal government had been allowed to regulate slavery, which southerners worried set a dangerous precedent. Just before the commencement of the Missouri debate, Ohio senator Benjamin Ruggles feared that Missouri would lead to "animated discussion" and "acrimonious recrimination." Ruggles had the clairvoyance to anticipate the problems resulting from Missouri's desire to enter the union with slavery, but his use of the term "recrimination" proved to be correct as well.[15] The *New York Commercial Advertiser* published a letter in which an unidentified Yankee excoriated southerners and slavery. "They are educated in a contempt for labor," he declared, "because, from infancy, they see none perform it but slaves; and for this reason, I must confess, they would not be apt to relish any project which would give to freemen the immense advantages that would certainly accrue to them from having a monopoly of the home market." He then added, "as long as the anti-manufacturing section of the great community have an absolute sway over the political opinions of that portion most interested in the promotion of domestic industry, thee may expect to be thwarted in the laudable wishes thee entertains, and that thy exertions will avail nothing."[16] Another northerner, whose letter appeared in the *Philadelphia Aurora*, echoed this sentiment. "I have only to say, there is great opposition from the south, and partially from the east, to the encouragement of manufactures, insomuch that I have my doubts whether we shall be able to make any increase in the tariff. Whether the opposition from the south arises out of the Missouri question, or from a desire to purchase from foreigners rather than to encourage national industry, you will judge; but from that source arises my fears."[17] Using the pen name "Universal Emancipator," an opponent of Missouri's admission into the union with slavery contended that "no man, unless he be a hypocrite, can be elected to Congress in this State [New Jersey], who will not oppose slavery, and vote for the tariff. . . . The country is no longer to be trifled with by British rice and cotton planters, hawkers in negroes and foreign frippery. She is bleeding to death: the tariff must immediately be adopted."[18] Northerners believed that the South owed them something, because of their section's acquiescence over slavery in Missouri. A compromise had saved the union during the Missouri crisis, but now compromise appeared to be the furthest thing from the minds of most Americans as they prepared to debate a new tariff.[19]

While the Missouri debate raged, Peter Little of Maryland fired the opening salvo of the anticipated tariff debate by making a motion to separate the Committee of Commerce and Manufactures into two separate committees. Virginia's Thomas Newton, chairman of the committee about to be split, opposed the motion. He argued that Congress best served the interests of commerce and manufacturing by having a single committee instead of two. Newton stressed that the Committee of Commerce and Manufactures already came into conflict with the Ways and Means Committee. If the House separated the committee, more collisions and competition would ensue. Both commerce and manufacturing were important to the nation, James S. Smith of North Carolina declared, and by splitting the committee, each would receive adequate attention. After Smith finished speaking, the House voted eighty-eight to sixty-six to divide the committee. Tariff supporters approved the proposal, while its foes opposed it.[20]

Henry Baldwin of Pennsylvania became the first chairman of the Committee on Manufactures. This appointment surprised some because Baldwin differed with Clay on the bank issue, the Seminole war, and the sale of public lands. The Speaker obviously knew his man because Baldwin became an untiring advocate of the tariff and sectional compromise during his time in the House and later on the bench. A graduate of Yale College, Baldwin had left Connecticut for Pennsylvania at the end of the eighteenth century. Finding his opportunities limited in Philadelphia, Baldwin moved to Pittsburgh. There he became a successful iron manufacturer. Elected with the support of Federalists and Republicans, Baldwin entered the House in 1817 and voted with the South during the Missouri debates, making him what John Randolph referred to as a "dough face," or a northern man with southern principles. In a series of letters to Daniel Webster, Baldwin explained that he supported the South during the Missouri crisis, based on the belief that when Congress debated "subjects deeply interesting to the people of the North," it would be "desirable to conciliate the dispositions of the South."[21] In other words, Baldwin suggested that he voted with the South expecting that his vote might be rewarded at some later point. Five days after Baldwin's exchange with Webster, Rufus King mocked the quandary of Baldwin's Pennsylvania delegation. "Pennsylvania is assailed, coaxed, flattered, and menaced, in order to detach her from her union with the free states," King avowed; "her revolt on this occasion alarms, distresses, and calls forth all the resources of the slave States to regain Pennsylvania; they will make sacrifices for this purpose."[22] King seemed to believe that Baldwin voted with the South over Missouri in return for votes on his tariff.[23]

Baldwin served in the House in 1818 when Monroe approved three bills relating to the tariff. Passed with little debate, these bills offered increased protection to manufactured copper and iron. Congress also approved a bill extending the operation of the tariff of 1816 until 1826. The House refused to take a roll call on the final vote. When Edward Colston tried to amend the bill to keep it in effect until 1820 instead of 1826, the House defeated his amendment by a vote of 31 to 108. The House then approved a motion to engross the bill and send it to a third reading by a vote of 106 to 34. Since these bills and the tariff of 1816 passed with the assistance of southern votes, why would Baldwin need to curry favor with southerners? More than likely, he sensed the southern animosity over Missouri, and he voted with southern members hoping that they would remember his act during the upcoming debate on his tariff. Southern votes on the tariff would act as a hedge against potential northern defections.[24]

Since the Ways and Means Committee previously reported tariff bills, their apparent stalling prompted Baldwin to draft a bill that took over their primary function. In his bill, Baldwin proposed to raise duties on imported staples such as almonds, cinnamon, cloves, coffee, figs, nutmeg, peppers, plums, raisins, and salt. Duties paid on these items would provide the government with revenue that would offset lost revenue from goods whose duties would be increased. The increases would be on hemp, iron, sugar, cottons, and molasses. Baldwin's bill sought to raise the average duties on imported goods to about 33 percent. This made the bill much more protective than the tariff of 1816. But Baldwin gave the sharpest increases in duties to iron manufacturers. If Congress approved his tariff bill, Baldwin told the House, then the depressed American manufacturers would receive a new impetus, and the iron foundries, cotton looms, and other business enterprises would return to producing articles necessary for Americans. Baldwin reported the bill on March 22, less than three weeks after he voted with the South on the admission of Missouri and just sixteen days after Monroe approved the Missouri Compromise.[25]

On the day after Baldwin presented his tariff bill, Hugh Nelson made a resolution for Congress to set a date for its adjournment. Baldwin answered him first and opposed his resolution, because the House had just commenced the important business of the session. In an unrecorded vote, the House agreed to lay Nelson's resolution on the table. This tactical victory boded well for Baldwin and his followers, but the House delayed debating the tariff until April 21. By that point, most members had grown weary of the extended session and desired to return to their districts and families.[26]

While Baldwin waited for a chance to begin debating his bill, foes of increased duties attacked the system that he recommended. On April 14, Samuel Smith, the chairman of the Ways and Means Committee, issued a report calling for retrenchment and reductions in federal spending. On that same day, Arthur Livermore, a Republican from New Hampshire, asserted that Congress should not modify the nation's revenue system during a financial crisis. Speaker Clay ruled Livermore out of order, but Philip P. Barbour, a Republican from Virginia, moved that Baldwin's bill be postponed indefinitely. The House rejected this motion by twenty-five votes. The next day, William Lowndes, the author of the tariff of 1816, offered a resolution requesting Baldwin to provide evidence as to why manufacturers needed additional encouragement and protection. The House tabled this resolution. Though Baldwin's tariff bill survived these skirmishes, they occupied precious time.[27]

On April 21, Baldwin took to the House floor and attacked the Ways and Means Committee for failing to act in the middle of a financial panic. As a result, Baldwin believed that it fell to his committee to assist the country. The peace in Europe, Baldwin declared, meant a revived European economy. Baldwin also acknowledged that the abundant harvests of Europe now deprived American farmers of a market. He next turned to the report that Secretary of the Treasury Alexander Dallas gave in 1816 and showed how the House Committee on Ways and Means in 1816 lowered most of Dallas's proposed duties. Baldwin desired to restore the duties that Dallas had advocated four years earlier. He contended that the United States had to offer protection to its manufacturers because other nations protected their own. "We are independent in name, have the powers of self government, but tamely content ourselves with being dependent on our rival for articles of necessity and the means of defense," Baldwin said. Cognizant of the opposition and bitter feelings still festering over Missouri, the Pittsburgh congressman concluded by asking his colleagues to look at the entire bill and not just any particular section that injured their districts. Every item in the bill had foes in some portion of the country, he admitted, but each region of the country had sections that favored them as well. With customs receipts dwindling owing to the panic, the American people would have to endure direct taxation if Congress failed to act, Baldwin predicted.[28]

The *National Intelligencer*, the mouthpiece of the administration and all things Jeffersonian, seemed to support Baldwin's bill. The paper admitted that the bill embraced provisions of "great importance" because "it proposes a small increase of the present duties, and, on the present rate of duties, on coarse woolens and cottons, an increase at the rate of from twenty-five to thirty-three and a third percent."[29] The editor misinterpreted Baldwin's proposed bill. Cotton and woolens would be increased by a little more than 33 percent. Iron manufacturers stood to become the biggest winners, but they were not alone. Imported hemp saw a protective level of 67 percent. Baldwin's bill marked a major upward revision of the tariff. An editor in New York City observed that Baldwin's tariff doubled most duties on imports. "The object is to protect and cherish domestic manufactures to force the people to buy at home those articles, which may be bought any where else for half the price—to create and support a new interest, that of manufacturing at the expense of agriculture and commerce—and finally to create a monopoly in the hands of a certain portion of the community, while the other parts of it are virtually taxed for its support."[30] While the initial skirmishes in Congress over the tariff had been resolved in Baldwin's favor, the public remained unconvinced of the necessity of increasing the tariff.

When editors discussed Baldwin's tariff, they could not refrain from comparing the tariff with the Missouri question. "This will be another real Missouri question, in warm discussion, if we are to judge of the hostility manifested towards it, or any thing connected with it, by many members," one announced.[31] "Next to the Missouri question, it is a subject the most important that has been before Congress the present session," a Massachusetts editor declared; "while the manufactures greet the bill as the precursor of golden days of individual and national prosperity, other classes of the community view it with alarm as the harbinger of distress and ruin."[32] The Panic of 1819 and debate over Missouri had delivered a death blow to most of the era's good feelings. Few expected the pending tariff to resuscitate those feelings.[33]

For Baldwin, the new tariff symbolized the main part of a defensive citadel against foreign importations. In addition to his tariff bill, Baldwin presented an auction bill and a cash duties bill. The auction bill laid duties on imported goods sold at auctions. If a foreigner or his consignment agent in the United States refused to pay duties on goods and thus forfeited those goods, they would be sold at an auction. Under Baldwin's bill, the winner at the auction would now have to pay the duties. The cash duties bill of Baldwin required that cash duties be applied to all goods imported into the United States. Foreigners and merchants in America could no longer use credit payments to pay the duties on imported goods. Baldwin wanted this bill to curtail the amount of imports entering the United States, but he also wanted it to bring specie or hard currency into circulation. If Congress acted on all the proposals of the Committee on Manufactures, Baldwin's system would make it difficult for foreigner manufacturers to sell their products at a profit in the United States. Hezekiah Niles rejoiced over Baldwin's plan. "The passage of this bill, together with those directing the prompt payment of duties and for regulating sales at auction, would cover our country with smiles in less than six months," Niles proclaimed.[34]

Congressmen debated Baldwin's three separate bills as if only a single bill had been presented. Even though the cash duties bill might have been before them, House members praised or assailed Baldwin's tariff and vice versa. The entire protective system became a topic for discussion. Nathaniel Silsbee and Ezekiel Williams, both of whom represented Massachusetts, defended the shipping interests of New England. The high rates would reduce imports and fewer imports would mean fewer jobs for the mariners of New England. Only a few Americans stood to benefit by Baldwin's scheme, Whitman declared. "It is certainly not for the interest of this nation to make any one class of men a privileged order, and allow them to live by extracting assistance from the hard earning of others." He feared the powers that manufacturers would assume if they succeeded in passing this tariff. "Ours is a government of sentiment," Whitman avowed. "Whatever the people *will*, at any particular moment, must be done. These great manufacturing interests have but one interest. It is an interest adverse to commerce, and oppressive to agriculture." He concluded with a rhetorical question that Andrew Jackson would ask when he battled the Second Bank of the United States in the 1830s. "Have we not, in this country, an aversion to aristocracy? And yet, here is to be erected a moneyed aristocracy—the worst of all aristocracies."[35]

Mark Alexander of Virginia likewise discussed the effects of the tariff on commerce. According to Alexander, the tariff taxed farmers to aid manufacturers. "And I must confess, that I do not understand this way of taxing the right hand to support the left," he remarked. At the end of his speech, he read from Adams Smith's *The Wealth of Nations*. Originally published in the year that Americans declared their independence from Great Britain, Smith's text argued against the mercantilist philosophies of the eighteenth century. Instead, Smith believed that economies flourished best when left free of government restraints and control such as tariffs. Smith's canon became the quintessential text for critics of commercial restrictions, and more and more Americans examined his arguments.[36]

On April 26, only five days after Baldwin initiated the deliberations, Clay descended from the speaker's chair and entered the debate. House speakers rarely joined the debate, but Clay had already begun to set a new precedent. According to the "Star of the West," congressmen spent too much time obsessing about the present. They needed to shift their thought process to think in terms of six-, eight-, or even ten-year periods. This applied especially to the development of American manufacturing. These establishments survived only with continued care and attention by governments. By fostering manufacturers, Clay avowed, the federal government kept the nation out of wars. He contended that foreign commerce remained the "great source" of wars and that the protective policy sought to keep the United States out of expensive conflicts. By decreasing dependence on foreign nations, the likelihood of war diminished. "Our late war would not have existed if the councils of the manufacturers in England had been listened to," Clay reasoned.[37]

Clay appealed to the patriotism of House members in his speech. He suggested that Americans might have to endure direct taxation to replace a drop in revenue caused by a more protective tariff. Congressmen habitually made references to the return of direct taxes, especially during the tariff debates, but few congressmen like Clay had the audacity to suggest that the country should embrace direct taxation. Clay viewed the nation as a young man who had just inherited an estate. He argued that the nation had to cultivate its vast resources and appropriate them toward manufacturing so it would not follow in the steps of a young man who squandered his inheritance. Over time, the nation would be rewarded with a substantial return on its investment. For Clay, it made little sense for the growing nation not to support manufactures. Manufacturing seemed the safest course for the American nation and its economy, because Americans had the resources and materials at hand for manufacturing at home. Once Congress enacted this protective tariff, Clay noted, it would ensure the United States' complete independence.[38]

In his conclusion, the Speaker notified the House that the people expected Congress to enact a new tariff. He asked them to look at all of the petitions that had been sent to the House imploring its members to offer increased protection to American manufactures. "Let us not turn a deaf ear to them," Clay admonished his colleagues.[39]

From the galleries, one observer composed a letter to a friend in Philadelphia while Clay spoke. "Make your mind easy. The tariff bill will pass our house by a large majority, the auction bill with little opposition, and the cash bill on imports, with modifications, enlarging the credits a little," he noticed. "Clay is making a noble speech, the best he ever made, a truly great one, on the subject. The Senate is with us."[40] Two days later, the *National Intelligencer* offered a different assessment of the tariff's chances in the Senate. "It is yet our impression that the Tariff Bill will pass the House of Representatives at the present session. Its fate in the Senate, however, is entirely a matter of conjecture."[41] William Plumer Jr., who expected the tariff to pass the House but run into difficulties in the Senate, referred to the tariff as "one of the most important to be discussed at the end of a long session. It is like trying an important jury case on Saturday afternoon."[42]

Louis McLane of Delaware voiced his opinions a few days after Clay's address. He offered to help opponents modify the tariff, but he objected to the sectional terms and "narrow prejudices" that had arisen during the debate. He believed that the tariff embraced every interest of the American community and was thus, a national object. Should the government not assist the displaced laborer, the Delaware Federalist warned, the impending consequence would be a rebellion. "Insurrections are the fruits of an idle, discontented population," McLane reminded the House. By no means was McLane making an empty threat. With thousands of workers suddenly unemployed and wandering the streets of manufacturing cities such as Pittsburgh, Philadelphia, Boston, Cincinnati, Lexington, and New York, Congress had to respond, or the horrors of the French Revolution might appear in the United States.[43] In McLane's opinion, Baldwin's proposed measures assisted all classes of American society and every segment of the American economy. In this sense, he fully concurred with Clay's argument that the tariff created a home market. With no home market, the American economy remained trapped in the continued cycles of boom and bust. "If our market is abroad," he declared, "the arrival of every ship will produce a fluctuation, and either reduce our prices, or raise them, to be again suddenly depressed." More important, the establishment of the home market alleviated sectional animosities between North, South, and West. Northern states required the raw materials of the South. The South exchanged their rice, cotton, and sugar for the manufactured articles of the North and the West. This trade became "equally beneficial to all parts of the community," McLane noted. With each section depending on the other sections of the union for either manufactured goods or raw materials, the chances for disunion became limited. The tariff also helped to alleviate the economic problems brought about by the 1819 panic. Since Congress refused to create a national currency, it had to seek another remedy to the panic; and for the Delaware Federalist, the fostering of national industry represented the best way to escape the carnage of the economic downturn.[44]

William Lowndes, who framed the tariff bill of 1816, spoke in opposition to Baldwin's plan. According to Lowndes, the House wasted too much time arguing a point that all admitted—that manufactures performed a necessary service to the nation. The South Carolinian viewed the American economy in zero-sum terms. If Congress benefited one interest, then it assisted that group at the expense of another. Baldwin's tariff could not aid farmers, mariners, and manufacturers at the same time. To compensate for this unfortunate aspect of tariffs, Lowndes urged Congress to follow the advice of Alexander Hamilton and offer temporary bounties to manufacturers in place of commercial restrictions. By making temporary payments to manufacturers, merchants and farmers would not be injured in Congress's attempts to assist manufacturers. Should Congress enact Baldwin's plan, Lowndes warned, it would result in higher prices for all Americans. Lowndes contended that the tariff made southerners the most highly taxed of all Americans. He arrived at this conclusion because the tariff increased prices of goods that southerners purchased but also because the tariff allegedly drove down the value of agricultural products. This point would be expanded on to great effect by other southerners in the upcoming years. It seems that Lowndes harbored bitter feelings from the House's rejection of his resolution asking for more information from Baldwin. If American manufactures needed so much assistance, Lowndes announced, surely Baldwin's committee could produce information confirming this. Since Congress prepared to embark on a new financial scheme, proof should be given that manufacturers required such a dramatic shift. Lowndes concluded by maintaining that the tariff of 1816 should be retained, because it furnished ample encouragement to manufactures without levying duties that half of the nation considered "partial and unjust."[45]

In private, Lowndes worked to forge an alliance between southern planters and New England merchants to defeat the bill. He penned two letters to Massachusetts Federalist Timothy Pickering. Lowndes informed Pickering that he and his friends in the South were "astonished" that any New Englander could contemplate supporting a protective tariff such as Baldwin's. The proposed system of the manufacturers, the South Carolinian wrote, threatened the North's shipping industry and the South's agriculture. Ninety percent of Americans would suffer for the benefit of only 10 percent, Lowndes contended. It therefore behooved northern navigators and southern farmers to join forces and resist future attempts to augment the tariff. Although Pickering's response is lost, Lowndes's attempts to solicit assistance from the New Englander would not be the last made by a southerner to unite regional interests.[46]

Charles Kinsey of New Jersey delivered the final speech on Baldwin's tariff bill. "The object of the present tariff is to make this country independent of the world, to lay the foundations of its future greatness on the solid basis of its own internal strength, and, from the profitable employment of the labor of the country, create durable riches," he announced. "By such a course of policy we disconnect ourselves from the entangling alliances of Europe, and become what we ought to be, a nation truly American."[47] After Samuel A. Foot's motion to postpone the bill until the next session failed, the House voted on the final passage of the bill and passed it by a vote of ninety-one to seventy-eight. The comfortable margin that had allowed the tariff of 1816 to pass the House had been cut in half in four years.[48]

As in 1816, the middle states of Delaware, Maryland, New Jersey, New York, and Pennsylvania ensured House approval of the tariff. Only four southerners voted for the bill, while fifty House members from the South voted against the measure. In only four years a dramatic swing had occurred in how southerners viewed the tariff. The 1820 vote reveals that the middle states could do whatever they wanted in the House, so long as they picked up a handful of votes from either New England or the West. If this occurred, the South could do nothing to curtail the agenda and power of this section. The question that remained was whether the Senate would follow the same pattern as the House.

The change in southern opinion in only four years can be traced to several factors. First, southerners linked a high tariff with an increase in taxes. Baldwin and Clay had both recommended direct taxes to offset the protection that would be given to northern manufacturers. Southern Republicans could stomach direct taxes in a time of war, but taxes would be difficult to swallow in a time of peace. Second, the Missouri crisis had stoked sectional feelings that ended the euphoric postwar nationalism. Some southern members tried to defeat Baldwin's tariff because their way of life had been attacked. Third, the Panic of 1819 not only injured the few

Table 2.1. House vote, 1820

	Republicans		Federalists		Unknown		Total	
	For	**Against**	**For**	**Against**	**For**	**Against**	**For**	**Against**
New England	14	15	3	2	0	0	17	17
Middle	47	5	10	1	1	2	58	8
South	4	43	0	4	0	3	4	50
West	11	3	1	0	0	0	12	3
Total	76	66	14	7	1	5	91	78

Source: *House Journal*, 16th Cong., 1st Sess., 29 April 1820, 467.

southern manufacturing establishments; it also revealed the importance of cotton to the southern economy. Decreased cotton prices meant less cash for southerners to buy manufactured goods. They needed to get their supplies and tools as cheaply as possible, but the tariff forced them to dispense with extra capital, with which many southerners could not part. Southern farmers received no benefits from Congress, yet Congress appeared willing to assist northern manufacturers with a protective tariff that hurt southern farmers. Fourth, the Corn Laws of Great Britain excluded foreign grain products from the British Isles. Southerners feared that Great Britain might also exclude southern cotton. But the British Isles remained the largest purchaser of southern cotton. Southerners, therefore, needed to placate them, and a low tariff represented the best way to accomplish that goal. Finally, Baldwin rushed his tariff through the House. Lowndes and the House spent months on the tariff of 1816, and he solicited the advice of numerous Americans when he crafted this bill. Baldwin, however, sought the counsel only of iron producers in Pennsylvania. As a result of this, southerners viewed the bill as imperfect and one that assisted only northern manufacturers.[49]

A shift had also begun to take place in the economic mindset of Americans. Although southerners led the change, some northerners began embracing free-trade opinions as well. Typical was Condy Raguet In 1816, he had worked as an agent for Pennsylvania manufacturers. Following the Panic of 1819, he abandoned protectionism and easy credit and became the leading proponent of free trade in the North. He edited several newspapers and published pamphlets. Merchants in northern port cities, especially New York City, resisted the move to protectionism. But most calls for lower tariffs came from the South. Lowndes, who had opposed Baldwin's tariff, became a hero to those who disapproved of the government interfering with commerce. "I am fully convinced that commerce will flourish best when least shackled by legislative interference," an unidentified man notified Lowndes.[50] A protective tariff stood to injure both manufacturers and farmers alike, this man reasoned. The calls for free trade would only grow louder in the upcoming years.[51]

Before Baldwin's bill arrived in their chamber, senators anticipated that they would have to confront the tariff question. Since the beginning of the year, they had presented petitions both for and against the tariff. Pennsylvania senators Jonathan Roberts and Walter Lowrie offered several memorials relating to the tariff. The Ohio legislature sent resolutions to the Senate calling for an increase of duties. Residents of Philadelphia had their sentiments in favor of an increase in duties presented by Nathan Sanford of New York. The Senate received all but one of these petitions before the House passed Baldwin's bill. These memorials show that Americans observed the movements of Congress and expected its members to assist them either by passing the tariff or rejecting it.[52]

Several senators wanted to dispose of the tariff as quickly as possible so they could return home. Harrison Gray Otis desired to leave Washington in order to address his financial situation, but he knew that he could not leave Washington City until the House defeated the tariff or until after the Senate acted on it. "I really consider the interests of Boston and indeed of commerce as jeopardized by this bill, and my vote and exertions may be very much wanted," Otis informed his wife.[53] He acknowledged that he wanted to assist manufactures; but since the duties proposed in Baldwin's bill injured the commercial interests of Boston, Otis's commitment to his constituents prompted him to oppose it.[54]

John Williams Walker, a senator from Alabama, desired an early adjournment so that he, too, might return to his home. He grumbled that the passage of the tariff by the House forced the session to continue. "I am sick to death of their everlasting delays and postponements and wish to be at home," he complained. Walker wanted the bill to be defeated and believed that a majority of his colleagues in the Senate shared his view. However, he also worried that the tariff might yet become the law of the land. "But such a clamor has been raised out of doors that the nerves of some may be too delicate to resist the shock," he lamented; "there may be a few others who may desire to avail themselves of it for purposes and aims of personal ambition, making it the pivot of a new party."[55] Walker suggested that the "clamor out of doors" had been raised not by politicians but by the people.

Williams's trepidation hints that he and other senators found themselves in a conundrum. They believed Baldwin's bill to be unjust and a bad remedy to the depressed economy, but they sensed that public opinion favored its passage. If the Senate yielded to these passions, it might set a new precedent whereby the people forced senators to act against their own best judgment. Walker also feared that a northern-based manufacturing party might emerge and become a viable force in American politics. If a manufacturing party came to fruition, it would be a sectional party composed only of northerners. A southern party would emerge in response, and every issue would be debated along sectional lines. The establishment of a political party committed to assisting American manufacturers would be detrimental to the interests of the South, and for this reason, Walker worked against Baldwin's tariff in the Senate.

The Senate spent only one day on Baldwin's tariff bill. James Barbour of Virginia moved that the bill be postponed until the next session. Mahlon Dickerson of New Jersey admitted that this had been a long and tiring session, but he argued that senators should not use the approaching adjournment as an excuse to avoid an issue. He reminded his fellow senators that the people had sent them to Washington to confront the difficult topics. Dickerson announced that he had seen this same pattern before. Important bills would be delayed until the end of the session, and then when they finally came before the Senate, opponents complained that no time remained for a full discussion of the bill. "In this way," he exclaimed, "bills of the greatest importance are defeated by minorities." After dispensing with these preliminary pleas to his colleagues to give the tariff a fair hearing, the New Jersey senator then echoed much of Clay's argument that a protective tariff created a home market. Competition among domestic manufacturers kept prices low for American consumers. If the country protected its own industries, then these manufacturers would improve and this modification would be seen in a savings in labor and expense passed on to the American consumer.[56]

Otis endeavored to answer Dickerson's arguments. He told the Senate that no person wanted to assist American manufactures more than himself. But the friends of the tariff wanted to create the "continental system" of Napoleon in the United States, according to Otis. He believed that the nation stood at the brink of a monumental decision. "On one side have been ranged the economists and cyclopedists of the Continent, and on the other side the disciples of the celebrated Adam Smith," he avowed. If the Senate approved this change in the political economy, it could not reverse the new policy without great difficulty. "The step which we are about to take, therefore, will be one which admits not of receding, under any circumstances," Otis pronounced, "nor, indeed, of halting, if it turns out to be inadequate to the attainment of its object." Great Britain and France, he explained to the Senate, are "chained to the manufacturing systems, and must, at all hazards, maintain their interests, whatever may be the imperfections and inconveniences resulting from them." Only after careful deliberation should the nation depart from a system that had worked for so many years. Furthermore, it made no sense to legislate under the excitement resulting from the recent panic. In Otis's opinion, the country should wait before making such a fundamental change in its economy.[57]

Once Otis finished his speech, the Senate voted on Barbour's motion to postpone the bill until the next session. The Senate approved the motion by a vote of twenty-two to twenty-one, thus killing the tariff for the time being. The voting pattern coincided with that of the House just a week earlier. Only one southerner, John H. Eaton of Tennessee, voted against the postponement.[58]

The Senate's vote stunned the tariff's supporters in the House and across the nation. One American observed that when he heard the news of the tariff's defeat, it resembled "a clap of thunder in a clear sky," because he expected the Senate to approve a measure for so many Americans in economic distress.[59] The tariff symbolized the main pillar of Baldwin's system, and, without it, no reason remained to pass the auction and cash duties bills. Keeping congressmen in Washington to debate these bills after it had defeated the tariff only hindered the chances of the next Congress passing a protective tariff, so Baldwin decided to postpone these issues in order to allow the tired congressmen to go home to their families.[60]

When the news that the Senate had killed the bill arrived in Kentucky, the editor of the *Lexington Public Advertiser* lined the announcement with bold black lines. "Mourn, oh, ye sons and daughters of Kentucky—Oh, ye inhabitants of these United States, put on sackcloth and ashes, for the great enemy of your independence has prevailed," he whined. "You must still remain tributary to the workshops of Europe. Your factories must continue prostrate. Your agricultural productions must lie and rot on your hands."[61]

Foes of the tariff recognized that they had only postponed the tariff. Like their adversaries, they too began to organize. "When the manufacturing interest conspires, it is necessary for the agriculturalists and merchants to combine," the pseudonymous "A Citizen—but no Merchant" declared in a New York City paper. Since the tariff's supporters formed town meetings, published essays in newspapers, issued pamphlets, presented memorials, knocked on the doors of congressmen, solicited the assistance of lobbyists, and remonstrated, the tariff's opponents were

Table 2.2. Senate vote to postpone, 1820

	Republicans		Federalists		Total	
	For	Against	For	Against	For	Against
New England	2	2	4	2	6	4
Middle	5	1	3	0	8	1
South	1	15	0	0	1	15
West	6	2	0	0	6	2
Total	14	20	7	2	21	22

Source: *Senate Journal,* 16th Cong., 1st Sess., 4 May 1820, 376. Note: "For" votes indicate support for Baldwin's tariff.

required to respond in kind. "They [tariff supporters] are rallying all their forces, preparing new schemes of action, that they may appear before the next Congress with a new and more imposing front," the anonymous writer declared. He offered the Virginia Agricultural Societies as an example for the tariff's foes to emulate. "You must fight them with their own weapons. *You* too must hold meetings. *You* must hold conventions. *You* must address the public. *You* must memorialize Congress."[62]

The increased coverage that newspapers devoted to Missouri and the tariff, along with the number of petitions, shows that more and more Americans began to take an active part in the political process. Throughout the 1820s and 1830s, numerous states revised their constitutions and offered the franchise to previously disfranchised groups. In 1820, less than one hundred thousand Americans voted for president. In 1824, that number increased to a little less than four hundred thousand Americans. In 1828, that number exceeded one million. Some Americans, however, believed that the tariff hindered the growth of democracy. For example, Churchill C. Cambreleng published a lengthy treatise against Baldwin's tariff. He charged that Baldwin's tariff stifled democracy because its highest duties fell on articles utilized by the poorer classes, while its lowest duties targeted items consumed by the upper classes. A democratic tariff, he argued, imposed its highest duties on luxury items used by the rich and not vice versa. "Under the New Tariff," Cambreleng declared, "the duties which would be paid by the mass of this nation, average about 75 per cent on all the articles of necessity; while the duties on fine goods and luxuries used only by the rich, would not average more than 30 per cent." He suggested that the tariff duties granted more power and privileges to the aristocracy of the nation. "We copied enough of the British system in 1790," he exclaimed, "when we took only the form. Pursue that system as we have done or as Mr. Baldwin would have us, and there is no probability; that this republic will last 100 years."[63]

Since it came up for debate immediately after the conclusion of the Missouri crisis, Baldwin's tariff only widened the breach between the North and the South. A more prudent course for Baldwin might have been to wait until the next session before bringing the tariff up for debate, but the economy stood in ruins, and no other congressmen seemed willing to offer the American people some form of assistance. The caustic words and close votes revealed that it would be a long time before Americans put the bitter memories of Missouri behind them. Virginia congressman James Pleasants looked to the future with little optimism in the beginning of 1821. "I fear in spite of all things to the contrary," he observed. "A geographical division of parties in future is to be that of our country."[64]

3

"A step between the throne and the scaffold"

A TTEMPTS BY PROTECTIONISTS to increase the tariff had failed after 1820. Henry Clay resigned his House seat in order to repair his wrecked financial condition, while Henry Baldwin retired from the lower chamber to engage in his own manufacturing business. Their departures removed the strongest advocates for a protective tariff from the House. Clay's resignation allowed Virginia's Philip P. Barbour to become Speaker. Barbour, a strict constructionist foe of the expansion of federal powers, opposed all efforts to bring the tariff issue before the House. As Speaker, he urged retrenchment in the economy and wanted Congress to slash federal spending. The less Congress spent, the sooner it could extinguish the public debt, he reasoned. Decreased federal spending removed the necessity for revenue from tariffs, so Barbour's policies represented a clear and present danger to proponents of a protective tariff.[1]

The first session of the Eighteenth Congress commenced on December 1, 1823. This became the first Congress to assemble after the 1820 census went into effect. As a result, states that had supported the Baldwin tariff increased their membership in the House. New York gained seven seats, while Ohio gained eight seats. Pennsylvania received three more seats, and Indiana and Kentucky each acquired two more. Of the twenty-six new seats in the House, twenty-two went to states that had supported the Baldwin tariff by large majorities. Hezekiah Niles noted, "The congress which shall be chosen after the next census will do all that is necessary to rescue the nation from its present poverty and distress, so far as these are to be relieved by an attention to domestic industry."[2] In another fortunate sign for protectionists, Clay returned to the House and regained the Speaker's chair on the first ballot by a vote of 139 to 42 over Barbour. His crushing defeat revealed that House members favored Clay and his policies over the Virginian's proclivities of retrenchment. Clay packed the Committee on Manufactures with friends of the tariff. John Tod of Pennsylvania became its chairman, while only one southerner, Henry W. Connor of North Carolina, received a post on that committee.[3]

Although an accomplished legislator and proficient in the art of compromise, Clay did not look forward to another tariff battle. "Of all subjects it is the most disagreeable affair of legislation," he wrote during the early stages of the 1824 debate. "The numerous conflicting and irreconcilable interests render it impossible to do all that I could desire."[4] Maine and Missouri's admission into the union after 1820 added to Clay's apprehension. No one could predict with any certainty how the new congressmen from those states might vote on the tariff. If Missouri's members voted like the members from the western states of Illinois, Indiana, Kentucky, and Ohio, then protectionists would have the required votes necessary to win passage of a protective tariff. But if Missouri's members voted with the South, then the tariff would be defeated once again. Also, both of Massachusetts's senators had opposed the tariff in 1820, so protectionists worried that the new state of Maine, formerly a part of Massachusetts, might vote along similar lines.[5]

President James Monroe's seventh annual message to Congress provided a promising sign for protectionists. In this message, which articulated the Monroe Doctrine, the president cryptically reminded Congress that he had recommended a new tariff in his previous messages and that his views on that subject remained "unchanged." While not a full-fledged endorsement of the protective policy, Monroe's message indicated that he wanted a new tariff and that he would not veto a bill if Congress presented him with one. The House's increased membership, Clay's return, and Monroe's recommendation left no doubt that the tariff would be a major topic during the upcoming congressional session.

When the House received Monroe's message, John W. Taylor of New York moved that the portions of the message relating to the tariff be referred to the Committee on Manufactures. One Virginian immediately viewed the pending debate as yet another assault on the southern way of life. "The Tariff subject will be the last measure which we agriculturalists shall have of making head against northern and eastern encroachment," he announced.[6]

On January 9, 1824, John Tod presented a new tariff bill from the Committee on Manufactures. Tod lived in Bedford, Pennsylvania, located just over one hundred miles east of Pittsburgh. A follower of Thomas Jefferson, Tod rose in Pennsylvania politics and became speaker of the state's lower chamber. He next served in the Pennsylvania senate and became president of that body. In 1820, he won a seat to the House of Representatives. As he was an economic nationalist, it surprised few that Clay tabbed him to shepherd the tariff bill through Congress. Tod rewarded Clay by serving as a presidential elector for him that fall.[7]

Tod's proposed tariff raised the minimum valuation on imported cloths from twenty-five cents a square yard to thirty-five cents; it levied a specific duty of six cents per square yard on cotton bagging; coarse cottons received the highest duty of 100 percent. The bill also offered increased protection to woolens, hemp, lead, glass, and iron. All told, Tod proposed to raise import duties to about 35 percent. This bill offered more protection to more interests than Baldwin's failed bill of 1820. Throughout January, Tod waited for the opportunity to begin the debate. On February 11, he got his chance. At that moment, no member of the House could have anticipated that the debate would rage until the end of April.[8]

Tod asked Congress if it desired to make the United States dependent on European monarchies for its necessary articles. He then argued that the country never offered manufacturers ample protection against European imports. Only because of trouble in Europe, he said, had Americans won "command of the home market." Wealthy foreigners, who could "throw away cargoes of their goods," made a mock-

ery of the 1816 tariff. Foreigners glutted American markets with the goal of destroying American manufactures. "There is nothing so intolerable as the dependence on
foreigners for what we may have as good or better at home," Tod declared. Accordingly, Americans could produce lead, hemp, woolens, cotton, glass, and iron. Owing to the ignorance of Congress, however, Americans paid a "tribute to foreigners." Tod then attacked the point that protective duties allowed manufactures to sell
their goods at exorbitant prices. Quite the opposite, he contested, "it is protection
only, which enables the manufacturer to sell them cheaply because protection assured the manufacturer a market and a steady demand for his goods."[9]

For four weeks after Tod delivered his speech, the House debated specific items
in the bill. Members refrained from debating the general principle of a protective
tariff. Instead, they praised or criticized the levels of protection that the proposed
bill offered to specific manufactured goods or agricultural items that were important in their districts. Congressmen sniped at one another over economic interests
that carried sectional overtones. Cotton growers argued that high duties on hemp,
which was used for cotton bagging, forced them to pay higher prices to bundle
their product and transport it to markets. The hemp grown in Kentucky came
into competition with Russian hemp, so Kentuckians such as Charles A. Wickliffe
worked hard to guarantee as much protection as possible to this native product,
which was used not only for bagging cotton but also in the rigging of ships. When
George W. Owen of Alabama secured the floor, he lamented that the tariff pitted
members of the House against one another on sectional terms. Owen felt "sorry to
perceive that every member who entered the discussion, referred to its operation
on his own individual district alone. State was set in opposition to State." As a cotton planter, Owen objected to the high duties on hemp and sugar. Because of these
duties his district "would have to help Louisiana in paying her tribute to Kentucky."
He then acknowledged that some interests would have to be sacrificed in order for
the bill to become law.[10]

George McDuffie of South Carolina reiterated Owen's argument. "What is the
question before us? It is not a question for providing for the common defence and
general welfare, or for maintaining the independence of the country. It is not a
question which is urged upon us on national grounds at all, but it is a question
distinctly arraying against each other the interests of two different sections of the
Confederacy."[11] Henry C. Martindale of New York responded to McDuffie several
weeks later and suggested that McDuffie seemed to recommend a course that might
lead to disunion—a topic that had become more and more popular with each passing day. "Gentlemen talk of a Confederation—of a Confederated Government," he
declared. "Sir, this language is new to me. I have not read it in the Constitution.
It sounds foreign to my ears, and it is foreign to the feelings of my countrymen
generally."[12]

Robert S. Garnett of Virginia believed that the actions of Congress attacked the
livelihood of southerners. He maintained that if southerners did not work together
to resist the encroaching danger of the tariff, then the liberties that they had fought
for and won during the Revolution would be for naught. Virginia's most prominent
statesman, Thomas Jefferson, just like Garnett, viewed the tariff as a means whereby

the North plundered the wealth of the South. The Sage of Monticello informed a visitor that the tariff took "a shilling off of every dollar the southern people paid."[13] James Hamilton of South Carolina echoed Jefferson's sentiments when he told a colleague that if the North intended to lay prohibitive duties, then "the section of the Union that I represent will be driven either into ruin or disunion—evils of equal magnitude."[14] A Virginian minced no words when he wrote, "The tariff bill is a miserable, mean, unprincipled, rascally 'pick-pocket' scheme to steal and defraud from one portion of the people their property for the exclusive benefit of another."[15] As the bill worked its way through the House, southerners held public meetings to protest the protective tariff. By the time the first session of the Eighteenth Congress concluded, seemingly every southern town, village, and city had met to announce their opposition to the tariff.[16]

The slow progress of the bill caused much consternation among its supporters, while opponents contended that the endless debate prohibited Congress from accomplishing anything else of importance. "I see you are on with the tariff bill slowly—every inch of ground it appears is to be disputed," a Pennsylvanian informed Tod. "You have a powerful force to contend against. I hope the apparent majority may prove firm—one and indivisible."[17] Nathaniel Macon, an Old Republican stalwart and US senator from North Carolina, admitted that the friends of the tariff seemed confident of their eventual success in spite of the delays. "I am tired of the session, more so than I ever was of one and think much of the debate on the tariff has been of too plodding character," he complained to a friend. "One plain principle is involved in the bill, which everybody understands and is this, ought one part of the people, to contribute their labor to support another?"[18] The *Raleigh Register* noted, "As there are *two hundred and sixty* articles in the bill, and each seems to be contested, it is probable that the session will be a tedious one."[19]

On March 26, Philip. P. Barbour of Virginia attacked the principle of protection itself and changed the nature of the debate. "No subject, of a more important character has occupied the attention of the national legislature, during its present session," he declared. A high tariff, according to Barbour, would make it difficult for the federal government to pay off its debt. Instead, Americans would be forced to suffer direct taxation to make up for the revenue lost by increased duties. He next argued that the tariff would increase the wealth of a few Americans, while it forced many others to pay higher prices. Congress, he maintained, could not create capital by legislation. As for the protectionists who held up the example of Great Britain as a model for America to follow, Barbour reminded the House that the success of British manufacturing had occurred alongside a steep rise in the price the British people paid for their goods. He declared, "The British example then, sir, should be to us a beacon, to warn us of the rocks and shoals which lie in the way of this policy."[20]

Barbour employed a new argument against the tariff in his speech, endearing himself to his southern colleagues. He maintained that the federal government habitually overstepped its bounds and assumed powers not granted to it under the Constitution. The Virginian informed the House that he regarded a protective tariff as unconstitutional. The Constitution stipulated that all taxes must be uniform,

Barbour announced, and since the tariff operated differently on the sections of the union, it followed that it had to be considered unconstitutional. Other orators would make a more nuanced argument about a protective tariff being unconstitutional, but Barbour's cursory argument became the first time that a congressman broached the unconstitutionality of a protective tariff.[21]

After Barbour's speech against the bill, Henry Clay descended from the Speaker's chair and delivered an extended address in favor of the tariff. Clay wanted to shift the terms of the House debate. For almost two months, members had sparred over the duties assigned to specific items. Clay confined his speech to the general principles of the bill. At the beginning of his speech, he asked the House members to define a tariff. "It seems to have been regarded as a sort of monster, huge and deformed, about to be let loose among our people, if not to devour them, at least to consume their substance," Clay announced. He then clarified the purpose of a tariff. "The sole object of the tariff is to tax the produce of foreign industry, with the view of promoting American industry." From there, Clay mocked his southern colleagues who insisted that the South could not engage in manufacturing. So long as the South persisted in its viewpoints, he chuckled, it would make the rest of the union "the slaves of slaves." "But, does not a perseverance in the foreign policy, as it now exists, in fact, make all parts of the Union, not planting, tributary to the planting parts?" he asked. Clay poked more fun at his southern colleagues when he implied that Great Britain duped them. According to the Speaker, Great Britain would never refuse southern cotton if the United States raised its tariff levels because the United States supplied Great Britain with better cotton at cheaper prices than any other area.[22]

Clay responded to Barbour by defending the constitutionality of a protective tariff. The Constitution gave Congress the power to regulate commerce with foreign nations, he reminded the House. "What is a regulation of commerce," he asked. "It implies the admission or exclusion of the objects of it, and the terms." In the past, Congress had enacted embargos and nonintercourse laws, and none argued that Congress did not have the power to do this. Statesmen such as Benjamin Franklin, Thomas Jefferson, James Madison, Alexander Hamilton, and George Washington had recommended tariffs before. If these men did not have constitutional objections, Clay suggested, how could anyone else insist that the Constitution did not sanction a protective tariff? For Clay, the Constitution should not stand in the way of progress. "If we attempt to provide for the internal improvement of the country, the constitution, according to some gentlemen, stands in our way. If we attempt to protect American industry against foreign policy and the rivalry of foreign industry, the constitution presents an insuperable obstacle. This constitution must be a most singular instrument! It seems to be made for any other people than our own."[23] Clay wanted to make sure the tariff did not divide the different sections of the union like slavery. This remained the core of his political philosophy for his entire career. Whereas many of his political adversaries thought in terms of sectional interests, Clay tended to think of the whole nation and not any particular region. More than anyone else, he recognized how close the country had come to civil war over the Missouri question. He argued that the tariff before Congress represented another example of compromise and mutual concession between Americans of different opinions. If the South had no members in Congress, Clay charged, then the North and the West would lay prohibitory duties on foreign goods. Southern opposition kept tariff levels at a low rate. Clay suggested that the South gained much from a tariff, and this belief became the most important part of his speech. The tariff created what Clay and others referred to as a "home market." In order for American manufacturers to succeed, they required control of the home market. Foreign manufacturers encountered all the same problems that hindered American manufacturers. But foreigners had the advantages of cheaper labor and a hundred years' worth of experience on their side. These advantages allowed them to compete for a share of the American market. High tariffs guaranteed a market for the American manufacturer and farmer, Clay stressed. He began articulating the notion of a home market at the end of the War of 1812, and several members had already referenced the concept during the 1824 debate. Under Clay's vision of a home market, northern and western manufactures used the South's cotton in their factories. Reciprocal exchanges created a market in America for American manufactured goods and American agricultural products because workers who earned their livelihood in manufacturing establishments used the agricultural products of the South and the West. The tariff brought into harmony all the discordant elements of the American economy and created an American System whereby the federal government promoted economic development.[24]

Clay's American System set the foundation of national unity. It granted the farmer and the manufacturer a steady and certain market for their labors. The British Corn Laws excluded American grain products, while foreign tariffs, tonnage duties, insurance, and shipping costs hindered American manufacturers in their attempts to compete in Europe. Americans had to sell their goods to their own countrymen because of the actions of Europeans. Clay told his audience that all the American interests had been confided to the protection of one government, which he equated to a "noble ship" with a "gallant crew." If the ship survived its travail through stormy seas, every member of the crew prospered because their fates had become intertwined. The same could be said of America. If one region succeeded, the other regions succeeded as well. Clay never viewed the American economy in terms of a zero-sum game as other mercantilists of the era. One section's benefit would not be at the expense of another's. "I appeal to the South," Clay said at the close of his speech, "with which I have so often cooperated, in attempting to sustain the honor and to vindicate the rights of our country. Should it not offer, upon the altar of the public good, some sacrifice of its peculiar opinions?" By using the term "peculiar opinions" to refer to the South, Clay suggested that the South stood out of step with the rest of the nation on this issue and could block the wishes of a majority of the American people. Clay perhaps sensed that even though southerners represented a minority in the House, they still might use their numbers to thwart the will of the majority of Americans who wanted tariff protection.[25]

The speeches of Barbour and Clay established the general theme of the tariff debate. For example, Mississippi's Christopher Rankin argued for free trade by telling the House that this principle of economics "produces lowness and uniformity in the price of everything we desire to purchase, by inviting competition, and enabling you to purchase from those who can produce or manufacture cheapest." Rankin also warned that once adopted, the restrictive policy would be difficult to abandon. The foes of this policy had to arrest it in its infancy, or it would be fastened around their necks for generations. "Be of good cheer, ye tariff men, in the end you will triumph," Rankin joked at the close of his address; "there is but a step between the throne and the scaffold."[26]

Daniel Webster followed Rankin and spoke for two days. Webster had not planned to participate in the tariff debate. He hoped that the tariff might "die a natural death" in committee before it came to the House floor, but since it survived, he decided to speak against it. The Webster of 1824 had not yet become the great defender of Yankee capitalism. Southerners endorsed his 1824 speech because of its free-trade doctrines. However, the Massachusetts representative had a more practical motivation. Webster opposed the tariff in 1824 because it hurt the commercial interests of his Boston constituents. He admitted that he approved of certain sections of the bill, but these sections did not overcome his overall objection to the fact that protectionism hurt commercial interests.[27]

Defending New England's commercial interests became the major focus of Webster's speech. The conclusion of the European wars hurt this interest the most. Instead of offering mariners assistance, Congress now proposed to add new burdens in the form of the tariff. "Protection," Webster charged, "when carried to the point which is now recommended, that is, to entire prohibition, seems to me destructive of all commercial intercourse between nations." Although protectionists like Tod and Clay argued that the fostering of home manufacturers made a nation great, Webster announced that he dissented from this viewpoint. To the contrary, he informed the House, the promotion of foreign trade made a nation great. "What I object to is the immoderate use of the power, exclusions and prohibitions; all of which, as I think, not only interrupt the pursuits of industry, with great injury to themselves and little or no benefit to the country, but also often divert our own labor, or, as it may very properly be called, our own domestic industry, from those occupations in which it is well employed and well paid, to others in which it will be worse employed and worse paid." Although he had a reputation as one of the nation's foremost constitutional authorities because of his successes at the bar before the Supreme Court, Webster refrained from addressing the constitutional aspect of a protective tariff. Near the end of his speech, he did try to make a rhetorical flourish and best Clay. "There is a country," he began, "not undistinguished among the nations, in which the progress of manufactures has been far more rapid than in any other, and yet unaided by prohibitions or unnatural restrictions. That country, the happiest which the sun shines on, is our own." Like John C. Calhoun's 1816 speech favoring the tariff, Webster's 1824 speech in opposition to the tariff caused him embarrassment after he changed this position.[28]

George Cassedy of New Jersey addressed the constitutionality of a protective tariff and in so doing rebuked Barbour. Having lost the argument against a tariff because of its harmful effects, foes now resorted to a constitutional argument to defeat it, Cassedy maintained. He sensed a more sinister motive in Barbour's use of a constitutional argument against the tariff. "Its effort," he said, "is to lay the axe at once to the root of the bill before us, and to effect, not only its destruction, but, so long as the Constitution shall remain unaltered, to deny to the general Government the power of protecting the industry of the country, by similar legislative enactments, at any future period." If Barbour succeeded, Congress would defeat Tod's bill and then set a precedent whereby all future tariff bills would be defeated because they, too, would be considered unconstitutional. Cassedy reminded wavering supporters of Tod's bill that the fate of the protective system rested on this rather imperfect bill. To lose now was to lose everything, he announced.[29]

James Hamilton of South Carolina reminded his audience of the principles of Adam Smith, and particularly, how Clay had forgotten those principles. "Labor and capital, if left to their own direction, will always seek, and find, their most prosperous exercise and investment, and that this may be safely confided to the sagacity of individuals who, by a law of nature, invariable in its operation, will pursue that department of industry which promises to yield either immediately or ultimately, the greater profit." Hamilton here presented the southern alternative to the mercantilism of Clay and the northern protectionists. If the government refrained from intervening in the economy, then capital would flow to its natural channels. Like Clay's home market, a disinterested government would make all wealthy. A government that favored manufacturers through a tariff would enrich only the few, while it impoverished the many by increasing prices.[30]

Hamilton disliked the amount of attention that the tariff received in and around Washington. Every tavern house and inn contained Americans discussing the proposed bill. He referred to the discussion involving the tariff as "outdoor legislation" and the debates in Congress as "indoor legislation." He mocked what he called the "pilgrims" from the North who came to ask the assistance of Congress, but he also assailed Tod and Clay. The secretary of the treasury should have crafted this bill and not the Committee on Manufactures, he declared. "The poor wretch who suffers amputation should at least be comforted, under the knife, with a belief that his doctor know what he is at," he scoffed in reference to those who believed that they understood the question before the House. Even though he excoriated several members of the House, Hamilton made a special point that he did not want to be labeled as an apostle of disunion. "I know that South Carolina will cling to this Union as long as a plank of it floats on the troubled ocean of events," he said.[31]

Tod had left the chamber during Hamilton's speech. When he returned, his friends told him of Hamilton's critical remarks toward him and Clay. Tod apologized to the House for missing Hamilton's "dissertation" on political economy. The Pennsylvanian informed the chamber that he would not be setting a date to meet Hamilton on the field of honor. "I for one have no ambition to be martyr to the best tariff that ever was devised," Tod announced. But Tod did not want to appear to be a coward and announced that he would meet Hamilton in a duel under certain circumstances. "If the gentleman from South Carolina is determined to have a personal contest upon this tariff, he shall not have it with me, without an actual attack," Tod avowed. When Tod finished, Hamilton informed him that to prevent the passage of even the worst bill, he would never make an appeal to the sword, which Tod accused him of doing. The adjournment of the day perhaps prevented the two men from meeting each other on the field of honor. It shows how seriously some antebellum Americans took the tariff though.[32]

The House then agreed to engross the tariff and send it to a third reading by a narrow vote of 105 to 102. A two-vote switch here would have killed the bill. South Carolina's George McDuffie then delivered the final House speech. A supporter of Calhoun's interests, McDuffie had returned to the House after being wounded in two duels. The pain from his wounds and the Panic of 1819 had transformed McDuffie from an ardent nationalist into an unrepentant sectionalist. Few speakers in the House matched McDuffie's vitriol; Louis McLane told his wife that he had never seen such a blustering bully in all his life. Perhaps more than any other South Carolinian, McDuffie symbolized the shifting currents of political opinions in the Palmetto State. He began the decade as a nationalist who criticized nullification but ended it by defending the doctrine.[33]

In his speech, McDuffie excoriated the northern "capitalists" and contended that their protective system endeavored to destroy the southern economy. By annihilating foreign commerce via the tariff, northern capitalists then forced southerners to buy manufactured articles at elevated prices. These increased prices allowed northern manufacturers to extract their profits from southern consumers who depended on the North for their manufactured goods. Without using the exact words, McDuffie suggested that the tariff policy of the North and the West made the South a colonial appendage to those regions. McDuffie believed that the tariff taxed the American people for about four million dollars each year. A few manufacturers in the North, McDuffie announced, benefited from this unconstitutional taxation, while the rest of the American people paid a tribute to them. McDuffie worried that the British would retaliate against American tariffs by refusing to purchase southern cotton, instigating a trade that carried high risks.[34]

On April 16, the House finally voted on the passage of the tariff bill. The bill passed by a vote of 107 to 102. The importance that members of Congress attributed to the tariff is revealed by the fact that several members, although gravely ill, stayed in Washington City so as to vote on the bill. This prompted a correspondent for the *Boston Courier* to write, "I might almost say the *dead* were called in to their assistance."[35] "So full an attendance has never been known during the time that we have been acquainted with the House of Representatives," the *Pittsburgh Gazette* reported.[36] Clay breathed a sigh of relief once the clerk announced the vote total. "We have done pretty well today," an observer commented to the Speaker. "Yes, we made a good *stand*," Clay responded, "considering we lost both our *Feet*." In saying this, Clay vented his frustration at New York's Charles A. Foote and Connecticut's Samuel A. Foot, both friends of the tariff expected to vote for the bill but who did not in the end.[37]

Unanimous support from the western states of Illinois, Indiana, Kentucky, Missouri, and Ohio ensured the tariff's passage. "The union of the west saved the bill," Hezekiah Niles reported to his readers.[38] The southern states gave the tariff only three votes of approval and sixty-four votes of disapproval. Every representative from the Deep South opposed the tariff in 1824. New England representatives, torn between supporting their recently established cotton and woolen looms and their traditional allegiance to the maritime industry, supported commerce over manufacturing. Fifteen New England representatives voted for the tariff, and twenty-three voted against it. The middle states had the greatest impact on the fate of the bill. These states provided the tariff with sixty positive votes and only fifteen negative votes. The fifty yea votes of New York and Pennsylvania alone nearly nullified the southern opposition to the bill. If New England leaned more toward its commercial interest, then the tariff might be lowered or reduced to a revenue level. But if New England realized that its interests coincided with those of the middle and western states, then the South would be unable to parry higher tariff bills in the future.[39]

Petitions had already arrived in the Senate, but after the House passage of the tariff, more appeared. The Senate then wasted little time in amending the House bill. In the first three days, the Senate struck out the duties on hemp and iron from the bill by single-vote margins. Senator John H. Eaton of Tennessee now considered the bill worthless. The editor of the New York Statesman avowed, "Striking out the duty on iron and hemp is like knocking out the bolts and bars, and stripping off the sails of a ship—the timbers and planks will fall to pieces."[40] Most observers in the federal capital recognized that the bill would either pass or fail by one or two votes. Several observers waited anxiously for the arrival of the new Illinois senator who would take Ninian Edwards's place. Assuming that this new senator supported the tariff, observers hoped he would arrive before the final vote and allow the bill to pass. However, these two amendments, which the Senate made while in Committee of the Whole, did not survive when the bill came out of Committee of the Whole. Henry W. Edwards of Connecticut reversed himself, which allowed the stricken items to be returned to the protective list; protectionists breathed a sigh of relief.[41]

With the approaching adjournment, few senators wanted to extend their time in Washington any longer than necessary. As a result, only six senators delivered extended speeches on the tariff. Robert Y. Hayne insisted that the ultimate goal of the bill's proponents remained to lay prohibitive duties on imported goods. The South Carolinian believed that soon all American ports would be closed to foreign imports. He also objected to the principle of government planning in the economy. "Labor and capital," he argued, "should be permitted to seek their own employment, under the guidance, entirely of individual prudence and sagacity."[42]

Mahlon Dickerson of New Jersey spoke in favor of the bill. Since all branches of the American economy suffered under the financial distress, Dickerson noted, Congress had a duty to try to remedy the situation. "The prosperity of a nation can only be secured by fostering and protecting its industry," he responded. In order for a nation to achieve greatness, it had to protect and nurture its manufactures, agriculture, and commerce. Congress had protected the latter two since the adoption of the Constitution but ignored manufacturers. This bill leveled the field, according to Dickerson. Whereas the bill's opponents had assailed speculating capitalists, Dickerson praised them. "Manufactures cannot succeed," he said in conclusion, "unless capitalists can be induced to vest their capital in establishments

Table 3.1. House vote, 1824

	For	Against
New England	15	23
Middle	60	15
South	3	64
West	29	0
Total	107	102

Source: *House Journal*, 18th Cong., 1st Sess., 16 April 1824, 428–29.

Table 3.2. Senate vote, 1824

	For	Against
New England	9	3
Middle	5	4
South	2	14
West	9	0
Total	25	21

Source: *Senate Journal*, 18th Cong., 1st Sess., 13 May 1824, 401.

necessary for those purposes."[43] For Dickerson, those who took risks would make America great.

On May 13, the Senate passed the tariff by a vote of twenty-five to twenty-one. The distribution of votes in the Senate somewhat paralleled that of the House, with the South nearly unanimous in its opposition to the bill and the West unanimous in its support. However, New England senators gave the bill nine votes of approval and only three negative votes. They favored the bill much more than New England members in the lower chamber. The biggest surprise in the Senate became the votes of Tennessee senators Andrew Jackson and John H. Eaton, both of whom supported the bill. If Jackson and Eaton had voted against it, then vice president Daniel Tompkins would have decided its fate. Charles Hammond, a Cincinnati editor who supported Clay and wanted the tariff defeated so that Clay could campaign on the issue, believed that the Pennsylvania legislature had goaded Jackson into voting for the tariff by nominating him for the presidency. "Had not Penn. played the fool and nominated him for President," Hammond exclaimed, "he would not have voted for the tariff, neither would his colleague Eaton. We may thank the double folly of Penn. and of Jackson for the tariff."[44]

After the final vote in the Senate, the House still had to agree to that chamber's amendments or force it to accept the House version. If House members decided to play a game of brinkmanship, they risked losing the entire bill. When the amended Senate bill came back to the House, McDuffie groaned that "Pandora's Box" had returned. He then blamed Clay for all the evils that had befallen the South. "The conduct of the Speaker was highly improper and tyrannical, and from the symptoms exhibited, I should not be surprised if we yet have a storm," he said.[45] McDuffie's fears proved to be unwarranted. Although the Senate made thirty-two amendments to the House bill, a conference committee of both chambers smoothed out the differences. Monroe signed the bill, and the tariff of 1824 supplanted the tariff of 1816 as the law of the land. Average rates on imports would now stand at around 33 percent.

4

Judicious and Injudicious Tariffs

EVEN BEFORE PRESIDENT JAMES MONROE had approved Tod's 1824 bill, the tariff became an issue in a presidential campaign for the first time. The five presidential candidates dealt with the tariff in their own ways, not because they wanted to but rather because they had to. The American people wanted to know the opinions of the candidates before they selected their next president. "To the voice of the people, all parties must yield," one American announced at a July 4 dinner.[1] Presidential aspirants recognized that the tariff, if handled properly, could gain them necessary electoral votes. Therefore, the five candidates and their supporters had to explain their position on the tariff.

The most popular and often evasive way to confront the tariff issue became to use the clever term "judicious." Several politicians contended that they favored a judicious tariff but never clarified just what they meant by the term. John Quincy Adams, John C. Calhoun, Henry Clay, William H. Crawford, and Andrew Jackson all sought to win the presidency in 1824 and some of the candidates referenced a "judicious tariff."[2]

On February 18, 1824, Pennsylvanians convened in Harrisburg and nominated Andrew Jackson for the presidency. As the leading manufacturing state in the union, Pennsylvania threw its support behind a candidate who had not yet taken a position on the tariff. While the campaigns of the other candidates ebbed and flowed, Jackson's continued to surge. He began picking up supporters from all his rivals.[3]

It appears that after Jackson learned of the action of the Pennsylvania legislature he began endorsing a protective tariff. "Jackson goes full length," North Carolina's Romulus Saunders wrote at the end of March. "This will injure him in the New England States, as they are all opposed to it and must injure him in the South."[4] But Saunders had misread the situation. Jackson defended the tariff in a way that probably made Clay blush. Clay's followers, who recognized that Jackson's candidacy would deprive them of western votes, desperately wanted to force him to vote on the tariff in the Senate. Before the Senate vote, however, Jackson penned a letter to elucidate his views on the tariff. "You ask me my opinion on the Tariff," Jackson wrote to Littleton Coleman. "I answer, that I am in favor of a judicious examination and revision of it; and so far as the tariff bill before us embraces the design of fostering, protecting and preserving within ourselves, the means of national defence and independence, particularly in a state of war, I will advocate and support it." Jackson reminded readers that the tariff would help prevent the calamities that befell the nation during the War of 1812 from happening again, but he also believed that the tariff would help in the distribution of labor. "Draw from agriculture this superabundant labor; employ it in mechanism and manufactures; thereby creating a home market for your breadstuffs, and distributing labor to the most profitable account; and benefits to the country will result," Jackson avowed. Clay had never gone to this extreme in defending a protective tariff. The tariff also provided the federal government with revenue that it could use to extinguish the national debt more quickly, Jackson wrote as a sop to southerners. He also endorsed the tariff as a means to hurt British merchants. "It is time that we should become a little more americanised; and, instead of feeding the paupers and labourers of England, feed our own," he offered. "Or else, in a short time, by continuing our present policy, we shall all be rendered paupers ourselves." Although a blatantly protectionist doctrine, Jackson's carefully chosen words in his Coleman letter allowed his southern supporters to remain with him and overlook his vote in favor of the tariff.[5]

Numerous newspapers and periodicals reprinted Jackson's letter. The letter itself represented political brilliance. Jackson conveniently neglected to define precisely what he meant by a "judicious" tariff. When Clay read Jackson's letter, he shrugged his shoulders and allegedly declared, "Well by——, I am in favor of an *injudicious* tariff!"[6] Jackson's clever term was not the first use of "judicious" in the 1820s. The term "judicious tariff" received attention on March 30 and again on March 31, 1824. A letter by an unidentified "Member of Congress" appeared in the *National Intelligencer* on March 30, in which this congressman called for a "judicious revision of the tariff." The next day, Clay mocked the concept of a "judicious tariff" and contended that no member of Congress could have used such language.[7]

Jackson's letter to Coleman, in spite of the fact that it never defined a "judicious tariff," was the most naked defense of a protective tariff that had yet to be written. It contained every argument that protectionists had made in Congress: creating a home market, giving employment to the American laborer, securing national defense, and promoting patriotism. His desire to pay off the federal debt, which remained a core issue for the southern Radicals or supporters of Crawford in Congress, gave southerners a reason to support him even if other parts of the letter troubled them. As a political tool, the Coleman letter secured Jackson's support in Pennsylvania and chipped away at Clay's strength in the West. In essence, this allowed disgruntled Clay supporters who did not think that their man could be elected to move into the Jackson camp because there appeared to be no difference between the two candidates on the tariff, and Jackson may have been the man who would go further to secure the protection of American industry. Crawford's supporters interpreted the Coleman letter as a protectionist document and hoped to use Jackson's position on the tariff against him in the South. Who can southerners support, Crawford's friends asked. "They have but one choice left. They must take Mr. Crawford, as the only man on the list who is indisposed to sustain the industry and labor of our country," a Crawford man responded.[8]

In spite of his cold demeanor, Secretary of State John Quincy Adams had supporters and newspapers devoted to his candidacy in every state of the union. The lack of a record benefited Adams the most. Adams had not served in Congress since he resigned from the Senate in 1808. Thus, he had not voted on the tariff or any internal improvements bill, and, because of this, congressmen and editors asked his opinion on the issues of the day. Like Jackson, Adams prepared a letter on the tariff, but unlike his opponent, he decided against submitting it for publication.[9]

Writing from Mississippi, Joseph Gibbs described the presidential campaign in that state to his friend, Louis McLane. Gibbs hoped that Jackson would win by a large majority, but he lamented the Old Hero's course on the tariff. "The vote of J on the tariff has had a very powerful effect against him with the ignorant," he wrote. "And the friends of Adams have made this their hobby on which they hope to ride their candidate into office or at least so far as the votes of the Southwestern states will effect it." Gibbs then described how the supporters of Adams used the tariff issue to their advantage. "If you know the opinion of Mr. Adams on this subject I would thank you particularly to let me know," Gibbs wrote. "His friends deny that he is in favor of even a judicious revision of the tariff while his enemies here say that he is an advocate of it. If this is the fact it would operate as much against one as the other. I should really like to see the contest on fair grounds."[10] Adams's friends in the South wanted to know where he stood on the tariff because of conflicting reports. The *Richmond Whig* told its readers that Adams disapproved of the tariff. "It is with the utmost satisfaction that we can assure the people of Virginia, that J. Q. Adams is *opposed* to this ruinous policy." However, the *Troy Sentinel* stated the opposite: "We assert, upon good authority, that Mr. Adams is, and has been all along, a friend to the Tariff policy."[11] The equivocation of Adams's supporters on this issue left the voters scratching their heads as they tried to discern Adams's true feelings regarding the tariff.

On March 1, 1824, Adams wrote a letter discussing his views on the tariff to Robert Walsh, editor of the *National Journal*. Although Walsh never published this letter, it appears that Adams composed it for public consumption. Adams called protection for American manufactures "necessary" but added that it "ought to be done with great caution with a tender and sincere regard to the agricultural interest of the South and the commercial interest of the North." The secretary of state added that he had not formed an opinion on the pending bill in the House. Adams worried that if American manufacturers pushed too forcefully for protection, then the public would turn against them and oppose their plans for a higher tariff. "The government of this country must be administered upon the principle of conciliation and not of conflicting interests," Adams believed.[12]

After the tariff passed the Senate, Walter Forward, a member of the Committee on Manufactures from western Pennsylvania who occupied Baldwin's old House seat, visited Adams and asked his opinion on the tariff. Adams told him that he favored the bill that had just passed. Before leaving for South Carolina, George McDuffie called on Adams and discussed the tariff with the secretary. At first glance, it seems surprising that southerners like McDuffie would seek out Adams's views and even contemplate supporting him. But in 1824, New England remained divided over the tariff. Daniel Webster, who often acted as a surrogate for Adams even though Adams considered him to be a tool for his presidential rivals Crawford and Calhoun, spoke against the tariff. When some newspapers loyal to Adams reprinted Webster's speech, Adams's opponents seized on this and argued that the secretary of state supported the "anti-tariff policy." McDuffie had every reason to believe that Adams shared these same views and might be interested in repealing the tariff if he had the chance as president. Adams did not flinch on the tariff when he met with McDuffie. He informed the South Carolinian that he considered the tariff as "one of those subjects in which great opposing interests were to be conciliated by a spirit of mutual accommodation and concession." Adams then told McDuffie that he remained "satisfied" with the recent bill.[13]

Secretary of the Treasury William H. Crawford had perhaps the best claim to the presidency. He had finished second to Monroe in the 1816 Republican Party caucus and stood aside with the expectation that he would succeed Monroe. Crawford drew his support from the "Radicals" in Congress. This coalition of southern Jeffersonians desired retrenchment in the economy. The Radicals opposed a central bank, a federally sponsored program of internal improvements, a standing army, most federal expenditures, and a protective tariff. However, as a congressman, Crawford supported the Bank of the United States in 1810 and 1811. As treasury secretary, he endorsed the Second Bank of the United States. While a member of Madison's, and then Monroe's, cabinet, Crawford did not have to take a public stand on the tariff. If voters looked at the views of Crawford's southern followers in Congress who opposed the tariffs in 1820 and 1824, they would conclude that the Georgian likewise opposed the tariff. A Pennsylvanian acknowledged that he could not support Crawford because of his tariff views. "Crawford was my man but I understand he is an anti-tariff man and as the best interests of our Pennsylvania is connected with the success of the tariff bill I will drop any man who supports a policy for the opposition," he announced.[14] But another Pennsylvanian argued that Crawford had gained supporters because he is a "*thorough going Tariff man*."[15]

The political waters were then muddied by developments beyond Crawford's control. Martin Van Buren, who acted as Crawford's campaign manager, voted for the tariff of 1824 after being instructed to do so. Van Buren's organ, the *Albany Argus*, abstained from commenting on the tariff until the beginning of March, when the New York legislature "requested" its members in Congress to vote for the tariff. At the end of the month, the *Argus* announced: "We have all along been favorable to a judicious modification of the tariff, which should combine the protection of the commercial, manufacturing, and agricultural interests of the country."[16] As treasury secretary, Crawford had called for tariff revision as the means to prevent the federal government from engaging in deficit spending. Crawford couched his pleas for augmenting the tariff with the warning that a failure to do so would lead to direct taxation. In his 1822 report to Congress, the Georgian wrote that the revenue might be increased "by a judicious revision of the tariff."[17]

Crawford secured the nomination of the sparsely attended congressional caucus on February 14. Even before the caucus convened, Crawford suffered a debilitating stroke. Bled over thirty times and blinded in one eye, the secretary was expected by few to recover. His friends refused to admit that his wrecked physical condition prevented him from performing the duties of the president. The treasury secretary's detractors made the most of his illness, however, and his chances of winning plummeted.[18]

The Radicals' plan of retrenchment of federal finances fell hardest on the war department that John C. Calhoun led. The South Carolinian's vision of a series of frontier forts and coastal fortifications succumbed to the tightening of the purse strings by Crawford's congressional supporters. Having failed to win approval of a federally sponsored program of internal improvements because of a presidential veto and retrenchment, Calhoun next tried to circumvent the president and Congress by having the army construct roads and canals. The Panic of 1819 stymied this maneuver. When the Radicals suggested that Calhoun had engaged in corruption, the South Carolinian fought back. He established a newspaper, the *Washington Republican and Congressional Examiner*, and for much of 1823, the residents of the capital witnessed two cabinet secretaries blazing away at one another in a print war. Just like Crawford, Calhoun did not have to vote on the tariffs of 1820 or 1824. Unlike Crawford, however, Calhoun voted on the tariff of 1816, and he gave the tariff his support. During his years as secretary of war, Calhoun advocated tariffs on imported cloths as a way to ensure that the army had proper clothing. The economic nationalists in Pennsylvania who coaxed Calhoun to enter the canvass represented the strongest supporters of a protective tariff. Some of these politicians hoped to forge a political alliance between Pennsylvania and South Carolina that could challenge the domination of Virginia. Some New York leaders supported Calhoun because they considered him to be a "northern man" and a "uniform democrat." In early 1824, Calhoun's support in Pennsylvania evaporated, and the state abandoned him for the insurgent campaign of Andrew Jackson. Recognizing that his chances lay elsewhere, Calhoun accepted the nomination for the vice presidency.[19]

Calhoun's advocacy of the tariff began to wane even before he withdrew from the race. An anonymous campaign biography published on his behalf made only a passing reference to Calhoun's support of the tariff in 1816.[20] The Washington *Republican and Congressional Examiner*, Calhoun's organ, criticized Tod's bill. It contended that the bill destroyed foreign trade and deprived the nation of a home market and that high tariffs led to direct taxes. In the end, the bill enriched only a few "greedy manufactures at the expense of all other classes of the community."[21] Clay sensed that his old messmate had changed his opinion on the tariff and that Calhoun disapproved of the 1824 tariff. The Kentuckian also worried that potential tariffs could be lost in the Senate because Calhoun would be vice president and might defeat future bills if they ended in a tie.[22]

Henry Clay likewise believed that his services to the country warranted presidential consideration. He supported the tariff more vociferously than any other candidate, his love of the tariff prompting John Randolph to dub him "Count Tariff."[23] The problem for Clay became that his rivals also supported the tariff, just not as strongly as he did. "The difference between them and me," Clay wrote privately in reference to his opponents on the tariff, "is that I have ever been placed in situations in which I could not conceal my sentiments."[24] Clay's friends published a broadside that reminded readers that even though Jackson supported the tariff, his friends in Congress opposed the measure. A man should be judged by the company he keeps, the broadside suggested, and it warned that if Jackson won the presidency, American ports would be filled with British goods.[25]

As Speaker of the House, Clay had no patronage to dispense like his rivals who held positions in Monroe's cabinet. This hindered Clay throughout the campaign. Although a shrewd politician, Clay also made a serious blunder when he prevented his friends from establishing newspapers devoted to his candidacy. Only near the end of the campaign did he abandon his republican sensibilities and allow his friends to finance newspapers on his behalf. With no patronage, no press, and another western candidate running on his popular appeal, Clay's chances dwindled. In particular, the Crawford forces spread rumors that Clay had withdrawn from the contest. Clay and his friends believed that no candidate would get a majority of the electoral votes and that the House of Representatives, as it had in 1801, would decide the election. Thus, Clay and his followers waged a campaign designed to ensure that Clay would be one of the three candidates left eligible after the general election. If Clay became one of the final three, he and his friends continually wrote, the House would choose him to be the president.[26]

During the summer and fall of 1824, white males cast their ballots for president. Jackson emerged as the leader by receiving over 152,000 popular votes. Adams came in second with 114,000 votes. Clay and Crawford ran a distant third and fourth, respectively. Jackson received a little more than 41 percent of the popular vote. In Pennsylvania, Jackson won 76 percent of the popular vote. Unlike his rivals, Jackson garnered votes from every section of the nation except New England, where he did not appear on the ballot. In the electoral college, Jackson won ninety-nine votes. This represented 38 percent of the electoral vote. Adams came in second with eighty-four electoral votes. Crawford finished third, while Clay came in last. Jackson carried the most states with twelve. He nearly swept the South, failing to carry only Georgia and Virginia. His stance on the tariff aided him in the North and the West and did not hurt him in the South. "We find Jackson, notwithstanding his vote on the tariff, a favorite of the south, and having a strong hold on the affections of the people of the north, while all the west is united in his favor," one editor observed.[27]

Since no candidate received a majority of the electoral votes, the House would have to decide who would be the nation's new president. Only Jackson, Adams, and Crawford would be eligible in the House. Many in Washington City speculated that if Clay's friends had managed his candidacy in New York better, he would have won enough electoral votes to be considered by the House and once there Clay could have used his charm and political skills to win the presidency. As Speaker, Clay now found himself in the role of kingmaker.[28]

Rumors of deals and the offering of cabinet positions spread throughout the city in the weeks before the official opening and counting of the votes. Adams once again clarified his position on the tariff. On January 22, 1825, James Barbour, a senator from Virginia, pressed Adams for his opinion on the tariff. The secretary of state informed him that "the ultimate principle of my system with reference to the great interests of the country was conciliation, and not collision." He then told Barbour that he remained "satisfied" with the recent tariff, but if it should be changed, he would "incline rather to reduce than to increase" the duties. If the tariff fell too hard on the agricultural interests of the South, Adams reported that he intended to alleviate that problem. Before concluding the interview, Adams remarked that he refused to consider the tariff as a constitutional question.[29]

Clay, too, visited with Adams. The secretary left only a cryptic message regarding their meeting in his diary, but more than likely, they discussed the tariff. After meeting with Adams, Clay decided to support him for the presidency. Clay, who despised Crawford just as much as Calhoun and Jackson did, viewed the Georgian's poor health as a disqualification for the highest office in the land. Only Jackson and Adams remained. Clay regarded the Tennessean as a military chieftain whose presidency would threaten the liberties of the American people. In words that would be repeated by his opponents for the rest of his lifetime, Clay claimed that killing twenty-five hundred Englishmen at New Orleans did not qualify someone to be president. With Jackson removed, only Adams remained. Clay assured his friends that the New Englander would protect the interests of the West, including its concerns about the tariff.[30]

John C. Wright, a supporter and close associate of Clay, penned a lengthy letter to Charles Hammond before the House voted. He expressed his belief that Adams would be elected on the first ballot. Wright did not consider Jackson to be a westerner but, rather, viewed him as a southerner, and he regarded southern politicians as being more opposed to the interests of the West than the commercially oriented eastern politicians such as Adams. Wright singled out the state of South Carolina for particular condemnation, calling them "too wild" and "too much tortured with the ambition of Mr. Calhoun and too strongly determined, right or wrong, to make him president." Should Jackson win the presidency, he speculated, southern politicians would rule his administration, and Calhoun would be the "master spirit." Thus, Wright, a member of the House Committee on Manufactures who aided in the passage of the bill the previous spring, decided to cast his lot with John Quincy Adams. Other westerners followed his example.[31]

Jackson had every reason to expect the House to choose him. He had the most popular and electoral votes. Also, almost all his electoral votes came from states where the people selected their electors. Of the seventy-one electoral votes that were given to candidates by state legislatures, Jackson received only fifteen. When the opportunity had been given to them, the people seemed to voice their preference for Jackson. But on the first ballot in the House, Clay persuaded enough House members to support Adams, making him the nation's sixth president. Five states that had supported Jackson in 1824 abandoned him in the House in 1825. When Adams appointed Clay to be secretary of state, the recognized stepping-stone to the presidency, Jackson and his supporters cried "bargain and corruption." "So you see," Jackson growled on learning of the offer by Adams to Clay to join his cabinet, "the Judas of the West has closed the contract and will receive the thirty pieces of silver." Jackson predicted that Clay would suffer the same fate as the disciple who betrayed Christ.[32] The question that now surfaced was what would be the course of the administration on the divisive issues of the day such as internal improvements and the tariff.

As the people learned of Adams's victory, they began adjusting to the new tariff. Protectionists argued that they had won a major victory, because Tod's tariff had proposed to set average duties at about 33 percent. The average rate under the tariff of 1824 during its four years of operation was just under 29 percent. Woolen manufactures voiced their discontent over what they perceived to be insufficient protection against foreign woolens. They increased their calls for greater protection after 1826, when the British Parliament removed its restrictions on foreign wool. Since British woolen manufacturers now had a cheap supply of raw wool, American woolen manufacturers feared that the British would be able to undersell them in America. Southerners denounced these calls for increased protection. But for those northerners who wanted more protection, southern indictments of the protective system seemed hypocritical because most of the South embraced Jackson, a man who had voted for the despised tariff.[33]

The tariff of 1824 demonstrated to the union that the western states had emerged as a pivotal voting bloc. No longer could northern and southern congressmen ignore the West. More importantly, the 1824 tariff became the last time that New England and the South acted in unison. After the final vote, these two regions became increasingly opposed to each other on most issues. Within three years, New England manufacturers took over the protective tariff movement, and southerners bemoaned the unconstitutional acts that Congress passed in 1824, which included the tariff. Nathaniel Macon looked back to 1824 and the passage of the tariff that year as the cause for all the South's future problems. "In the year 1824 the constitution was buried in the Senate," Macon recalled.[34]

In the midst of his lengthy speech on the tariff in 1824, James Hamilton announced that he considered Clay's restrictive system to be an "evil omen." "It looked as if some more tremendous tariffs were yet in reserve, as the *ne plus ultra* of the 'parental policy,'" Hamilton announced. Although the South Carolinian did not recognize the democratic insurgence spreading across the land, he sensed that the most oppressive tariffs loomed on the horizon.[35]

5

Scratching an Itch

"THE CARDING MACHINE, SPINNING WHEEL and Loom—Cursed be the American who prevents their progress, with an intent to aid a foreign foe," one man toasted after the 1824 tariff went into effect. Three cheers then went up, and guns fired announcing support for government protection of woolens.[1]

Woolen manufacturing had become a major business as investors, particularly in New England, diverted their capital from commercial shipping to woolen manufacturing. Ships along the New England seaboard began rotting at the wharves, and others were sold at a loss so that new woolen manufacturers had the capital necessary to commence the manufacturing of wool. Farmers in the region succumbed to the temptations of profits from wool and abandoned growing crops on their lands, instead using their fields to raise sheep from which wool might be sheared. All the New Englanders who shifted their resources to woolens and wool expected to enjoy the same success as cottons enjoyed under the 1816 tariff. By the end of 1827, Americans had invested over forty million dollars of capital into woolen manufacturing. However, a stagnant economy, smuggling, and the actions of the British ministry dashed the hopes of American wool investors. In order to recoup their financial losses, manufacturers, farmers, and capitalists urged Congress to increase the duties on foreign woolens and wool. By scratching this itch, woolen manufacturers and wool farmers met with the expected resistance from the South, but they also encountered opposition from some of the strongest quarters of tariff support. The debate over the tariff entered a new phase: Should Congress use its legislative powers to bail woolen manufacturers and wool farmers out of debt, and, if so, would Congress assist the woolen manufacturer, the wool grower, or both?[2]

The varying opinions over assisting the farmer or the manufacturer also showed the differences between the emerging political factions as the nation approached its fiftieth anniversary. New England manufacturers wanted high duties on manufactured wool but low duties on raw wool. These men, who supported President John Quincy Adams, claimed to be the true friends of the American System. But these men had embraced the American System only after Adams secured the presidency. The Jacksonian opposition noticed this change and exploited it for political purposes. The New England manufacturers, who supported Adams, maneuvered so that only the finished product would be protected under the tariff. Thus, woolens would be protected, but raw wool would not. The Jacksonians sought to offer protection to manufacturers and the producers of the materials used in manufacturing. Jacksonians used the wool issue to prove that their definition of the American System was "American" because it offered assistance to all regions, and perhaps more importantly, it offered protection to all classes of American citizens. The administration, the Jacksonians charged, aided only greedy capitalists while ignoring the farmer.[3]

On October 14, 1825, the Tennessee state legislature nominated Andrew Jackson for the presidency. Tennessee legislators knew they acted rashly, but circumstances forced their action. If they delayed, New York might bring forward DeWitt Clinton, or Vice President John C. Calhoun might induce the South Carolina legislature to nominate him for the highest office. Jackson's supporters in Tennessee did not want a rival candidate for the presidency stealing the initiative. The Tennessee legislature's move prompted the other opponents of Adams to coalesce around Jackson.[4]

President Adams made several blunders as president, which his opponents took advantage of. His first message to Congress, while visionary, demonstrated his detachment from the American people and provided his enemies with ample ammunition to hurl back at him. In particular, the president's foes mocked his proposed program of public works. Adams called for new patent laws, a national university, federally sponsored internal improvements, and the construction of astronomical observatories. Adams ended his message by telling members of Congress that they should not be "palsied by the will of our constituents."[5]

By the end of 1826, most Jackson supporters seemed reasonably certain about the Old Hero's prospects to defeat Adams. "From present appearances, I think it almost certain, that Mr. Adams's reign will close with his present term, unless by intrigue, and the dexterous management of his extensive patronage, this important election shall again be made to devolve upon the H. Repts," James K. Polk wrote. "This is his only prospect; neither the man nor his measures will be sustained by the voice of the American people."[6] Other Jackson men asserted that as long as Jackson remained in good health, nothing could prevent his elevation to the presidency. With only two candidates in the field this time, Jackson stood to gain support from Calhoun's followers, as well as those of William H. Crawford. He could even pick up new friends who refused to follow Clay into the Adams camp. The disgruntled supporters of Calhoun, Crawford, and Clay merged with Jackson not so much because they endorsed Jackson, but because they disliked the policies of the Adams administration. Adams offered nothing to the South, and his policies on public lands enraged westerners. Only a major mistake by Jackson could deprive him of the presidency. "Judging from the news we have from every quarter, the Presidential contest is ended—unless some cause should arise to produce a reaction," James Buchanan wrote in the beginning of 1827.[7] Yet in spite of their assurances of their ultimate success, Jacksonian leaders fretted over the tariff.[8]

Jackson's presidential defeat coincided with an accelerated shift in southern political thinking reoriented toward states' rights. The decisions handed down by the Marshall court, the tariff of 1824, and Adams's desire to send delegates to the Panama Congress, which would include former slaves as representatives, convinced southerners that they had made a mistake by supporting the nationalistic programs after the War of 1812. Southerners recognized that northern states had gained more members in the House of Representatives, and this increase in northern membership led to the implementation of measures that southerners deemed detrimental to their livelihood.[9]

South Carolina took the lead in announcing the danger posed by the federal government's acquisition of unwarranted powers. At first, South Carolinians focused their wrath not on the tariff but on federally sponsored internal improvements. No longer did war loom on the horizon, and some South Carolinians even argued that if a war did occur, an invading army would use newly constructed roads against the nation. William Smith, an upcountry farmer and inveterate foe of Calhoun and his policies, fought the South Carolina brand of nationalism at every step. Smith believed in the strictest interpretation of the Constitution and grudgingly threw his support behind Crawford in the canvass of 1824 because Crawford's hatred of Calhoun matched his own. In 1822, Smith lost his Senate seat to Charleston attorney Robert Y. Hayne. Returning to South Carolina, he plotted revenge against Calhoun and took a seat in the state House of Representatives. There, he pushed through a series of resolutions, originally drawn up by Stephen D. Miller, opposing the encroachment of the federal government. The fifth resolution stated, "That it is an unconstitutional exercise of power, on the part of Congress, to lay duties to protect domestic manufactures."[10] Smith's resolutions served as a notice to other states that South Carolina had abandoned any support for economic nationalism. Shortly after the legislature adopted Smith's resolutions, Calhoun began corresponding with Andrew Jackson. If Smith and his faction joined a soon-to-be victorious Jackson first, South Carolina's patronage would flow through Smith and his followers, leaving Calhoun and his supporters with little influence in the state. It seemed unlikely that Smith and his followers would embrace a man who voted for both the tariff and an internal improvements bill in 1824, but in the wake of Adams's first annual message, Jackson's prior transgressions might be more easily forgiven and overlooked. Therefore, it behooved Calhoun to support Jackson for his own political survival.[11]

Virginia followed South Carolina in denouncing the unconstitutional acts of Congress. William B. Giles, a veteran of the political battles stretching as far back as the first Congress, presented three resolutions to the Virginia assembly. Like South Carolina in 1825, Virginia coupled internal improvements with the protective tariff as measures that proved Congress acted in an unconstitutional manner. Indeed, Giles said that the protection of domestic manufactures involved "the most despotic and dangerous power that can be exercised by government." Giles said that nowhere could the power to "protect manufacturers" be found in the Constitution. He concluded by warning that if the American people acquiesced to this violation by Congress, the power assumed must "eventuate in the most frightful, consolidated despotism, or in the severance of the union of these states."[12] Talk of secession had disappeared after the controversy surrounding Missouri's entrance into the union had been settled. Veiled suggestions about it began resurfacing in 1824 when Congress confronted the issues of internal improvements and the tariff.

If Congress revisited these issues it might imperil the union. The antitariff movement in Virginia suffered a crushing defeat when James Madison published a letter affirming his belief that the Constitution granted Congress the power to enact a protective tariff. This setback would be only temporary.[13]

In his second annual message, delivered in December 1826, Adams announced that customs receipts had declined and had failed to match expectations. The president put a positive front on this by declaring, "The diminution, however, is in part attributable to the flourishing condition of some of our domestic manufactures, and so far is compensated by an equivalent more profitable to the union."[14] But woolen manufacturers maintained that they were not in a "flourishing condition." Just as in 1824, they flooded Congress with petitions and memorials. Farmers who sheared raw wool from their sheep also called for more protection, but most of the clamor came from the woolen manufacturers, who organized public meetings and had their state legislatures pass resolutions calling for increased rates on manufactured woolens. Opponents of increased protection seized on the manufacturers becoming the primary force and endeavored to depict the entire movement as a plot by wealthy New England aristocrats.[15]

On January 10, 1827, Rollin C. Mallary, chairman of the House Committee on Manufactures, reported the woolens bill. According to Mallary and other friends of the bill, wool manufacturing gave value to the hills and mountains of New England, New York, Ohio, Pennsylvania, and western Virginia. Only wool could be transported from these rugged regions to market at a profit. More important to the friends of the bill was the fact that this bill gave the revenue laws of the nation more teeth. Foreigners allegedly committed numerous frauds when they landed their woolens at American ports. They used false invoices but also imported woolens in an unfinished state. Customs officials appraised unfinished woolens at a low price, and the foreigner paid a low duty. Foreigners then improved these cheap woolens at a minimal cost in the United States and sold them cheaper than Americans could afford to sell them. The proposed bill prevented future frauds from occurring by establishing the minimum principle on woolens. The minimums proposed by the bill were 40¢, $1.50, $2.50, and $4 per square yard of manufactured wool. Coupled with the shift to specific duties, friends of the bill believed that this now allowed American wool manufacturers to compete with their British counterparts. These increased duties would offset the actions of the British Parliament, particularly since Parliament slashed the duties on raw wool imported into Great Britain. With a ready supply of cheap wool not only from Great Britain but also from its colonies and parts of northern Europe, British woolen manufactures undersold their American rivals. Since many Americans invested in woolen manufacturing after the 1824 tariff went into effect, the flood of British woolens ruined American manufacturers.[16]

Foes of this bill included those opposed to any tariff. But some of the strongest supporters of protective tariffs voiced their opposition. Enemies of the bill made it a point to tell the House that just because they opposed this bill did not mean that they opposed the entire protective system. The fact that the increased duties on woolens went into effect immediately while the increased duties on raw wool did not go into effect until the following year upset foes the most. This delay would allow foreigners to dump their raw wool in the United States, and American wool manufacturers would have an abundant supply of raw wool from which to manufacture woolens. This scheme helped woolen manufacturers but would ruin Americans who raised sheep. This seemed unfair to even the most vocal advocates of a protective tariff. They also wondered why only woolens received increased protection when the 1824 tariff offered protection to over ninety items. The tariff of 1824 granted woolen manufacturers a duty of 33⅓ percent. Under the provisions of the woolens bill, woolen manufacturers received a protective duty of over 200 percent. Thus, if a foreign manufacturer sent five dollars' worth of woolens to America under the 1824 tariff, he had to pay a duty of $1.60. Should the woolens bill take effect, that foreigner now paid a duty of $11.65. If a duty of 33 percent induced foreign importers to commit frauds, an increased duty of above 200 percent would prompt even more foreigners to evade the customhouse.[17]

Opponents of the bill objected to the type of monopoly the bill proposed to create. The woolens bill allowed fine woolen goods to enter into the country without a high duty, but coarse and rough woolens received a high duty. This duty hurt the poor and lower classes of American society since they could afford only cheaper woolens. In an appropriate pun, James Hamilton reminded the House to be wary of the wolf in sheep's clothing. Samuel Ingham charged the bill's supporters with trying to secure a bailout from Congress. "The truth of all this is, disguise it as you may," Ingham admonished his colleagues from New England, "an effort among a powerful class of men, as we now perceive, to persuade Congress to make up to them the loss of a bad season's business."[18]

The woolens bill passed the House by a vote of 106 to ninety-five. Only one southerner, Joseph Johnson of Virginia, voted for the bill. The most important observation from the geographical distribution of votes on the woolens bill is the switch that occurred in New England. Its House members had opposed the tariff of 1824. Now its House members had reversed their position. Thirty-three New England House members supported the woolens bill, and only six opposed it. In 1824, only one member of the Massachusetts House delegation voted for the tariff. In 1827, only one member opposed the woolens bill. Daniel Webster, who delivered a crushing speech against protectionism in 1824, voted for the woolens bill in 1827. Webster delighted in the fact that the bill split the members of the Jackson coalition, especially those from Pennsylvania. Webster hoped that this might allow Adams to carry the state in the upcoming election.[19]

At first, the attention that the woolens bill attracted paled in comparison to the tariff of 1824. Only those engaged in the business of wool cultivation or manufacturing watched the progress of the woolens bill. One editor suggested that 999 out of 1,000 Americans knew nothing about the woolens bill. Roused from their slumber, opponents of the protective system finally began to move. In Boston, a memorial against the woolens bill obtained five hundred signatures in only three hours. The woolens bill had fought its way inch by inch through the House, and opponents of the restrictive system feared that it would do the same in the Senate.[20]

The Senate wasted little time with the woolens bill. After minor skirmishes over the question of whether the bill should be referred to the Finance Committee or Manufactures Committee, Robert Y. Hayne proposed to table the bill. Twenty senators voted for the motion, and the exact same number opposed it. The fate of the woolens bill rested with Vice President John C. Calhoun. His tie-breaking vote on a tariff bill or a bill offering protection to a particular interest would win him both friends and enemies. Calhoun's failed presidential campaign had hinged on support from tariff-friendly Pennsylvania. At this time, most southerners disapproved of Calhoun's political positions. Although Pennsylvania did not support the woolens bill as enthusiastically as other tariff bills, a vote against the woolens bill would lose Calhoun support in Pennsylvania and damage his future presidential aspirations. Unbeknownst to official Washington, Calhoun had reevaluated his opinions on the political issues of the day. As secretary of war, he made few trips to his home state of South Carolina. Once he assumed the duties of the vice president, however, Calhoun traveled home while Congress recessed, and he acquired an upcountry plantation. Back in the Palmetto State, Calhoun saw the effects that the American System had on his friends and supporters. The South Carolina economy, more than the economy of any other state, languished from the Panic of 1819. The price of cotton continued to fall, the depleted South Carolina soil did not return as much yield as the soil of the Southwest, and more and more South Carolinians contracted "Alabama Fever" and left their native state. Rumors also continued to arrive in South Carolina that Great Britain might levy a tariff on southern cotton or might abandon the crop altogether in favor of Egyptian or Indian cotton. After weighing his political options, the economic situation of his state and region, and his own economic opinions, Calhoun voted to table the bill. Whereas previous vice presidents John Adams and George Clinton had asked the Senate to allow them to make a few remarks when they broke ties in the Senate, Calhoun did not ask the indulgence of the Senate. Even before he gave his vote, he sensed that the tariff would be a critical issue when Congress reconvened in December. "The South ought to send forth to the next Congress all of her talents, her character, and experience," he wrote.[21]

The vice president had to vote on the bill because eight senators missed the vote. Four of these senators—Josiah S. Johnston, William R. King, John McKinley, and Thomas H. Williams—represented southern states, while the other four absentees—Ephraim Bateman, Dudley Chase, Martin Van Buren, and Calvin Willey—represented northern states. More importantly, four of these senators—Bateman, Chase, Johnston, and Van Buren—supported Andrew Jackson, while the other four sided with the administration. With only a few days remaining in the session, it seemed doubtful the Senate had enough time to act on the woolens bill, so the strategy of forcing Calhoun to take the blame for the defeat of the bill appealed to both political camps. Few men in Washington could orchestrate such a daring strategy. One of the men with the political shrewdness to carry out a maneuver such as this, Van Buren, also missed the vote, but he had been in the chamber earlier in the day and voted on other matters. When it appeared likely that the woolens bill would come before the Senate, Van Buren asked his friends back in Albany for their advice. "I am disposed to protect woolen factories but am not very willing to commit highway robbery to affect the object," he wrote.[22] Another correspondent

Table 5.1. House vote, woolens bill of 1827

	Jackson		Adams		Total	
	For	Against	For	Against	For	Against
New England	2	3	31	3	33	6
Middle	20	14	33	3	53	17
South	1	53	0	9	1	62
West	1	6	18	4	19	10
Total	24	76	82	19	106	95

Source: *House Journal*, 19th Cong., 2nd Sess., 11 Feb. 1827, 282–84.

informed him that more bills similar to the woolens bill might threaten the permanency of the union. With conflicting advice, Van Buren opted for the less perilous course and avoided the issue by allegedly taking a visitor to the congressional cemetery when the vote occurred. Thurlow Weed, an enemy of Van Buren and the Albany Regency, wrote that he sacrificed his friends and the interests of his state by ducking the question.[23]

Support for the principle of protection among the New England delegation was the most important part of the woolens bill. Although some historians point to New England as a bastion of free-trade ideology because of Daniel Webster's speeches against the tariff, New England opposed tariffs not because of their understanding of economics but, rather, because tariffs hurt the shipping industry, which remained the foundation for the New England economy. This is why most of New England opposed the 1820 and 1824 tariffs. If the principle of free trade was so prominent in New England, why did the region abandon it in only three years? The people of New England recognized that the protective system could not be reversed. If they continued to oppose the protective system, western states might surpass their region both politically and economically. After the passage of the woolens bill, New England congressmen admitted that their opposition to the tariff of 1824 had been in vain. The tariff of 1824 levied high duties on iron, hemp, and other articles necessary for the shipping interest. Since duties on these goods made shipping less profitable than it had been in previous years, New Englanders shifted their capital into manufacturing, particularly woolen manufacturing, and believed that since Congress decided to support manufactures with the tariff of 1824, it must continue to do so. If Congress chose to abandon manufactures, it would be, according to New England manufacturers, a breach of trust.[24]

As the debates showed, some in Congress thought that New England acted selfishly. Most of the sharpest attacks against the protective system came from New Englanders in 1820 and 1824. But now the strongest arguments in favor of the system came from that region. "I should like to see domestic manufactures flourish," Hugh Lawson White announced in a speech given in Knoxville, Tennessee, after the passage of the woolens bill, "but would never wish to see them brought into existence or nourished in one section of country at the expense and positive loss of another."[25] White must have spoken for many other Americans. New England wanted all the benefits of protection but did not want to share any of its burdens. This zero-sum mercantilist mindset that southerners such as White charged New England with advocating coincided with New England's strong Federalist heritage. This ideology, however, ran counter to the original Jeffersonian, and emerging Jacksonian, ethos of a level society that redistributed wealth. The stockjobbers, the speculators, and those who profited from the public debt had long been the enemy of republicanism. The woolens bill, by offering protection to a small group of manufacturers, symbolized what the Jeffersonians fought against in the 1790s. When southerners talked about a return to the principles of 1798, this is partially what they meant—an economy that did not favor one interest over another.[26]

At the end of the session, Van Buren journeyed south to conclude a political alliance that he had worked to complete since Adams became president. Believing that a healthy and competitive two-party system ensured individual liberty and hindered corruption, Van Buren hoped to forge a union between the "planters of the South and the plain Republicans of the North." In an extended letter to Thomas Ritchie, editor of the *Richmond Enquirer* and leader of the Richmond Junto, Van Buren reasoned that this political coalition, if consummated, would quell threats to the union by suppressing agitation over the question of slavery. Thus, northern and southern Republicans should unite and ensure that Jackson defeated Adams in the presidential election of 1828. Accompanied by Cambreleng, the most outspoken northern opponent of the tariff but also a man who had been born in North Carolina, Van Buren met with political leaders in the Carolinas, Georgia, and Virginia. Although they despised Calhoun for his treatment of their leader while both served in James Monroe's cabinet, Crawfordites in Georgia learned from Van Buren that Calhoun must remain on the ticket. Back in New York, Van Buren's mouthpiece, the *Albany Argus*, periodically published editorials praising Crawford. More than likely, Crawford provided Van Buren with intimate details regarding Calhoun's opposition to Jackson's incursion into Florida in 1818. It appears Van Buren con-

Table 5.2. Senate vote to postpone woolens bill of 1827

	Jackson		Adams		Total	
	For	Against	For	Against	For	Against
New England	3	0	7	0	10	0
Middle	2	2	2	2	4	4
South	0	11	0	1	0	12
West	0	4	6	0	6	4
Total	5	17	15	3	20	20

Source: *Senate Journal*, 19th Cong., 2nd Sess., 28 Feb. 1827, 245–46.
Note: "For" vote indicates support of the woolens bill and opposition to the motion to table.

vinced Crawford to sit on this damaging information until the right moment. If Crawford exposed Calhoun at this point in time, then the second position on the Jackson ticket might go to DeWitt Clinton of New York. Van Buren did not want a rival New Yorker involved in the Jackson administration because that blocked his chances for success. More than likely, Van Buren told Crawford that he would expose Calhoun at a time that not only would do the most damage to the South Carolinian but also would assist himself. Henry R. Storrs, an Adams man from upstate New York, maintained that Crawford and his Virginia allies joined the Jackson coalition with the understanding that the tariff policy would be abandoned.[27]

The alliance that Van Buren crafted in 1827 had more to do with political expediency than policy. This is most evident in regards to the tariff. Jackson supported the tariff in 1824, as did Van Buren and other northern Jacksonians. Western Jacksonians voted for Tod's bill in 1824, too. However, some of the most vociferous opponents of the tariff joined the Jackson ranks at the same time as some of its strongest supporters. Neither side seemed willing to compromise its beliefs on the protective tariff. When Jacksonians talked about the "judicious" tariff, they meant a tariff that lowered the federal debt but one that gave assistance to a wide range of Americans and not one particular interest. Getting protariff and antitariff Jacksonians to coalesce tested all of Van Buren's political skill and nearly wrecked his political party in 1828.[28]

6

The Harrisburg Convention

ANGERED OVER THE DEFEAT of the woolens bill, woolen manufacturers held meetings throughout the northern and western states. On April 30, a Pennsylvania editor proposed that friends of the American System form a central committee and meet in Harrisburg. Woolen manufacturers and their editors seized on the idea of a national convention. On May 14, 1827, the Pennsylvania Society of Manufactures and the Mechanic Arts reiterated the call for farmers and manufactures to hold conventions in their states and appoint delegates to attend a national convention at Harrisburg, Pennsylvania, on July 30. The call requested that each state send at least five delegates. "Public opinion, which, in a government like ours, directs all things and conquers all things, is on the side of domestic industry," one editor exclaimed. By capturing the attention of the American people, manufacturers hoped to use the defeat of the woolens bill to shift wavering public opinion to their cause.[1]

Southerners thundered against the convention. To them, this "Manufacturing Convention" sought only to promote the reelection of Adams. At the end of the summer, planters in the city of Columbia, South Carolina, increased the stakes when they asked Thomas Cooper to deliver a speech on the history of the acts that the British Parliament used to support woolen manufactures. Cooper addressed the requested topic but spent much more time excoriating the American System. This corrupt system, he exclaimed, took 25 percent of the annual income of every southern planter. And where did this tribute go? It went to the manufacturing capitalists in the North. "Manufacture is a hydra," Cooper announced. "The motto of a manufacturer now and always, here and every where is a *monopoly*: to put down all competition, and to command exclusively every market." Cooper continued to assail the northern manufacturers by insisting that they sent representatives to do their bidding and not the people's. He described John Tod, the architect of the tariff of 1824, as a failing lawyer who had no idea about the operations of a tariff. Nonetheless, iron manufacturers in western Pennsylvania sent him to Congress to secure their interests. Cooper maintained that the same could be said of Henry Baldwin, the author of the failed tariff of 1820. "These gentlemen must be considered as lawyers employed by local communities; pleading the cause of particular interests," he argued, "not as independent advocates for great national rights, or strictly what they ought to have been, national representatives." Lobbyists, Cooper announced, stood ready to fill the void if the carefully chosen representatives failed to do the bidding of the manufactures. By bargaining for votes, the lobbyists assisted in riveting the chains on the southern planters. Although Cooper's condemnation of monopolies can be viewed as an early salvo of Jacksonian democracy, it is what he mentioned at the very end of his oration that caught the attention of the nation. "I have said," Cooper concluded, "that we shall 'ere long be compelled to calculate the value of our union; and to enquire of what use to us is this most unequal alliance." The southern people, according to him, could either submit or separate. What good did the union serve if it plundered one section for the benefit of the others, he demanded? He insisted that the American System and more particularly the protective tariff stole from the South for the benefit of the North. The question that remained now was whether other disgruntled southerners would follow Cooper and assist him in throwing the tea overboard or whether they would continue to submit.[2]

In the weeks after Cooper delivered his speech, the *Charleston Mercury* published a series of essays by Robert J. Turnbull. In the fall of that year, these essays were bound together and published under the title of *The Crisis*. Using the pen name "Brutus," Turnbull's essays showed the dangers of a consolidated government. The more power that the federal government assumed, Brutus warned, the more it threatened the interests of the South. *The Crisis* became the most important southern pamphlet before the Civil War. Turnbull's sharp prose, slashing rhetoric, and fears of consolidation spoke to many southerners, especially in South Carolina.[3]

Two issues in particular worried Brutus—federally sponsored internal improvements and the protective tariff. He mocked both John C. Calhoun and George McDuffie for their support of federally sponsored internal improvements, but McDuffie, who supported the General Survey Act of 1824, received much more criticism than Calhoun, whose primary sin had been to issue a report favorable to federally sponsored internal improvements while secretary of war. State governments and private enterprises should fund internal improvement projects, Brutus believed; New York and Maryland had proved that point. In Brutus's opinion, the person most responsible for the federal government assuming powers not granted to it by the Constitution was James Monroe. With no wars to fight, he had urged Congress to turn its attention to internal improvements and the protection of American manufactures. Congress overreached itself, Brutus argued, because federally sponsored internal improvements and a protective tariff were unconstitutional. Looking back at the debates in the constitutional convention of 1787, Brutus concluded that since the delegates debated internal improvements and the promotion of domestic manufactures but did not include a provision in the finished document, these measures should be considered unconstitutional. "Monopolies to the manufacturers cannot be created by an act of Congress, without a departure from the Constitution, and *yet they may be given* in the shape of *protecting* and *prohibitory* duties, because Congress 'has the power to lay imposts.' Canals *cannot* be dug in the States, or military roads constructed, because it is to exercise sovereignty over soil and territory, and yet *money may be voted* for the *same* objects, because Congress can promote the 'general welfare.'" The chartering of a national bank in 1791 represented Congress's first violation of the Constitution, according to Brutus. This began a long series of usurpations that plundered the South and threatened to turn it into a colonial appendage of the North. For Brutus, the protective tariff symbolized the worst of northern aggression over the South because the tariff was a double-edged sword. It acted as an onerous tax on southerners, and then the federal government spent those tax dollars on projects in the North. Southerners, according to Brutus and other strict constructionists, received nothing in return from their tax dollars and only had to pay increased prices through the tariff.[4]

Where were southerners to look to stop federal usurpations of power? Brutus contended that the Supreme Court could not assist the South and rule the protective tariff unconstitutional because the authors of the tariffs framed them as revenue measures. Turnbull lamented that the Supreme Court could not base its decisions on the motives of the architects of a bill. If it could, then it would declare a protective tariff unconstitutional; but since tariff bills were revenue bills, they passed constitutional muster. As a result, Brutus believed that the "Constitution is a *dead letter*. It may mean *any thing*, or it may mean *nothing*." When a state government had a difference with the federal government, the federal judiciary became the arbiter. But Brutus believed that this was unfair because the federal judiciary had a vested interest. The people of the South had to look to their state legislatures for redress. "If the people of three fourths of the state legislatures, for this purpose, cannot be obtained, it would prove that the power ought not to be exercised," Brutus wrote. "Whether disunion shall approach us, rests not with ourselves, but with our Northern brethren." In the same number in which Brutus broached the notion of disunion, he concluded his essay with a more direct warning to the North: "Let Congress beware, how it approaches us with any extension of the Tariff, or it may tread upon the Rattlesnake of the South. It is Slow in its resistance, Generous in its warning, but may be Deadly in its Blow."[5]

In his first issues, Brutus only hinted at the dangers that a consolidated national government posed to South Carolina, but in his later numbers, he explicitly stated that a consolidated federal government menaced the institution of slavery. By allowing Congress to do whatever it wanted under the general welfare clause, it could abolish slavery. Through the general welfare clause, Brutus warned, "the ultra fanatics and abolitionists of the north contend, that Congress can alter, whenever it pleases, the whole domestic policy of South Carolina." To prevent this, southern congressman should resist every effort of the American Colonization Society. If Congress appropriated money to this organization, it would only be a matter of time before that organization began clamoring for the abolition of slavery. To make the point more direct, Brutus reminded his readers that Henry Clay, the foremost proponent of the American System, was a member of the Colonization Society. "Domestic servitude is the policy of our country, and has been so from time immemorial," Brutus averred. "It is so intimately interwoven with our prosperity, as a member of the confederacy, and with our comfort as a society, that to talk of its abolition, is to speak of striking us out of our civil and domestic existence." During the Missouri debates of 1820, the tariff was only tenuously connected with the slave question; but now Turnbull presented the tariff as the means by which the North accrued more power. And with that power, he argued, the North planned to wage war on the institution of slavery.[6]

Pennsylvania supporters of Andrew Jackson joined southerners in opposing the Harrisburg Convention. They had to do this in a manner that showed they did not oppose the principle of protection, however. Both James Buchanan and Samuel Ingham took to the stump and called the convention a trick to deliver the state's electoral votes to Adams. Buchanan warned that if tariff supporters called a convention, tariff opponents would hold their own convention. "What a mournful spectacle would be presented to the friends of this Union," Buchanan declared. "If two conventions, the one composed of Northern, the other, of Southern states, should assemble at the same time, for the purpose of acting in direct hostility to each other." At Fourth of July celebrations in Pennsylvania, the friends of Buchanan and Ingham excoriated the convention. In a fitting toast, Joel Bailey said, "The national convention at Harrisburg. Guess the woolen bags won't be as destructive to General Jackson as the cotton bags were to the British army at New Orleans."[7]

Northern opposition to the pending convention did not confine itself solely to Pennsylvania. Van Buren prevented any member of the Albany Regency from attending. Louis McLane, a Federalist who had joined the Jackson movement, was elected as a delegate from Delaware. When he learned of his selection, he penned a public letter declining the appointment. McLane defended his vote against the woolens bill, claiming that woolen manufactures did not need the protection that they demanded. McLane admitted that his vote against the bill emerged from "no change of previous opinions" on the tariff. Isaac Hill, an editor from New Hampshire sympathetic to Andrew Jackson, reminded his readers that "New England federalists" (his term for the supporters of the administration) began supporting domestic manufactures in the past three years. These manufactures had arisen to maturity almost in spite of the opposition of the "New England federalists." Daniel Webster led the opposition to the system in 1824, but once the "Dons of Boston" invested large sums of capital into woolens, "Mr. Webster, in the twinkling of an eye, becomes the champion of American manufactures."[8]

Perhaps more so than any other Jacksonian politician or editor, Hill captured the mindset of the opposition to Adams and the growing Jacksonian movement in his editorial. The Jacksonians used populist and class-based rhetoric to win converts. They depicted Adams as an aristocrat who lavishly spent the people's money on his diplomatic missions and then on a billiard table while president. The tariff continued this trend of waste and extravagance, Jacksonian editors argued, because it fostered a monopoly, and this monopoly made the tariff inconsistent with the republican values that they wanted to restore. For the Jacksonians who supported the protective tariff, Hill suggested that a proper tariff assisted the farmer, the manufacturer, and the navigator. No particular interest received special favors from the government, and no interest was injured. The main problem for Hill became convincing northern Jacksonians that they could survive and grow in a market economy with minimal tariff protection. Northern Jacksonians disliked monopolies just as much as their southern colleagues, but the protection that the tariff afforded northerners kept their wages high and their jobs secure in a fluctuating market-oriented economy. The removal of tariff barriers by Congress jeopardized the livelihood of northern laborers.[9]

On July 10, a large group of citizens from the city of Albany held a meeting to select their delegates for the Harrisburg Convention. Most attendees, however, sensed that the meeting had been called to criticize Van Buren's absence during the vote on the woolens bill. In Albany that day, he decided to attend the meeting, even though his friends urged him not to go, arguing that a leading statesman should not place himself in the line of fire. When Van Buren entered the chamber hall, he smiled to his friends and enemies, spoke with some of them, and waved to others too far in the distance to extend a hand. The allegedly nonpartisan meeting grew quiet when the attendees noticed his arrival.[10]

Van Buren waited patiently as ten speakers castigated him. When he took the floor, he explained in a speech of about an hour that he missed the vote because the chairman of the Committee on Manufactures informed him that there would not be a vote on the bill the day that the vote actually took place. Years later, Van Buren modified his story and wrote that he missed the vote because he gave a friend a tour of the congressional cemetery. If Van Buren told his angry constituents that he missed a vote critical to their interests because he viewed the interests of the dead more favorably than he did theirs, he may not have left the chamber alive. In his speech, Van Buren reminded his audience of his support for the tariff of 1824 and told them that all his efforts to improve the woolens bill were defeated. He told his anxious audience that he wanted the increased duty on raw wool to go into operation at the same time as the increased duty on manufactured wool. This would have prevented manufacturers from injuring woolgrowers. After Van Buren equivocated on whether he approved or disapproved the measure, he then addressed the pending Harrisburg Convention. "We have the strongest reason to believe that political designs did not enter into the motives that led to the call of this morning," Van Buren declared. He then added, "We ought not, nevertheless, to shut our eyes to the fact that reaches us from every quarter, and is present to us everywhere, that a deep rooted conviction has fastened itself on the public mind that recent movements upon this subject have proceeded more from the closet of the politician than the workshop of the manufacturer." Van Buren observed that farmers and manufacturers in Kentucky and Pennsylvania denounced the woolens bill and the Harrisburg Convention. "Although they all agree as to the principle, they differ as to the best means of supporting it, and those differences being embittered by personal and political contentions, are becoming every day more inveterate," he said. Van Buren implied that the Adams administration sought to use the plight of manufactures to further its political interests.[11]

Beneath the surface of Van Buren's remarks, however, was a deeper political agenda. By missing the vote, Van Buren brought attention to the issue while flushing New England congressmen into the open on the question of protection to woolen manufactures. The switch of New England from free trade to protection for woolens had become common knowledge, and Van Buren wanted to exploit this switch as much as possible. Van Buren now knew that as long as any tariff bill offered protection to woolen manufacturers, New England congressmen would have to vote for it or be accused of inconsistency.

Van Buren's equivocation did not go unnoticed. After the meeting, a wool grower known as Mr. Wood approached Benjamin Knower, one of Van Buren's lieutenants, and wanted Knower to express his compliments to Van Buren on a very "able" address. Before letting Knower take his leave, Wood asked him: "On which side of the tariff question was it?" Van Buren's noncommittal on the issue was by design. He gave a lengthy address that demonstrated careful thought and reasoning. By no means did he make an off-the-cuff speech that evening. When Knower related the story to Van Buren, they no doubt shared a good laugh. Van Buren said nothing that would worry his southern friends, and he had exposed the Harrisburg Convention as an attempt to secure a second term for Adams.[12]

By the time the delegates arrived in Harrisburg, the Jacksonians had convinced the public that the Harrisburg Convention had more to do with politics than woolens. At a Jackson rally in Pittsburgh, Henry Baldwin reminded Pennsylvanians that Jackson voted for the tariff of 1824. It made no sense for them to abandon Jackson for Adams at this point in time. "As there is little hope of electing Mr. Adams without the vote of Pennsylvania," Baldwin declared, "we must expect that efforts will be used by his friends correspondent with the magnitude of the object to be effected." In South Carolina, George McDuffie told an audience that Clay convened the convention and that the administration planned to win a second term by offering millions of dollars in the form of tariff protection to American manufacturers in return for their votes. This threatened American democracy, according to McDuffie. "Liberty cannot exist—it is not the nature of things that it should—where large masses of the people, are taught to look habitually to the government for pecuniary favors and support," he declared. Clay's return to Kentucky, which took him through most of Pennsylvania, provided Jacksonians with more opportunities to tie the administration to the convention.[13]

Although the Jacksonians opposed the convention in every state, delegates were elected in a democratic manner that the Jacksonians would have supported. Most of the identifiable delegates tended to be influential men involved in manufacturing. Towns, villages, and counties held meetings to elect delegates to attend a convention in the capital city. Oftentimes, an editor issued a call for a meeting. Some state meetings were attended by obscure manufacturers, while in Massachusetts, prominent manufacturers such as Abbot Lawrence participated alongside political leaders such as Governor Levi Lincoln, Lewis Tappan, Edward Everett, and Harrison Gray Otis. With precious time between the calls for the convention and the announced start of the convention, some of these meetings took place "at early candle light." Some of the meetings had as many as five hundred citizens in attendance. Once these early evening meetings elected delegates, the selected men next attended a statewide convention that elected the state's delegates for the Harrisburg Convention. At the local meetings, the attendants always issued resolutions in favor of granting increased protection woolens and other American manufacturers. Meetings at the local level often ended with committees of correspondence being created to open a dialogue with other communities that felt wronged by the rejection of the woolens bill.[14]

The Harrisburg Convention commenced on July 30. Of the ninety-five men who attended the Convention, only fourteen of the attendees came from slaveholding states. The slaveholding states of North Carolina, South Carolina, Georgia, Alabama, Mississippi, Louisiana, Tennessee, and Missouri sent no delegates to the convention. Mathew Carey opened the convention by moving that it elect a president. The delegates unanimously elected Joseph Ritner of Pennsylvania to be president of the convention. The following day, the convention divided into committees to prepare a memorial to Congress and an address to the people of the United States. Although the convention had been called to agitate for increased protection to woolen manufactures, the delegates appointed committees to examine the necessary levels of protection on iron, hemp, glass, and cotton goods as well. The reports of these committees were forwarded to the committee assigned to address a memorial to Congress. Hezekiah Niles instructed the committee that the "interests" of woolgrowers and manufactures should be made the "chief and leading object of the memorial."[15]

The delegates completed their work on August 3. They printed ten thousand copies of their petition for immediate distribution. In this petition, the delegates contended that both woolen manufacturers and wool farmers lost twenty million dollars per group as a result of inadequate protection. The memorial recommended a series of increased rates duties on imported raw wool and manufactured wool. It asked Congress to impose the minimum system on manufactured wool too. Manufacturers other than wool manufacturers secured a place in the memorial as well. The petitioners asked Congress for increased protection on flax, hemp, distilled spirits, and cotton goods, but they did not offer any specific level of duties for any of these items. This memorial resembled a congressional tariff bill in many ways. The protection to wool and woolens pleased New England and New York while the proposed increase of duties on iron would receive the support of Pennsylvania. Higher duties on hemp and flax garnered the support of Kentucky while a higher duty on imported wines or foreign spirits would assist grain growers in the West, who could distill their grain into whiskey. Senators Samuel Bell and Ashur Robbins refused to sign the memorial, but three members of the House of Representatives, Ichabod Barttlet, Rollin C. Mallary, and John C. Wright, had no qualms about fixing their signatures to the memorial.[16]

The Harrisburg Convention represented the first meeting of an interested group who sought redress through legislative channels since the Hartford Convention. In the upcoming years, other groups followed the initiative set forth by the Harrisburg Convention. Free traders held their own convention in New York City in 1831 and issued a detailed report to Congress. Southern industrialists held numerous commercial conventions across the southwest in the 1840s and 1850s. Sabbatarians, women's rights advocates, temperance advocates, and abolitionists all mimicked the Harrisburg Convention in the years before the Civil War. In 1831 and in 1832, political parties adopted the scheme of the Harrisburg Convention, and the Anti-Masons, National Republicans, and Democrats all held nominating conventions in Baltimore. A convention became the best expression of democracy in America.[17]

On October 10, Hezekiah Niles completed the address of the Harrisburg Convention. Using restrained language, Niles bridged the gap between the North and the South over the tariff. "The will of the majority ought to prevail; but the minority have also interests and feelings that must be respected by all who respect themselves as they ought," Niles wrote. When Americans looked to the mountains of New Hampshire, they found the sugar of Louisiana. When they looked at the Mississippi delta, they found the cotton cloths of Rhode Island. Wool sheared from sheep in Ohio found a market in Massachusetts, while lead from Missouri and Illinois could be found in most American cities. The raw materials from Pennsylvania and Virginia fueled the furnaces of factories in New York. Niles's arguments in the memorial reiterated Clay's "home market" argument without acknowledging its original author. To do so would arouse more suspicion of political involvement. The protection of American manufactures did not corrupt the morals of American society, Niles declared. It led to a higher quality of goods and cheaper prices for consumers. As more and more Americans accrued capital, they invested that capital into internal improvements and other public works. Furthermore, if Congress assured the home market to manufactures of clothing, it would "fill up all the spare time of 100,000 women and girls." Sensing that the constitutional argument would dominate the upcoming debate once Congress reconvened, Niles showed that the Constitution allowed Congress to protect manufacturers. The preamble to the tariff of 1789 proclaimed, "Whereas, it is necessary for the support of government, for the discharge of the debts of the United States, and the encouragement and protection of manufactures, that duties be laid on goods, wares and merchandise imported." Niles then declared in the address that Washington, Franklin, Jefferson, Hamilton, Madison, and Monroe "are all on our side."[18]

Southerners wasted little time in denouncing the Harrisburg Convention. Some branded the convention as "unconstitutional" while others called it "treasonable." At a Richmond dinner, several guests offered disparaging toasts toward the convention. "The Harrisburg Convention, whilst they profess to encourage the growth of wool, may they not fleece the people of their rights," one guest declared. Virginians found themselves in a difficult situation. The alternative to four more years of John Quincy Adams was Andrew Jackson, who, as a senator, voted for both the General Survey Act and the Tariff of 1824. Southerners despised the General Survey Act of 1824 because they viewed this legislation, which allowed the army to survey potential routes for roads and canals, as a violation of the Constitution. Virginians often denounced Jackson with as much vitriol as they did Adams and the Harrisburg Convention. "State rights as understood by Jackson," one Virginian intoned, "establish roads where you please, cut canals where you please, and cut the throats of those who oppose you."[19]

Overall, the Harrisburg Convention has to be regarded as a success because Congress made the tariff a primary concern once it reconvened. By the commencement of the next summer, Congress had increased most tariff duties. Some of these increases exceeded the recommendations of the convention. In the fall of 1828, however, Adams lost the presidency to Jackson in a landslide. If manufacturers called the convention to aid Adams's reelection, then the convention has to be viewed as a failure. While many delegates wanted to see the incumbent reelected, they preferred a new tariff with increased duties, which they received in 1828.

Furthermore, the man who defeated Adams voted for the tariff in 1824. The Harrisburg Convention, when viewed in this light, has to be regarded as a success.

The Harrisburg Convention scared Calhoun back in South Carolina. He may have begun to regret his vote on the woolens bill at this point. "It is the selected instrument to combine with greater facility the great geographical Northern manufacturing interest in order to enforce more effectually the system of monopoly and extortion against the consuming states," he wrote of the convention. If the delegates to the convention "should succeed in electing its President and passing its Tariffs of monopoly," the South could, as Cooper and Turnbull suggested, either acquiesce in its oppression, or it could secede. But how should the "consuming states" resist the tariff system? "After much reflection," Calhoun wrote to Littleton W. Tazewell at the end of August, "it seems to me, that the despotism founded on combined geographical interest, admits of but one effectual remedy, a veto on the part of the local interest, or under our system, on the part of the States." Just three weeks after the Harrisburg Convention, Calhoun began formulating the doctrine of state interposition or nullification as a means to defeat the protective system.[20]

7

"Wolves in sheep's clothing"

T HE TARIFF OF 1828, dubbed the "tariff of abominations" because it set
average rate on imported goods at an all-time high, remains the most controversial tariff enacted in American history. The Smoot Hawley tariff of 1930 exacer-
bated the hard times of the opening phases of the Great Depression, but it did not
bring the country to the brink of disunion like the tariff of 1828. After Congress approved the 1828 tariff, southerners began complaining that they had been tricked by
Martin Van Buren and Silas Wright. They, along with numerous historians, maintained that the New Yorkers had told them that they wanted to defeat the tariff of
1828. Wright and Van Buren sought to create a bill that would fail on the basis of its
own flaws. The chief culprits, however, would appear to be the New England members of Congress who supported incumbent president John Quincy Adams. If the
New England delegation defeated the tariff, the New Yorkers could present their
presidential candidate, Andrew Jackson, as the friend of the tariff and domestic industry and their rival, incumbent president John Quincy Adams, as its enemy.[1]

In actuality, Wright and Van Buren wanted the 1828 tariff to pass all along.
They desired the tariff's passage because the people of New York favored increased
protection. Wright and Van Buren recognized that all politics was local. But this
interpretation leaves one question unresolved: if Van Buren and Wright wanted
the tariff to pass into law, what did they tell their southern colleagues such as Vice
President John C. Calhoun of South Carolina? Perhaps the question that should be
asked regarding the tariff of abominations is "what did the vice president know and
when did he know it?" According to Calhoun, the New Yorkers tricked him and
his colleagues. "I have its author in my eyes," Calhoun said in 1837 while scowling
at Silas Wright. The tariff of 1828, Calhoun continued, "was passed by a breach of
faith. We were deceived then." He next outlined the steps that led to the passage
of the tariff of abominations. The South Carolinian said that southerners had two
options available to them in 1828. They could join with the New England delegation and support the amendments that these members desired to make the bill less
objectionable, or they could resist all amendments in the hope that the New England members would then join southern members in defeating the bill on a final
vote. The first option, Calhoun recalled, would make the system of high tariffs permanent in America and would also lead to the reelection of John Quincy Adams.
The second option offered southern members a chance to defeat the system of high
tariffs once and for all and also deny Adams a second term. The problem with this

strategy was that the tariff supporters of the North, regardless of politics, might fuse together in the end and pass a less than perfect bill. "To guard against that result," Calhoun remembered,

> assurances were given which placed the representatives of the South at ease on that point. I speak not of my own personal knowledge. It was generally so understood at the time; and I was informed by individuals who had a right to know, and who consulted with me what course, under the pressing difficulties of our situation, ought to be adopted. . . . Our friends accepted the assurance, and accordingly resisted all amendments that would make the bill acceptable to the Eastern interests, as the only possible means of defeating an odious and oppressive system.[2]

Exactly who made "assurances" was something Calhoun failed to elaborate, but he must have meant Van Buren, Wright, or one of their intermediaries. Who else could have been in a position to make an "assurance?" In 1842, George McDuffie, Calhoun's top lieutenant in the House in 1828, referred to an understanding that the tariff of 1828 was framed to be defeated. "We saw that this system of protection was about to assume more gigantic dimensions, and we determined to put such ingredients in the chalice as would poison the monster. This is what is sometimes called 'fighting the devil with fire,'" McDuffie recalled. "A policy which I altogether did not approve, I adopted in deference to the opinions of those with whom I acted."[3] Although these statements appeared in the years after the tariff of 1828 had been passed, evidence from 1828 confirms that some sort of accord had been reached between Calhoun and other Jackson men to defeat the tariff. Therefore, it appears that Van Buren played a cunning game. He wanted to pass a bill, all the while he never revealed his true intentions to his political colleagues from the South. The resentment over this trick would have long-lasting ramifications.[4]

When Congress reconvened in December 1827, the Jackson men found themselves in a majority in both the House and Senate. Andrew Stevenson of Virginia, a Jackson supporter, defeated John W. Taylor of New York, an Adams man, for the position of Speaker of the House. Stevenson won on the first ballot by ten votes. John Tyler, another Jackson man from Virginia, wrote that if this same thing occurred in Great Britain, the ministry would be forced to resign. Adams had no intention of resigning, though. Stevenson's defeat of Taylor demonstrated that this would be yet another difficult session for Adams.[5]

Congressmen from New York and Pennsylvania pushed Stevenson to his victory. The defeated Taylor suspected that the New York and Pennsylvania Jacksonians struck a deal with Stevenson. For their votes, the Virginian would appoint tariff supporters to the appropriate committees and allow the tariff to come to floor. This would allow northern Jackson men to present themselves as the friends of protection to their constituents. Conversely, South Carolina representative James Hamilton believed that Stevenson's victory boded well for the foes of the tariff and the American System. "It is impossible to determine what sort of session we shall have," he wrote, "but as the opposition have now become the government, I think it will be a short one in which there will be little excitement and little legislation."[6]

Petitions, memorials, and resolutions concerning the tariff arrived from citizens throughout the union as members of the Twentieth Congress faced the new session. Americans had expressed their opinions on the tariff to their representatives and senators in 1816, 1820, 1824, and 1827, but more papers on the tariff arrived on the desks of congressmen in 1828 than in all those years combined. At one point, Henry R. Storrs of New York reminded the House that their tables were "groaning under the weight" of the petitions.[7] David Woodcock of New York added, "Memorials and resolutions, either for or against the system which the bill proposes further to protect, have been presented from all the states, adopted either by their Legislatures, or by public meetings."[8] The documents from Americans of all regions, classes, and sections reveal the democratic impulse of the 1820s.[9]

Several southern state legislatures adopted resolutions in opposition to any increase in the tariff. These resolutions typically addressed the constitutional question. For instance, South Carolina resolved that the Constitution did not grant any power to the federal government to promote domestic manufactures. On the same day that the Palmetto State adopted its resolutions against the tariff, North Carolina did the same. Members of the Tar Heel State legislature admitted that Congress could lay an impost solely for revenue purposes. "There is nowhere to be found in the Constitution an express power given to Congress to encourage science, agriculture, or manufactures," the legislators avowed. They then declared that any assistance to manufacturers should be done at the local government, not the federal, level. In a joint remonstrance, members of the Alabama house and senate announced their fear of the eventual effects of the decision of Congress to encourage manufacturers: "Its natural offspring is monopoly, and its natural tendency is to divide the community into nabobs and paupers, to accumulate overgrown wealth in the hands of the few, and to extend the poverty, the vices, and the miseries of the many." Since the protective, or "British," system threatened the liberties of every American citizen, Alabamians warned that they would not surrender their liberties without a fight: "If our rights must be usurped, and our wealth drained to pamper monopolists, we will yield them only when the last inch of ground has been defended with the spirit of freemen."[10]

Northern states sought to influence the debate as well but from the opposite direction. The Pennsylvania legislature instructed its senators to work for a new tariff. "The best interests of our country demand," the legislature announced, "every possible exertion should be made to procure the passage of an act of Congress imposing such duties as will enable our manufacturers to enter into fair competition with foreign manufacturers, and protect the farmer, the growers of hemp and wool, and the distiller of spirits from domestic materials, against foreign competition." Ohio legislators tackled the constitutional question by focusing on the general welfare clause of the Constitution and by restating the arguments of Washington, Jefferson, Madison, Hamilton, and Marshall supporting the protective tariff. Since these statesmen approved the tariff to protect American industries, Ohioans reasoned, a protective tariff had to be constitutional. The reactions by both northerners and southerners reveal that that the tariff had helped to bring more and more Americans into the political process. "There is no lack of sensitiveness, no defect of energy, among the people, on a topic which involves so many, and such essential interests," the *National Journal* announced.[11]

Politics, more than expertise in wool manufacturing, guided the selection of the key House committee. On December 6, Speaker Stevenson appointed Rollin C. Mallary of Vermont, an Adams supporter and a delegate to the Harrisburg Convention, to be chairman of the Committee on Manufactures. In addition to Mallary, Stevenson placed Silas Wright of New York, Lewis Condict of New Jersey, William D. Martin of South Carolina, Thomas P. Moore of Kentucky, James S. Stevenson of Pennsylvania, and William Stanbery of Ohio on the committee. While it included strong supporters of the tariff, it had only one member, Mallary, who knew the details of woolen manufacturing. Moore, a Jackson man, knew the intricacies of hemp manufacturing, while Stevenson, another Jackson man, looked after the interests of iron manufacturers. Stanbery, yet another Jacksonian, claimed no knowledge of woolen manufacturing, and Wright, Van Buren's surrogate and a Jacksonian, began to examine the subject only after he had been placed on the committee. These appeared to be odd appointments because protection for woolens constituted the sole reason for revisiting the tariff question. Some whispered that Stevenson allowed Mallary to serve as chairman so that when the upcoming tariff bill failed, an administration supporter would be blamed.[12]

This committee also reflected an odd system of alliances that had emerged in the nation. Southern Jacksonians, opposed to protection on principle, could be counted on to provide at least fifty negative votes in the House. Jackson men from New York and Pennsylvania, with the assistance of Adams supporters from those states, would offset southern opposition. The key became New England and the West. Would the New England men favor the shipping industry or manufacturing? Westerners had no love for eastern capitalists, but if the tariff protected raw materials such as lead, flax, hemp, and whiskey, they would support it. Because of the conflicting interests involved and since the debate occurred during an election year, the popular refrain became that the tariff needed to be saved not from its enemies but rather from its friends. "That the present bill has been designedly so framed as to defeat the object of those who were in favor of such a modification of the existing rate of duties, as to afford an equal and proper protection to the farmer and manufacturer, there cannot exist a doubt in the mind of any intelligent man," an administration paper announced once Congress began debating the bill. The paper then added, "but we are strong in the assurance that the deception cannot avail, and that the people will soon discover who are the real friends of Domestic Industry, and will discover, also, who are its *pretended* friends—'wolves in sheep's clothing.'"[13] A Boston newspaper loyal to the administration warned its readers that woolen manufacturers needed to worry more about northern defectors than southern opponents of the protective system. The editor used the term "dough face" to describe the Jackson men from New York and Pennsylvania who he expected to side with the South on the tariff question.[14] A western Adams paper made the same argument. This editor believed that just enough northern Jacksonians intended to vote with the South to defeat the bill and place the blame on the administration. "When the bill comes up, the sheep's clothing will be torn off of the wolves who are plotting its destruction," he observed.[15]

In his third annual message to Congress, Adams failed to mention the tariff. Many saw this as a blunder. The president explained to Henry C. Martindale of New York that he left the topic out of his message so as not to injure his southern supporters. But this omission left his northern friends bitter. They began asking the president to introduce them to his southern friends, since they believed he had little support in the South. It seemed to them as if Adams had resigned himself to defeat and desired his supporters to share the same fate. "I consider it the final blow that renders his reelection out of the question and am myself disposed to ground my arrows," Charles Hammond cried in disgust. The Cincinnati editor and Adams supporter believed that Adams should stand aside and let another candidate run for the presidency instead.[16] Moreover, Jackson's supporters in the North took notice of Adams's omission of the tariff. Since the tariff had been the key topic of discussion after the close of the last session of Congress, and because the friends of the Adams administration claimed to be the friends of domestic industry, the *Albany Argus* declared, the president's failure to mention the tariff demonstrated his lack of commitment to the issue. The president and his friends opposed increased protection and only wanted to use the tariff as a "hobby horse" to win a second term, Jacksonians charged. Adams defended his omission of the tariff by allowing Secretary of the Treasury Richard Rush to elucidate the administration's position on the tariff in his annual report on the finances of the nation. Adams's silence allowed the Jacksonians to capture the initiative.[17]

When Rush submitted his "Annual Report on the State of the Finances" to Congress, he defended the tariff of 1824 but asked for increased duties on woolens, wool, cotton cloths, bar iron, and hemp. Rush's report defended Clay's home-market argument. Rush explained how a protective tariff assisted settlement in the West. A highly protective tariff assisted western lead miners and fur trappers. Since westerners lived closer to many of the raw materials needed for manufacturing, it would only be a matter of time before manufacturing developed in that region, he argued. Thomas Hart Benton of Missouri, who spoke for many Jackson men from the West, attacked Rush's report and charged that the administration only wanted to aid eastern capitalists. High prices for western lands deprived the Treasury of revenue, leaving the federal government to resort to higher tariffs, which, according to westerners, meant higher prices for all goods. Expensive western lands hindered emigration to the West, trapping more eastern laborers to work in the cotton and woolen factories.[18]

On New Year's Eve, Mallary offered a resolution asking that the Committee of Manufactures be given the power to call witnesses. This represented an unprecedented request, because the House had given this power only to the Judiciary Committee in cases of contested elections and malfeasance in office. Mallary announced that he disapproved of the resolution but submitted it because his position as chairman compelled him to. Supporters of the resolution argued that calling witnesses before the chamber and forcing them to testify under oath allowed the House to comprehend the true state of American manufacturers. If Congress based the bill on the sworn testimony of American manufactures, then it could not be held liable for any defects in the bill, James S. Stevenson of Pennsylvania argued. Edward

Livingston, a close associate of Jackson from Louisiana who had served with him at the Battle of New Orleans, endorsed the resolution by claiming that all the petitions before the House came from Americans with an interest in the tariff. He wanted the input of disinterested Americans. Silas Wright echoed Livingston's statement and admitted that the House had numerous petitions and memorials on the tariff before it, but almost all these expressions of opinion had some connection with a "National Convention in Pennsylvania."[19]

Some House members suggested that the resolution represented a delaying action. If Congress adopted the resolution, it served the same function as a motion for the indefinite postponement of a tariff bill. Since Congress had taken five months to pass the tariff of 1824, it would be unable to pass one in 1828 if it had to call witnesses from throughout the union. Other members viewed the resolution as redundant. The petitions and memorials that the people presented accomplished the same goal as sworn testimony, in their opinion. Some members opposed the motion because the committee intended to call only manufacturers. The House should subpoena farmers, merchants, and mariners to get their opinions on a subject that affected all branches of the American economy, they contended. Still other members feared the precedent that would be set by this action. "Should the grant of such a power become common, it would lead to the exercise of inquisitional powers," John C. Wright warned.[20] The resolution's opponents, such as John C. Wright, feared the precedent that the House would establish if it approved the resolution. Congress would create a regiment of sergeants-at-arms who would go to the doors of the American people and force them to come to Washington City to testify. The House agreed to the resolution by a vote of 102 to 88. Most Jackson men voted yes, while most Adams men voted no. Only five southern members voted against the resolution. When the votes on the woolens bill and the resolution are compared, it suggests that tariff foes desired to use the resolution as a means of obstruction. Seventy-six members voted on both issues. Of the forty-four members who voted for the woolens bill, forty-three voted against the resolution. The thirty-two members who voted against the woolens bill gave unanimous support for the resolution.[21]

For sixteen days, the House Committee on Manufactures deposed twenty-eight manufacturers. When testifying, all the woolen manufacturers presented a dire picture of their industry. Some of them had manufactured wool since 1809 and said that they could not recall such a bleak period. Others admitted that they had recently ceased to operate their mills. A few witnesses who continued to produce woolens stressed that they knew of many failures near their mills. Manufacturers notified the committee that they had as much as $350,000 of capital invested in their enterprise. Most of the manufacturers had not paid out any dividends since the tariff of 1824 took effect. They had high hopes after Congress passed the tariff of 1824, but the British dashed these hopes by repealing their wool laws and evading American duties. One manufacturer said that in 1825, he sold his woolens in Boston for seventy-five cents a pound. Two years later, in the same market, his cloths fetched only fifty-five cents per pound. The importation of woolens was the reason for the drop in prices, the witness contended. "Should I continue business, at present prices of the raw material, and prices of the fabric, I must wholly fail," William Phillips informed the committee. Most of the manufacturers maintained that they competed mostly with foreign and not domestic woolens. Abraham Marland went so far as to ask for prohibitive duties on foreign wool and woolens. This would allow him to restore his losses and give American manufacturers, such as himself, control of the market. "We dread the foreign, but would be glad to encounter domestic competition," E. I. DuPont told the committee.[22]

The bill that Silas Wright drafted offered generous protection to a variety of interests: a seven-dollar increase for iron bars from thirty dollars per ton to thirty-seven, a ten-dollar increase on hemp from thirty-five dollars to forty-five dollars, a fifteen-cent increase on most types of spirits. Whiskey distillers were rewarded a second time by a big increase of the duty on molasses, which went from five cents a gallon to ten cents a gallon. This made rum production unprofitable so Americans would turn to whiskey. Flax would be charged a duty of thirty-five dollars a ton. This rate would increase by five dollars every year until it reached fifty dollars a ton. Under the tariff of 1824, flax was levied a duty of 15 percent. Wool farmers emerged as big winners in Wright's bill because the new tariff set a duty of seven cents a pound on raw wool along with an additional 40 percent duty. Under the tariff of 1824, raw wool paid a duty ranging from 15 to 30 percent depending on the quality of wool. The seven cents per pound and the duty of 40 percent represented a major increase and a victory for the wool farmer at the expense of the woolen manufacturer.[23]

Woolen manufacturers believed that the committee had ignored them. Instead of the duties that the Harrisburg Convention had recommended, the Committee on Manufactures placed the minimum points on woolens at fifty cents, one dollar, two dollars and fifty cents, and four dollars. This was generous protection, but it was well below what woolen manufacturers thought they needed. The Harrisburg Convention had recommended that the minimum points be at fifty cents, two dollars and fifty cents, four dollars, and six dollars. Silas Wright declared that the minimums recommended by the committee offered adequate protection for woolen manufacturers. The lowest minimum point equated to a duty of 33 percent while the highest minimum was 100 percent. The average of the minimums became a duty of about 67 percent, which was double the rate that woolens paid under the tariff of 1824. Since the proposals of the Harrisburg Convention on woolens amounted to prohibition, Silas Wright perhaps had devised a clever trap. Surely, some protectionist would try to make the rates on woolens conform to the Harrisburg Convention's rate, and when that happened, the Jackson men could show that the greedy woolen manufacturers wanted prohibitory rates so they could have a monopoly over the American marketplace.[24]

On February 13, James Buchanan wrote, "I expect the Tariff will be up next week. It will pass unless a division among the friends of the system should defeat it. I fear the Eastern members will not be willing to concede to Pennsylvania and New York a protection for those articles in which they are most deeply interested."[25] Buchanan anticipated that the bill could be rejected because of differences among the friends of protection. The high duties that New Yorkers wanted on raw wool hurt

New England woolen manufacturers, while the high duties on iron injured New England shippers who needed iron for anchors and chains. A high duty on hemp benefitted Kentuckians, but it hurt New England shippers who preferred Russian hemp for the rigging in their ships. David Barker, an Adams supporter from New Hampshire, noted that the Jackson coalition included what he referred to as "unpalatable provisions" in the bill to force New England members to oppose it. "Their only object is to defeat the measure," he said of the Jacksonians.[26] Willis Alston, a Jackson man from North Carolina, noted, "the pretended American system is certainly losing ground with the intelligent, almost every where, if the Tariff is defeated it will certainly be by the administration."[27]

Like Buchanan, President Adams's supporters believed that the tariff would be rejected in 1828. In Ohio, an Adams editor wrote, "the bill by laying a duty on molasses, was intended to be made so objectionable to the New England Navigation interest, as to render it necessary that the delegation from that section of the Union should vote against it, and thus the bill be lost."[28] John Bailey, a member of the House from Massachusetts and a follower of Adams, had the most succinct statement on the tariff proposal of 1828. "The bill . . . was framed precisely to defeat itself," he noted.[29] It appears that most observers who had followed the debate expected the bill to be defeated.

Aside from Van Buren and his fellow members of the Albany Regency, it appears most members of Congress and those who followed the debate, regardless of who they supported for president, expected the tariff to be defeated. The question remained—who would be responsible for its defeat? But the clever Jackson strategy of forcing the Adams men to kill the tariff could backfire. "If this bill should fail or its most important features be so modified as to render it of little efficacy, the whole responsibility say they [Adams men], must inevitably fall upon the Jackson party, who claim a majority in the House," a Jackson man from Pennsylvania cautioned.[30] The most telling comment came from Henry Clay. Although unable to participate in the debate, the secretary of state directed strategies for the administration. "I anticipate a tremendous discussion," he observed to John Crittenden. "The Jackson party is playing a game of brag on that subject. They do not really desire the passage of their own measure; and it may happen, in the sequel, that what is desired by neither party commands the support of both."[31] Clay was no stranger to high-stakes card games, having allegedly bet fifty thousand dollars in a card game in 1812. In 1828, the Kentuckian hoped to force the Jacksonians to show their cards.[32]

As soon as they saw the tariff, Adams supporters called Wright's measure a worthless bill. According to them, it had more to do with politics than economics. New England would be punished, while the West would be rewarded. "This is Jacksonism with a vengeance," the *Scioto Gazette*, an Adams paper, roared. "But let not the friends of Domestic Manufactures despair. This great interest is sustained by public sentiment, and will be triumphantly supported at the polls, it is the cause of the country and must finally and eventually succeed."[33] Adams men with ties to the woolen industry believed that the bill did not offer adequate protection to their enterprise. The American people would be able to purchase only woolens that had been made in Europe, they contended. Furthermore, the minimums, instead of protecting American woolen manufacturers, encouraged foreigners to send their woolens in America. New England shippers, particularly those in Maine, believed that the tariff discriminated against them because of the doubling of the duty on molasses. Since many Maine shippers transported lumber and fish to the West Indies and exchanged those products for molasses, they argued that the duty of ten cents a gallon on molasses would drive them out of business. This bill, New England editors asserted, had been framed with the intention that it would be killed by the votes of New England members. "The very high duty on molasses and some other articles, were obviously inserted for the purpose of giving the bill such a character as that the Northern and Eastern members could not vote for it," a Connecticut paper announced. "The whole proceeding is apparently designed to produce two results: first, to defeat the measure altogether; second, to throw its defeat on the friends of the Administration."[34]

Northern and western Jacksonians contended that the Committee of Manufactures had crafted a "national tariff" that offered "abundant protection" to a variety of interests. The bill benefitted both the farmer and the manufacturer. The Jacksonians tried to convince the public that they better understood the American System and that they would be the better custodians of it. "The American System consists in affording an equal and just legislative protection to all the great interests of the country," James Buchanan said for the Jacksonians. "It is no respecter of persons. It does not distinguish between the farmer who ploughs the soil in Pennsylvania, and the manufacturer of wool in New England. Being impartial, it embraces all."[35] According to Amos Kendall, the Adams men acted "selfish" and "sectional." Since New Englanders would not accept half a loaf of bread, no interest or section would benefit, he charged. Jacksonian editors also utilized Adams's recent annual message omission to demonstrate their opponents' disregard for American manufacturing. "Honest men of all parties will now be enabled to perceive," Duff Green proclaimed, "who are the real friends of a fair National Tariff, protecting not only the Woolen Manufacturers of New England, but the Wool Growers of New York, Pennsylvania, New Jersey, and Delaware, the Iron Mongers of Pennsylvania, and the Growers of hemp, and Distillers from Grain of Ohio, Kentucky, Indiana, Missouri, and Illinois."[36]

Once the debate commenced, Mallary proposed a series of amendments that would adjust the minimum points in Silas Wright's bill. The minimums for woolens included four points, just as in Wright's bill. Mallary's first minimum was the same as Wright's: fifty cents. After that first minimum point, however, Mallary's and Wright's proposals diverged. Under Mallary's changed system, the next minimum would be two dollars and fifty cents. This would be followed by a minimum point of four dollars and then a final minimum point of six dollars. Mallary's proposal would mean that the rates on woolens would go from about 33 percent to 250 percent. The Vermont representative also sought to lower the rate of raw wool from seven cents a pound to four cents a pound. If the House concurred with these amendments, then the bill would conform to what the Harrisburg Convention had proposed for every part of the wool industry.[37]

The task of defending an imperfect bill fell to Silas Wright. The proposed tariff offered sufficient protection to both the wool grower and the woolen manufacturer, he announced. The farmers who raised sheep in New England, New York, Pennsylvania, Ohio, and Virginia would all benefit from the seven-cents-a-pound duty on raw wool. According to Wright, there were more than enough domestic sheep to meet the demands of American woolen manufacturers. Wright ascertained that woolen manufacturers required a tariff of about 65 percent to offset the fact that British manufacturers obtained their wool cheaper than American producers. The committee's bill gave American manufacturers protection but not as much as they desired, he maintained. Woolen manufacturers demanded protection at a level of 65 percent, but the minimums in the proposed bill ranged from almost 33 percent to just under 100 percent. The average of the two ends came out to be just above 65 percent, which woolen producers desired. This was a compromise—some forms of woolens obtained more protection than necessary, while others received less. Wright charged that Mallary's amendments amounted to prohibition. If the House adopted these changes, American woolen manufacturers stood to have absolute control over the market. Mallary's amendments, because they bordered near prohibition, would encourage foreigners to commit frauds and thereby deprive the Treasury of revenue.[38]

Protectionists argued that Silas Wright's bill would destroy both the wool farmer and the woolen manufacturer. The poorly conceived minimums would allow foreign woolens to flood the American market. This would put both the woolen manufacturer and the wool farmer out of business. Isaac Bates, a wool farmer and House member from Massachusetts, captured this point in a single sentence on the House floor. If the tariff before the House became law, he warned, it would "put the knife to the jugular vein of every sheep in the country."[39] Many editors seized on this statement to show the danger of Silas Wright's bill. Hezekiah Niles echoed Bates's fears. "From fifty to sixty millions of dollars will be instantly sacrificed, in the reduced value of lands and sheep and the manufactories of wool," he warned. "Already, the farmers stand with whetted knives to kill off these useful animals."[40]

The prevailing opinion in Washington City held that Wright's bill would have to be modified in order to pass the House. Hezekiah Niles informed John W. Taylor, "I will not say that the bill was reported to be defeated, but it will be unless materially altered."[41] At the end of March and early April, northern Jacksonians and southern Jacksonians combined to reject Mallary's efforts to amend the bill. Several New York and Pennsylvania Jackson men dodged the question and failed to vote. On one amendment, the vote stood 78 for and 102 against. On another, the vote was 80 for and 115 opposed. "No combination of wool growers and woolen manufactures, should ever attempt to dictate a tariff to the people of the United States," James Buchanan scolded Mallary.[42] Peleg Sprague of Maine then tried to remove the duties on hemp, iron, and molasses since they hurt the shipping industry. The House rejected his amendments as well. "While affecting friendship for the manufacturing and agricultural interests, they [the Jacksonians] have secretly given them the fifth rib stab," one administration sheet announced.[43] With the amendments rejected, the prevailing opinion throughout the country that editors and observers shared was that the bill would be repulsed. "These votes are strong indications that the bill will be defeated," an observer noted.[44]

The southern strategy had worked. Since woolen manufacturers had failed to receive increased protection, they would urge their representatives to vote against the bill in the end. Thus, New England and southern votes would defeat the bill. But just after the House defeated one of Mallary's amendments in early April, southerners gloated and told their New England colleagues that they had wanted to make the bill as bad as possible to force them to vote against it. Southerners had tipped their hand. McDuffie, who immediately recognized that the battle had not yet been won, cursed his southern brethren for revealing their plan. Northern members might now agree to an imperfect bill just to spite southern members. "We have not only disclosed our plan, but defeated its success," Augustine B. Shepperd of North Carolina groaned.[45] Henry R. Storrs added, "I am quite sure that the South will be 'taken in' by their own contrivances."[46] The time for celebrating had not yet arrived.

As these events unfolded, Clay pondered what course the administration should adopt. Unlike Adams, he knew the political importance of the tariff. The secretary recognized that the bill had been reported to damage the Adams party. He called it a "trick" and the "vilest of cheats." "With the professed purpose of protecting our Woolen manufactories, it demolishes them. With the purpose avowed of encouraging the growth of wool it destroys the Home market," he exclaimed.[47] If the House failed to amend the bill, Clay predicted that two-thirds of the members would vote against the tariff. However, he worried that his party might suffer at the polls as a result. How should the administration act to avoid being blamed for the defeat of a bill that neither party wanted to become law?[48]

The Adams members found a way out of their situation on April 10 that ultimately led to the defeat of the southern strategy. Joel B. Sutherland, a Pennsylvania Jacksonian, offered an amendment to decrease the duty on raw wool. Wool would be subject to a duty of four cents a pound instead of seven. This amendment passed by a vote of one hundred to ninety-nine. Ninety-one of the yes votes came from Jackson men, and nine came from Adams men. Eight of the nine Adams men who voted for this amendment represented southern districts. Only one northern Adams man, Joseph Wingate of Maine, voted yes. A single reversal would have killed the amendment. On the no side, fourteen Jackson men concurred with eighty-five Adams men. The Jackson men who voted no came from Indiana, Kentucky, Maryland, New Hampshire, New York, Pennsylvania, and Ohio. No southern Jackson man voted against Sutherland's amendment.[49]

"The woolen manufacturers are well taken care of, and by their friends in this House," Bates announced shortly after the amendment had squeaked through.[50] Cheaper wool would make woolen manufacturing more profitable. Clay now began telling his friends to pass the bill. He reasoned that a bill passed with Jackson and Adams votes would be of little use to either side during the presidential election. E. I. DuPont, a gunpowder manufacturer who had followed the debate, concurred with Clay's decision. "It is essential at this time not to give a triumph to the Jackson party, who never intended that the bill should pass, and had manufactured it at purpose to be only a political instrument," he informed a friend.[51] On April 15, the House agreed to send the tariff bill to a third reading by a vote of 109 to 91. This

virtually guaranteed passage through the House. Southerners had assisted northern Jacksonians in making the bill as bad as possible with the understanding that
New England votes would kill the bill, but now this bad bill would pass the House
with its most objectionable features injuring the interests of the South. Henry R.
Storrs recorded a telling entry in his diary after the House engrossed the bill: "They
[southern House members] are now satisfied that the N York and Pennsylvania
leaders who contrived the scheme of operations with Mr Calhoun on the Bill have
been 'blind guides' to them." Storrs added that southerners should have joined New
England members in striking out the duties on molasses and hemp. This would
have then allowed the bill to be defeated.[52] Storrs's diary entry links Vice President
Calhoun to the southern strategy. As an Adams man from New York, Storrs would
have had no inside knowledge of any plan or what Van Buren had told his southern friends. But he did proclaim that southerners had been tricked. A Pittsburgh
observer, who agreed with Storrs, wrote home, "The bill was preserved by the lib-
erality of the south, as they prevented all that was contained in the bill, beside the
woolens, from being struck out." He then noted, "the north and south could have
pared down the bill to the mere bill of last year. The bill was, by the middle and
southern states, preserved in its original form nearly."[53] The southerners' strategy
had failed, and they had little to brag about.[54]

Since they had remained silent all throughout the debate, southerners now began a weeklong assault on the bill. Unfortunately, many of these speeches went unrecorded. In the recorded speeches, no member mentioned being duped by their
northern colleagues. John Randolph of Virginia commenced the attack. Three
South Carolinians followed him. These southerners made the same argument—
protective tariffs injured the southern economy. Southern planters had to suffer
solely for the economic gain of a few manufacturers in the North. McDuffie said
that the high duties "amount to an enormous and permanent tax upon the great
mass of the community, for the benefit of a very small number of wealthy capitalists." He amplified this populist thrust near the end of his address. "The wealthy
cotton planter of the South fights by the side of the small farmer, the mechanic,
and the laborer, in New York and Pennsylvania, because they all have a similar interest in opposing a system on which the burden falls upon them for the benefit
of others."[55] Rhetoric similar to this would soon be found in Jackson's messages.
McDuffie refrained from making a constitutional argument, but William Archer of
Virginia and James Hamilton of South Carolina could not resist.[56]

The House then approved the measure by a vote of 105 to 94. As with previous
tariff bills, nearly unanimous support from the middle states of Delaware, Maryland, New Jersey, New York, and Pennsylvania offset southern opposition. The
western states of Illinois, Indiana, Kentucky, Ohio, and Missouri likewise gave the
tariff nearly unanimous support. Only Edward Bates from Missouri voted against
the bill. New England members remained divided over this tariff. The region gave
the bill sixteen positive votes and twenty-one negative votes. If six New England
members switched their vote, the tariff would have been defeated. After the clerk
announced the final House vote, Silas Wright wrote that he "trembled" over the fate
of the tariff in the Senate.[57]

Table 7.1. House vote, 1828

	Jackson Men		Adams Men		Total	
	For	Against	For	Against	For	Against
New England	1	3	15	20	16	23
Middle	30	7	27	4	57	11
South	0	50	3	9	3	59
West	13	0	16	1	29	1
Total	44	60	61	34	105	94

Source: *House Journal*, 20th Cong., 1st Sess., 22 April 1828, 607–9.

While the geographic distribution of the House vote mirrored that of the votes on the tariffs of 1820 and 1824, the vote on the tariff in 1828 became the first vote on a tariff between two political organizations. The tariff had friends and enemies in both the Jackson and Adams camps. Administration members supported the tariff by giving it sixty-one votes. The three Virginians who voted for the tariff supported the administration. However, thirty-four Adams members in the House voted against the tariff. More than half of these votes came from New England. The distribution of votes among Jackson men became a topic for boardinghouse conversation as well. Sixty Jacksonians voted against the bill, but forty-four endorsed it. "The bill seems to be an acceptable one to nobody, and to be urged on its passage as much by the objections to it as by the arguments in its favor," the *National Intelligencer* announced. "Party considerations have had too much to do with it."[58] Again, a switch of only six northern Jackson men would have killed the bill.[59]

In the Senate, the bill received the title by which it has since been known. Samuel Smith of Maryland referred to the bill as a bill of abominations, and the phrase has stuck. Smith regarded the new tariff as an abomination because the excessively high rates injured merchants, shippers, and farmers. The high duties in the bill would mean higher prices that consumers would have to pay. Since Smith had business interests in Baltimore, he believed that the tariff would reduce his profits.[60]

John Tyler of Virginia still hoped to salvage the plan of defeating the bill by keeping it unchanged in the Senate. "The hated Tariff bill, that curse to the whole South, is reported to the Senate with sundry villainous amendments," Tyler wrote. "Its fate rests on our ability to preserve the bill in its present shape. If we can do so it will be rejected."[61] Vice President Calhoun informed a friend that the fate of the tariff in the Senate remained "doubtful." It appears that Calhoun, perhaps with "assurances," still expected the tariff to be defeated in the Senate either because something had been communicated to him or because the numerical majority that the North enjoyed in the House had been removed and southerners now found themselves on a more level playing field. If a few New England or western senators voted against the bill, it could be defeated. Also, in the event of a tie, Calhoun could break it in favor of lower duties.[62]

As expected, the Senate Committee on Manufactures reported the bill with several amendments. It kept the minimum points on woolens that the House had refused to change. However, the committee had included an additional duty of 40 percent to each of the minimum points. This 40 percent duty would increase to 45 percent the following June. While not going as far as the Harrisburg Convention had desired, this additional duty offered significant protection to woolens. It was not a prohibitory duty, but it came close to being that. Woolen manufacturers applauded these changes. They came up for a vote on May 5 and 6. They passed the Committee of the Whole and then the full Senate by a vote of twenty-four to twenty-two. When the New England members sought to reduce the duty on molasses from ten cents a gallon to seven cents a gallon, the Senate rejected this amendment by a vote of twenty five to twenty-one. Dominique Bouligny, an Adams man from Louisiana, and Martin Van Buren switched their votes. Their votes allowed woolen manufacturers to obtain more protection, but they refused to remove any of the other burdens that had been imposed by the bill. After Van Buren supported the amendment on woolens, Littleton W. Tazewell of Virginia, according to one observer, appeared as if "he had been struck by a bullet" since Van Buren's decision changed the dynamic of the vote. "Sir, you have deceived me," Tazewell grumbled to Van Buren.[63]

These woolens amendments prompted the Adams men to reevaluate their position once again. Webster sought advice from New England manufacturers. Their response: pass the bill. "What reconciles me, in some measure to the bill," Webster noted, "is that N. E. will, certainly, on the whole, be benefited by it."[64] Most manufacturers throughout the region now agreed with Webster's assessment. Abbott Lawrence believed a better bill could have been obtained but still believed that New England would have the last laugh. "This bill if adopted as amended," he observed, "will keep the South and West in debt to New England the next hundred years."[65] With manufacturers falling into line in support of the bill, the administration now joined them. A bad bill had become somewhat acceptable, and any chance that southerners had of defeating the tariff disappeared with the Senate amendments on woolens.[66]

The amendments concluded, it now became time for senators to express their views on the bill. Jackson men Richard M. Johnson and Thomas Hart Benton both grumbled over certain sections and rates in the bill. They then announced their intention to vote for the bill because they regarded it as a "whole tariff" and a "national tariff." Robert Y. Hayne of South Carolina called it "an unconstitutional measure." Albion Parris of Maine charged that the high duties would almost ensure the destruction of the New England shipping industry. He argued that the Atlantic Ocean was the farmland of New England. By planting salt in their farms through high duties on molasses, iron, hemp, and sail duck, the rest of the country would force shippers to go out of business, he declared. But the lengthiest speech that survived came from Daniel Webster. Webster had opposed the tariff in 1824. Now, in 1828, he declared that the protective policy had become the fixed policy of the land. New Englanders could either fight a losing rear-guard action or lead the winning protective movement to new levels. Webster announced that New England had chosen the latter. But Webster also criticized the ongoing southern strategy. Southerners in the Senate, just like their colleagues in the House, had resisted every effort to remove

Table 7.2. Senate vote, 1828

	Jackson Men		Adams Men		Total	
	For	Against	For	Against	For	Against
New England	0	3	6	2	6	5
Middle	5	1	3	1	8	2
South	1	13	1	1	2	14
West	4	0	6	0	10	0
Total	10	17	16	4	26	21

Source: *Senate Journal*, 20th Cong., 1st Sess., 13 May 1828, 406.

the high duty on molasses. These same men had claimed that, overall, the protective tariff represented an onerous tax on the poorer classes. Why would they not remove one of the most despised taxes in the bill, he asked. Webster no doubt enjoyed pointing out this apparent hypocrisy of southerners. "Let them not, complain. Let them not hereafter call it the work of others. It is their own work," he avowed.[67]

The Senate approved the tariff by a margin of twenty-six to twenty-one. Sixteen Adams men voted for the bill along with ten Jacksonians. John H. Eaton of Tennessee and Bouligny were the only southern senators to vote for the measure. But nearly unanimous southern opposition, just like in the House, could not stop passage of the tariff. Every senator from the western states of Ohio, Indiana, Illinois, Kentucky, and Missouri, regardless of party, voted for the bill. Of the eleven New England senators who voted, six favored the tariff of abominations, and five opposed it. The two Massachusetts senators divided over the tariff. "We both saw in the measure something to approve and something to disapprove," Webster said when he returned to Boston.[68]

Although Adams said little regarding the tariff as the debate raged around him, he signed the new tariff into law. Only one of his letters discussing the tariff has been preserved. His failure to mention the tariff in his annual message, the limited treatment that the tariff received in his diary, and the absence of the tariff in his correspondence suggest that Adams never grasped the importance of the tariff. Adams blamed the Jacksonians for the excessive features of the bill that hurt New England shippers. "They have passed a bill for the protection of American manufactures, and found no better expedient for turning it against the administration than by encumbering it with some odious appendages because they bear with peculiar hardship upon New England," he complained. Adams's wife, however, rejoiced over the passage of the bill, not because she supported the measure; rather, because this allowed the presidential family to leave the swamps of the capital for the more comfortable climate of Braintree, Massachusetts. As the presidential family left Washington, the American people discussed the new tariff and thought about who they wanted to lead them for the next four years.[69]

8

"The people are generally greatly excited on the subject of the Tariff"

THE PASSAGE OF THE TARIFF of abominations with the aid of Jackson and Adams men meant that neither would be able to use the tariff as an issue to campaign on during the election of 1828. That did not stop both sides from trying, however. As politicians endeavored to figure out how they could use the tariff to advance the cause of either Andrew Jackson or John Quincy Adams, the American people examined the new legislation. While the tariff of abominations did not influence as many voters as had been expected, it created an incredible amount of anger in the South. Southerners began calling for a lowering of the tariff. The animosity became so intense that talk of disunion, which had subsided after the debate over Missouri, resurfaced.

When news of the tariff's passage arrived in South Carolina, ship captains lowered their flags to half-mast in protest. South Carolinians and many other southerners viewed this new tariff as yet another unconstitutional burden that affected their economy. On June 30, at a gathering in Columbia, a mob burned Mathew Carey, Henry Clay, Edward Everett, Rollin C. Mallary, John W. Taylor, and Daniel Webster in effigy. Then, at an Independence Day feast, Governor John Taylor added to the outrage by declaring, "It is true, the late tariff, and all the tariffs of congress, enacted to regulate the labor of the citizens, to control them in the choice of professions and pursuits, possess the very essence of tyranny."[1] No one in South Carolina focused their anger on Martin Van Buren, the man who had tricked them. A public attack on Van Buren could have sewn divisions in the Jackson party that the Adams coalition might have exploited. While South Carolinians refused to castigate the New Yorker publicly, James Hamilton addressed a lengthy letter to him. He informed Van Buren of affairs in South Carolina and told him that he and other southerners blamed their northern brethren for forcing them into their current situation. "But resist we will," he declared, "and our friends at the north who love us yet in spite of our probable rebellion must be prepared to expect it and in some degree thank themselves for attempting to play 'brag' with '*the Blackleg*' on this most foul and corrupting subject."[2]

Jackson's friends warned him to remain silent on the tariff question. At first, the Old Hero followed their advice. "My real friends want no information from me on the subject of internal improvements, and manufactories," he announced.[3] If he published a further explanation of his views, Jackson feared that he would be charged with electioneering. But John H. Eaton, his most trusted advisor, sensed that Jackson could not remain silent amid the unceasing calls for a clarification of his views. Eaton counseled his friend to compose a "very laconic note" that referenced his "old letter of 1824 to Dr. Coleman." "Upon so complex and difficult a subject no man can venture to go into detail," Eaton cautioned Jackson. "Or do more, than speak in terms the most general: this you did do in your letter to Coleman, while your votes in 1824 give opinions more in detail, than the letter did."[4]

The Indiana legislature tried to force Jackson to take a more committed stand on the questions of internal improvements and the tariff. Jackson believed that he saw the "finger of Mr. Clay" in the matter. Since Jackson's friends in the South advocated his election to the presidency because he opposed the tariff and internal improvements, while his supporters in the northern and western states claimed that he favored those issues, Hoosier State Jacksonians wanted to know where he stood on the issues. Members of the Indiana legislature passed a resolution asking Governor James B. Ray to write Jackson a letter seeking his opinion on the leading questions of the day. The Tennessean answered him on February 28. "My opinions, *at present*, are precisely what they were in 1823, and '24," Jackson wrote to the governor, "when they were communicated, by letter, to doctor Coleman, of North Carolina, and when I voted for the present tariff and appropriations for internal improvement." Jackson restated many of the themes addressed in his 1824 letter to Coleman, but he no longer talked about sending farmers to work in factories. He told Ray: "To preserve our invaluable constitution, and be prepared to repel the invasions of a foreign foe, by the practice of economy, and the cultivation, within ourselves, of the means of national defence and independence, should be, it seems to me, the leading objects of any system which aspires to the name 'American,' and of every prudent administration of our government."[5] As in 1824, Jackson appeased foes of internal improvements and the tariff by appealing to their patriotism and reminding them that he wanted to preserve the Constitution and keep government spending at a minimum. With the possibility of a British invasion declining every year, Jackson's primary reason for supporting a tariff weakened. Since he hinted that he wanted to practice a rigid economy, foes of internal improvements and the tariff sensed that the Old Hero would support a tariff only for a limited time. James K. Polk applauded Jackson's handling of the Indiana resolutions and told him that he had avoided a political trap. Amos Kendall, editor of the *Argus of Western America*, likewise praised his course. If the people of Indiana wanted Jackson's explicit opinion, Kendall laughed, the Indiana legislature should have written out a tariff bill with proposed duties and then asked his opinion of it.[6]

The administration, however, mocked Jackson's newest statement on the tariff. To them, Jackson simply continued to avoid the question. "The reader cannot but observe that the General has very dexterously evaded the principle question, in relation to *protecting* our own manufactures to the exclusion of those of foreign countries," one Adams editor informed his readers. Administration supporters scratched their heads over the fact that southern Jacksonians cited the Coleman letter as proof of Jackson's opposition to the tariff, while western and northern Jacksonians used the same letter to prove that he supported the tariff. "The Senate of Indiana asked the General for a direct avowal of his sentiments, upon certain public concerns, and he sends them, in answer, a puzzle which has been perplexing all parties for about four years," the editor claimed.[7] The *Connecticut Courant* called this epistle a "shuffling letter" and said that Jackson refrained from taking a recognizable position so as not alienate his southern friends. "He dare not avow himself, in plain terms, to be a friend to manufactures, because he knows such a declaration would sacrifice, for his interests, all the support of the Southern states," the editor wrote.[8] Henry R. Storrs scribbled the following into his diary: "All parties are puzzled to know whether Genl J's letter to Governor Ray '*commits*' him or not to either side of the Tariff Question. His friends in the Tariff States faintly insist that it does so in favor of the system of Protection. His friends from Virginia and the South claim that it is directly the reverse!"[9]

Since Jackson dodged the tariff question in his public statements, Adams editors told the public to examine the actions of his congressional friends. The company that Jackson kept revealed his position on the tariff, they believed. "Where do we find the most numerous body of General Jackson's supporters?" one Adams editor asked. "Among southern planters, who feel a fraternal feeling for the general, as one who favors their anti-tariff doctrines, and like themselves, hold slaves, and rolls his chariot, with a retinue of negro servants in attendance."[10] The joining of the tariff and slavery had been done in 1820 after Missouri. Now, slavery was being linked with the expansion of power by the federal government. The biggest manifestation of federal supremacy was no longer federally sponsored internal improvements. It had become the tariff.

At parties commemorating Independence Day, South Carolina citizens denounced the new tariff. Every dinner gathering included multiple condemnations of the tariff of abominations. A Colonel Cruger toasted it as follows: "The Tariff—Come it from the East or the West—from the banks of the Potomac or the summits of the Alleghany—we denounce it on principle, and will resist it to the death." John Rutledge, a member of the South Carolina bar, said, "The Tariff of 1828—An act of oppression, passed not for the general welfare, but to exact tribute from the minority." William S. Gaillard, another lawyer avowed, "The Tariff—May it recoil like the viper, and destroy the bosom that fostered it."[11] At a dinner honoring George McDuffie's return to South Carolina, B. F. Whitner declared, "the advocates of the late oppressive Tariff—May we teach them their dependencies on us, by showing our independence from them." James Terry declared at the same dinner, "The Tariff—in resisting its odious policy, our measures should be characterized by manly firmness, tempered with a sacred regard to the principles of the Union."[12] Terry's toast demonstrated an attachment to the union while Cruger's suggested he planned to fight the tariff to the death regardless of the consequences.

Throughout July, the South Carolinians who preached the sanctity of the union began to qualify their allegiance to the union. "The Union of the States—To be preserved only by mutual concession—not by unequal taxation," one unidentified South Carolinian toasted. Richard Pinckney's toast revealed that his allegiance to South Carolina superseded his attachment to the union: "Carolina—Right or Wrong, I pledge my devotion to her." At the end of July, John C. Calhoun lamented to Samuel Smith that if Congress did not retrace its steps, the end would be either despotism or disunion. All summer, South Carolinians formulated ways to transform their words into action on the chance that the federal government refused to address the state's grievances. The actions of South Carolinians during the summer of 1828 suggest that even though the Palmetto State would not entrust its citizens with the choice of presidential electors until after the Civil War, democracy made advancements across the state. Spontaneous outbursts of anger flourished in the most undemocratic state owing to numerous public meetings and the animosity leveled against the tariff.[13]

Some residents of the Palmetto State believed that the Adams administration passed the tariff to throw the southern states into a state of rebellion. If South Carolinians revolted over the tariff, New York and Pennsylvania might give their electoral votes to Adams, allowing him to retain the presidency. "The people are generally greatly excited on the subject of the Tariff, but this has nothing whatever to do with the Presidential question," Hayne wrote to Jackson. Couching his true feelings so as to avoid angering the Old Hero, he apologized for some of his state's rash actions but told Jackson that the tariff of 1828 passed because some of the General's friends supported it. "A persevering refusal to make any of the modifications to the Bill which were designed for the exclusive benefit of the East, at the expense of the West and South," Hayne informed him, "deprived us of the advantage of exposing to the world the hollow pretensions of those who under the pretext of supporting American Industry, were merely driving a bargain for their own personal advantage." But he reminded Jackson that the protests against the tariff came not from the politicians but the common people. The statesmen of the South, he suggested, had been "hurried away" by the groundswell of opposition. Once they saw the direction of public opinion, they took over and began to lead it. He confirmed to Jackson that his state had no desire to secede from the union so long as the administration avoided interfering with the institution of slavery. Should Adams interfere with slavery, he would not be responsible for the consequences, Hayne warned.[14]

Jackson informed James Hamilton Jr. that he "regretted" the protests taking place in South Carolina. He urged him, Hayne, and other disgruntled South Carolinians to act with prudence and caution. Jackson possibly feared that his tariff-supporting followers in the North might abandon him if his southern followers continued to agitate over the tariff. "To regulate a Judicious tariff is a subject of great difficulty at all times," Jackson told Hamilton, "and ought to be discussed, with great calmness and due deliberation, with an eye to the prosperity of the whole Union, and not of any particular part viewing the whole as one great family, and extending impartial justice to every branch, with feeling of Mutual concession, extending to all equal benefits, and each bearing a Just portion of the burdens the Tariff may impose."[15] Although the actions of South Carolinians focused attention on their state, Georgians voiced their displeasure over the tariff as well. In Milledgeville, Governor John Forsyth opined, "We are all anti Tariff mad here."[16] Another Georgian, Hines Holt, observed that the tariff continued to empty the pockets of southerners. "Is there no constitutional measure which we can adopt, to disappoint those who are manufacturing shackles to manacle us as well as woolens to clothe our nakedness on their own terms?" he asked.[17] Milledgeville residents resolved to refrain from using anything produced in the "tariff states" and to rely on their own industry for the articles that they consumed. Students at Franklin College in Georgia issued a similar resolution and urged the members of the faculty to assist them in using goods manufactured in the South.[18]

Always keeping his finger on the pulse of the electorate, Van Buren, perhaps apologizing for the storm that his actions had created, lamented, "the whole country is yet greatly Tarrified."[19] Van Buren had failed to anticipate the outrage that passage of a bad tariff would produce. This was surprising for such an astute politician. He did not begin to discuss the tariff of 1828 until 1840, when he needed southern votes to secure his reelection. He said in 1840 that he did not want the bill to pass but voted for it because he had been instructed by the New York state legislature. Also, the "Little Magician" failed to mention the tariff of abominations in his autobiography. Van Buren muddied the waters on several occasions regarding the tariff.[20]

Adams supporters welcomed these demonstrations against the tariff in the South. They hoped that the states with early elections, Kentucky, Indiana, Illinois, Louisiana, New York, Ohio, and Pennsylvania, might reevaluate their support for Jackson and stay with the incumbent. Jackson men scolded their brethren in South Carolina for threatening Jackson's elevation to the presidency. Both Samuel Smith and Duff Green urged Calhoun to curtail the protests in his home state. Once a Jackson administration came into power, the violence toward the tariff would subside, Calhoun assured Van Buren. The New Yorker accepted this explanation after administration candidates suffered defeats in both Kentucky and Louisiana at the end of summer. These defeats doomed the administration and signaled the triumph of Andrew Jackson in the coming presidential election.[21]

Throughout the North that summer and fall, northerners arrived at the belief that southerners exaggerated the effects of the protective system. Pennsylvanians hailed the tariff of abominations as a "judicious tariff" that saved the American System from destruction by the administration. "The Glorious Tariff of our last Jackson Congress," one Pennsylvanian stated, "unlike that of our 'Wool Gathering' opponents, it is neither partial nor local in its operation, but extends equally its various blessings to the American People—'May it be perpetual.'"[22] Southerners' actions more than likely contributed to this change of opinion. It could also be argued that many northerners wanted to give the new bill a fair chance before passing judgment on it. Perhaps the new president, not having to worry about an election, might urge Congress to modify the tariff and remove some of its more objectionable features. At a dinner in Cincinnati, Henry Baldwin defended the new tariff and said, "It is the most important bill which was ever adopted." A bill that pleased nobody at first had now become somewhat palatable at least for those in the North.[23]

In the fall, Jackson won the presidency, sweeping the South and the West. He secured Pennsylvania and more than half of New York's electoral votes. In Pennsylvania, already committed to a high tariff, Jackson won 101,000 popular votes to Adams's 50,000. Adams carried only New England, New Jersey, Maryland, and Delaware. All told, Jackson won 56 percent of the popular vote.[24]

After the election, however, the South Carolina opposition to the tariff reached a crescendo. The state's economy had never fully recovered from the Panic of 1819, largely because the price of cotton continued to fall. More and more commerce flowed to the North to the exclusion of southern merchants. Southerners still provided the nation with the majority of its exports in the form of cotton, tobacco, and rice, yet southerners received little compensation. Wealth seemed to be diverted from the South to the North, and when southerners looked around for the cause of the draining of their wealth, they focused on the actions of the federal government but particularly the protective tariff. "They [the people of the South] feel that they have been reduced to a condition almost tantamount to colonial vassalage," the *Charleston Mercury* cried. "They see their commerce, which once whitened the ocean, about to be destroyed, and their smiling fields about to be ruined and deserted. They see and feel, in short, that the great sources of their wealth are about to be dried up, and that their dignity as a State, and prosperity as a people, are upon the eve of leaving them forever."[25] The primary reason why southerners resisted the tariff with increased energy came from the belief that protective tariffs meant higher prices on the goods that southerners purchased. Southerners conducted most business transactions with cotton. As the price of cotton fell, southerners needed more cotton to complete a business deal. Since Congress levied duties on the items that southern planters required, they needed extra cotton to balance the transaction. Another reason why southerners opposed the tariff, although neglected during the debates prior to 1824, was that they considered a protective tariff a violation of the Constitution. They now began thinking of ways to end this violation. Clairvoyant southerners sensed that if the numerical majority that the North enjoyed in Congress violated the Constitution in one respect, it might begin legislating on the institution of slavery.[26]

Although the tariff of abominations caused much controversy, it provided the federal government with a financial windfall. While this tariff remained in effect, veterans' pensions increased, internal improvements continued, Native Americans were evicted from their ancestral homelands, White House improvements were authorized, and federal government expenditures increased. President Jackson informed Congress in 1832, "within the four years for which the people have confided the Executive power to my charge $58 million will have been applied to the public debt."[27]

As Americans looked forward to the day when the federal debt would be removed, South Carolinians continued to complain over the injustices of the tariff. It seemed as though they were swimming against the current. The middle states continued to endorse protectionism. Most in New England had changed their position on the protective tariff. Westerners endorsed it by large majorities as well. "The principle of protecting the domestic manufactures of the country, has been so often advanced by every branch of the government, and so firmly upheld by constantly increasing majorities of the people, that it is now too late to enquire whether it be right or wrong, just or unjust," Edward Bates notified the people of Missouri. "Protection is now the settled policy, not of the government merely, but of the people of the United States, and all republicans will submit to the unequivocal expression of the public will."[28]

Immediately after Congress passed the tariff of abominations in 1828, the entire South Carolina delegation, except William Smith, convened at Robert Y. Hayne's lodgings in Washington City to vent their anger. They agreed to go home to their constituents and discourage discussion of the tariff until after the presidential election. But the people would not yield. In November, William C. Preston decided to channel that outrage into an announcement of South Carolina's opposition to the protective tariff. Preston asked Calhoun to compose a document articulating the state's grievances against the tariff and asserting ways that the state could protect its sovereignty against encroachments by the federal government. Calhoun had begun thinking about these issues and had been formulating the methods by which a state might nullify a federal law or "interpose" its sovereignty as early as 1827. Preston's letter gave Calhoun a reason to put his theory of state interposition down on paper.[29]

Calhoun presented Preston with a draft of what came to be known as the *South Carolina Exposition*. The *Exposition*, whose authorship was known to only a few, represented the final act in Calhoun's transition from nationalism to sectionalism. Calhoun's *Exposition* was two documents in one. First, the *Exposition* articulated the economic arguments against the tariff. Second, it proposed a remedy to alleviate these grievances. This remedy, which Calhoun drew from the resolutions of 1798, came to be known as state interposition or nullification. The *Exposition* served as a massive broadside against the protective system.[30]

Calhoun charged that the protective system operated unfairly on the people of the South. This argument had been made by countless others since 1820. But Calhoun had the statistics to back up this argument. Southern farmers exported $37 million worth of goods. The rest of the country only exported $16 million worth of goods. With the tariff of abominations imposing an average duty of 45 percent, Calhoun contended that southerners would contribute $16.7 million to the federal treasury. Although southern exports doubled the exports of the rest of the country, the South had only seventy-six House members, while the rest of the country had 137.[31] Thus, a third of the country produced two-thirds of the country's exports. The high tariffs imposed by the majority of the North and the West diminished the value of southern agricultural products because most farmers traded agricultural goods for manufactured items. The high tariff increased prices and prompted southern farmers to spend more to obtain manufactured goods. "It is by this very increase of price, which must be paid by their fellow citizens of the South, that the indemnity to the manufacturers, is effected," Calhoun declared. "And by means of this the fruits of our toil and labour, which on every principle of justice, ought to belong to ourselves, are transferred from us to them." Thus, the tariff stole the labor of southern planters. Calhoun made the point more explicitly: "We are the serfs of the system, out of whose labour is raised, not only the money that is paid into the Treasury, but the funds out of which are drawn the rich reward of the manufacturer and his associates in interest. . . . The duty on imports which is mainly paid out of our labour gives them the means of selling to us at a higher price." This system would soon lead to the decay of the South. Calhoun next added, "The case then, fairly stated between us and the manufacturing States, is, that the Tariff gives them a prohibition against foreign competition in our own market, in the sale of their goods, and deprives us of the benefit of a competition of purchasers for our raw material." Northern manufacturers' desire to prohibit European goods from entering America gave American manufacturers a monopoly, according to Calhoun. However, he and other South Carolinians feared that European states would retaliate against the United States by excluding American cotton. This would force southern planters to turn to manufacturing, leaving southerners unable to compete against northern manufacturers. Eventually, Calhoun observed, "those who now make war on our gains would then make it on our labour." Here Calhoun linked the tariff with slavery. The end result of the protective tariff would be to make agriculture unprofitable. Southern planters would abandon their fields and use their slaves as a labor source for manufacturing. Northern manufacturers would not want to compete against slave labor, so the North would use its numerical majority to free every slave. All the economic problems that had dogged the South since the Panic of 1819, according to Calhoun, could be attributed to the tariff. Internal improvements, a high debt, and the emancipation of every slave could all be blamed on the tariff. "The Tariff is the soul of the system," he declared. In order for the South to succeed economically, the tariff had to be lowered.[32]

The South Carolina legislature refrained from endorsing the *Exposition* but still ordered four thousand copies to be printed. Copies of the *Exposition* circulated throughout the union, and Americans began shuddering at the renewed prospect of disunion. Calhoun and other southerners hoped that the threat of nullification would force Jackson to make tariff reduction his primary goal. Protectionists did not agree. "He [Jackson] was a tariff man in 1824," a New England Federalist laughed while discussing the situation of South Carolina. Robert T. Hubbard, a Virginia tobacco planter, confirmed this when he argued that regarding the tariff, Jackson would act in the same way as Adams had acted.[33]

9

"Every American must give up a little for his country"

OVER THE SPAN OF EIGHTEEN months in 1828 and 1829, a wolf killed thousands of sheep near the town of Sandwich, Massachusetts. Foes of the 1828 tariff of abominations deemed the wolf an "anti-tariff wolf," because this animal injured the interests of men who had benefitted from the 1828 tariff. "There are huge gangs of anti-tariff wolves prowling about in the most civilized parts of South Carolina every day," a Columbia editor warned. "They whet their teeth most ferociously, in the true spirit of 'blood and carnage' for the throats of manufacturers."[1] Although extreme, this anecdote reveals the outrage directed toward the tariff among South Carolinians. Outside of South Carolina, other southerners wanted the tariff of abominations ripped to shreds as well. This desire soon brought the nation to the brink of civil war, however.

With South Carolinians calling for a destruction of the protective tariff and northern manufacturers claiming that they would be ruined if Congress removed tariffs on foreign goods, how could a compromise be reached? Compromise had ensured the creation and ratification of the Constitution. It allowed most bills of importance to become law. It saved the union during the Missouri crisis. Yet, on the tariff, Americans could not reach an agreement. "It seems to be understood that Congress will hand over the most difficult subjects to their successors," James Madison mused in 1829, "particularly the tariff, on which the discord between the South and the Centre and the West will be not a little embarrassing, and require the compromising management of a masterly hand."[2] Southerners wanted a return to a tariff modeled after the tariff of 1816. This would make the cultivation of cotton profitable once again. Northerners believed that southerners exaggerated the problems of the protective tariff. Its reduction to the levels demanded by southerners would jeopardize the capital that northerners had invested in manufacturing. "A modification of the Tariff is loudly called for in the South and stoutly opposed in the north but the west I hope will be able to bring the extremes nearer each other and save the Country," John Tipton of Indiana announced in 1832.[3] "Every American must give up a little for his country," a Pennsylvanian noted in 1832. "It is in this way only we can expect to live together as a nation."[4] Peleg Sprague of Maine captured the notion of compromise best when he announced on the Senate floor in 1832: "By compromise was the government formed; by mutual concession only can it be preserved."[5]

Some type of compromise had become necessary because the hints and threats of disunion became serious throughout the 1820s. The decisions of the Supreme Court under John Marshall, the calls for federally sponsored internal improvements, and the tariffs of 1824 and 1828 had convinced southerners that northerners sought to end the concept of a federal government and replace it with a consolidated national government. Southern animosity against the doctrine of consolidation reached an apogee in the fall of 1828 with John C. Calhoun's *South Carolina Exposition*. Shortly after South Carolina broached the concept of nullification, former president James Madison sensed the inherent dangers in the doctrine. If nullification succeeded, Madison noted, it "would convert the Federal Government into a mere league, which would quickly throw the States back into a chaos."[6] But for many Americans, the problem with nullification was not that it would return the nation to the unwieldy Articles of Confederation, but that it would lead to secession.

Andrew Jackson entered the presidency on March 4, 1829. In mourning as a result of the recent death of his wife, Rachel, Jackson delivered a short inaugural address. Jackson announced his plan to observe a "strict and faithful economy" so as to extinguish the federal debt. He then added: "the great interests of agriculture, commerce, and manufactures should be equally favored, and that perhaps the only exception to this rule should consist in the peculiar encouragement of any products of either of them that may be found essential to our national independence." This last statement appeased southerners because it suggested that all but a few manufactured items would have their tariff rates lowered. However, Jackson's inaugural secured approval from northerners, because if they could justify that their product aided the independence of the country then Jackson would not recommend a lowering of the duties on that product.[7]

The tariff did not influence Jackson's thinking when he entered the executive mansion. For Jackson, the high rates of the 1828 tariff would allow the federal government to extinguish its debt by the close of his first term. Committed to Jeffersonian ideals, Jackson wanted to remove the debt more than anything else. But the tariff also had political ramifications that complicated matters. A call to lower the tariff would cost Jackson support in Pennsylvania, New York, and the western states of Ohio, Kentucky, Illinois, Indiana, and Missouri. The loss of these states could hinder Jackson's chances for reelection. Furthermore, if Jackson alienated members of Congress from these states, they might retaliate by opposing his other reforms such as curtailing the power of the courts, eliminating the Electoral College, evicting Native Americans from their ancestral lands, or destroying the national bank. Therefore, Jackson demurred.[8]

When Jackson had to address the tariff, he chose his words carefully. Jackson's tariff position provided flexibility to himself and his supporters. While the nullifiers in South Carolina had called for a drastic reduction of the tariff, Pennsylvanians had offered resolutions in support of a protective tariff through nearly unanimous majorities in their legislature. By not committing, Jackson could bring the opposing sides together at the most opportune time. William Smith, a South Carolinian opposed to nullification, complained that he found "little disposition in Congress for any kind of legislation" on the tariff but believed that if Jackson threw himself into the debate, "the question is settled forever."[9]

While Jackson's early words as president offered few clues as to his tariff goals, his actions spoke louder. Original members of Jackson's cabinet, such as Martin Van Buren and John H. Eaton, had supported the protective tariff. The executive department that would have the most input on the tariff, the Treasury Department, went to Pennsylvania's Samuel Ingham. Ingham had missed the final votes on the 1824 and 1828 tariffs, but all recognized that this paper manufacturer supported protectionism. William Cullen Bryant opined about Ingham, "He is a tariff man, infected with the leaven of the American System."[10] Jackson's other cabinet positions went to John M. Berrien, William T. Barry, and John Branch. Attorney General Berrien and Navy Secretary Branch had voted against the 1828 tariff. Barry, the postmaster general, however, had never served in Congress. Jackson's cabinet appointments disappointed Vice President Calhoun and Jackson's own southern supporters because of their stances on the tariff.[11]

Jackson sent another signal that tariff reform was not a high priority for his administration when a vacancy opened on the Supreme Court in early 1830. He nominated Henry Baldwin, a protectionist and author of the failed tariff of 1820, to fill the vacancy of the deceased Bushrod Washington. Baldwin had labored tirelessly for Jackson since 1824. His efforts warranted a cabinet appointment, but Baldwin yielded his claims to his fellow Pennsylvanian Ingham. The Senate confirmed Baldwin's nomination with only two senators dissenting: South Carolina's Robert Y. Hayne and William Smith. The New York Daily Advertiser editor hailed Baldwin's appointment and subsequent confirmation. For this editor, Baldwin's appointment by Jackson signified that the judiciary would continue to adhere to precedents when deciding constitutional questions and not new theories such as nullification. If the constitutionality of a protective tariff came before the high court, Baldwin, who had not yet begun his descent into insanity, would rule in favor of the tariff. Before he departed for Washington City, Baldwin's friends dined with him at Griffith's Hotel in Pittsburgh. Baldwin refrained from making a political speech and simply toasted his adopted home city of Pittsburgh. When he took his seat, an unidentified man rose and said, "The Tariff—The friends of domestic industry rejoice in the elevation of one who was their early, their faithful, their zealous, and their eloquent advocate."[12] Baldwin's appointment and easy confirmation showed the nullifiers that the nation supported the protective system.[13]

As the Senate prepared to confirm Baldwin, the tariff became entwined with the issue of public lands. Westerners, led by Thomas Hart Benton, a Missouri senator who had traded gunshots with Jackson in a barroom brawl but who had since reconciled with the Old Hero, wanted Congress to sell western lands for only a few cents an acre. For northerners, cheap western lands could mean the departure of laborers for western farms. To stop this, Connecticut Senator Samuel A. Foot, an opponent of Jackson, offered a resolution that sought to curtail western land sales. Benton rose and announced that he sensed a conspiracy. The plot involved high prices for western lands and the protective tariff. "The manufactories want poor people to do the work for small wages; these poor people wish to go to the West and get land," Benton announced. He then exclaimed, "A most complex scheme of injustice, which taxes the South to injure the West, to pauperize the poor of the North!"[14]

South Carolina's Robert Y. Hayne sensed that Benton's speech offered an opportunity to forge an alliance between the South and the West. In return for southern votes on a bill to lower the price of western lands, southerners expected westerners to assist them in lowering the tariff. The *Boston Courier* discerned what southerners might be able to accomplish. "It is believed that the understood compact which the South are disposed to form, was to give the public lands to the West, provided the West could go with the South in producing some modification of the Tariff," the editor announced.[15] On January 19, Hayne endorsed a reduction in prices for the public lands. He announced that the South had become a colonial appendage of the North. It had also been exploited just as much as the West. What Ireland was to England, Hayne declared, the South was to the North. All the ills of the South could be traced back to the tariff, Hayne wrote. "The people of America are, and ought to be for a century to come, essentially an agricultural people; and I can conceive of no policy that can possibly be purchased in relation to the public lands, none that would be more 'for the common benefit of all the States,' than to use them as the means of furnishing a secure asylum to that class of our fellow-citizens, who in any portion of the country may find themselves unable to procure a comfortable subsistence by the means immediately within their reach."[16]

Massachusetts senator Daniel Webster heard Hayne's attacks on the East and responded the next day. Webster endeavored to show that the East had long supported western interests. As for the tariff, "it was literally forced on New England," Webster lamented. Hayne quickly offered a rejoinder to Webster. "The gentleman may boast as much as he pleases of the friendship of New England for the West, as displayed in their support of internal improvement; but, when he next introduces that topic, I trust that he will tell us when that friendship commenced, when it was brought about, and why it was established." Hayne suggested that easterners, including Webster, had supported western interests only once Adams became president in 1825. After implying that easterners had granted favors to the West for political purposes, Hayne began to wander away from the public lands, internal improvements, and the tariff. Instead, he began discussing the Northwest Ordinance of 1787, slavery, the principles of 1798, the Hartford Convention, and nullification.[17]

This was the opening that Webster had been waiting for. He charged Hayne and other South Carolinians with inconsistency. The tariff of 1816 passed with the votes of South Carolina, he reminded the audience in the Senate chamber. Her delegation had supported the General Survey Act of 1824. Now, Webster announced, the Palmetto State declared that these programs are unconstitutional and believed that it could break up the union over the tariff. Webster then reiterated how New England had reluctantly supported the tariff after fighting it from 1816 until 1824. "What, then, were we to do?" he asked. "Our only option was, either to fall in with this settled course of public policy, and accommodate ourselves to it as well as we could, or to embrace the South Carolina doctrine, and talk of nullifying the statute by State interference." Webster next responded to Hayne's charge that he had acted inconsistently on the tariff. "Does political consistency consist in always giving negative votes?" he asked. The Baldwin tariff of 1820 and the tariff of 1824 did not aid his constituents, so he opposed them. Since the woolens bill and the 1828 tariff afforded them protection, he supported them both. Webster declared that he had been a consistent custodian of the people of New England's interests.[18]

Although at one point Webster said, "No more of the Tariff," he kept coming back to it. "In Carolina, the Tariff is a palpable, deliberate usurpation; Carolina, therefore, may nullify it, and refuse to pay the duties. In Pennsylvania, it is both clearly constitutional, and highly expedient; and there, the duties are to be paid. And yet we live under a Government of uniform laws, and under a Constitution, too, which contains an express provision, as it happens, that all duties shall be equal in all the States! Does this not approach absurdity?" With the Senate galleries overflowing, Webster next maintained that the union preceded the states. Because of this, when disputes arose between the federal government and a state, the Supreme Court became the final arbiter. Turning to Hayne, Webster hallowed the significance of the federal union and articulated the nationalist interpretation of the Constitution: "It is, sir, the People's Constitution, the People's Government; made for the People; made by the People; and answerable to the People." If a state such as South Carolina could pick and choose which laws it wanted to obey, then the country would revert to the condition that existed under the Articles of Confederation, Webster concluded. Henceforth, the union would become "a rope of sand."[19]

Webster's second reply to Hayne became the high-water mark for the debate, but it was not the last word. For five months, the Senate debated Foot's resolution. Over twenty senators offered their own insights into the public lands, the tariff, and internal improvements. William Smith, South Carolina's other senator and an enemy of Calhoun, Hayne, and nullification, put his faith in the people to remedy the problem of the tariff. "Public opinion must, and will correct this mighty evil, and in its own way, and leave the States still further to cultivate their Union, upon those pure principles that first brought them together," he declared.[20] But most senators articulated their viewpoints on the nature and the origin of the federal union. History and subsequent events gave Webster the victory, but in 1830, he won what can only be regarded as a split decision. Northern papers touted Webster, who quickly published his second reply, as the victor, while southern papers believed that Hayne had defended the rights of the states against federal consolidation.[21]

Thinking that he had bested Webster, Hayne sent a copy of his speech to James Madison. The retired president thanked him for providing a copy of his Senate address. He then informed Hayne that he disagreed with him regarding the constitutional right of a state to nullify a federal law. Edward Everett, the editor of the *North American Review*, subsequently published Madison's rebuttal to Hayne. Madison's public refutation became a grievous setback for the nullifiers. They had based the doctrine of nullification on Madison's arguments in the Virginia Resolutions of 1798 and the Virginia Report of 1799. Now, the "Father of the Constitution" disapproved of their theory. Moreover, Madison endorsed Congress's right to pass a protective tariff. Throughout the early 1830s, Madison penned several letters refuting arguments that his and Thomas Jefferson's resolutions supported nullification.[22]

Once the Senate concluded its debate over the public lands brought on by Foot's resolution, Congress debated bills relating to federally sponsored internal improvements. While wrestling with a bill to fund a road from Buffalo to New Orleans, James K. Polk, a Jackson man from Tennessee, used the opportunity to attack the tariff. "Each individual does not see the amount of tax which he pays go into the hands of the collector; but, notwithstanding, he pays the tax in the increased price he pays upon almost every article of necessity which he eats, drinks, or wears," Polk announced.

> He pays it upon every bushel of salt he uses, upon every pound or iron, upon coffee, tea, sugar, upon every blanket and great coat that protects him from the inclemency of the season in winter. In short, every head of a family, whether rich or poor, pays a tax, and a heavy tax, in the increased price he pays upon every article himself or his family buys or are compelled to use, and which he does not furnish himself by his own labor or the domestic industry of his family. The tax is an indirect one. It is a tax on consumption; but it is as much a tax, and is as oppressive upon the people, as if it were a direct tax.[23]

In Polk's eyes, the tariff inflated the prices of goods that Americans purchased.

Although this bill failed to clear congressional hurdles, another internal improvements bill, the Maysville Road bill, passed Congress. Southerners recognized that the appropriation of federal dollars toward internal improvements would perpetuate the system of high tariffs. If they could block funds from going to public works projects such as this, then they could alleviate the necessity for a high tariff. Southerners smiled when they learned that Jackson would veto the Maysville Road bill, but they frowned when they recognized his reasons for vetoing it. The president vetoed the Maysville Road bill because he regarded the appropriation of federal dollars to a local project as unconstitutional. He then united federally sponsored internal improvements and the tariff. Local projects, such as this, Jackson announced, would never receive his sanction. The same held true with domestic manufacturers that did not manufacture a good for the national defense. A high tariff on certain goods functioned as a tax on that good that the people had to bear. Jackson affirmed that so long as the goals of domestic manufacturers remained directed to national ends they would receive his "temperate but steady support." However, if a tariff protected a single interest, he would not support it. He once again reminded Congress that he came to Washington on a platform of reform, and a primary reform remained the elimination of the federal debt. Internal improvement projects only added to the debt. This was an odd place for Jackson to suggest his views on the tariff, but it reveals the political difficulties that he faced over this issue.[24]

In Jackson's 1830 annual message, the president included a more forceful statement on the tariff. Jackson wanted all to know that that he considered a protective tariff to be constitutional. "The power to impose duties on imports originally belonged to the several states," Jackson announced:

> the right to adjust those duties with a view to the encouragement of domestic branches of industry, is so completely incidental to that power, that it is difficult to

suppose the existence of the one without the other. The states have delegated their whole authority over imports to the General Government, without limitation or restriction, saving the very inconsiderable reservation relating to their inspection laws. The authority having thus entirely passed from the States, the right to exercise it, for the purpose of protection, does not exist in them, and, consequently, if it be not possessed by the General Government, it must be extinct.

Jackson next added that the opinions of Washington, Jefferson, Madison, and Monroe on the protective tariff confirmed his position.[25]

The nullifiers began to force Jackson's hand on the tariff in 1831. George McDuffie argued that the tariff took forty bales from every cotton planter in a speech at Charleston. Essentially, the tariff taxed southern cotton planters at a rate of 40 percent. Northern manufacturers did not have to endure this onerous tax. William W. Freehling succinctly summarized the forty-bale theory of McDuffie as "poor economics but superb propaganda." "The great fundamental and conservative principle of a Confederative Government, should be equal taxation," McDuffie shouted to thunderous applause. "The inevitable consequence of violating it is to enrich and corrupt one portion of the Union to impoverish and enslave another." McDuffie then offered a solution. Manufactured goods that received protection should be taxed at the same rate as foreign manufactured goods. This would equalize the tax burden between the North and the South, he contended. If the North failed to relieve the sufferings of the people of the South, he warned, "I believe this confederacy cannot possibly be held together under a permanently unequal and unjust system of taxation." All that remained, McDuffie concluded, was nullification.[26]

With most roads for political advancement now blocked because of a public falling out with Jackson over his criticism following from the Seminole controversy of 1818, Calhoun endorsed nullification in his "Fort Hill Address" at the end of July 1831. Unlike the *South Carolina Exposition* of 1828, this address focused primarily on the precedents and legality of nullification. Only near the end of his statement did Calhoun discuss the economics of the tariff. He calculated that once the debt had been paid, the government would have an annual surplus of ten million dollars. This surplus would lead to extravagant expenditures or, worse yet, an unconstitutional distribution of the surplus back to the states. Distribution, according to Calhoun, would "perpetuate forever" the system of high duties. To protect against this, Calhoun wrote, the only remedy was a reduction of the tariff to "the wants of the government."[27]

The "Fort Hill Address" quelled the more extreme nullifiers in South Carolina, but Calhoun enraged them by not demanding an immediate reduction of the tariff and the abandonment of the protective principle. His critics outside of South Carolina saw nothing in the address to approve of since nullification threatened the union. "He contends for nullification in its wildest sense, and entrenches himself behind the names of Jefferson and Madison," a New England editor declared.[28] The *National Intelligencer* condemned Calhoun's "heresy" and his "wild doctrine" of nullification, while a North Carolina editor informed his readers that nullification applied to the Articles of Confederation and not the union established by the Constitution.[29] From his home in Quincy, Massachusetts, John Quincy Adams avowed, "the doctrine in all its parts is so adverse to my convictions, that I can view it in no other light than as organized civil War."[30]

Calhoun's decision to issue his "Fort Hill Address" had been prompted by the actions of the more militant nullifiers who accelerated their calls for a nullifying convention. They formed the States' Rights and Free Trade Association of South Carolina. This political organization, branded a "Jacobin Club" by opponents of nullification both within and outside of the state, rallied South Carolinians behind the "Carolina doctrine." Candidates for office extolled the benefits of nullification and how it protected the people against encroachments by the federal government. Governor James Hamilton stressed that the new political organization sought to unite every South Carolinian toward a common object—the lowering of the tariff to the standard that met the needs of the government. At an 1831 Fourth of July celebration in Charleston, Hayne prepared South Carolinians for the possibility of more militant action by reminding them of the exploits of Francis Marion, William Moultrie, and Thomas Sumter. Even though he reached back into the state's Revolutionary past, Hayne stressed the nonrevolutionary aspect of nullification by continuing the argument that both Jefferson and Madison sanctioned it when they composed the Virginia and Kentucky Resolutions of 1798. If South Carolina continued to allow the federal government and the "tariff party" of the North to acquire powers not granted to them by the constitutional compact, he argued, then every South Carolinian would be reduced to a state of slavery.[31]

The opposition to the tariff extended to areas beyond South Carolina. Every southern state had pockets of opposition to the tariff, and most of these states included nullifiers who agreed with South Carolina. Jackson's refusal to address the tariff, along with his decision to allow Congress to take the lead in formulating a new tariff policy, pushed other southerners closer to the nullifiers' position. Jackson had always wanted to isolate the nullifiers, but keeping the rest of the South content had become more and more difficult.[32]

In spite of New England's reversal on the tariff, a vocal element of tariff opposition remained in the North as well. These men would not go as far as South Carolina and recommend a nullification of the tariff, but they could be counted on to provide votes in Congress for a reduced tariff. Condy Raguet, who had worked as an agent for iron manufacturers in 1820, emerged as the leader of the free-trade forces in the North. His journals, the *Banner of the Constitution* and then the *Examiner and Journal of Political Economy*, spoke for those in the North who opposed the American System. Although it reached fewer people than *Niles' Weekly Register*, the *Banner of the Constitution* helped to articulate a different viewpoint to the people of the northern and middle states. Unfortunately for Raguet, northern protectionists ignored his arguments against the tariff and his calls for unfettered trade. "The Free Trade Party contend that every individual is a better judge of how he can obtain more profit on his capital, or more wages for his labor, than any Government possibly can be," Raguet announced.[33]

On September 30, 1831, 212 delegates assembled for a free-trade convention in Philadelphia. Westerners avoided the convention, but one 134 southerners attended along with 78 delegates from the middle states. Modeled after the Harrisburg Convention of 1827, the free-trade convention of 1831 reiterated the southern argument that high tariffs were unjust and oppressive. The convention completed an "Address to the American People" and then submitted a memorial to Congress. Thomas R. Dew helped Albert Gallatin compile arguments and statistics for the memorial. Gallatin's association with the convention and memorial gave it increased legitimacy, but many northerners still saw the convention as an effort to support nullification. In the memorial, Gallatin argued for a uniform system of duties. If Congress adopted Gallatin's plan of a horizontal tariff, all imported items would be assessed the same duty. Aside from a passing reference, Gallatin avoided discussing nullification or the unconstitutionality of a protective tariff, reasoning that this would taint the convention and make it appear as a tool of southern extremists. Calhoun lamented that the convention refused to address the grievances of the South.[34]

Over five hundred protectionists held their own convention in New York City a month later. The southernmost delegates came from Virginia, which had a representation of only three men. New York sent 146 delegates, while Pennsylvania sent 100. William Wilkins, a senator from Pennsylvania who supported Jackson, became the president of the convention. A committee of fourteen members composed an address to the people of the United States. The free-trade convention had avoided the constitutional issue, but this convention devoted considerable attention to the constitutionality of a protective tariff. The report asserted that the Founding Fathers drafted the Constitution to give the government the power to levy countervailing duties against nations that excluded American products. Every American president, including the current chief magistrate, sanctioned the protective policy, the report contended, which had been in operation for forty-two years without interruption. If Congress relinquished the power to protect manufacturers, the committee predicted a return to the conditions that existed while Americans lived under the Articles of Confederation. Prosperity and happiness would be replaced by depression. The report incorporated many of the arguments that Clay had used in 1824. The tariff lowered prices, it offered farmers a market for their crops, and it kept the wages of workers high. According to the report, the tariff also secured the bonds of union. "Sugar, and iron, hemp, and lead, wool, and cotton, and the other productions of our diversified soil, elaborated by our own indefatigable industry, and protected by our own free government, are, in effect, the government that holds us together and make us one people," the report claimed. No doubt, this section had been included in response to the recent actions of South Carolina.[35]

Jackson's mercurial position on the tariff, Calhoun's public support for nullification, and the two conventions on the tariff all contributed to keeping the tariff before the people as 1831 drew to a close. All hoped that when Congress reconvened in December that it would be able to find a compromise that pleased all parties.

10

"Repeal the Tariff or Repeal the Union"

BEFORE CONGRESS RECONVENED in December 1831, every member and observer must have sensed that this session would be a momentous one. All the divisive issues—the tariff, the national bank, internal improvements, and public lands—would be debated. They would all have a bearing on the presidential election as well. "Much and great interest is felt to the proceedings of the present Congress," a North Carolina judge noted. "The tariff is the great subject upon which the eyes of the public are turned. That it will be modified I have but little doubt. It would seem that all parties express themselves favourable to a modification and reduction. . . . I suppose the difficulty will be in the detail."[1] Daniel Webster observed, "We are to have an interesting and arduous session. Every thing is to be attacked, every thing is to be debated, as if nothing had ever been settled."[2]

President Andrew Jackson now decided to try to outflank the nullifiers. Since the debt would be eliminated by the end of his first term, he recommended a "judicious reduction of duties to meet the wants of government" in his third annual message. If this did not placate the nullifiers, then nothing would, Jackson believed. The lowering of duties "will annihilate the Nullifiers as they will be left without any pretext of complaint," Jackson wrote to Martin Van Buren. "And if they attempt disunion, it must be because they wish it, and have only indulged in their vituperations against the Tariff for the purpose of covertly accomplishing their ends."[3] The leading Jacksonian sheets naturally applauded the president's decision to lower the tariff. Jackson's opponents saw other motives for his decision to recommend a tariff reduction. Virginia governor John Floyd said of Jackson's message, "it is in much more subdued tones than before. The old man is afraid of losing his reelection."[4] "The longer a modification of the Tariff is delayed," the *Albany Evening Journal* announced, "the stronger will be the arguments against the protective system, by the accumulation of unnecessary funds in the treasury. The longer it is delayed, the stronger will be the feeling of disaffection at the South."[5]

After Jackson delivered his message to Congress, Secretary of the Treasury Louis McLane submitted his annual report. McLane urged Congress to sell the federal government's remaining shares of stock of the Bank of the United States. This would give the government eight million dollars of revenue and allow it to pay off the debt by the time Jackson's first term ended. With the debt removed the tariff could then be reduced. "If the measure proposed is rejected, if the American System is riveted down upon us, as the firm, fixed, and settled policy of the nation," a southern Jackson paper cautioned, "the spirit of revolt now in its incipient state, we fear will burst forth in open blaze, in all the violence of determined opposition."[6]

Henry Clay, who had just taken his seat as a senator from Kentucky, connected the dots: the payment of the debt ended the necessity for a high tariff. Jackson would then call for the removal of the protective tariff to undercut the nullifiers. This would ensure Jackson's reelection. By calling for the end of the federal debt, Jackson had laid siege to the American System. "I fear that there will be no agreement among parties either as to the amount of the reduction of the revenue, or the objects on which it shall be effected," Clay informed a colleague. He also worried that the unwavering stance adopted by the nullifiers might make adjusting the tariff difficult. "They appear to be bent on the destruction of the system of protection, or on their own destruction," Clay mused.[7]

Protectionist congressmen and editors held a series of meetings at Washington boardinghouses at the end of 1831 and the beginning of 1832. The group formulated strategies to protect the American System and defeat the administration. Clay became the leader of these meetings. All the men who attended the meetings supported American manufacturing, but they also opposed the administration. Clay urged resistance to Jackson's desire to pay off the debt before the end of his first term. Since the Jacksonians wanted to destroy the American System through an accumulation of revenue, the opposition must decrease revenue. Clay proposed to repeal duties on items not produced in the United States. This would cut revenue by about seven million dollars annually. Clay next recommended that items already protected under the tariff of 1828 be given increased protection. Manufacturers would receive more protection, but it would also decrease the revenue coming into the government's coffers. When members suggested to Clay that this course might enrage the South, he laughed. According to Clay, "the discontents were almost all, if not entirely, imaginary or fictitious, and in almost all the southern states had, in a great measure, subsided."[8]

Clay had little time for the suggestions of the other members. His demeanor (he arrived at one meeting inebriated) bothered the other members, particularly the puritanical John Quincy Adams. After losing the presidency to Jackson in 1828, Adams returned home to Braintree, Massachusetts, reread the classics, became bored with life, and won a seat in the House. Although no other American had been treated worse by the Jacksonians than Adams, the Massachusetts representative argued that the payment of the debt should not be made a partisan issue. Adams suggested that instead of an immediate removal of duties on certain goods and the increase of duties on others, Congress should lower duties over the span of several years. This would allow Jackson to pay off the debt by the close of his first term, and it would alleviate the tensions between regions. Adams said that it would be a dereliction of duty to his constituents to abandon protection altogether, but he agreed that some concessions must be made to the South. Clay rejected this idea. "To preserve, maintain, and strengthen the American System he would defy the South, the President, and the devil," Clay informed the former president. After meeting with Clay in Washington, Joel R. Poinsett, the leader of the South Carolina Unionists who opposed nullification, reported that the Kentuckian would do nothing to alleviate the tensions that had arisen as a result of the tariff.[9]

On January 11, 1832, Clay submitted a resolution urging the Senate to abolish duties on goods that did not come into competition with American goods. The only exceptions to this proposal were duties on silks and wines, which he asked the Senate to lower. He believed that this proposal would slash the revenue from the tariff by seven million dollars. Clay then delivered a lengthy speech defending his resolution, presenting it as an olive branch to the South. "I came here, in a spirit of warm attachment to all parts of our beloved country, with a lively solicitude to restore and preserve its harmony, and with a firm determination to pour oil and balm into existing wounds, rather than further to lacerate them," Clay announced. However, he wanted senators to add more teeth to American tariffs. For instance, he asked the Senate to change the location of valuation. Since foreigners decided the value of American goods, Clay reasoned that this led to frauds. To eliminate these frauds, Clay desired to see duties assigned by Americans at American ports. This became known as "home valuation." He next recommended that Congress curtail the credit system whereby foreigners paid duties on credit. Clay also urged Congress to lay prohibitory duties on foreign spirits. The exclusion of foreign liquors would assist sugar, grain, and fruit farmers because their products would be used in the domestic production of alcohol.[10]

Clay delivered a more elaborate defense of the American System on February 2. The American System accounted for the prosperity that the nation enjoyed, he argued. It gave employment to most professions in the union, including obscure professions such as makers of buttons, baskets, bonnets, mustard, and umbrellas, as well as cork cutters and stocking weavers. Every region of the nation from the Louisiana Delta to the northern shores of Maine enjoyed the benefits of the American System. If southerners succeeded in destroying the American System, he claimed, it would lead to the loss of immense amounts of capital but also the ruin of thousands of American laborers. Clay reminded the Senate that the protective tariff guaranteed employment for females in the Northeast. If Congress removed the duties on cotton and woolen cloths, female laborers would lose their positions. He also challenged the arguments of the recent free-trade convention and mocked Albert Gallatin. "The call for free trade," Clay avowed, "is as unavailing as the cry of a spoiled child, in its nurse's arms, for the moon or the stars that glitter in the firmament of heaven. It never has existed; it will never exist." The Kentucky senator concluded by defending the tariff against charges that it catered to the aristocracy. In fact, Clay declared, it promoted democracy. The joint stock companies of the North allowed men of modest means to pool their resources together to gain more wealth. Manufacturing, therefore, allowed for wealth to be distributed among many individuals. "Nothing can be more essentially democratic, or better devised to counterpoise the influence of individual wealth," he avowed.[11]

The nullifiers' economic arguments did not escape Clay's attention, either. The tariff, he declared, ensured competition among American manufacturers, which drove down the prices of goods. In 1817, cotton fabrics fetched twenty-nine cents per yard. In 1831, a yard of cotton fabrics sold for eleven cents. The tariff on cotton goods had actually lowered the price. Northern manufacturers had not created a monopoly, Clay stated. The tariff allowed for more manufacturers to have a share of the market, and this increased competition had reduced prices. Clay never answered Calhoun's charge that the tariff lowered the price of raw cotton, but the Kentuckian suggested that the tariff augmented the demand for the principal staple of the South. Southerners, Clay hinted, should actually be thankful for the tariff. The galleries interrupted his speech on several occasions. Not even the icy glare of the vice president could restrain the spontaneous outbursts of applause.[12]

Hayne rose to answer Clay. Whereas in 1830, Hayne tried to solidify an alliance between the South and the West, now he wanted nothing that Clay offered because any agreement between the West and the South would have to include southern support for federally sponsored internal improvements. Hayne called this a "left handed marriage" and announced that it would never be consummated. He blamed all the problems of the South, and more particularly his home state of South Carolina, on the tariff. There is no justice, Hayne roared, in a system that makes the manufacturing system of the North profitable while it devalues the agricultural system of the South. His greatest fear was that Clay's American System would lead to the closing of British ports to southern cotton. Thus, close to one million bales of cotton would rot in America. "All we ask, is to be let alone," Hayne declared. And the best way for Congress to do this would be to abandon the American System and adopt a policy of free trade. According to Hayne, free trade promoted commerce in every part of the union. With the approaching end of the federal debt, he urged Congress to return the nation to the tariff levels of 1816, which provided enough revenue for the government and offered manufacturers incidental protection. Hayne believed that this represented a fair compromise to all parties involved.[13]

The Senate debated Clay's resolution sporadically for most of the winter and early spring. This became the first time that the Senate debated its own tariff and not one that the House had passed. Numerous senators joined the debate. George M. Dallas noted that the debate over Clay's resolutions reminded him of the debate over Foot's 1830 resolution. After the debate over his resolution concluded, Clay received a letter from James Madison. The former president told Clay much depended on his course. If he failed, Madison feared the calling of a southern convention. This convention would more than likely end in disunion. The animosity over the tariff, the former president claimed, had to be resolved, and perhaps only Clay could institute some sort of nation-saving compromise to which all parties would agree.[14]

Some senators considered this bill unconstitutional because article 1, section 7 of the Constitution stipulated that "all bills for raising Revenue shall originate in the House of Representatives." John Holmes presented a simple answer to this problem. The Maine senator suggested that the Senate could originate this tariff because the bill "lowered" revenue instead of raising it. It was all for naught, however. The Senate eventually tabled the bill. Tariff supporters such as Clay, Dallas, and Webster voted to table it, while almost all the southern antitariff members opposed the motion. It seems that Clay and his followers had grown tired of the debate. Perhaps the

Kentuckian wanted to appear as willing to lower the tariff so as to help his prospects in the South in the upcoming election.[15]

While the Senate grappled with Clay's proposal, others in Washington City worked publicly and privately on plans to modify the tariff. Supreme Court Justice Henry Baldwin crafted a compromise plan. Baldwin resurrected his failed plan of 1820 and recommended it to Jackson, McLane, Adams, McDuffie, and Hayne. Under Baldwin's plan, all imported items would pay a duty of only 20 percent. Credit payments would be abolished in favor of cash payments. The 20 percent component made Baldwin's plan attractive to southerners. Baldwin hoped that the cash payments and auction duties would offset manufacturers' opposition to the low 20 percent duty. The South Carolina delegation liked Baldwin's plan, but they asked that a Pennsylvanian present it. No member of the Keystone State's delegation agreed to do so, however, because the state legislature had just passed a resolution in favor of a high tariff. Edward Everett disapproved of Baldwin's plan since he sensed that Baldwin wanted to sacrifice northern manufacturers to make himself chief justice when John Marshall died. Thus, nothing became of Baldwin's proposal.[16]

House members formulated plans to change the tariff as well. Although he did not want the position, John Quincy Adams became chairman of the Committee of Manufactures. "I know no Gentleman in Congress who is more generally acceptable to all parties," Willie P. Mangum wrote about the former president.[17] On January 19, the House passed a resolution asking Secretary of the Treasury McLane to provide information on American manufacturing. As chairman of the Ways and Means Committee, George McDuffie did not wait for McLane's report. He submitted a report and a bill to reduce the duties on imports. When he delivered his oration in favor of his bill, McDuffie situated himself next to Nathan Appleton, a freshman Massachusetts representative who had been involved in textile manufacturing in New England since the War of 1812. McDuffie's position and his personal attacks against Appleton increased the sectional tension over the tariff. McDuffie proposed that all foreign goods entering American ports should be levied a duty of 12.5 percent. The South Carolinian criticized the entire protective system, contending that it taxed southern farmers at a rate of 40 percent. He avoided discussion of the constitutional question and nullification. Adams confided to his diary that McDuffie's report reminded him of one of the South Carolinian's dinner speeches against the tariff without its usual fury. Ralph Ingersoll issued a minority report with which only he and John Gilmore agreed. Ingersoll warned that if Congress adopted McDuffie's plan, it would make the repayment of the federal debt more difficult because the revenue would decrease. Furthermore, Ingersoll reminded Congress, never before had an American tariff contained a single uniform duty.[18]

On April 27, McLane presented his report, which he called a "scheme of compromise." McLane had battled an illness most of the winter, which accounted for his delay. Nullifiers charged that McLane took three months to prepare his report, because he had to consult with men "North of the Potomac." The secretary recommended a ten-million-dollar reduction of revenue. This would be achieved by lowering the duties on woolens, raw wool, iron, hemp, salt, and sugar. McLane also urged the abolition of the hated system of minimums because it encouraged frauds. All told, if Congress adopted this scheme, the tariff would be lowered to 27 percent.[19]

Clay believed that McLane's plan sacrificed the American System. He called it a "Southern judicious tariff." New York senator William L. Marcy believed that McLane's bill removed too much protection. "I am anxious to go as far as the public interest will permit," he wrote.[20] Wool growers denounced it as a "cut throat bill." The duties on raw wool recommended by the secretary meant that millions of sheep in America would be slaughtered, they charged. A North Carolinian opined, "the North and East are greatly dissatisfied with Mr. McLane's Bill. I further see that most of the South is equally so. Can this vexed question be settled, as to reconcile the two parties and sustain the Union?"[21] Even in McLane's home state of Delaware, a plan emerged to burn him in effigy. Papers loyal to Jackson praised the report and presented it as a fair compromise. McLane's report contained the approval of the president, making it an administration piece. Clay and the nullifiers would oppose it for this reason alone. Washington insiders now began whispering about an alliance between Clay and the nullifiers. Nullifiers were crestfallen at McLane's proposal because they had expected more reductions. "We see no other hope for a restoration of the principles of the constitution, or the preservation of the Union, but—*nullification*," Duff Green announced.[22]

Others believed that McLane issued his report in order to protect Van Buren's interests in the South. Shortly after McLane presented his report, the Democratic Party nominated Van Buren to be Jackson's vice president. A modification of the tariff by the administration would hold southerners to the Jackson ticket. "The law which, in 1828, was necessary to promote Gen. Jackson's election, is now sought to be repealed, to prevent his defeat," Thurlow Weed, a constant critic of Van Buren in Albany, roared.[23]

As chairman of the Committee on Manufactures, Adams took McLane's proposal, made several changes, and presented a new tariff bill to the House on May 23. The former president reconciled the propositions of Clay and McLane. Clay's proposal granted too much to northern manufactures, while McLane's gave too much to the South. Adams split the difference and offered what he conceived to be a compromise tariff. He recommended the abolition of the system of minimums. Adams also urged that all coarse woolens be admitted free of any duties.[24]

All told, the Adams tariff reduced rates to levels comparable to the 1824 tariff. The tariff would be protective but not as protective as the tariff of abominations. This prompted a series of public meetings to be held in the North in opposition to Adams's tariff. Hezekiah Niles crowed, "We have the proceedings of perhaps one hundred different meetings—held in the open face of day, and not in 'nooks and corners,' after the manner of our opponents."[25] In Philadelphia, ten thousand people planned to attend an outdoor meeting on the tariff. Many editors, however, expected little to come from Adams's proposal.[26]

Adams's bill became known as the "Compromise tariff" even though it pleased neither the protectionists nor the free traders. The proposal angered some of Adams's New England colleagues, who viewed the bill as one that made too many concessions to the South. Charles P. Huntington noted that Adams had become an

"Anti-tariff man" and contended that Adams allowed the "golden fleece of New England" to be stolen by "the Southern Argonauts."[27] For as much criticism as Adams received from his constituents in New England, southern opponents of protection criticized him as well. The bill still offered protection, and some southerners, perhaps to arouse public opinion, contended that the bill afforded more protection than the tariff of abominations.[28]

According to Joseph Gales, editor of the *National Intelligencer*, most House members attended every session and listened to their colleague's speeches. Some speeches occupied two days of the House's calendar. As the debate continued, most members of Congress and most observers could not discern the fate of the measure. Littleton W. Tazewell, a senator from Virginia, believed that only a tariff increasing duties could pass. Adams informed his wife, "I have been fully convinced that no serious tariff question will be settled at this session of Congress."[29] Jackson remained skeptical as well. "The tariff bill is before them and all agents of the ultras and nullifiers are at work to defeat it," Jackson observed. "I have still hopes, that a majority of Congress will pass the bill, and give harmony to the Union."[30]

But to the surprise of many, the House approved the Adams tariff by the comfortable vote of 132 to 65. One correspondent wrote that the large margin shocked every House member. No previous tariff bill had passed the House by such a wide margin. "A most unexpected and astonishing result," Everett said. "The Southern men saw that the Manufacturers would not vote for a bill, by which they would be sacrificed and they knew that if no bill passed, the whole South would be thrown into the hands of the Nullifiers."[31] Duff Green sneered that this margin failed to represent the true southern opposition. He called the new bill the "Van Buren tariff" and argued that southerners voted for it so Van Buren and his supporters could cry, "Compromise" and "the Union is saved."[32] However, the four nullifiers from South Carolina all voted against the measure.[33]

Tired of dealing with the tariff after debating it all winter, senators spent little time on the Adams bill. They proposed a series of amendments, which passed or failed by one or two votes, with Calhoun breaking several ties. In the end, the Senate added more protection to the bill, including the restoration of the minimum principle on woolens. Protectionists outside of Congress approved these amendments. Hezekiah Niles rejoiced at the senate's amendments and believed that Congress had successfully navigated the nation through stormy seas. Other protectionists grumbled about some of the provisions of the bill but remained content to see that the principle of protection had not been repudiated. After the motion to engross the bill passed, Clay rose from his desk and congratulated the friends of the American System on the success of the protective policy.[34]

The Senate approved the Adams tariff by a vote of thirty-two to sixteen. The Senate amendments, however, resulted in nearly unanimous southern opposition. The only southern senators who voted for the tariff were Josiah Johnston and George A. Waggaman of Louisiana, both of whom were National Republicans or foes of Jackson. In a conference committee, the House refused to acquiesce in the Senate amendments, so the amendments were lost. Jackson then signed the measure.

Table 10.1. House vote, 1832

	Democrats		National Republicans		Anti-Masons		Nullifiers		Total	
	For	Against	For	Against	For	Against	For	Against	For	Against
New England	10	1	7	16	0	0	0	0	17	17
Middle	37	7	14	10	1	1	0	0	52	18
South	29	20	7	3	0	0	0	4	36	27
West	14	3	13	0	0	0	0	0	27	3
Total	90	31	41	29	1	1	0	4	132	65

Source: *House Journal*, 22nd Cong., 1st Sess., 28 June 1832, 1023–24.

Table 10.2. Senate vote, 1832

	Democrats		National Republicans		Nullifiers		Total	
	For	Against	For	Against	For	Against	For	Against
New England	1	0	11	0	0	0	12	0
Middle	6	0	4	0	0	0	10	0
South	0	12	2	0	0	2	2	14
West	4	2	4	0	0	0	8	2
Total	11	14	21	0	0	2	32	16

Source: *Senate Journal*, 22nd Cong., 1st Sess., 9 July 1833, 431

Most northerners applauded the new tariff. They had surrendered some pro-tection, but they could have given up the system altogether. Some northerners ar-gued that this tariff, passed with southern votes, settled the question of protection once and for all. "Although the mad ambition of the South will not now receive it [the new tariff] as an act of equal justice, yet the sober sense, and patriotism, of the yeomanry of the South, will by it, be induced to pause from any overt acts of resistance," James Tallmadge believed.[35] Right after the bill passed, John Quincy Adams informed his wife, "The present Tariff Bill operates as a universal anodyne. All parties are claiming it exclusively as their own, each for itself."[36] Furthermore, neither side would be able to use it in the fall elections. "Happy the present bill is as far removed as possible from being a party bill," a Massachusetts editor an-nounced. "It neither helps Clay nor Jackson to the presidency, and the partisans of both are found among the yeas and nays."[37] Other protectionists cheered this new tariff because it increased protection on manufactured goods, while it lowered lev-els on raw materials. For the most part, the people of the North took comfort in the fact that Congress had reached a compromise. "We rejoice that the spirit of com-promise is still found able to exercise its legitimate duty, to soften and stay partisan feuds, when 'the greatest good of the greatest number' is endangered," a Massachu-setts paper observed.[38] The *National Intelligencer* announced, "It is emphatically, whatever may be said of it by those who have opposed it, a *Bill of Compromise*."[39] From Philadelphia, Henry Horn, a Jackson man, notified James K. Polk, "The tariff as modified is decidedly popular even the ultras who clamored loudly against any change in our protective system are obliged to acknowledge the Judiciousness of the change or to acquiesce in silence in a measure to which their opposition would be utterly useless."[40]

Southerners gave the new tariff partial support. To many, it appeared as a fair compromise that would avert civil war. Southerners hoped to see the bill modified in the upcoming years, though. Other southerners viewed this new bill as a wedge by which they could destroy the entire protective system and place the country on the path to free trade.[41]

The nullifiers were still enraged and increased their attacks on the protective sys-tem. The pronullification members of the South Carolina delegation published an "Address to the People of South Carolina." The tariff of 1832 was the worst of all the tariffs, they argued. From 1824 until the present, each tariff had grown more protec-tive, but these tariffs also received more support. The tariff of 1824 passed the House by five votes, the 1828 tariff passed by eleven votes, and now the tariff of 1832 passed by a two-to-one margin. For the nullifiers, this proved the progressive nature of the tariff. With each tariff, Congress eased the burdens on the North, while it increased those on the South. The tariff of 1832 solidified the protective system, according to the nullifiers. Newspapers throughout the Palmetto State repeated these arguments. "Nullification will be put in practice in the winter," John L. Hunter observed.[42]

All summer and into fall, the nullifiers assailed the compromise tariff, because it retained the principle of protection. "We find it a difficult matter to hold the people back," one nullifier wrote. "We will try to keep the war dogs chained until after the convention lets them loose, or removes altogether the necessity for it."[43] A New England visitor observed, "Should the cholera come to South Carolina, it can hardly be worse than the political mania, which is raging here at present."[44] At dinners across the state, nullifiers issued a series of toasts announcing their disapproval of the new tariff. "*The Tariff of 1832, the requisition of a master on the property of his vassals. It shall never become the law of the land in South Carolina*," one nullifier toasted.[45] At another, a South Carolinian raised his glass and said, "The tariff of 1832—Submission to such an act would rivet upon the country irretrievably and forever, a system hostile to general welfare, utterly unconstitutional and destructive of the best interest and dearest rights of the Southern states."[46] For the nullifiers, it had now become a question of liberty or slavery. If the state failed to act in response to this act of Congress, it would rivet the chains of oppression on the people of the state forever. "We know that *now* we are enslaved, when we have a right to be free," the *Columbia Telescope* reported.[47] At a militia gathering in South Carolina, one unidentified South Carolinian stood up and announced, "The compromise which has been offered by Congress: a compromise which South Carolina will not accept. Let her next legislature do their duty, and her sons will support them."[48] By the end of summer, Calhoun knew that the summer campaign had achieved its goal and that the nullifiers would be able to nullify the tariffs after the fall elections.[49]

The violent denunciations of the tariff in South Carolina prompted northerners to realize that only a complete surrender of the principle of protection would appease South Carolina. Mathew Carey, one of the leading economic nationalists, expressed his remorse over the predicament of his country and regretted what his actions and writings may have caused. "A dissolution of the Union is inevitable," he wrote. "We are a spoiled, selfish, money loving race. We are unworthy of the splendid bequeathment we inherit from our ancestors. Nothing short of a miracle can save us."[50]

Seemingly, every city, town, village, hollow, and hamlet held some form of a meeting on the tariff in 1832. "It is not a time for Republicans to be idle in any part of the Union; when the question is, whether our government was instituted for the benefit of the people, or whether our legislation is to be controlled by a few hundred large capitalists," the *Richmond Enquirer* noted.[51] These meetings ranged in size from a few hundred participants to over ten thousand in New York City. Every meeting adopted a series of resolutions either praising or assailing the protective policy. Several observers believed that these meetings influenced Congress to modify the tariff. "But these circumstances, and others which go to show the deep feeling existing among the people in regard to the Tariff, have had, a decided effect to stimulate Congress to an adjustment of the question," one observer noted.[52] Jackson's mouthpiece in particular pushed the democratic spirit. An anti-Jackson paper in Connecticut likewise discussed how the events brought more and more Americans into the political process. "Nullification and the Tariff continue to be the all absorbing topics, not only with the politicians and editors, but appear also to agitate the whole mass of the population from one end of the Union to the other," it argued.[53] However, the best expression of the tariff spreading democracy appeared at the beginning of 1833. "What until lately was the opinion of politicians, has now become the feeling of the people," one editor avowed.[54]

Democracy spread throughout New England as a result of the tariff as well. Manufacturers and merchants exerted an influence beyond their numbers, but the people of New England wanted manufacturing to succeed. At a meeting in a Connecticut hotel, residents of the state announced that they remained "aware that all political power is inherent in the people, and that all free governments are founded on their authority." In 1828, over four thousand Bostonians signed a single petition asking for increased protection. This and subsequent petitions maintained that the protective system had been established through the democratic process and that New Englanders had shifted their capital into manufacturing. Mechanics, farmers, and other laborers in Essex County, Massachusetts, sent a memorial to Congress saying that a reduction on woolens would reduce the value of their labor. In 1830, National Republicans, champions of a protective tariff, swept every House race in Massachusetts. The most contested race pitted Nathan Appleton, a prominent cotton manufacturer, against Henry Lee, author of the free-trade Boston Report of 1828. Appleton bested Lee by over one thousand votes, and he captured 56 percent of the votes. The attainment of large majorities across the Bay State by Appleton and others sympathetic to manufacturing revealed that the people of Massachusetts approved the protective tariff. In neighboring Connecticut and Rhode Island, the people endorsed protectionist candidates in almost every election as well.[55]

"It is not the democracy, it is the aristocracy that is complaining," John Holmes announced in 1832 during a Senate tariff debate. According to Holmes, the tariff injured the people, while it padded the pockets of rich manufacturers. However, when he used the term "aristocracy," it had a sectional connotation. Southern aristocrats, Holmes declared, threatened democracy. Holmes disliked the protective system, but he argued that the Constitution gave Congress the power to assist manufacturers. To him and other northerners, the actions of wealthy South Carolinians threatened democracy. The minority should not dictate how the majority should act, they announced. As southerners tried to establish a regional identity by constructing a phalanx against the assumption of powers by the federal government, New Englanders likewise forged a sectional identity. "Depend upon it, if we do not behave better, we shall be beaten out of the field by the unanimity, good fellowship, and constancy of the south; and after a few years, New England will have no representation worthy of her," a Boston paper warned.[56] This emerging regional identity prompted wavering New Englanders to rethink their views on the tariff question. Some championed a protective tariff simply because the South opposed it. Since northerners refused to relinquish the protective system, southerners threatened to dissolve the union. Residents of Sharon, Connecticut, reminded southerners that the revolutionary heroes of New England refused to buckle under the oppression of the British government. Their sons would not be bullied into lowering the tariff. Most New Englanders criticized nullification as a doctrine that threatened democracy.[57]

Jackson's biggest mistake of his presidency was his failure to perceive that nullification had begun as a grassroots movement. Throughout the nullification crisis, he, just like Abraham Lincoln thirty years later, maintained that the state's politicians had led the people of South Carolina astray. Joel R. Poinsett, who reported to the president about the movements in the state, confirmed Jackson's belief that a few misguided leaders had hijacked the hearts and minds of the people. "We had rather die, than submit to the tyranny of such an oligarchy as J. C. Calhoun, James Hamilton, Robt. Y. Hayne and McDuffie," Poinsett informed Jackson.[58] But the meetings against the tariff and the petitions written by the people of South Carolina are at odds with the opinions of Poinsett and Jackson. In spite of his misunderstanding the nature of nullification, Jackson still prepared to use force to bring the people back to their senses, and he talked openly of hanging the leading nullifiers. Jackson's harsh stance pushed wavering South Carolinians and other southerners into the nullifiers' camp.[59]

The march of democracy in South Carolina during the nullification crisis came at a price. Violent acts defined society in the Palmetto State during the crisis. Few South Carolinians traveled unless they carried a pistol or a knife. Benjamin Perry, an upcountry unionist, traded shots with Turner Bynum and wounded the nullifier. Bynum eventually succumbed to his wound. His brother then confronted Perry and told him that the nullifiers used Bynum as a tool in an effort to silence Perry, a critic of nullification. Bynum's brother informed Perry that he harbored no ill will toward him, even though Perry had killed his brother. The cities and more populated areas of South Carolina became particularly precarious. Unionist and nullifier mobs roamed the streets of urban areas, looking to break up the demonstrations and meetings of their opponents. Samuel Cram Jackson, a unionist, confided to his diary that "many are looking for civil war and scenes of bloodshed." A religious individual, Samuel Cram Jackson regretted the course adopted by his state. "His [God's] wrath is about to be visited over this guilty land," he scribbled into his diary.[60]

Jackson defeated Clay for the presidency in a landslide that fall. Neither Jackson nor Clay could use the tariff since it had passed with bipartisan support. Van Buren, Jackson's new running mate, issued a public letter on the tariff. Van Buren announced his support for the president's position on the tariff, especially Jackson's call to extinguish the debt. Deprived of the tariff, Clay sought to use Jackson's veto of the bank against him, but this strategy boomeranged and probably contributed to the president's strong showing. However, nullifiers also won enough seats in the South Carolina legislature to call a nullifying convention. "You will have seen by the public papers, that the Union party throughout the state of So. Carolina have been beaten at the ballot box," Poinsett informed Jackson. "You must be prepared to hear very shortly of a State Convention and an act of Nullification."[61]

On November 24, delegates from across South Carolina declared that the tariffs of 1828 and 1832 would be considered null and void within the state on February 1, 1833. They required all state officials, except members of the legislature, to take an oath. This oath forced officials to support nullification and any act of the legislature passed in support of it. The ordinance of nullification warned Jackson that any forceful act by the federal government or any attempt to close the ports of South Carolina would be interpreted by the people of South Carolina as an act of aggression, resulting in the dissolution of the state's ties to the federal union. "We may now rejoice that the day of our deliverance from the Tariff is at hand," a nullifier declared, while another avowed, "There is but one question now left for the decision of the other states—'*Repeal the Tariff or Repeal the Union*.'"[62]

The nullifiers issued a series of reports and addresses defending nullification. Hayne's "Report of a Committee" restated the familiar arguments against the protective tariff. It maintained that the protective tariff had "crept insidiously" into the halls of Congress. The protective system had been established as a temporary system to pay off the debt from the War of 1812. But, according to Hayne, greed prompted manufacturers to enact the tariffs of 1824, 1828, and 1832, which increased the level of protection from 25 to over 50 percent. Hayne declared that northerners used federally sponsored internal improvements to perpetuate the protective system. Very quickly, Hayne noted, the American people championed an unconstitutional system, because they enjoyed the spoils of internal improvements. His report addressed the constitutional question as well. It maintained that nowhere in the Constitution did the Founding Fathers make any allusion to manufacturers. The right to regulate commerce applied to foreign nations and not manufacturing, he argued. But the core of Hayne's report declared that the protective system favored the North at the expense of the South. Northern manufacturers received a monopoly, while southerners found themselves in a state of "cruel bondage." The longer South Carolinians waited to act, he announced, the stronger the protective system became. The only remedy remained the doctrine of state interposition. "We cannot again petition, it would be idle to remonstrate, and degrading to protest," the report said in conclusion; "in our opinion it is now a question of Liberty or Slavery." If Congress refused to recognize the errors of its way, Hayne warned, it "would transform our confederated Government, with strictly limited powers, into an absolute despotism."[63]

When Jackson learned of the victory of the nullifiers, he announced to Van Buren that South Carolina "is in a state of perfect excitement and the nullifiers in a state of insanity. I still hope the Unionists will have sufficient strength to check them in their mad and wicked course and preserve the state from Civil War and bloodshed."[64] Americans began referring to February 1, 1833, as the "fatal first" since this is when nullification would go into effect. Even a Unionist lamented that "there will be no peace until the Tariff be greatly reduced, for it has become an article of faith with Southern men that its oppressions are galling."[65]

After nullifying the tariffs of 1828 and 1832, the nullifiers played a game of musical chairs. Hamilton resigned the governorship, Hayne resigned his Senate seat, and Calhoun resigned the vice presidency. Hayne became governor, and Calhoun took the vacated Senate seat, while Hamilton remained in reserve in case he needed to command the state militia. This arrangement put the leading nullifiers in positions where they could do the most good for their state and perhaps the most damage to the union. All eyes now turned to Washington City as the lame-duck second session of the Twenty-Second Congress began arriving.[66]

11

"Our country is at an awful and momentous crisis"

T HE PRESIDENT IS IN ADMIRABLE HEALTH and beams with patriotic firmness," George M. Dallas wrote. "He is a much abler man than I thought him, one of those naturally great minds, which seem ordinary, except when the fitting emergency arrives."[1] Dallas, who lived until 1864, was not referring to Abraham Lincoln. He wrote those sentences on December 1, 1832. Instead, Dallas referred to President Andrew Jackson, who, like Lincoln after him, faced a threat to the union during his presidency. Jackson, who had recently won reelection by a large margin over Henry Clay, had to confront the people of the state of South Carolina who claimed the right to nullify a federal law that violated the Constitution. "The result of the late election is a political phenomenon and established more conclusively to my mind the correctness of the theory of our government than anything which has taken place since the formation of that government," Charles Jarvis wrote to his brother, a member of the House of Representatives. "We have yet however to encounter one more severe trial and if we pass that unscathed my confidence in the perpetuity of our Union will be more firmly established than ever."[2] The severe trial about which Jarvis spoke had arrived. If Jackson tried to coerce South Carolina into respecting federal authority, he might push the rest of the South into rebellion and provoke a civil war. As a result, Jackson had to move cautiously, but also firmly, in order to ensure that the actions of South Carolina were not repeated.

South Carolina's ordinance of nullification declared that after February 1, 1833, no tariffs would be imposed at any port in the state. The expected train of events would go as follows: When a foreign good arrived in the Palmetto State, the federal customs collector would demand that the duties be paid. The merchant or importer would refuse to pay since the tariff was no longer in force at this port. The federal official would next seize the goods, and the importer would subsequently go to a South Carolina state court. The court would rule with the importer and issue a writ of replevin allowing him to retake his goods. Next, the federal customs collector would ignore this court, whereupon he would be arrested for contempt. These opening steps were expected by all. What would happen next became anyone's guess. If the foes of nullification in South Carolina decided to support the customs collector, the nullifiers would oppose them. One itchy trigger finger could quickly lead to bloodshed at a South Carolina customhouse. How then could nullification be peaceful, many pondered? "If South Carolina is put down or drawn out of the

Union upon the principles she has adopted, will not all future resistance to the pro- tective system, or to the exercise of any other powers by the general Government be useless and unavailing," one nullifier asked. "Will it not establish the right in Congress to pass and compel obedience to any laws which she may think proper to enact and render ours instead of a Confederation, a consolidated government?"[3]

A single state telling the other twenty-three states what was and was not con- stitutional seemed to threaten democracy. Furthermore, if South Carolina could threaten disunion and civil war since the people of that state considered the tar- iff to be too high, then why could not the people of a northern state do the same over another issue or over a lowered tariff? "If the principle of protection be aban- doned, the Northern and Middle States will have much greater reason for nullifi- cation, than South Carolina pretends to have," a New England editor announced.[4] Another editor from the same region added, "If the tariff should be destroyed, and the people of the Middle and Eastern States should become dissatisfied and hold a Convention for the purpose of seceding from the Union, would not our Southern brethren say that it was rank treason, and that the traitors ought to be hung." After all, this editor declared, had not the southerners objected to the Hartford Conven- tion?[5] Thomas A. Marshall, an anti-Jackson House member from Kentucky, pon- dered, "will not the immediate abandonment of protection under the dictation of the ordinance of 1832 be considered by all as affording strong countenance to the right set up in that ordinance of dictating to the Union the terms on which alone a State will continue one of its members?"[6]

As members of the lame-duck session of the Twenty-Second Congress filtered into Washington, Jackson finished his fourth annual message. From Maine to Loui- siana, Americans anticipated what the reelected president would say. "No part of the President's Message will be read with greater interest by the people of New En- gland than that which relates to the Tariff," a Connecticut editor announced. "It is a subject in which the whole people are concerned. It affects not merely the wealthy, the monopolists, the joins-stock companies, but the industrious, hard working classes, who earn their subsistence by their daily labor."[7] A correspondent for the *Richmond Enquirer* believed that he had a solution to the problem and urged the president to take his advice: "If the president could be prevailed upon to recom- mend to Congress a gradual reduction of the duties on the protected articles, say only five percent a year, until they are brought down to twenty percent, or lower, I think it would be attended with the happiest consequences."[8]

Jackson submitted his annual message on December 4. The tone and overall contents of this message befuddled many in Washington and those who had fol- lowed the recent events in South Carolina. He nearly ignored the nullifiers, devot- ing only a passing reference to them. The majority of Jackson's message contained criticisms of the emerging market economy. "Independent farmers are everywhere the basis of society and the true friends of liberty," he declared. Federally sponsored internal improvements, the national bank, high prices for western lands, and the protective tariff all sought to force yeoman farmers into a state of bondage to the speculators of the Northeast. The main thrust against the market economy came when Jackson endorsed a "gradual" reduction of the tariff. Since his calculations revealed that the debt would be eliminated by the end of 1833, a "gradual" reduction would actually be a rapid reduction. The president noted that the grant of protection to domestic manufacturers had never been intended to be permanent. American manufacturers had anticipated "temporary" and "incidental" protection from the federal government. The benefits of the protective system were "counterbalanced by many evils," Jackson declared. High tariffs had led to "a spirit of discontent and jealousy dangerous to the stability of the Union." With the debt about to be paid and with ample revenue still in the government's coffers, a reduction in the tariff could be made without any difficulties. Jackson struck a populist chord when he stated, "those who have vested their capital in manufacturing establishments can not expect that the people will continue permanently to pay high taxes for their benefit, when the money is not required for any legitimate purpose in the administration of the Government." Two days later, Secretary of the Treasury Louis McLane submitted his annual report to Congress. In it, he recommended that Congress cut six million dollars from the tariff.[9]

Reaction to Jackson's annual message varied. "I have just finished the Presidents message," Archibald Yell noted from Tennessee. "Upon the Tariff he is *perfection*. . . . He says but little about S. Carolina and at that I am pleased. I am no Nullifyer. Yet I am with the South in every thing but the *Means* to rid themselves of a very obnoxious Tariff."[10] The *Charleston Mercury*, the leading organ of the South Carolina nullifiers, praised Jackson's message. To this editor, and no doubt most of the nullifiers, it appeared as if the president had given in to their demands. "Its doctrines as to the relative powers of the Federal and State Governments, are genuine Carolina doctrines, and it recommends such an arrangement of the Tariff as would satisfy the South," the *Mercury* announced.[11] "The Spy in Washington," a correspondent for James Gordon Bennett's *Morning Courier and New York Enquirer*, concurred with the *Mercury*'s pronouncement: "There is no doubt that the administration are prepared to go the whole length in modifying the tariff laws, demanded by South Carolina."[12] A northern newspaper correspondent commented, "the friends of the Tariff, Internal Improvement and the Bank regard the tone of the message as indicative of a determination on the part of the President, to put a check on that policy which had been permanently deemed to be established by the repeated sanctions of public opinion."[13] John Quincy Adams, who had supported Jackson's desire to eliminate the federal debt just six months earlier, could hardly restrain his anger. "It [Jackson's message] recommends a total change in the policy of the Union with reference to the bank, manufactures, internal improvement, and the public lands," Adams noted. "It goes to dissolve the Union into its original elements, and is in substance a complete surrender to the nullifiers in South Carolina."[14] E. I. Dupont, a gunpowder manufacturer from Delaware, despaired when he read Jackson's message. "From the tenor of the president's message, and the known wish of the ruling party, we manufacturers have a bad prospect before us," he wrote.[15] George Poindexter, a Mississippi senator who would soon have a falling out with Jackson over nullification, wrote, "the views discussed by the president are moderate and *particularly* judicious; more in accordance with Southern policy than any of his previous messages, and if carried out by legislation, may restore tranquility to the Union, without impairing the prosperity of any branch of industry now in operation in any section of our country."[16] A Pennsylvania editor whose paper had supported high tariffs observed that Jackson "recommends the reduction of the tariff down to the revenue standard," while the *New York Evening Post* noted that Jackson's message advised "an absolute abandonment of the protecting policy."[17]

Jackson ignored the nullifiers on purpose. Throughout the looming crisis, he sought to isolate them. Some observers suspected that Jackson omitted a discussion of South Carolina's nullification in his annual message because he had prepared a special statement. Jackson confirmed this with a proclamation on nullification that he delivered on December 10. The president vowed that tariff duties would be collected in South Carolina because he had taken an oath to ensure that federal laws were executed. The opening sections of Jackson's proclamation assailed the Carolina doctrine of nullification. If South Carolina could nullify a federal statute, he suggested, then the country would revert to the condition of the Articles of Confederation. But, Jackson announced, the Constitution gives "explicit supremacy to the laws of the Union over those of the states." The power to tax, he continued, has been given to "the representatives of all the people, checked by the representatives of the States and by the Executive power." The doctrine of nullification gave the taxation power to "the legislature or the convention of a single state, where neither the people of the different States, nor the States in their separate capacity, nor the Chief Magistrate elected by the people have any representation." Therefore, nullification allowed one state to dictate to the other states what passed constitutional muster. For the president, nullification left the nation with two choices: a repeal of the revenue acts, which would leave the nation with no means of support, or an end to the union. Jackson refused to accept a no-win scenario.[18]

The significance of Jackson's proclamation became his use of the nationalist argument. This argument had already been pronounced by both John Marshall in *McCulloch v. Maryland* in 1819 and by Daniel Webster in his debate with Robert Hayne in 1830. The union, Jackson declared, predated the states. "The Constitution of the United States, then, forms a government, not a league; and whether it be formed by compact between the States or in any other manner, its character is the same," he proclaimed. "It is a Government in which all people are represented, which operates directly on the people individually, not upon the States." Jackson rejected the idea that the states had retained their sovereignty under the Constitution. The people of each state had transferred their allegiance to the federal government, and they owed obedience to the Constitution. Therefore, a state could not nullify and a state could not secede. The union would be preserved at all costs. The overall thrust of the proclamation, which Marshall and Webster both approved of, prompted southerners to distance themselves from the president. They may have disapproved of nullification, but they still endorsed the doctrine of secession. Jackson's overtly nationalistic position weakened his credibility among many of his southern followers and even began pushing some into the arms of the nullifiers.[19]

Jackson's political opponents in the North embraced the proclamation. Thurlow Weed remembered that it was a "thunderbolt unexpected and effective."[20] At Faneuil Hall in Boston, Webster delivered a short address praising the doctrines of the proclamation. Webster sounded just like Jackson when he said that nullification "is resistance to law by force, it is disunion by force, it is secession by force: *it is civil war.*"[21] John Davis of Massachusetts, another political opponent of Jackson, noted that the proclamation overturned all of Jackson's previous statements on states' rights. The president, according to Davis, now pushed the powers of the federal government to a point further than Alexander Hamilton. John Reynolds told James Buchanan that the proclamation had won Jackson many new friends in Pennsylvania. Men who had opposed the president during the last election now supported him. Edward Everett, a National Republican from Massachusetts, believed that the proclamation contained "sound" doctrines. A Pennsylvania editor praised Jackson's resolve. "The Union is in no danger while Andrew Jackson has the helm; if the nullifiers disregard his generous appeal, they will be made to feel and respect an argument more potent, an argument of arms, which no one knows better how to wield, than Andrew Jackson."[22]

Southerners, on the other hand, divided over Jackson's proclamation. Some referred to it as a noble state paper that would be immortalized like George Washington's Farewell Address. "No American citizen can possibly rise from the perusal of this address, without being convinced that nullification is treason in theory, and if put into practice, in practice can only result in rebellion," an Alabama editor noted.[23] From Jackson's home of Tennessee, one man wrote, "The Deluded South Carolinians has caused the Lion to Shake his mane—as he has come out in the Majesty of his Strength. It is without Doubt the greatest Document that was ever written by man."[24] Most southerners, however, criticized the proclamation's tone and arguments. In North Carolina, a Tar Heel announced, "Genl Jackson proclamation will not satisfy the South. It is thought to be an abandonment of the rights of the states."[25] "His [Jackson's] proclamation has swept away all the barriers of the constitution and given us in place of the federal government under which we had fondly believed we were living, a consolidated military despotism," John Tyler raged.[26] When John Randolph read the proclamation he contemplated ending his retirement from public life. The proclamation, Randolph avowed, went far beyond what Hamilton or John Adams would have approved. Another Virginian announced that prior to the proclamation, the people of Virginia wanted to put down the nullifiers. In the wake of Jackson's proclamation, however, Virginians planned to support South Carolina. "The Executive can never march troops against South Carolina, through eastern Virginia, *but over our dead bodies,*" another Virginian avowed.[27] In Alabama, James H. Pettigrew contended that the state's Unionists had now become nullifiers as a result of the doctrines espoused in the proclamation. In New Orleans, where the residents still considered Jackson a hero because of the victory that he won in that city in 1815, the proclamation was greeted with applause. In the Crescent City, every time someone mentioned Jackson's name, those who heard it cheered as loud as possible.[28]

When Jackson's proclamation arrived in South Carolina, it created a "sensation." The *Charleston Mercury* called it a "declaration of war" against the sovereign state of South Carolina. James H. Hammond exclaimed, "It is the black Cockade Federalism of 98 revived fearfully invigorated by its long sleep, and seems destined to bring about another reign of terror."[29] William C. Preston, who had urged Calhoun to draft the *South Carolina Exposition* in 1828, traveled to Virginia to try to gain support for nullification. Preston told an audience in Richmond, "If South Carolina, is put down to-day, it will be Virginia's turn, to-morrow; and North Carolina's the day after."[30] The nullifiers believed that the nationalist doctrines espoused by Jackson would aid their cause by prompting more southerners to rally behind them.[31]

Jackson's proclamation, while it galvanized many in the North and enraged numerous southerners, blurred his political position. In less than a week, Jackson had issued his annual message, which championed agrarianism and states' rights, but also his proclamation, which one New Yorker referred to as "just such a paper as Alexander Hamilton would have written and Thomas Jefferson condemned."[32] A Georgia representative, Augustin Clayton, seemed befuddled by the president's abrupt swings. "The inconsistency of Gen. Jackson passeth all understanding," Clayton wrote. "His best friends cannot unravel the mystery. That his Message and Proclamation should come from the same mind in the short space of six days beggars all speculation."[33] Henry Clay perhaps spoke for many when he observed, "One short week produced the message and the Proclamation—the former ultra, on the side of State rights—the latter ultra, on the side of Consolidation." Clay wondered, like most Americans, how Jackson's two positions could be reconciled.[34] John Quincy Adams maybe had the best explanation of the inconsistency between the president's annual message and his proclamation. Adams sensed that Jackson's policy had been crafted with an eye to ensure Van Buren's elevation to the presidency. "They [Van Buren's New York supporters] are now tenacious of States rights, and politically leagued with the anti-tariff policy of the South, but as Jackson men they must be anti-nullifiers; and to these two incoherent elements, subserviency to the slave-holding policy and the personal animosities of President Jackson against Vice-President Calhoun, may be traced the glaring inconsistencies of principle between the message of this year and the proclamation."[35] The president may have overplayed his hand, however. He interpreted his smashing victory over Clay as a sign that a large majority of the people would support him at all costs. But the tariff and nullification had not been before the people when they went to the polls. The 1832 campaign had focused on the question of whether the national bank should be rechartered. Other issues that influenced voters in 1832 were fears of a conspiracy by Masons and also whether the government should endorse a day of fasting and prayer owing to an outbreak of cholera. Mahlon Dickerson lamented to Van Buren that Jackson owed his recent victory to his popularity. "The people supported him tariff or no tariff," Dickerson observed.[36]

Jackson found encouragement from the reactions of numerous states whose legislatures issued reports and resolutions on the nullification crisis. Every state criticized the course of South Carolina. Southern states were particularly severe toward the "Carolina doctrine." North Carolina resolved that nullification was "revolutionary in its character, subversive of the Constitution of the United States and leads to a dissolution of the Union."[37] Alabama criticized the protective tariff, but then referred to nullification as "unsound in theory and dangerous in practice."[38] The Mississippi legislature avowed, "We are opposed to Nullification. We regard it as a heresy, fateful to the existence of the Union."[39] The harshest condemnation of nullification came from the state of Georgia, which had been attempting to nullify a recent decision by the Supreme Court. The Georgia legislature issued a resolution saying, "we abhor the doctrine of nullification as neither a peaceful, nor a constitutional remedy, but, on the contrary, as tending to civil commotion and disunion; and while we deplore the rash and revolutionary measures, recently adopted by a Convention of the people of South Carolina, we deem it a paramount duty to warn our fellow citizens against the danger of adopting her mischievous policy."[40]

As 1832 drew to a close and 1833 began, most of the nation held its breath and wondered what would happen. A misstep by members in Congress or the nullifiers in South Carolina might plunge the nation into civil war. Jackson, who seemed to be spoiling for a fight, might not be able to control his passions. "I, at this moment, feel assured we will soon be by that monster and villain, Jackson, involved deeply in a civil war," John Floyd noted in his diary.[41] The nullifiers sought to prepare for Jackson's wrath by trying to purchase 120,000 pounds of gunpowder from the E. I. Dupont Company in Delaware. The business politely declined the order. "Our country is at an awful and momentous crisis," Jackson's organ announced. "If we weather this storm, the ship of the Union may ride out the tempests and tornadoes of a thousand years."[42] Most Americans would have agreed with the first part of that statement, because Jackson had now begun to talk openly about hanging his own vice president. "I should like to have a rope round the necks of Calhoun, McDuffie, Hayne, and Hamilton and if they escaped me then heaven forgive them," a Maine resident wrote evincing his approval of Jackson's measures.[43] Cave Johnson of Tennessee perhaps had the simplest solution to the problem. Johnson wrote, "It would be a blessing to the country if the leading tariff men, who made the law and the leading nullifiers could be all beheaded. We could then adjust the differences without difficulty and get on prosperous and happily."[44]

But Jackson was not the only one willing to use violence. In South Carolina, one nullifier warned that if Jackson came to South Carolina, it would be "war to the knife" and that Jackson would more than likely sleep "under the sod." Samuel Cram Jackson, no relation to the president, noticed how the proclamation had inspired a certain group of South Carolinians who had yet to participate in the struggle against the tariff. "Even the women would shoot him, for they are as strong nullifiers as any, and in some cases, urge their husbands and sons to revolution," he noted.[45] From the pulpit, ministers exhorted their congregations to resist Jackson and the federal government. The state of South Carolina became an armed camp. One female reported that her drawing room had been converted into a war room where nullifiers gathered to discuss military strategies. Few could have anticipated that the tariff would have the nation on the precipice of disunion.[46]

12

The Winter of Discontent

PRESIDENT ANDREW JACKSON ended 1832 with an olive branch in one hand and a sword in the other. Some Americans still held out hope for a peaceful resolution to the nullification crisis, while others began to fear the worst. Martin Van Buren recalled that Thomas Ritchie, the editor of the *Richmond Enquirer*, "scarcely ever went to bed in these exciting times without Apprehension that he would wake up to hear of some *coup d'état* by the General."[1]

While the country digested Jackson's swings in philosophy, Secretary of the Treasury Louis McLane and House Ways and Means Committee chairman Gulian C. Verplanck collaborated on a new tariff bill. Verplanck was a free trader from New York City. In 1831, he had published an open letter to William Drayton of South Carolina, in which he defended the constitutionality of a protective tariff. Verplanck supported President Andrew Jackson, but he had no allegiance to Martin Van Buren and the Albany Regency even though he came from New York State. Many observers made the mistake of associating Verplanck with Van Buren.[2]

Verplanck's report stated the sum of fifteen million dollars would be necessary for the operation of the federal government. "All beyond this must be a needless burthen upon the people, a tax falling directly or indirectly upon the land and labor of the country, certainly injurious in its effects, and probably unequal," he announced. Verplanck next added that the recently passed tariff of 1832 would bring in eighteen million dollars of revenue. When added to other sources of income, the Treasury would still have a surplus of between five and nine million dollars annually. To eliminate this surplus, he proposed a "progressive reduction" of the tariff. Rates should be imposed at a duty of between 10 and 20 percent. His accompanying bill had been modeled after the tariff of 1816. "The vast increase in manufactures, of all sorts, in the United States, during the eight years between 1816 and 1824, proves, that the framers of that tariff, in providing revenue, had not only given ample incidental security to existing manufactures, but even induced new investments of capital," Verplanck proclaimed. Verplanck's bill would reduce most rates to the 1816 levels in only two years. There would be a significant reduction in 1834 and then another in 1835. Coffee and tea would no longer be duty free but would now be taxed at a rate of 20 percent. Rates on woolens and cotton fabrics would be drastically reduced. The only industry that would continue to have a high duty was iron. This had been done because Verplanck deemed iron essential for national defense. A high duty on iron would also curry favor from Pennsylvania representatives. "If this bill passes both Houses, it will pour oil on the stormy waves of discontent in South Carolina, and the awful crisis will be averted," Thomas Ritchie announced after he read the proposal.[3]

The *United States Gazette* called Verplanck's plan a "bill of concessions," while the *Norwich (Connecticut) Courier* referred to it as a "Submission bill," because it sacrificed the protective policy to the interests of the nullifiers. These statements typified the northern response to Verplanck's bill. Many northerners complained that the nullifiers had acted too rashly because they had not even allowed the tariff of 1832 to go into effect. If Congress decided to pass this bill, manufacturers warned, they would be prostrated. They contended that this bill sacrificed their livelihoods to appease southern malcontents, and a surrendering of the principle of protection would be akin to a breach of contract. By passing protective tariffs, Congress had encouraged Americans to invest in manufacturing, but a sudden removal of the tariff would threaten the investments that northerners had made based on a pledge from the federal government.[4]

Observers divided over the fate of Verplanck's bill. When the debate began, the "Spy in Washington" wrote, "I am now satisfied, that there is a decided majority favorable to a large reduction of the tariff."[5] The opinion of the "Spy" seemed to be the exception. The prevailing opinion within Washington held that the administration would force the bill through the House by the narrowest of margins. "The Tariffites in the House of Representatives are said to be under the impression that their case is hopeless in that body," the *Richmond Enquirer* announced.[6] The Massachusetts delegation convened a caucus at Edward Everett's house just before the House took up Verplanck's bill. "The opinion was unanimous that it [Verplanck's bill] should be opposed," John Quincy Adams recorded in his diary. "But no hope could be entertained by any one that the passage of it in the House could be prevented." A few Bay State officials expressed a "feeble" hope that the bill could be defeated in the House. Other observers expected Verplanck's bill to have a tougher fight in the upper chamber but still feared that Jackson's use of patronage could force the bill through.[7]

Four days before the House began debating Verplanck's bill, Richard Henry Wilde of Georgia predicted what the opponents of the bill would do. Wilde recalled an old maxim, "when you are in a majority, act: when you are in a minority, talk."[8] Northern protectionists, who belonged to the National Republican Party, did exactly what Wilde said they would do: they tried to defeat the bill by talking it to death. Their lengthy speeches all predicted the downfall of American manufacturing if Verplanck's bill became law. Several members delighted in reminding their House colleagues that South Carolinians, including Calhoun, had supported the tariff of 1816. A few members suggested that if South Carolina could nullify a protective tariff, then a northern state could nullify a tariff designed for revenue purposes only. "By the very spell by which you would lay one troubled ghost, might you awaken from the tomb another spectre, still more terrifying than the former?" Edward White of Louisiana asked.[9] Many of the arguments presented by protectionists had been made as early as 1816. The more novel arguments suggested that this proposed reduction symbolized a threat to democracy. Why should one state, which incorrectly blamed the tariff for all its woes, be able to dictate to the other twenty-three what and was not constitutional? Jabez Huntington of Connecticut said that Verplanck's tariff "had been brought into the House without the least warning to the country."[10] Another Connecticut representative, William Ellsworth, echoed Huntington's claim that the people had not called for this bill. "Not a breath had reached that House declaring such was the people's will," he declared.[11] Thomas McKennan, a Pennsylvania Anti-Mason, said, "have we heard a voice, sir, from home—from our constituents—thundering in our ears, and demanding the immediate reversal of the act which we did, with so much deliberation, not six months ago."[12]

Verplanck offered a more detailed analysis of his bill on January 18. With the impending elimination of the debt, the country would be left with a surplus. Therefore, high rates on imports represented an unfair burden on the people. This bill, he announced, sought to relieve the tax burden on the American people. Verplanck declined to explain the details of the bill, and Daniel Jenifer of Maryland challenged him to give more specific facts. Jenifer also asked why the other members of the Committee on Ways and Means remained silent. One of the committee members requested by Jenifer to provide information to the rest of the House was James K. Polk of Tennessee. Polk, who had aided Verplanck in drafting the bill, responded a few days later. Since Verplanck had failed to discuss the finer points of the bill, the Tennessee representative decided to explain the functions of the bill and why the rates had been set at the proposed levels. He argued that American manufacturers had been making immense profits under the protective tariffs, using recent testimony that manufacturers had given to substantiate his point. According to Polk, manufacturers had been successful during the years between 1816 and 1824, and since Verplanck's tariff resembled the tariff of 1816 but with more protection, manufacturers would continue to prosper. By offering a more refined explanation, Polk no doubt hoped to hasten the debate and bring about a final vote. But the high-tariff men wanted to voice their disapproval of the bill before letting a vote take place.[13]

The delaying tactics seemed to be accomplishing their goal. The "Spy in Washington," however, bemoaned this tactic. "No man's vote will be changed by the speeches that are to be made," he observed.[14] But with the session set to conclude on March 3, the filibustering strategy seemed logical. Of the first twenty-eight speakers on Verplanck's tariff, twenty-two spoke against it.[15]

Surprisingly, the nullifiers also disapproved of Verplanck's plan, even though it alleviated almost all their grievances. Pure politics forced the nullifiers into opposition. If Congress passed the Verplanck tariff, then Jackson and Van Buren would receive the credit. This would pave the way for Van Buren's coronation in 1836 as Jackson's successor. If Congress rejected Verplanck's bill and did so with northern votes, William R. King of Alabama cautioned Van Buren, then southerners would hold Van Buren accountable, jeopardizing his chances to succeed Jackson. Van Buren no doubt already recognized this, but he also knew that a resort to force would destroy the alliance he had forged between the planters of the South and the plain republicans of the North. Therefore, Van Buren needed a peaceful resolution to the crisis. To that end, the New Yorker adopted a simple strategy—stay out of Washington. With mixed signals from Jackson and unyielding positions being assumed by northern protectionists and the nullifiers, prospects for a peaceful settlement dwindled. "The Yankees are determined to protect their spinning jennies and the Southerners are determined to legislate them out of the country," a House clerk noted.[16]

The Verplanck tariff had been a final peace offering from the Jackson administration. If the nullifiers refused this olive branch, then Jackson would resort to the sword. To ensure the nullifiers recognized this, the president sent his third major paper on the nullification crisis to the Senate on January 16. This message became known as the "Force Bill" message, which John Davis said was as long as "a line of rail road cars."[17] Jackson summarized what South Carolina had proposed to do on February 1. "In fine," he declared, "she has set her own will and authority above the laws, has made herself arbiter in her own cause, and has passed at once overall intermediate steps to measures of avowed resistance, which, unless, they be submitted to, can be enforced only by the sword." Since the nullifiers vowed to secede if the federal government made any attempt to collect the revenue, Jackson noted, they could be mollified only if the entire protective system was abandoned. Nullification allowed the state of South Carolina to enjoy all the benefits of union without enduring any burdens, he charged. The president showed his resolve and announced his intention to ensure that federal laws remained in effect in South Carolina after February 1. Even though Congress passed pieces of legislation in the 1790s and as late as 1815 that gave him the power to enforce the laws, Jackson wanted more explicit authority through a new bill. In essence, Jackson sought congressional approval to lead an army into South Carolina. Since Jackson asked for power that he already had, some suspected that the president wanted to discern who supported him and who stood with the nullifiers.[18]

After Jackson's message had been read in the Senate, Calhoun jumped to his feet and demanded the floor. No doubt agitated, the former vice president exclaimed that South Carolina "entered the confederacy with the understanding that a State, in the last resort, has a right to judge of the expediency of resistance to oppression or secession from the Union. And for doing so it is that we are threatened to have our throats cut, and those of our wives and children." Calhoun quickly apologized for his outburst. After calming down, he notified Hamilton back in South Carolina that "Jackson is anxious for force." Calhoun now believed that Jackson's latest move would benefit the nullifiers. "It has roused the Southern members more than any event, which has yet occurred," he wrote. Perhaps Jackson's tone would end South Carolina's isolation.[19]

In spite of the efforts of Verplanck and Polk, supporters of the Verplanck tariff could not muster enough votes to bring the bill to a final vote. Protectionists continued to assail the bill, and Jackson's Force Bill message now emboldened them. Why surrender protection to South Carolina if Jackson desired to execute the nullifiers in the Palmetto State? One editor referred to Verplanck's bill as a "carcass," while a group of House members told Webster that they regarded it as a "corpse." With Congress at an impasse, the gossip in Washington became that it would adjourn without lowering the tariff. If that happened, the nullifiers would put nullification into effect, prompting Jackson to send the army down to South Carolina. In order to do this, he would have to march through Virginia and North Carolina. The president would also call on the other states, including southern states, to help suppress a rebellion. While every southern state disapproved of nullification, a president leading an army through the South and demanding the aid of the state militias might force some southerners into the waiting arms of South Carolina. If South Carolina seceded and Jackson used force against it, he might lose the South—an area where he had just won 80 percent of the popular vote.[20]

In early February, John Quincy Adams proposed to kill the Verplanck bill by striking out the enacting clause. The House defeated this maneuver. A correspondent still thought the bill stood no chance of passage even though it had survived this move: "Many of the adversaries of the Bill were opposed to the motion, because they considered that the mode of destroying the Bill was too summary; and they desired, with true Indian taste, to see it tortured a little, before any mortal stroke was given to it."[21]

A potential way out still remained for Jackson and the nation. The president could call a special session of the newly elected Congress to convene immediately after March 4. This idea became a topic for discussion among members of Congress and editors. An unidentified member of Congress predicted the calling of a special session in a letter written to a Mississippi friend on December 21. "This body, elected under the new census, with a considerable increase of members, particularly from several of the states where there will be more who are friendly to the views of the president," the *Knoxville Register* reported, "will the more certainly remove the burthen from the South and administer relief to their sufferings."[22] "It appears to be the general impression at the seat of government, that the new congress will be called together immediately after the term of the present congress expires, which will be on the evening of the third of March," the *Albany Evening Journal* predicted.[23] A pro-Jackson paper in New Hampshire declared, "It is said that in case the Tariff question is not satisfactorily settled by the present Congress, the president will call the new Congress together in May, the monopolists, who had rather the Union would be dissolved, than to give up a cent of their enormous profits, are already whining about the destruction of manufactures. They had better make the best terms they can, and settle the question the present session, for we think they will find little favor at the hands of another Congress."[24] The editor of the *New York Evening Post* urged protectionists to quit stalling and accept the Verplanck tariff. "Let them recollect that next winter another Congress assembles; a body far less favorable to the restrictive system than the present one. Let them consider the current of reaction has already begun to flow, and that it is not in the nature of public to remain stationary."[25] John M. Clayton of Delaware no doubt spoke for many supporters of manufacturing when he wrote, "We believe that some such bill as Verplanck's will pass next session unless something can now be done to save the system."[26] William Hammett of Virginia noted, "Nullification is first to be put down and then next session the whole weight of the Executive influence will be thrown against the protective system and it goes down. I should not be surprised if Verplanck's bill is lost nor should I be surprised if a better one were to pass so uncertain are things here."[27] It appears, however, that Jackson did not give the idea of calling the new Congress into a special session any attention.

Clay also recognized that the next Congress might remove all elements of protectionism in one fell swoop. He told his colleagues that Jackson's reelection meant the destruction of the protective tariff. Jackson "has marked out two victims," Clay moaned. "So. Carolina, and the Tariff and the only question with him is which shall be immolated first." The Congress that would assemble when called by Jackson would carry out the president's wishes because many of these men would owe their offices to him, Clay argued. Near the end of January, John Tyler of Virginia wrote, "All prospect of settling the tariff, except through Clay is gone, from him I still have hope. If he strikes at all it will be at a critical moment." Unbeknownst to Tyler, Clay visited manufacturers in Philadelphia and asked their opinions about a modification of the tariff in order to save the protective system. He now waited for the moment when he would have the most leverage.[28]

With Congress unable to adjust the tariff to a level that satisfied both the nullifiers and northern manufacturers, a mass meeting of nullifiers convened in Charleston, on January 21. Led by James Hamilton, the meeting recommended that nullification be postponed until after Congress adjourned. This would give Congress more time to pass some tariff modification. The leading nullifiers, Hamilton among them, now announced that they would hold their imported goods in federal customhouses and not pay the tax on them. If Congress lowered the tariff, as all in attendance hoped, the nullifiers would pay the lowered duty. If Congress failed to lower the protective duties on imported items, then the nullifiers vowed to go to the death for their imports.[29]

Meanwhile, in Washington, the Senate judiciary committee acted on Jackson's recommendation for a measure authorizing him to use force to collect the federal revenue. This committee, filled with Jacksonian protectionists, presented the Revenue Collection Bill, more commonly referred to as the Force Bill. This bill proposed to clothe the president with increased powers to ensure the enforcement of federal laws. Southerners branded it the "Bloody Bill," the "Boston Port Bill," and the "Botany Bay Bill." When Calhoun observed the proposed legislation, he called it the "bill to repeal the constitution." Jackson wanted the bill passed immediately. "Surely you and all my friends will push that bill thro the Senate," Jackson cajoled Tennessee's Felix Grundy. "This is due to the country—it is do to me, and to the safety of this union and surely you and others of the committee who reported it will never let it slumber one day until it passes the Senate."[30] Most National Republicans, including Daniel Webster, supported Jackson's efforts to get the Force Bill passed. "We now stand in the awkward predicament of having the leading measure of the administration ardently supported by the bitterest enemies of the President—ultra Federalists and ultra tariffites, who would delight to see the North and South arrayed against each other," Cambreleng informed Van Buren.[31] On February 15, Calhoun delivered a two-day speech against the legislation. Grundy prevailed on Webster to make the administration's case. Webster, although he disagreed with Jackson's politics, accepted the offer. The Massachusetts senator concluded his oration with a dramatic appeal to the people. "I shall exert every faculty I possess in aiding to prevent the Constitution from being nullified, destroyed, or impaired," he declared. "And even should I see it fail, I will still, with a voice feeble, perhaps, but earnest as ever issued from human lips, and with fidelity and zeal which nothing shall extinguish, call on the People to come to its rescue." The galleries erupted in thunderous applause when Webster sat down.[32]

Although both men claimed victory, Jackson, who had grown close to Webster in spite of their differences over the bank, believed that the Massachusetts senator had destroyed Calhoun. Jackson's badgering of Grundy, along with Grundy's desire to be reelected to his Senate seat, prompted the Tennessee senator to defend the administration and deliver the final speech on the Force Bill. In an anticlimactic finish, the Senate passed the Force Bill on February 20 by a vote of thirty-two to one. Calhoun led most of the southern senators out of the chamber before the final vote in a symbolic protest, leaving John Tyler to cast the lone negative vote.[33]

The nullifiers and other southerners had abandoned their delaying tactics against the Force Bill owing to an unanticipated event on February 11. Henry Clay announced his intention to introduce a bill that would modify the tariff the next day. "The tariff stands in imminent danger." Clay decreed. "If it should even be preserved during this session, it must fall at the next session." After consultations with Calhoun, Clay proposed to reduce tariff duties over ten years.[34] In his plan, the sharpest reductions would take place in 1841 and 1842. This delay, Clay argued, would give manufacturers almost a decade worth of protection and prevent an economic crisis by the sudden withdrawal of protection. If the bill passed with the approval of both parties or with the approval of both manufacturers and antitariff southerners, Clay announced, this would preserve the peace and settle the issue once and for all. When he concluded, cheers erupted from the galleries. Calhoun announced his support of Clay's proposal, prompting the people seated in the galleries once again to erupt in applause. The Kentuckian then proposed that his bill be referred to a select committee instead of either the Senate Finance Committee or the Manufactures Committee, because both of these committees would more than likely make an unfavorable report on the bill. President Pro Tempore Hugh Lawson White, a staunch Jackson supporter from Tennessee, agreed to send the bill to a select committee and appointed Calhoun, Clay, John M. Clayton, Dallas, Felix Grundy, William C. Rives, and Webster to that committee. One observer, whose opinion must have been shared by many, predicted that Clay's bill served as a "death warrant" for Verplanck's House tariff bill.[35]

The passage of the Force Bill in the Senate and the presentation of Clay's tariff bill did not resolve the situation, however. The men who had opposed the Verplanck bill would have to be reconciled to Clay's legislation. But the Kentuckian's bill offered Calhoun and the nullifiers an honorable retreat. They needed it because rumors circulated that Jackson had begun turning knots in a hangman's noose for his former vice president. To Robert Letcher of Kentucky, Jackson allegedly promised that "he would try Calhoun for treason, and, if convicted, he would hang him on a gallows as high as Haman."[36]

One unexpected hurdle remained, however. If northern protectionists had to swallow the new tariff, they demanded that home valuation be included. Under home valuation, imported goods would be assigned their values at American ports by American customs collectors. Manufacturers argued that this would reduce frauds, noting that the practice of allowing foreign merchants or their agents in America to assign the value of the good encouraged false valuations. Also under home valuation, shipping and insurance costs would be added to the overall value. Home valuation could add an additional 10 to 20 percent to the overall cost. Clay was reluctant to insist on home valuation but Clayton of Delaware demanded that home valuation be included on imports after 1842. If this demand was not met, Clayton vowed to encourage his friends to scuttle the bill and leave the nullifiers at the mercy of Jackson. Furthermore, Clayton demanded that Calhoun and his allies vote for home valuation and then the bill itself. Under no circumstances would they be allowed to walk out in protest as they had over the Force Bill. Clayton wanted the nullifiers on record so they could not later claim that they regarded either home valuation or this tariff bill as unconstitutional. Clay asked Clayton to drop his demand, but the Delaware senator would not budge. "If they [the nullifiers] can't vote for a bill that is to save their necks from a halter, their necks may stretch," Clayton informed his colleague. "They *shall* vote for it, or *it shall not pass*." If the nullifiers refused to support home valuation, Clayton notified South Carolina senator Stephen D. Miller, he would move to table the bill. Miller did not know what to make of this order from the young Delaware senator, but then Clayton took out his watch and said he had fifteen minutes to convince Calhoun to vote for home valuation. If the nullifiers called Clayton's bluff, then he and the protectionists would kill the bill. With five minutes to spare, Calhoun conceded and announced that he opposed the provision but informed the Senate that he would vote for the amendment to save the bill. The amendment calling for home valuation after 1842 passed. Van Buren's mouthpiece, the *Albany Argus*, saw Clayton's amendment as a poison pill to defeat the bill. But manufacturers had made this a sine qua non for their relinquishment of protection.[37]

Most of the nation received Clay's proposal with enthusiasm. They saw it as a compromise. It addressed a grievance of the South and provided manufacturers with another decade's worth of protection so that they would be able to modify their business practices to adapt to the upcoming era of lower tariffs. It was better than Verplanck's tariff and would be better than anything manufacturers would get from the next Congress. Many manufacturers, however, particularly their representatives in Congress who had not been consulted over the details of Clay's plan, excoriated it because they believed it surrendered too much too fast. Hezekiah Niles said that Clay's bill "will be received like a clash of thunder in the winter season." Webster opposed the plan, calling it "Clay's pretty little bill." He possibly worked against the bill simply because Clay had not consulted with him before he formulated it. John Davis of Massachusetts said that "Clay had stepped over the Potomac," implying that the Kentuckian presented this compromise to curry southern votes that would allow him to win the presidency.[38] One Pennsylvania paper even charged Clay with committing "parricide" since he strangled his own child, the American System. Even though Verplanck's House bill lowered duties more quickly and to lower levels, Calhoun and the nullifiers embraced Clay's scheme because it would end protectionism. More importantly, it denied Jackson and Van Buren the credit for resolving the crisis. "The South Carolina Senators appear like men whose shoulders an intolerable load has been removed!" a Mississippi correspondent noticed after Clay introduced his bill.[39]

The other opposition, although not as loud as the complaints from northeastern manufacturers, came from Jackson men. Since Clay and Calhoun supported the new tariff proposal, the Jackson men found themselves in a difficult spot politically. The crisis would be settled amicably, but Jackson's two enemies would be seen as saviors and not the president or Van Buren. Thomas Hart Benton, who grumbled over every tariff before voting for it, now opposed Clay's bill because it struck at protection. According to the Missourian, Clay's tariff removed protection on an item that would be necessary in the event of a war—lead. This would hurt Benton's constituents in Missouri but also lead miners in Illinois and Indiana. Furthermore, Clay's bill threatened democracy, he argued, because the people had elected members to Congress who would eliminate the protective system once and for all. Clay's bill deprived them of that opportunity. Old Bullion also did not think that one Congress should bind future Congresses to a policy. These arguments allowed him to mask his real reason for opposing the bill—that it benefitted his and Jackson's enemies politically.[40]

While the galleries and the nation cheered Clay's proposal, it still had to pass both the House and the Senate and receive Jackson's signature. Clay's bill had many hurdles to clear and little time to spare. The Kentuckian also had to ensure that both the tariff and the Force Bill passed. While the protectionists had killed Verplanck's bill by delivering extended speeches against it, a handful of nullifiers and southern House members could do the same with the Force Bill. The two bills, even though they were separate, had become linked. The first sign that the logjam might be broken occurred on February 25. As House members put on their overcoats to go back to their messes for dinner, Robert Letcher, a Kentucky National Republican and Clay loyalist, offered an amendment to the Verplanck bill. Letcher proposed to strike out Verplanck's entire bill after the enacting clause and insert Clay's Senate bill in its place. Most members stood in stunned silence as they tried to discern what had just been proposed. Suddenly, the members realized that Letcher had offered them a path out of the malaise into which they had gotten. In a matter of minutes, the House agreed to Letcher's amendment by a vote of 105 to 71. "It swept like a hurricane," John Quincy Adams wrote.[41] Even Verplanck voted to kill his own bill. Most of the no votes were cast by New England tariff supporters such as John Quincy Adams, Nathan Appleton, Tristam Burgess, John Davis, and Edward Everett. Although most of Washington was thunderstruck at this sudden and unexpected development, observers quickly realized its importance. Letcher's proposal broke the deadlock in the House. "We have now a fair prospect of having such an adjustment of the Tariff, as will, I am certain, restore peace and harmony to our distracted country; for this measure we are indebted to Henry Clay, who I must say, has acted nobly," Mitchell King of South Carolina exclaimed.[42]

On the next day, after only three hours of debate, the House passed Clay's tariff bill by a vote of 119 to 85. The Senate threatened to table Clay's tariff bill if the House refused to vote on the Force Bill. Led by McDuffie, southerners planned to use a series of parliamentary tricks to avoid having a final vote take place on the despised "bloody bill." Jacksonians called this a new form of nullification. "I have learned the important fact that an understanding, or agreement has been effected by a majority of the Senate, to reject the tariff bill, if the House of Representatives should not pass the enforcing bill," a correspondent noted.[43] Thurlow Weed applauded the Senate's course: "The prompt and proper ground taken by the Senate, in holding the Tariff bill, as hostage for the Enforcing bill, through the House of Representatives, no doubt brought the Nullifiers to their senses."[44]

Most of the opposition to Clay's tariff in the House came from northern representatives who supported manufacturers. Twenty-seven of the eighty-five negative votes came from New England. Southern House members, however, supported this measure by a large majority. All told, sixty-three southern representatives supported the measure, while only two opposed it. Every South Carolinian gave the measure his support.

Shortly after midnight on March 1, the House approved the Force Bill. All throughout March 1, the Senate debated the new tariff bill. Several senators complained about certain sections of the bill but announced that they would support it to maintain the peace. Democrat John Forsyth of Georgia quoted from *Richard III*: "Now is the winter of our discontent, made glorious summer by the son of York." After he finished with this soliloquy, George M. Bibb, a Democrat from Kentucky, embraced Forsyth's use of *Richard III*. However, Bibb suggested to Forsyth that he might need to make a change to it. The winter of discontent had ended, Bibb announced, not by the son of "Old York, or New York, but a son of the Old Dominion—from the slashes of Hanover." Bibb was referring to the efforts of his Kentucky colleague, Clay. Later that day, the Senate passed the new tariff by a vote of twenty-nine to sixteen. Clay called March 1 the most important day in the history of Congress because the actions of that day saved the union.[45]

In the Senate, every Southerner approved the compromise tariff. New England divided on it, giving the tariff six pro votes and six negative ones. Maryland, New Jersey, New York, and Ohio each divided, while both of the senators from Indiana, Maryland, Missouri, and Pennsylvania opposed the bill. Delaware, Illinois, and Kentucky provided the tariff with unanimous support in the Senate.

A final part of the compromise involved Clay's land bill. This bill had languished during the session and then pushed through on March 1. It proposed to distribute the proceeds of the public lands to the states based on their population. Clay could have linked this bill with either his tariff or the Force Bill but opted not to. Although Clay had not joined it to the other bills, distribution was tied to the tariff because if land sales went to the states, the tariff would be the only source of revenue for the federal government. This more than likely would have required an increase in the tariff at a later date. Jackson recognized this. Fearful of having his veto overridden, Jackson opted to use a pocket veto. "It is an unwarrantable stretch of power, that finds no countenance in the spirit of the Constitution, and exhibits fully the disposition of the President to make his own will the sole measure of legislation," an editor averred in opposition to Jackson's use of the pocket veto. Distribution would become very important a decade later.[46]

Most Americans greeted the compromise package with joy because it preserved the union and prevented the effusion of any American blood. "The adjustment is one, at which all men must feel bound to rejoice," the *Columbia Telescope* announced. "The Tariff is overthrown, the corrupt majorities in Congress have yielded." The *New York Evening Post*, however, suggested that the compromise package emerged not from politicians in Washington but rather the people: "The truth is that this measure has been forced upon Congress by the authority of public opinion."[47]

Calhoun departed the capital and raced back to Columbia to ensure that the convention supported the new tariff. Nullifiers complained about some of its provisions, but they accepted it because it allowed them to claim that nullification had accomplished its desired goal. South Carolina rescinded its ordinance of nullification but then nullified the Force Bill to show the legitimacy of their course. "We have beat the nullifiers and things are quiet for a time," Poinsett boasted. "I verily thought we should have had a struggle and a short civil war, and was prepared once more to take the field. I was exceedingly indignant with these Radicals and rather desired to put them down with the strong arm."[48] Another South Carolinian noted, "We Carolinians are a lucky people, we have had the satisfaction of taking the lead in a most honorable resistance, we have had the satisfaction of displaying great courage to a threatened danger, and we have the still greater of seeing the danger quietly disappear."[49]

Why did the nullifiers accept Clay's proposal and reject Verplanck's, which slashed duties at a greater rate than Clay's? It cannot be argued that the nullifiers in Congress rejected democracy and the will of their constituents because the nullifiers at the convention in South Carolina approved Clay's compromise tariff by a vote of 153 to 4. The nullifiers in South Carolina and in Washington accepted Clay's tariff for many reasons. First, it deprived Jackson and Van Buren of the ability to claim victory. Second, it removed the tariff issue from politics for a decade. Third, no Southern state came to the nullifiers' aid, and they faced the grim prospect of confronting Jackson alone. Clay's bill also foretold the abandonment of the protective system in ten years, a goal in line with southern sentiment.[50]

"Nullification is triumphant," Duff Green crowed on March 9. "What has produced the settlement of the tariff question," he asked. "Nullification. Would we have seen Mr. Clay's bill had it not been for the action of South Carolina?"[51] Green maintained that nullification had worked in a peaceful manner since it had forced Congress to lower the tariff. Other contemporaries saw it differently, however. Jackson's supporters saw the resolution to the crisis as a victory for Old Hickory. After the compromise was approved, a New Hampshire man declared how the whole crisis had resulted in a great victory for Jackson. "Not only has the Champion of the Tariff been forced to give up his American System," he wrote. "But the mad Carolina Nullifier, too, has been forced to join him in doing homage to the superior wis-

Table 12.1. House vote, 1833

	Democrats		National Republicans		Anti-Masons		Nullifiers		Total	
	For	Against	For	Against	For	Against	For	Against	For	Against
New England	10	1	0	26	0	0	0	0	10	27
Middle	21	23	3	23	0	2	0	0	24	48
South	51	0	8	2	0	0	4	0	63	2
West	14	3	8	5	0	0	0	0	22	8
Total	96	27	19	56	0	2	4	0	119	85

Source: *House Journal*, 22nd Cong., 2nd Sess., 26 Feb. 1833, 428–29.

Table 12.2. Senate vote, 1833

	Democrats		National Republicans		Nullifiers		Total	
	For	Against	For	Against	For	Against	For	Against
New England		0	5	6	0	0	6	6
Middle	1	5	4	0	0	0	5	5
South	10	0	2	0	2	0	14	0
West	2	3	2	2	0	0	4	5
Total	14	8	13	8	2	0	29	16

Source: *Senate Journal*, 22nd Cong., 2nd Sess., 1 March 1833, 224.

dom of President Jackson."[52] The *Nashville Republican and State Gazette* concurred with this assessment: "The reduction of the tariff, therefore, down to the standard of revenue in compliance with the express and repeated recommendations of the President, may justly be regarded as a most signal triumph, the more glorious because marked by a total surrender on the part of Mr. Clay of the point in dispute."[53]

The public displays and meetings in favor of the union and compromise suggest that democracy had continued to spread. Political leaders were responding to the wishes of their constituents. "It is quite amazing to look around the country and see the great meetings and oratorical displays that have been made on the subject of nullification and the President's Proclamation," Newton Cannon of Tennessee observed.[54] The nullification crisis ended with all the participants able to claim victory, with the exception of New England manufacturers, who now had only ten years' worth of protection. Calhoun and the nullifiers crowed that nullification had accomplished its goal and that the doctrine had not been thwarted. They charged that far from leading to disunion, nullification had brought the country together and prompted statesmen to find a consensus. Clay returned triumphantly to the political arena after suffering a humiliating defeat the previous fall. The Kentuckian had now saved the union twice. "He has nobly and patriotically surrendered his hobby to the salvation of his country. We have censured him severely for his faults, why not praise him for his virtues?" a pro-Jackson paper declared. If the editor of this paper could salute Clay, perhaps the American people might remember his efforts and reward him with the jewel of American politics that had twice eluded him. Jackson emerged victorious even though he had to compromise. He sanctified the concept of a perpetual union, and the Force Bill gave him the unquestioned authority to crush any future rebellion against the federal government.[55]

The Compromise of 1833 represented a neat and tidy package that catered to a disparate group of interests. "This unnatural system, which is so much at war with the genius of the age, and the institutions of a free and a young country, will never be renewed after 1842, by all the Clays and the Calhouns in the country," the *Richmond Enquirer* declared. On the tariff, there would be peace and quiet for a decade at least, allowing Americans to focus their attention on different issues.[56]

13

"Democracy seeks the benefit of all at the expense of none"

O N THE EVENING OF JANUARY 8, 1835, 250 Democrats crowded into Brown's Hotel in Washington. A large portrait of Washington hung where all could see the "Father of His Country." A band had been assembled to play music. President Andrew Jackson, too ill to attend, remained the center of attention. When his cabinet arrived, the band began to play "Hail to the Chief." Thomas Hart Benton, the president of the ceremony, then stood up and announced, "Gentlemen, we have met for the commemoration of two great events—the anniversary of the victory at New Orleans, and the extinguishment of the national debt." This was met with loud applause. "The debt of two wars is paid off! And this beneficent consummation takes place under the civil administration of him, whose career, connecting itself with both wars, finishes the most brilliant event of our military annals," Benton proclaimed. "*The national debt is paid*! This month of January, 1835, in the 58th year of the Republic, ANDREW JACKSON being president, the NATIONAL DEBT IS PAID!"[1]

After Benton concluded his remarks, numerous attendees offered toasts of their own. They toasted the patriots of 1776, Jackson's subordinate officers at the Battle of New Orleans, hard money, the destruction of the national bank, the armed forces, and states' rights. Surprisingly, nobody referenced or toasted the tariff. This was odd since the tariff had been the primary reason why the country had paid its debt. At most dinner parties since the 1820s, the tariff had always played a conspicuous part. Now, it had disappeared.

The tariff had been removed from the minds of Americans for several reasons. The issue of a national bank had become the primary issue in American politics. Also, the speculation on lands in the West had provided the federal government with an unexpected source of revenue. In 1835, the federal government obtained just above 50 percent of its revenue from the tariff, but in the ensuing two years that number declined to under 50 percent. The income from the public lands had nullified the economic importance of the tariff. The years of 1836 and 1837 were the only two years before the Civil War during which the federal government did not obtain a majority of its income from the tariff. But the primary reason why the tariff failed to galvanize the people came from the fact that the compromise tariff of 1833 satisfied most Americans. Complaints against the tariff subsided, and the calls for disunion ended. Petitions dwindled, and memorials and public meeting on the tariff declined.

In the years that followed the passage of the 1833 compromise tariff, the second American party system crystallized in the United States. The Democrats remained the followers of Jackson and advocated rigid economy and states' rights. Jacksonians continued to regard federally sponsored internal improvements as unconstitutional. Since the Jacksonians drew support from tariff supporters in Pennsylvania and New York and free traders in the South, the best position for the party on the tariff was to maintain the compromise. The Whigs, at first, comprised an odd assortment of protectionists, free traders, nullifiers, probank men, hard-money advocates, supporters of paper currency, and men for and against internal improvements. The lone unifying principle for the Whig Party became opposition to Andrew Jackson. For some Whigs, this was based on Jackson's politics. For others, it was a dislike of the man whom they regarded as a Caesar-like figure who threatened to destroy the republic and install himself as a dictator.[2]

In the 1836 presidential election, the tariff influenced few voters. William Henry Harrison, one of three Whig candidates in 1836, spoke about the tariff just days before the people went to the polls. Whereas Harrison's remarks suggested that he favored a repeal of the compromise tariff, he subsequently issued a clarification that became known as the "Zanesville Letter." "I regret that my remarks of yesterday were misunderstood in relation to the tariff system," Harrison wrote to a group of Ohio protectionists. "What I meant to convey was, that I had been a warm advocate for that system, upon its first adoption, that I still believed in the benefits it had conferred upon the country. But I certainly never had, nor never could have any idea of reviving it. . . . I am for supporting the compromise act, and never will agree to its being altered or repealed."[3] Since this letter appeared at the end of the campaign, it had little to no impact on the presidential election. Democrat Martin Van Buren, Andrew Jackson's anointed successor, won the presidency.[4]

As Harrison noted, the Compromise of 1833 had become sacrosanct among the American people. Anyone who advocated undoing the compromise could be seen as attempting to revive sectional tensions between the North and the South. "The reason why the compromise tariff ought not to be repealed is simply this. It is not merely a law, but it is a contract; a treaty of peace and amity entered into between two great parties that had divided the country for nearly twenty years previous to its passage," one editor observed.[5] But during Andrew Jackson's final days in office, however, Democrats attempted to break the compromise and lower the tariff. In early 1837, House Ways and Means Committee chairman Churchill Cambreleng introduced a bill that would reduce the tariff by one-third on September 30, 1837, then another third on March 31, 1838, and a final third on September 30, 1838. The final reductions would eliminate all elements of protection. This bill violated the Compromise of 1833, but Cambreleng believed that he had a good reason to break the agreement and hasten the demise of protection. Cambreleng pointed to the surplus that the government enjoyed and calculated that the federal government would soon have a surplus of forty-four million dollars. Excess revenue, he argued, led to increased expenses. Increase revenue tempted politicians, the New Yorker warned. He even suggested that the efforts to subdue Native Americans would not have happened had there not been so much revenue. "To avoid these evils, the only safe and prudent course is to diminish the income of the government," Cambreleng concluded.[6]

Since Cambreleng had always been identified as a spokesperson for the incoming president, Martin Van Buren, Whigs believed that the Little Magician wanted to lower the tariff in order to stand on good terms with his southern supporters. Van Buren had not directed Cambreleng to offer this measure. Silas Wright, Van Buren's top lieutenant in Washington, recognized that the proposed reduction would drive the antitariff nullifiers into the arms of northern Whigs because Van Buren would be seen as the one who had broken the peace over the tariff. Wright opposed Cambreleng's movements and talked with him for three hours in an attempt to persuade him not to introduce his bill. But Cambreleng vowed to press forward. Since his colleague would not relent, Wright decided to offer his own tariff reduction scheme in the Senate. Wright probably presented this bill to demonstrate unity among Van Buren's supporters.[7]

Southern senators, however, greeted Wright's bill with howls of anger. John C. Calhoun sensed a trap. Although the leading nullifier favored a reduction of the tariff, he feared that a drastic reduction would bring the tariff issue to the forefront of American politics once again. "Have you forgot the tariff of 1828, that bill of abominations," Calhoun growled staring at Wright. "I have its author in my eyes, and he knows the fact. He well remembers the part he bore in the passage of that act, and the means by which it was effected. We were deceived then. It will not be my fault if we be deceived now."[8] A violation of the compromise, he warned, would prompt northerners to try to increase the tariff to levels that exceeded those in 1828. Therefore, Calhoun reasoned that the best strategy for the South would be to abide by the 1833 compromise.[9]

Few expected Cambreleng's bill to pass. Only the most pro-Jackson sheets endorsed the proposal. A Georgia editor noticed that the compromise act had been crafted by Clay and Calhoun and not by Jackson; therefore, Jackson could urge his supporters to repeal it. "If the faith of the government is pledged, are we bound by it, when it is demonstrated that the operation of the act for which that faith was pledged, is productive of the most serious evils to the country?" one editor asked.[10] "These recommendations are not without a motive," the *United States Telegraph* opined. "To agitate, and throw the various interests of the country into conflict, is a part of the settled policy which has distinguished this administration."[11]

Most eyes focused on the Senate and not on the House. "It [Wright's bill] is far less odious to the manufacturing interest than Mr. Cambreleng's bill," one editor avowed.[12] Wright's bill passed the Senate by a vote of twenty-seven to eighteen. It failed to win approval in the House owing to the end of the session. One editor called Wright's bill a mere "humbug" and declared, "the changes proposed by Mr. Wright's bill amount to nothing, farther than to disturb the compromise, and again agitate the country with the tariff question."[13]

Discerning which party supported the proposed reduction is difficult, since this was a fluid period in American politics. Some Whigs would soon be Democrats and vice versa. Nevertheless, a majority of the Democrats favored the bill, while most Whigs opposed it. No more than three Whigs, all from the South, voted for the reduction, while only four Democrats opposed it and these Democrats came from Pennsylvania, Ohio, Illinois, and Indiana. Yet geography could not always trump sectionalism. For example, Calhoun and William Preston, both regarded as nullifiers in 1837, opposed the bill. Calhoun would soon become a Democrat while Preston later joined the Whig Party. While Wright's bill failed in the House owing to a lack of time; the Senate vote signaled that a majority of senators supported lower duties.[14]

When Jackson left the presidency in 1837, the Whig Party found itself at a crossroads, since their party had been established as an organization opposed to Jackson. The proper response to the bruising Panic of 1837, which erupted just after Jackson departed Washington City for the Hermitage, dominated the presidency of his successor, Martin Van Buren. But the panic and Van Buren's handling of it hardened the positions of the Whigs and Democrats on the critical issues. Those Whigs who had opposed the compromise tariff as National Republicans charged that reduced duties contributed to the panic. Presumably, their best argument rested on the fact that under Van Buren, the federal government expended eight million more dollars annually than it received. Since the new president spent so lavishly, particularly on improvements for the executive mansion, he should increase the tariff.[15]

By 1840, the Whig Party became the party of Henry Clay's program of federally sponsored internal improvements, a national bank, and a protective tariff. Whereas Democrats generally endorsed reductions in spending and strict economy, Whigs believed that the best way for the government to escape the financial Panic of 1837 was through an increase in both revenue and federal expenditures. Few dared to advocate direct taxes, so the obvious way to augment the government's revenue became high tariff duties, which would also aid manufacturers. Ira Eastman, a Democrat from New Hampshire, bluntly stated the positions of the two parties in an 1841 speech: "Opposition to the protective policy is clearly and unequivocally a Democratic doctrine. Go where you will, North, South, East, or West, and the Democratic party will tell you that they are opposed to the protective system. The protective system is essentially and virtually the Whig system." Eastman even put the differences between Democrats and Whigs on the tariff in populist terms. "Democracy seeks the benefit of all at the expense of none," he announced. "She guards the interests of all, whatever they may be. She knows no distinctions between any classes or any sections. She throws her broad mantle over the whole country and the whole people."[16] The Whig decision to embrace the tariff was by no means an empty gesture. In 1840, after the Whigs nominated William Henry Harrison, the hero of the Battle of Tippecanoe, and John Tyler as his running mate, Pennsylvania Whigs campaigned on the slogan of "Tip, Tyler, and the Tariff."[17]

Van Buren's inability to guide the country out of the Panic of 1837 gave the Whigs ample ammunition to use against a man they dubbed "Martin Van Ruin" in 1840. By that year the government had fallen $5.6 million into the red. Van Buren's final budget left the government with a projected debt of seventeen million dollars.

Whigs used the poor economy against the Democrats. Expecting to be the Whig nominee in 1840, Clay had begun to modify his positions on the issues. He hoped that this would win him southern support. While southerners were willing to give the two-time presidential loser another try, his southern strategy injured him in New York and Pennsylvania. Consequently, at their convention in Harrisburg, the Whigs nominated General William Henry Harrison, instead of Clay. An inconsolable Clay moaned, "I am the most unfortunate man in the history of parties: always run by my friends when sure to be defeated, and now betrayed for a nomination when I, or anyone, would be sure of an election."[18] As a sop to the Kentuckian, the Whigs picked John Tyler of Virginia, a Clay supporter, as Harrison's running mate.[19]

Democrats charged that Harrison was a Federalist of the school of John Adams. "He is in favor of a high protective Tariff, shinplaster currency, a national debt, surplus revenue, and splendid schemes of internal improvement, and consequently impost taxes," Joseph Duncan of Illinois charged.[20] Democrats also tried to show that Harrison had equivocated on every issue, including the tariff. With no other viable candidate available, the Democrats renominated Van Buren. The president issued a statement to the citizens of Elizabeth County in Virginia on the tariff: "I was seriously friendly to the passage of the compromise bill, and have always been, and still am, disposed to carry it into full and fair effect."[21]

In the 1840 election, Harrison defeated Van Buren for the presidency. For many Americans, regardless of their political affiliation, they welcomed Harrison's victory, since they had associated Van Buren with all their economic troubles. "I have never had any luck since Van Buren was elected," one man observed after the election of 1840. "I have lost Cattle, Hogs, and Horses. One of my sons run off and left me and one of my daughters has had her Leg Broke; but thank God, we got Harrison in and I think times will alter."[22] At the Hermitage, Jackson believed that the Whig triumph meant the return of a national bank, federally sponsored internal improvements, and a protective tariff. New England Whigs assumed that with Webster at the State Department, their interests would be a key part of the Harrison administration. New England congressmen such as John Quincy Adams, Nathan Appleton, and Caleb Cushing expected the new president to disregard the Compromise of 1833 and support a new protective tariff.[23]

Jackson's fears about the Whigs restoring a government of the few over the many turned out to be unfounded. Harrison delivered a lengthy inaugural address in front of thirty thousand spectators. "It was a scene every way more glorious than a Roman triumph," a Pennsylvanian recalled.[24] But the Whigs became the party of hard luck. Harrison died shortly after taking the oath of office. Tyler, a states' rights Whig and an enemy of protectionism, assumed the presidency and became known as "His Accidency." Jackson could not contain his euphoria. "Their [the Whigs'] plan of a national Bank, a national debt, high protecting Tariff and assumption of state debts etc. and all prepared for the action of the called Session of Congress, by the death of Harrison is blown sky high," Jackson informed Francis P. Blair.[25] Clay had expected Harrison to defer to his politics, and with his death, the Kentuckian hoped to find his friend Tyler even more sympathetic to his cause. "I have no confidence in Tyler," Robert W. Barnwell, a South Carolina Democrat complained. "He will be Clay's man."[26] Jackson too wondered what course Tyler would follow. "Write me what you think will be Tyler['s] course. Will he stick to a strict construction of the constitution or will he sell himself to Ball, or rather take that unprincipled swaggering demagogue, Clay, for his guide and worship him," Jackson asked Blair.[27] Barnwell, Jackson, and the rest of the country would soon realize that Tyler would not be a Clay man.

With total control of the federal government, the Whigs now pushed their economic program. They called for a national bank, a protective tariff, and the distribution of funds from the sales of public lands back to the states. If the Whigs distributed excess federal revenue back to the states, then the states would plan on this source of income. Since this source of revenue would no longer be available to the federal government, it would have to turn to the tariff to offset the loss. Therefore, distribution necessitated a high tariff. Finally, many Whigs advocated lavish expenditures by the federal government. William B. Campbell, a Tennessee Whig, related a conversation that he had to his uncle in Virginia: "One of the most intelligent of the protecting tariff men, said to me that their policy was to protect home industry and labor and to do that, they must create the necessity for a tariff by liberal expenditures."[28] A few Whigs, most notably William Cost Johnson of Maryland, endorsed the idea that the federal government should even assume the debts that states had incurred as a result of the panic. This would necessitate increased revenue for the federal government, which could be accomplished through a high tariff. Thomas Ritchie, the longtime editor of the *Richmond Enquirer*, likewise feared that Whigs would call for the assumption of state debts. The protective tariff, according to Whigs, functioned like the sun because every other program revolved around it.[29]

In the winter of 1841, southern Whigs, led by Edward Stanly of North Carolina, made overtures to increase the tariff. During a debate on the question of issuing more Treasury notes, Stanly stipulated that he intended to talk about the tariff, "a word which causes Southern gentlemen generally to start from their seats with affected dismay, as if they beheld some spirit bring 'blasts from hell' which were to desolate the country."[30] Treasury notes offered no relief to the people, he declared. To the government, they provided only temporary relief. For Stanly, increased tariff duties on luxury items seemed to be the best way to get the country out of the hard times.

Stanly advocated a new position for southern Whigs on the tariff, which would have been untenable just a few years earlier. The protective tariff was not a "monster as that described by Milton, as seen by Satan at the gates of Hell," he announced. Stanly decreed that southern Whigs like himself would support a protective tariff if the circumstances required it. A Tennessee editor, after listing the numerous manufacturers in the state, asked, "Are all these interests to be disregarded, because we are in the mass an agricultural people?"[31]

Statements by other southern Whigs demonstrate that the tariff had become a partisan issue, instead of a sectional issue, by 1841. "The great object of agitation now, is the Tariff. The true ground for our friends on that subject is that it is not now, as formerly, a question of laying duties for protection, and raising more money than is wanted for revenue," William Graham, a North Carolina Whig, observed. "But the simple state of the case is, that the Government costs 20 odd millions of dollars per year. The reduced duties now existing yields about 13 millions. Now, the question is, whether the balance is to be raised by a Tariff, in which men only pay as they consume foreign goods, or by direct taxes on lands and slaves, as was done during the war. He who is not for the latter must agree to raise the amount needed, by a Tariff. Or he is in favor of what is worse than either, and that is withholding supplies, and disgracing the Government."[32] In his gubernatorial campaigns of 1841 and 1843, James Jones, a Tennessee Whig, announced his support for a protective tariff. Jones bested former Speaker of the House James K. Polk in both elections. If southern Whigs joined southern and western Democrats in opposition to a tariff, the country would go bankrupt, or it would have to resort to direct taxation. Every congressmen feared retribution at the polls if they voted for direct taxes, which had not be levied since the War of 1812. When Congress took up the tariff in 1842, Alexander Stuart presented a petition from residents of Virginia praying for an increased tariff. This was greeted with cheers in the House and approval in the North. "It is especially gratifying to see Virginia—a state that exercises such a great moral influence over the South generally—leading off in this matter," a northern paper declared.[33]

The special session under Tyler proved both successful and frustrating for Whigs. They repealed the Independent Treasury, which had gone into operation only in 1840, and passed bills to increase funding on costal fortifications and to improve the navy. Finally, and most importantly, they passed a land bill, which would distribute the revenue from land sales to the states as long as tariff rates remained at or beneath the 20 percent level. Congressional Whigs had been forced to add on the 20 percent threshold in order to avoid a veto by Tyler. But these successes were offset by Tyler's refusal to sign bills into law creating a new national bank. Since a new national bank had become the centerpiece of the Whig program, Tyler's decision to veto these bills made this special session seem like a failure for the Whig Party. For Whigs such as Clay, Tyler had defied the will of the people by deploying the veto against these bills. His position on a national bank was similar to that expressed by most Democrats. One Whig allegedly said, "the Lord took our president—the demos have taken our vice president—and the Devil will take our party."[34]

The Whigs also tinkered with the tariff during the special session. A new tariff bill required that items admitted duty free or at a rate of less than 20 percent must pay a duty of 20 percent. The only exemptions were tea and coffee. Calhoun and his supporters howled that this bill violated the Compromise of 1833. Southern Whigs who supported this tariff augmentation became prime targets for southern Democrats. "The Southern Whigs who voted for this bill betrayed their constituents, and are deserving of eternal infamy. When a public servant, through devotion to party alone, disregards the dearest interests of his country, he should become a byword and reproach among honorable men," one observer noted.[35]

Just as Tyler signed this tariff increase into law, his cabinet, with the exception of Secretary of State Daniel Webster, resigned. An express rider traveling to New York City warned a curious onlooker that the messages that he carried amounted to "a declaration of war" between Whigs and their own president. Tyler assembled a new cabinet composed of states' rights Whigs, Whigs opposed to Clay, and southern Democrats. Walter Forward, a western Pennsylvania Whig and high-tariff supporter, became the new treasury secretary. A nearly bankrupt Treasury and a protariff man in the Treasury Department meant that the tariff would be an issue in 1842. But for several states, relief would not come soon enough. Starting in the summer of 1841, six states, Michigan, Indiana, Maryland, Arkansas, Illinois, and Mississippi, defaulted on their loans. In 1842, Pennsylvania and Louisiana joined them. Other states likewise stood near the brink of collapse. In mid-February 1842, Abbot Lawrence noted, "I have never known in my experience merchandise of all kinds sold at so low prices as at this moment."[36]

14

"Congress should be made to see &
hear that the People are in earnest"

JOHN TYLER'S ELEVATION to the presidency and his use of the veto had
created a fluid state in American politics. He appeared to be a Whig in name
only. As Whigs prepared to wash their hands of him, Democrats had a difficult decision to make. Should they align with the president since he opposed the bank, or
should they continue to oppose him? Active support for Tyler might anger some
of the Democrats who had their eye on the presidency in 1844 since the incumbent president might secure the nomination. The Democrats who had been with
the party since its inception would frown on a recent convert getting the nomination over them. "He [Tyler] differs with us on the Sub Treasury and also on many
other equally important measures, and besides he is *Judas to* and *renegade from* all
parties," one Democrat wrote. "Our party therefore will not touch him with a ten
foot pole."[1] Samuel Tilden spoke for many Democrats when he endorsed a middle-
of-the-road position. "While we render to Tyler liberal credit for every good act he
does, and sustain every right measure which he proposes, and defend him against
the unjust and unconstitutional attacks of the Whigs, we cannot give his administration an unqualified support, or commit ourselves in favor of his re-election," the
young New Yorker wrote.[2]

Democrats had problems of their own. Already, numerous men had begun to
position themselves for the party's 1844 nomination. Many Democrats believed that
Van Buren should be given another chance. Thomas Hart Benton, a man whom
many Democrats wanted to run for president, endorsed Van Buren in December
1840 and removed himself from consideration. Other Democrats disagreed with
Benton, however. They saw Van Buren as a hindrance to their 1844 chances and did
not want to stand for election in their own states with him at the top of the ticket.
For these Democrats, there was no shortage of "available" candidates to run instead
of Van Buren. James Buchanan had close to two decades' worth of party service as
his claim to the presidency. Michigan senator Lewis Cass had served in a variety of
posts with distinction. Former vice president Richard M. Johnson of Kentucky had
support as well. And John C. Calhoun seemed to have made amends for his past
sins.[3]

As Democrats positioned themselves to capture the nomination, a younger
wave of high-tariff supporters with new arguments emerged. Led by Horace
Greeley, protectionists now argued that Congress had a duty to aid the American

economy just like it had a responsibility to protect American shores from foreign invasion. According to these men, no difference existed between an invading army and cheap foreign goods, since they both sought to overthrow the country. Protectionists amplified the argument that a tariff protected American labor from the reduced wages that monarchs provided their subjects. James Tallmadge of New York insisted that Congress needed to offer American laborers increased protection because of technological improvements. An editor in Pennsylvania added: "The protection of American labor is of such importance to us, that it ought not to occupy any second place in our thoughts. What avails our declaration of independence, if we are to be subject to the burthens of British poverty? If we deny protection to our laborers to our own laborers, are they not immediately placed upon a level with their pauper competitors in Europe? As Americans, we are not willing this country should be converted into a national alms house for the support of foreign paupers."[4]

When Congress convened in December 1841, Tyler's annual message painted a bleak picture of the government's finances. To improve the economy, the president endorsed an increase of the tariff. "So long as duties shall be laid with distinct reference to the wants of the Treasury, no well founded objection can exist against them," Tyler announced.[5] However, he reminded Congress that if it increased duties beyond 20 percent, then it would have to abandon distribution. "I want a well digested tariff this winter, but I am afraid our movements for that will aid in the repeal of the distribution act," Horace Greeley confided to Millard Fillmore.[6]

Greeley and other Whigs realized that they had been placed on the horns of a dilemma: they could have a high tariff or distribution, but Tyler would not let them have both. The tariff was popular in the North, while distribution was favored in the South and the West. If Tyler could not be made to see the importance of distribution and a high tariff, then some section of the Whig Party would be sacrificed. "I do not remember any period of our political history when the people were in such a state of indecision and uncertainty in relations to public measures or public men as at this moment," a Massachusetts Whig wrote. "They seem to be looking for nothing from Washington and would not be surprised or disappointed at anything."[7]

The more dire news came after Tyler submitted his annual message. On December 20, Treasury Secretary Walter Forward submitted his annual report and painted an even bleaker picture of the nation's finances. The debt had soared to nearly eighteen million dollars and because of expenditures by the federal government, he predicted that the government would face a budget deficit of over fourteen million dollars. Whigs had promised to revitalize the economy in 1840, but in their first year in power, the debt had increased nearly three times. The easiest way to narrow the massive deficit and get the country's economy back on track would be to increase the tariff, according to Forward. "The situation of this country is much more perilous than is generally supposed," Abel P. Upshur noted in early January 1842.[8] James Buchanan confirmed this when he wrote: "The Treasury has been entirely empty for some weeks. The Whigs, by the extravagance and folly at the extra session, have reduced the Treasury to its present deplorable condition and instead of economy and retrenchment, they are now running up a national debt rapidly in time of peace."[9]

Whigs prepared for the upcoming tariff debate with mixed feelings. For example, Charles Hudson of Massachusetts believed that the opponents of protection outnumbered protectionists in Congress. Other Whigs, however, exuded confidence about the favorable votes that would come from south of the Potomac. "All Pennsylvania and Maryland go to the death for a tariff," the *New York American* claimed. "And so do large portions of New York, Connecticut, Massachusetts, New Jersey, *Virginia, North Carolina, Georgia, Tennessee and Kentucky.*" British cotton cultivation in Egypt and India had prompted some southern planters, according to this sheet, to see the necessity of supporting a high tariff.[10]

Despite a large majority in the House and the nation's financial distress, House Whigs delayed bringing a tariff bill to the floor. In the spring, the poor economy forced Tyler to stop paying some federal officeholders. Across the country, manufacturers closed their doors and released their workers. And still the Whigs in the House waited. They calculated that as the financial condition of the country worsened, Tyler might become more pliant to the Whig legislative agenda and would approve a tariff with distribution. "The Tariff is in a desperate condition, I fear," Robert C. Winthrop, a Massachusetts Whig observed. "The more meetings and memorials the better. Congress should be made to see & hear that the People are in earnest."[11]

While the House stalled, the Senate acted. On February 15, Henry Clay offered eleven resolutions, which all provided for higher duties. Clay wanted both a tariff above 20 percent and distribution of funds from land sales. The Kentuckian was at his best on March 7, when he presented a petition from female textile workers in Rahway, New Jersey. Turning to Calhoun, Clay expressed his hope that he could "rely on the chivalry of South Carolina to rush forward and protect their fair countrywomen from foreign competition." Calhoun refrained from taking the bait, but James Buchanan, a bachelor, snatched it. He offered his own petition from Pennsylvania iron manufacturers and said that he wished that Clay had let someone else offer protection to so many ladies. Clay apologized for leaving the iron manufacturers to Buchanan but added that since the "Senator had lived for thirty-five years, and upwards, without taking any lady under his protection," Clay felt compelled to do so.[12]

After Clay finished mocking Buchanan, he and Calhoun assailed each other over whether or not Clay's resolutions violated the Compromise of 1833. Calhoun believed the compromise to be perpetual, while Clay argued that succeeding generations could modify the tariff as needed. Quite possibly, Clay presented his resolutions with the expectation that they would not be acted on. Therefore, they served a political purpose. He also offered them as a form of a valedictory address, for on March 31, Clay vacated his Senate seat. He notified the General Assembly of Kentucky that he "desired to retire to public life," but everyone sensed that his departure had more to do with preparing for a presidential run than with becoming a simple farmer at Ashland, his home. Thomas Hart Benton, a onetime friend but now an inveterate foe of Clay, claimed that the Kentuckian "retired" because the public had repudiated all his programs, including a high tariff. Nathan Sargent recalled that when Clay took his leave, he and Calhoun embraced in silence—no doubt the two remembered past battles over the tariff. The fate of the tariff seemed even more uncertain with the departure of its leading advocate.[13]

The delays of the House and the politicking in the Senate did not go unnoticed. "There is a deliberate purpose to make Henry Clay president of the United States, even at the hazard of a revolution," Upshur wrote in March 1842. "The design is to embarrass the administration by withholding all needful facilities for carrying on the government; to distress the people by the severest pressure [of] all their interests, in order to throw the odium of their suffering upon the existing administration."[14] Upshur suggested that Whigs seemed willing to bring the nation to the edge of an economic collapse in order to put their hero, Henry Clay, into the White House. These politicians, according to Upshur, would use the tariff to get what they wanted. If they did not get their way, they would take the country over a fiscal cliff.

Throughout the spring, Fillmore, chairman of the Ways and Means Committee, conversed with manufacturers and Secretary of the Treasury Forward. His committee met each day from nine o'clock in the morning until four in the afternoon to craft a new tariff. While they worked, Tyler sent a special message to Congress on March 25. Once again, Tyler reminded congressional members of the depressed state of the nation's finances and urged them to do something to rectify the situation. Although Tyler recommended that Congress increase the tariff beyond the 20 percent level, he warned its members that they would have to forego distribution. Herein was the position of the president—if the legislature would abandon distribution, an increase in the tariff would receive his signature. For Tyler, the profits from the sales of lands should go toward eliminating the federal debt and not into the coffers of the states. Some Whigs charged that Tyler's actions revealed that wanted to curry favor with the Democrats and thereby secure their presidential nomination in 1844. In the wake of Tyler's message, Whigs pondered their strategy. Perhaps the president would approve a tariff with distribution, because the condition of the country had become so dire. Or perhaps Tyler was serious. Although already in "retirement" in Lexington, Clay urged his former colleagues not to give up distribution or the tariff.[15]

As Congress delayed, the American economy underwent its bleakest period since the Panic of 1837 had commenced. Manufacturers closed many of their factories. Others slashed their labor force. Federal contracts were canceled, and three thousand workers at federal navy yards lost their jobs. "Nothing will save us but a Tariff," Robert C. Winthrop, a Massachusetts Whig, moaned.[16] But the inaction of Congress prompted some people to begin blaming Congress for their predicament. A New York City resident overheard some workers who had lost their jobs in that city. "I have had reason to hear their complaints loudly made against the present congress as taking the bread out of their mouths and in some instances compelling American born citizens to send their children to the county poor house."[17] An editor in New York declared, "our languishing manufacturing establishments and the depressed state of every branch of industry, calls loudly upon Congress to lay aside, for a short season at least, their political broils and strife, and do something for their suffering country."[18] Whigs had calculated that the people would blame Tyler for their problems. But the people could blame the majority in Congress instead.

In early June, the House finally began to act as Fillmore offered two tariff bills. The first tariff, dubbed the "Great Tariff" or "Permanent Tariff," would include highly protective rates and distribution. This proposal sought to set rates at the level of the tariff of 1832, or around 35 percent. The protective rate was actually much higher because Fillmore had included numerous items in the free list to reduce the overall average. Under the "Great Tariff," duties would exceed 20 percent, and distribution would be continued. On June 9, Fillmore called up what became known as the "Little Tariff," or "Provisional Tariff," bill. Designed as a temporary measure, this bill sought to maintain tariff levels as they existed on June 1 and extend those rates until August 1. This measure also proposed to continue distribution. Thus, the "Provisional Tariff" would prevent the final cuts from the compromise tariff from taking effect. Caleb Cushing, a Massachusetts Whig representative who sympathized with Tyler, did not like this measure but regarded it as a necessity. He had agreed to support the "Provisional Tariff" based on a provision in the Compromise Tariff of 1833. This bill had said that after July 1, 1842, home valuation would take effect. However, Congress had never passed any subsequent legislation to say how home valuation would be enforced. With no defining statute, Cushing worried that no duties could be collected legally and therefore the country would become a free-trade nation on July 1. "There was," he insisted, "an imperative moral urgency to enact some tariff law. Without it, the treasury must be without money."[19]

Cushing was not the only one who feared what might happen on July 1. James W. McCulloch, formerly the plaintiff in the case of *McCulloch v. Maryland* and now the comptroller of the United States, sent instructions to American customs collectors. When foreign goods arrived, the collector would ascertain their value and then deduct one-sixth. Completing that task, the collector would assess the duty. Those who had longed for home valuation argued that they had been cheated, because under this method, foreign goods entered the United States with reduced, instead of increased, duties. McCulloch's instructions on home valuation alleviated the fears of many, however.[20]

With the home valuation issue resolved, the House turned to Fillmore's bills. The Ways and Means chairman announced that the government needed twenty-seven million dollars each year to pay its expenses and debt. If the country did not increase the tariff, then the only alternative would be direct taxes. Such a proposal was unpopular and very difficult to implement. Should Congress resort to direct taxes, it would result in an army of tax collectors who would owe their offices to the goodwill of the president. "They would be spread over the land, like the frogs of Egypt, until they would be found in every man's bedchamber," he asserted. Fillmore unveiled statistics from 1789 until 1840, which showed that the government had garnered almost 82 percent of its income from tariffs. Direct or excise taxes, Fillmore declared, would not work. Only a tariff could keep the government solvent. The bill before the House would raise enough revenue, and it would offer protection to American manufacturers.[21]

Fillmore's tariff contained specific duties that had to be paid in cash on arrival. Under the previous tariffs, foreigners could import their goods into the United States and pay the duties on credit, with full payment due three to six months later. This would no longer be allowed. Fillmore's proposal reinstated the minimum principle on raw wool. Democrats charged that Fillmore's tariff exceeded the 1828 tariff of abominations. Thomas Hart Benton moaned that it would take three months to digest this tariff. Congressmen now began to complain that they would be in session throughout the entire summer.[22]

The debate on the "Provisional Tariff" proved to be short. It hinged on distribution rather than the tariff. Western and southern Whigs would not swallow the tariff unless they got distribution. Northeastern Whigs did not want to lose the tariff over distribution, which divided about two million dollars between all the states each year. John Quincy Adams's wife, Louisa Catherine Adams, suspected a bargain between New England and the West. New England would get the protection that it sought, while the West would retain distribution. According to her, this strategy appeared to be the work of Clay. Thomas Gilmer, a Whig loyal to Tyler, proclaimed that if the Whigs wanted to aid the country, they only had to drop the distribution component. But he contended that the Whigs cared more about politics than aiding the country. The Whig policy, he predicted, "would place the country where it was at the end of revolutionary war, without means and in debt."[23] When Democrats lost on a motion to strike out the distribution clause by a vote of 102 to 113, everyone recognized that the House would approve the "Provisional Tariff."[24]

Indeed, on June 15, the House passed it by a vote of 116 to 104. The vote on this tariff confirmed that partisanship now trumped sectionalism. Only two Democrats voted for the "Little Tariff," while ninety-three voted against it. For the Whigs, 114 members supported the measure, and only eleven opposed it. Sixteen southern Whigs voted for this new tariff. The House now turned its attention to Fillmore's other tariff bill, the "Great Tariff."[25]

The Senate approved the "Little Tariff" by a vote of twenty-four to nineteen on an almost straight party-line vote. Six southern Whigs voted in favor. Winfield Scott observed the change in southern opinion on the tariff and notified Thaddeus Stevens that "many Southern Whigs are nearly up to the mark of a tariff for protection—*sufficient* protection."[26] Some Whigs now expected Tyler to sign the "Provisional Tariff." In a congratulatory statement, the *National Intelligencer* asserted, "Thus have the Whigs in Congress, acting up to their determination to do their whole duty, passed another necessary measure for carrying on the administration of the government."[27] When Robert Letcher heard a rumor that Tyler intended to veto the "Little Tariff," he wrote, "I rather think he wishes to render himself conspicuous by being hung. . . . I am inclined to say he is the damndest rascal and biggest fool of the age."[28] Meanwhile, an editor in Kentucky opined, "If Mr. Tyler choose, by vetoing revenue bills, to stop the wheels of Government, let him do it.

Table 14.1. House vote on the "Little" or "Provisional" tariff, 1842

	Democrats		Whigs		Total	
	For	Against	For	Against	For	Against
New England	1	9	26	0	27	9
Middle	0	34	40	0	40	34
South	0	35	20	12	20	47
West	1	13	28	1	29	14
Total	2	91	114	13	116	104

Source: *House Journal*, 27th Cong., 2nd Sess., 15 June 1842, 974–55.

Table 14.2. Senate vote on the "Little" or "Provisional" tariff, 1842

	Democrats		Whigs		Total	
	For	Against	For	Against	For	Against
New England	0	3	7	0	7	3
Middle	0	3	5	0	5	3
South	0	5	6	2	6	7
West	0	6	6	0	6	6
Total	0	17	24	2	24	19

Source: *Senate Journal*, 27th Cong., 2nd Sess., 24 June 1842, 428.

No Government at all would be about as good as a Government with him at the head of it."[29]

Tyler vetoed the "Little Tariff" because it violated the Compromise of 1833 and the Land Act of 1841. Moreover, he scolded Congress for uniting the tariff and the distribution of revenue from land sales. Whigs protested their president's decision. "Capt. Tyler in his recent and unnecessary and fool hardy veto has cut the last link that bound him to the Whigs, and has gone over soul and body to the Locos," Fillmore groaned.[30] Privately, Tyler complained that the Whig Party had broken from its moorings. It had reverted to the policies of Henry Clay and the old National Republican Party abandoning state's rights Whigs, such as himself. This became the first time that a president vetoed a tariff bill. It would not be the last.[31]

From Kentucky, Clay pressured the Whigs in Washington to pass the "Great Tariff" with distribution included. In his opinion, by using the veto, the president acted in the same manner as Andrew Jackson. If Congress blinked, then the legislative branch would surrender to the executive branch. Leading Whigs, dismayed at Clay's dictatorial style, warned that Tyler would surely veto the measure. The strategy of enticing vetoes could backfire, they warned.[32]

The Whigs' determination to maintain both the tariff and distribution began to fracture their party. "What shall we do?" John J. Crittenden nervously asked Clay. "Shall we pass the Tariff, giving up the lands, or adjourn, and let all got together? Write me immediately an answer to these questions."[33] Whigs reexamined the prospects before them. "A Tariff is indispensable—Distribution is not. The interests of the country may survive the loss of Distribution; but they cannot survive the defeat of the Tariff," a Whig paper proclaimed.[34] At a Whig meeting in Brooklyn, attendees resolved, "the Tariff is vastly paramount in importance to distribution, we shall not neglect the greater benefit."[35] Public opinion seemed to suggest that the Whigs should abandon distribution. John C. Calhoun enjoyed watching the Whigs' struggle with Tyler. "The Whig majority is in a sad state of distraction between defeats and vetoes," Calhoun observed. "The Western portion refuse to give up distribution for the Tariff, and the Northern the tariff for distribution."[36]

Deferring to Clay, Fillmore steered the "Great Tariff," or "Permanent Tariff," through the House after Tyler's veto of the "Little Tariff." The "Great Tariff" contained all the measures dear to protectionists—minimums, specific duties, cash duties, and distribution. Dozens of congressmen spoke on the subject. After one prolonged session, John Quincy Adams complained in his diary, "one drowsy orator succeeding to another, hour by hour, without intermission, and nobody listening to any one of them."[37] A few optimistic Whigs thought that Tyler would approve the bill, but most expected to receive another veto message. The House approved the "Great Tariff" by the close vote of 116 to 112. Only one Democrat, William Parmenter of Massachusetts, voted in favor of the new tariff. Fifteen Whigs voted against the bill. All but one of these hailed from the South, while the other came from Illinois. Thirty-three southern Whigs supported this protective tariff. "A tight fit, truly!" the *National Intelligencer* declared. "But then it must be remembered, that no tariff of duties can ever pass the House of Representatives except by a close vote. There are so many and such different reasons which influence men to vote against it, in many cases not so much with the intention of defeating the bill, as for the purpose of making their individual discontent at particular provisions of it, that the majority in its favor will always be diminutive in its proportion."[38]

In the Senate, the Whigs decided to remain silent and allow the Democrats to assail the bill. The key speeches against the tariff came from Levi Woodbury and John C. Calhoun. Both men warned that this bill would cause more harm to the country than the tariff of abominations. Calhoun also saw protectionism as an addiction. Once it began, its advocates craved only more. "Every protective tariff that Congress has ever laid, has disappointed the hopes of its advocates; and has been followed, at short intervals, by a demand for higher duties," Calhoun declared. "The cry has been protection: one bottle after another, and each succeeding one more capacious than the preceding."[39] The Senate approved the bill by a vote of twenty-five to twenty-three. No Democrat voted for the tariff. Three Whigs, William Graham of North Carolina, William C. Preston of South Carolina, and William C. Rives of Virginia, opposed it.

All eyes now turned to the executive mansion. "I would give almost my right hand if you could be persuaded to sign the bill," Secretary of State Daniel Web-

Table 14.3. House vote on the "Great" or "Permanent" tariff, 1842

	Democrats		Whigs		Total	
	For	Against	For	Against	For	Against
New England	1	8	27	0	28	8
Middle	0	35	43	0	43	35
South	0	39	17	17	17	56
West	0	13	28	0	28	13
Total	1	95	115	17	116	112

Source: *House Journal*, 27th Cong., 2nd Sess., 16 July 1842, 1107–9.

Table 14.4. Senate vote on the "Great" or "Permanent" tariff, 1842

	Democrats		Whigs		Total	
	For	Against	For	Against	For	Against
New England	0	4	8	0	8	4
Middle	0	3	7	0	7	3
South	0	7	4	3	4	10
West	0	6	6	0	6	6
Total	0	20	25	3	25	23

Source: *Senate Journal*, 27th Cong., 1st Sess., 5 Aug. 1842, 544.

ster pleaded to Tyler.[40] But the president remained unreceptive—the "Great Tariff" would be vetoed. Since it had been expected, most Whigs took the veto in stride. This latest veto cut any remaining links between the Whig Party and Tyler. When the news of his veto arrived in New York City, Democrats fired cannons in the president's honor. The Whigs had driven their adversary into the arms of their opponents. Would the Democrats accept him or refuse him?[41]

When the House received Tyler's latest veto message, John Quincy Adams asked that the veto be referred to a select committee. The Speaker agreed and appointed Adams as chairman. "Old Man Eloquent" subsequently issued a report excoriating Tyler's actions. The president, according to Adams, "thwarted the will of the people through his use of the veto. The power of the present Congress to enact laws essential to the welfare of the people has been struck with apoplexy by the Executive hand. Submission to his will, is the only condition upon which he will permit them to act." He proposed a constitutional amendment that lowered the threshold to override a presidential veto from a two-thirds majority to a simple majority. More importantly, Adams's report recommended that Tyler should be impeached for his transgressions against the people. By electing Whigs, the people had shown they wanted a new protective tariff, Adams suggested. At first, Whigs in the House liked the idea of impeachment. However, they distanced themselves from it, once they realized that the Senate probably lacked the necessary votes to convict Tyler. In fact, one editor speculated that only fifteen senators countenanced convicting the president.[42]

Whigs wondered what their next move should be. A large number of them wanted to go home and leave the Treasury empty. With the federal government unable to meet its obligations, many would be ruined. Blame would have to be assigned, and Whigs expected that the people would accuse Tyler and his new allies, the Democrats. Clay also endorsed this strategy. John Pendleton Kennedy, a Maryland Whig, warned that if the Whigs adjourned without enacting a new tariff, the Treasury would be empty in only fifteen days. "After that," he predicted, "the wheels will stop and the revolution, perhaps, begins to take an active shape."[43] Thurlow Weed, the politically savvy editor of the *Albany Evening Journal*, counseled against this strategy. Weed did not fear peasants with pitchforks like Kennedy, but rather fretted over the political consequences: "Depend upon it the people will not be satisfied to be deprived of a Tariff on account of the conflict of opinion between Congress and the President. But now, when Tyler adroitly offers to sign a Tariff, if you adjourn without putting him to the test, we are irretrievably lost."[44] Fillmore informed a group of Ohio residents: "We are at this moment trembling upon the verge of an awful precipice. Whether the president will permit the will of the people as expressed through their Representatives to become the law of the land and thereby restore at once the credit of the nation and the prosperity of the country, or whether, for the gratification of his own individual caprice, he will throw himself in the way of every effort to save the country and *veto* the *Revenue* Bill now before him, a few days will determine."[45]

If the Whigs left Washington without a tariff then Tyler would summon them back to a special session. Since the president had committed himself to signing a tariff without distribution, Whigs resolved to stay in Washington and pass a clean tariff bill. The western or "Distribution Whigs" would be sacrificed. The Whigs also decided to stay, because ten states had already held their elections. In eight of those states, the majority of Whig candidates lost. "I have never in my whole life known the people so savage towards Congress," one observer noted.[46] If the Whigs failed to enact anything of significance in the longest congressional session yet, then they would incur more defeats in the fall elections. "The astounding result of the late elections has warned these men that their power is going—that they must make haste or the people will overtake them before their labor of selfishness is done," the *Charleston Mercury* declared.[47]

Few days in the history of the House have been as riveting as August 22, 1842. "We do not remember ever to have witnessed, during the thirty-five years' attendance of the House of Representatives, a more exciting scene, a severer contest, a greater earnestness and self-devotion, than characterized the proceedings and votes of yesterday," the *National Intelligencer* asserted the next day.[48] Whigs needed to find a way out of their predicament, to be sure. Thomas McKennan of Pennsylvania seized on a solution. Through some parliamentary maneuvering, he brought the vetoed "Great Tariff" back to the floor, minus distribution, and with coffee and tea allowed to enter duty free. The House approved this motion by a close vote of 102 to 99. It next voted on the engrossment of this modified tariff bill. Charles Brown, a Pennsylvania Democrat, avowed that the bill was the "bitterest he had to swallow," but he voted yes because of the desperate situation of the country.[49] When the clerk had finished calling all the names of the House members, the vote stood tied at 101. All heads looked up to Speaker John White, a Kentucky Whig and supporter of Clay. The Speaker voted against McKennan's bill because distribution had been stripped. Richard Thompson of Indiana moved to reconsider the vote. The House approved this motion by the vote of 106 to 98. The House once again voted on the engrossment of the bill. Now the vote stood at 103 for engrossment to 102. Again, all eyes turned to the Speaker, and again, White voted no, producing a tie and thus defeating the bill. Suddenly, Edward Stanly of North Carolina and Landaff Andrews of Kentucky rushed to the Speaker's desk and demanded that their votes be counted since they had missed the previous vote. White agreed, and these so-called "Distribution Whigs" both voted in the affirmative. When Stanly walked away from the rostrum, he shouted, "God damn Tyler!"[50] The House then passed the tariff, minus distribution, by a narrow vote of 105 to 103. Twenty Democrats voted for this tariff, while thirty-five Whigs opposed it. The *Washington Globe* summarized the day's proceedings: "the big tariff was squeezed through today, under the severest screwing we have ever witnessed."[51]

Former president Martin Van Buren believed that the Whigs had offered this clean tariff bill with the expectation that it would be defeated by the votes of Democrats. After all, Van Buren knew a thing or two about playing tricks with a tariff. But just enough House Democrats had voted for the measure. However, Democrats could still reject it in the Senate. This would, in turn, give the Whigs a potent issue to use in the states that had not conducted their elections yet. The positions of Democrats James Buchanan and Silas Wright became the topic of widespread speculation. When each of these men rose to speak in the Senate, observers in the gallery whispered, "Well, his course decides the question."[52]

Buchanan went first, but both men made the same argument: the situation of the nation's finances demanded a new tariff. With so little time remaining before adjournment, the tariff represented the only hope for the country. "If you pass no bill, you will ruin a very large portion of all the mechanics and artisans throughout the country," Buchanan declared. "These are not to be counted by hundreds or by thousands, but by hundreds of thousands." He warned that some of the best lawyers in the land believed that the recent order of the Treasury Department was unconstitutional. He predicted that if Congress did not approve a new tariff, the Treasury Circular of McCulloch, outlining how home valuation worked, would be struck down and, thus, there would be no tariff at all in the United States.[53]

Wright followed Buchanan. Regarded by many as Van Buren's agent in Washington, he admitted that he disliked the bill before the Senate but announced that he had to vote in the affirmative to save the nation's finances. With distribution removed, this bill had become acceptable to Wright. While the friends of protection breathed a sigh of relief as he spoke, southerners cried treachery. "We are betrayed," one roared. Another grumbled, "I suspected as much from his vote in 1828." Cal-

Table 14.5. House vote on the final tariff with distribution, 1842

	Democrats		Whigs		Total	
	For	Against	For	Against	For	Against
New England	1	6	25	1	26	7
Middle	19	10	35	3	54	13
South	0	35	7	21	7	56
West	0	17	18	10	18	27
Total	20	68	85	35	105	103

Source: *House Journal*, 22nd Cong., 2nd Sess., 22 Aug. 1842, 1385–87.

Table 14.6. Senate vote on the final tariff with distribution, 1842

	Democrats		Whigs		Total	
	For	Against	For	Against	For	Against
New England	1	2	8	0	9	2
Middle	3	0	4	2	7	2
South	0	7	2	7	2	14
West	0	5	6	0	6	5
Total	4	14	20	9	24	23

Source: *Senate Journal*, 22nd Cong., 2nd Sess., 27 Aug. 1842, 629.

houn and his allies could not contain their excitement. Although they disapproved of Wright's vote, which allowed the tariff to pass the Senate, they reasoned that it would reflect poorly on Van Buren in the South and therefore hinder his chances for winning the nomination of the Democratic Party in 1844.[54]

The tariff without distribution passed the Senate by a vote of twenty-four to twenty-three. Nine Whigs voted against the bill. Most of these negative votes came from disgruntled members who wanted to preserve distribution. Switches by northern Democrats offset the high number of Whig defections. Four northern Democrats supported the bill. Some suspected that these Democrats approved the tariff, because they viewed it as only a temporary measure. "It is a horrible bill," Wright confessed before he endorsed it. "But as we ought to pass some bill and this one will kill distribution I think I shall vote for it, and shall do it knowing that it will make a great and produce great dissatisfaction both in the City of New York and at the South."[55] Wright was not mistaken. Southern Democrats charged that their northern brethren had betrayed them. "The idea is, that we had fought the battle—gained the victory and then in the very moment of triumph—we were delivered over into the hands of our enemies," Tennessee congressman Aaron V.

Brown complained.[56] Tyler signed the tariff of 1842. In the final hours of the session, Whigs passed a separate distribution bill, but the president pocket vetoed the measure and forwarded a veto message at the beginning of the next session.[57]

Presumably the Senate vote had more to do with the upcoming presidential election than with improving the American economy. Democrats were convinced that Whigs in both the House and the Senate voted against the tariff in order to force their opponents to save it, thus damaging Van Buren's presidential prospects. "This move on the political chess board must seriously affect Mr. Van Buren," Tennessee's William M. Gwin predicted. "The inevitable result must be to make Mr. Calhoun the Democratic candidate for the presidency."[58]

Democrats vowed that the tariff of 1842 would be repealed. New York Democrats James Roosevelt and Richard Davis promised that in the next Congress, their party would undo what the Whigs had done. Repeal became the watchword for Democrats throughout the country. One of the first public meetings in opposition to the new tariff occurred that fall in Buckingham County, Virginia. This group of Virginia citizens resolved that "the present tariff ought to be so altered that protection should be disregarded, and that not one cent should be collected further than is necessary for revenue."[59]

The tariff of 1842 represented a victory for protectionists. The new tariff set average rates at below 30 percent. However, this was deceiving. The average rate stood at such a low level, because Fillmore included more items on the free list. He actually increased protection on iron, woolens, cotton bagging, hemp, glass, flax, wood, books, and liquor. This tariff stipulated that all duties were to be paid in cash. Thus, if foreigners or their consignment agents failed to make a payment after sixty days, their goods would be sold at a public auction, and they would receive none of the proceeds. Opponents of the tariff of 1842 maintained that cash duties added another 10 percent to the value. Section 28 banned "indecent and obscene prints" so there was even a moral component to the new tariff. The only blemish for the Whigs with the tariff of 1842 was that they had surrendered home valuation.[60]

The Whigs proclaimed the tariff as the perfect tonic for all the country's ills. In the fall, American manufacturers reopened their doors and hired new laborers. But Whigs were playing the part of a false prophet. The years of 1842 and 1843 became the toughest in the financial panic that had started in 1837. Since many Democrats inside and outside of Congress had pledged that the tariff of 1842 would be repealed, few foreigners sent their goods to the United States after the new tariff went into effect. In 1843, the Treasury Department collected only seven million dollars in customs. "Now that the tariff bill is condemned, and has but an existence whose days are numbered," *Niles' National Register* announced. "The importation already so restricted is about naturally to experience a new arrest. Manufacturing Europe, which had but half opened its ports to the last tariff, is going to shut them entirely, and await the new era which is about to dawn."[61] Things began to improve in 1844, however. This prompted Tyler to report to Congress:

> The credit of the country, which had experienced a temporary embarrassment, has been thoroughly restored. Its coffers, which for a season were empty, have

been replenished. A currency nearly uniform in its value has taken the place of one depreciated and almost worthless. Commerce and manufactures, which had suffered in common with every interest, have once more revived, and the whole country exhibits an aspect of prosperity and happiness. Trade and barter, no longer governed by a wild and speculative mania, rest upon a solid and substantial footing, and the rapid growth of our cities in every direction bespeaks most strongly the favorable circumstances by which we are surrounded.[62]

Whigs believed that this favorable balance of trade kept specie in the country. When British merchants wanted to purchase American goods, they preferred to exchange broadcloths or calicoes for them. However, with the 1842 tariff in effect, British merchants now had to pay for American goods with specie. Of all the antebellum tariffs, only under the tariff of 1842 did the United States have a favorable balance of trade.[63]

Although the economy revived under the 1842 tariff, the battle over it hurt the Whig Party. Van Buren correctly believed that the Whigs had blundered over the tariff. In 1842, the Whigs controlled 139 House seats compared to the Democrats' 102. In the Senate, they had a seven-seat advantage. Defeats in congressional elections in 1842 and 1843 and redistricting as a result of the census of 1840 changed the makeup of Congress. Voters blamed the Whigs, not the Democrats, for the country's problems. In the next Congress, Democrats held 142 seats and the Whigs counted only 79. Democrats now had an almost two-to-one majority. Clay took the events in good stride and put his faith in the people: "I do believe that the people are greatly ahead of their representatives at Washington, in sustaining Protection."[64]

Clay's onetime friend and now rival, Calhoun, emerged from the tariff debate in a strong position. His speech against the "Permanent Tariff" received praise throughout the union. Significantly, both the *Washington Globe* and the *Nashville Union* endorsed Calhoun's speech. Calhoun had reason to believe that the presidency might be his in 1844. Either way, the battle over the tariff of 1842 had complicated the political calculus and paved the way for an intriguing presidential election. Unbeknownst to the American people, however, the next election would not hinge on an economic issue.[65]

15

"If you elect us, boys, the Tariff of 1842 is safe"

THE TARIFF OF 1842, DENOUNCED by northern Democrats and dubbed by some southerners as the "Black Tariff," helped to spark an economic turnaround in the United States. Manufacturers began hiring, and specie stayed in the country. Whigs trumpeted this new tariff as the reason why the country finally escaped the panic of 1837. The economic success attributed to the new tariff allowed more and more southern Whigs to endorse a protective tariff, because the improved economy provided them with necessary political cover. Robert Toombs, a Georgia Whig at this time, observed that on the tariff more unity existed among the Whigs than the Democrats. Toombs noted that he looked forward to taking to the stump to defend the 1842 tariff against the Democrats who had kept up a constant cry to repeal the new tariff.[1]

True to their word, Democrats decided to try to rescind the new tariff in 1844. This appeared to be an easy task because the Democrats had a sixty-three-seat advantage in the House. With such a large majority, James I. McKay, a North Carolina Democrat and chairman of the Ways and Means Committee, produced a bill that lowered the tariff of 1842 to the compromise levels of 1833. It contained specific duties on iron and coal but also sought to bring back duties based on the overall value of good on most other items. The retention of specific duties on iron and coal symbolized an olive branch to Pennsylvania Democrats. McKay, however, conducted a rather lackluster campaign on behalf of his bill. In fact, he left the capital for ten days to visit his wife in North Carolina. This prompted Cave Johnson to note that McKay lacked "energy." Perhaps more worrisome to southern Democrats were their New York colleagues. The New York delegation that remained loyal to Martin Van Buren wanted to avoid touching the tariff at this time. A downward revision of the tariff by Van Buren's friends in the House would be interpreted by other northern Democrats as a sign that Van Buren still could not be trusted on the tariff. A tariff that the South craved would resurrect the charges that Van Buren was a northern man with southern principles. Yet, in spite of McKay's failings and the hesitation of the New Yorkers, Johnson still predicted that the new tariff would pass the House by twenty votes simply because of the Democrats' large majority.[2]

In 1844, only a handful of Whigs engaged the tariff. The few who defended it attributed the recent upswing in the economy to the 1842 tariff. Abraham McIlvaine of Pennsylvania claimed that under the tariff of 1828, the coffers of the federal government had been full. However, after the cuts brought on by the 1833 compromise tariff, the coffers had become nearly empty. A protective tariff, such as the tariff of 1842, however, had restored funds and brought back confidence and prosperity throughout the country. Other Whigs charged that the 1842 tariff had not been in effect long enough to judge its merits. Give the new tariff a fair chance, they argued. Some other Whigs reiterated an old warning about how a reduction in rates would ruin American manufacturers.[3]

Southern Democrats once again attacked the concept of a protective tariff as unconstitutional. In addition to this line of attack, Robert Rhett and John Slidell championed familiar free-trade doctrines. Free trade would break up the monopolies of northern manufacturers, Rhett alleged. These men believed that a tariff brought to the revenue standard of 20 percent would be adequate for American manufacturers. Rhett assailed the tariff of 1842 but perhaps did more harm than good for the free-trade cause, since most members of Congress and many northerners viewed Rhett as Calhoun's spokesman and associated him with nullification. For the northern Democrats, approval of McKay's tariff signaled submission to the nullifiers in South Carolina.[4]

The high-water mark of the 1844 debate took place on April 23. Democrat George Rathbun of New York began discussing the politics of Henry Clay. He reintroduced the charge of "bargain and corruption" and equated Clay with Caesar, Caligula, and Oliver Cromwell. John White, a Kentucky Whig and former Speaker of the House, understandably took offense to these charges and suggested that Rathbun had lied. When Rathbun asked his colleague if he meant his accusation, White responded, "I do, God damn you!" The two men squared off and threw punches at one another. The sergeant-at-arms brought the mace to the floor of the House in a vain effort to restore order. As congressional members tried to break up the melee, William S. Moore of Kentucky fired his pistol and wounded John L. Wirt, a capitol officer, in the leg. This unexpected brush with possible death brought the combatants to their senses. Rathbun and White shook hands and professed their fidelity for each other. No one could deny that the tariff still inflamed passions unlike any other issue.[5]

The Rathbun-White incident aside, the debate surrounding the proposed tariff of 1844 lacked the passion of the previous debates. Alexander Stephens, a Georgia Whig, called the pending tariff a "humbug."[6] Whigs and northern Democrats joined together to table McKay's bill by a vote of 105 to 99. Twenty-five Democrats voted to table the bill, fifteen of whom represented districts in New York and Pennsylvania. Rhett, who had been sleeping on a sofa before the vote, roared that this latest action once again revealed the treachery of northern Democrats. Rhett and his like-minded South Carolinians discussed severing all ties with northern Democrats.[7]

In the Senate, George McDuffie of South Carolina tried to restore the tariff to the Compromise of 1833, but he received little assistance. Indeed, McDuffie complained that former nullifiers, such as Willie P. Mangum and John M. Berrien, who had become Whigs, supported the 1842 tariff. "I regard the policy as fixed in this Country, and whatever party may come into power, I think, the change or modi-

Table 15.1. House vote to postpone the tariff, 1844

	Democrats		Whigs		Total	
	For	Against	For	Against	For	Against
New England	5	10	15	0	20	10
Middle	23	12	29	0	52	12
South	0	43	15	1	15	44
West	1	33	17	0	18	33
Total	29	98	76	1	105	99

Source: *House Journal*, 28th Cong., 1st Sess., 10 May 1844, 895–96.
Note: "For" vote indicates support for a high tariff.

fication will be but slight," Mangum complained.[8] On a test vote taken just before the adjournment, McDuffie realized that protectionists outnumbered him by seven votes. Consequently, no reduction would be forthcoming from the Senate.[9]

Whigs, however, charged that the action of the Democrats proved that the tariff of 1842 was an effective piece of legislation. Henry Clay assured his supporters in central Pennsylvania, "This decision was an involuntary concession of our political opponents to the *wisdom and beneficence of whig policy*, produced by the returning prosperity, and the enlightened opinion of the people."[10] A Whig sheet echoed Clay's point when it asked, "Could there be a stronger affirmation of the wisdom of that great measure of Whig policy?"[11] The *Richmond Whig* boasted, "Now can we confidently say that the Tariff of 1842 will not be changed for years to come, and that it is the permanent, fixed and immutable policy of the Government. People may now go to work in confidence that enterprise will not be crippled by the actions of government, and bankruptcy caused by its unstable legislation."[12] For Clay and these Whig editors, Congress had finally given the people what they wanted—stability. But how long would the peace endure? William A. Graham of North Carolina, a Whig who voted against the 1842 tariff in its final form because it ended distribution, expected the upcoming presidential election to turn on the tariff. At Fayetteville, he took to the stump and avowed that he "felt sure that the people were about to settle this, as all other great questions, right, on a basis of protection to the Industry of the Country."[13]

After failing to reduce the tariff, Democrats turned their attention to selecting a nominee for the presidency. Former president Martin Van Buren wanted another chance at the presidency. When the Indiana legislature asked him for his opinion on the leading issues, he responded. The ex-president composed a fifty-four-page draft, which Silas Wright edited to a thirteen-page printed response. Van Buren professed that he favored a tariff for revenue purposes. He also admitted that he supported some protective duties, so long as they did not become "oppressive."[14] From the Hermitage, Andrew Jackson praised Van Buren's response. "Yours will stand the test, and be the text book of old school democrats," Jackson predicted.[15] Van Buren received numerous letters asking for a further explanation of his opinion, since many saw his letter as another dodge by the "Little Magician." The nullifiers especially groused over Van Buren's newest exposition. They talked about his duplicity over the tariff of 1828 and insisted that Silas Wright's vote in 1842 signaled that Van Buren still favored a protective tariff. But nothing stuck to the Little Magician. By the spring of 1844, seventeen states had held conventions to recommend nominees for the presidency. In twelve of them, Democrats endorsed Van Buren, while the other five states remained uncommitted. The party nomination appeared to be his to lose. "I have no doubt you will be the nominee," Jackson assured him in the fall of 1843.[16]

The other contenders for the Democratic Party's nomination included James Buchanan, John C. Calhoun, Lewis Cass, and Richard M. Johnson. Of the four, Cass and Calhoun posed the most serious challenge to Van Buren, since Buchanan and Johnson were simply favorite sons whose support would evaporate after the first ballot in a convention. Buchanan said that he had a better chance of being elected Pope than Johnson had of being the nominee of the Democratic Party. Whigs, however, respected Buchanan. "The plain truth is," Robert Letcher observed, "Buchanan is the cleverest man of all his party, and has the best capacity, Van Buren not excepted."[17]

Cass had been governor of the Michigan Territory, secretary of war, and minister to France. His executive and diplomatic positions meant that he had never taken a public position on the issues of the day. This caused some Democrats to wonder if Cass even belonged to their party. He opposed the national bank but supported state banks and paper money. Cass had been appointed to the French mission under Van Buren, but he had retained that post under Harrison. To counter these hesitations, Cass issued a series of public letters. In these letters, he presented himself as a Democrat in the Jeffersonian mold. Concerning the tariff, Cass announced that he favored one that offered "incidental protection" to American industries, along with a "judicious tariff."[18] Van Buren and his followers, however, viewed Cass as an opportunist who would trim his sails and say whatever it took to win the nomination.

Calhoun had hoped that 1844 would finally be his time. By the end of 1843, however, Calhoun realized that his chances for winning the nomination were thin. He bowed out of the race citing northern Democrats' adherence to the protective tariff as one of his reasons. Calhoun and his partisans now embraced Cass. The Michigander became acceptable, because he offered them an alternative to the treacherous Van Buren. "Our people will go for him as the 'Yankee Girl' did for her Beau who was rather annoying, Married him to get rid of him," one Calhounite declared.[19] Furthermore, if Cass won the nomination, it would break the alliance between New York and Virginia. Calhoun and his friends favored this, because a rupture between the Empire State and the Old Dominion would force Virginians to realize that their interests coincided with those of the South and not New York. Calhoun also believed that Van Buren would sacrifice his southern friends in order to win votes from the abolitionists and the "Tariffites." For Calhoun, this potential alliance of protectionists and abolitionists would be a grave threat to the South and its institutions.[20]

While Democrats tried to find common ground on the tariff, the annexation of Texas became the primary issue in American politics. Texas annexation and subsequent statehood almost certainly meant war with Mexico. Politically, Texas statehood meant at least one slaveholding and antitariff vote in the House and two more in the Senate but could mean many more. Since the tariff of 1842 had passed under the closest of margins, extra votes opposed to the tariff would make its repeal more likely. Joshua Giddings, an outspoken antislavery Whig from Ohio, warned Democrats in the West that Texas annexation would mean a repeal of the tariff of 1842. "Are the liberty loving democrats of Pennsylvania ready to give up our tariff—to strike off all protection from the articles of iron, and coal, and other productions of that State, in order to purchase a slave market for their neighbors?" Giddings pondered.[21]

In April 1844, Van Buren blundered when he announced his opposition to Texas annexation. On the same day, Clay, the presumptive Whig nominee, informed the public of his opposition to annexation as well. Southern Democrats hurriedly abandoned Van Buren, prompting northern Democrats to cry betrayal. The latter had made sacrifices on the tariff and the gag rule in Congress, only to have their southern brethren drop Van Buren when they disagreed with one of his decisions. Clay's letter did not immediately threaten his grip on his party's nomination, but it would hurt him in the general election. With both of the presidential frontrunners opposed to the annexation of Texas, proannexationists had no candidate espousing their position. Suddenly, Texas annexation had consumed all other topics in the political discourse. Buchanan, an annexation supporter, announced that he would stand for the nomination because "the Texas question has absorbed the Anti-Tariff feeling" in the South.[22] The Texas issue had made Van Buren vulnerable.[23]

Yet, in spite of this self-inflicted wound, Van Buren still hoped to secure the nomination. When the convention opened on May 27, the Democrats decided to maintain their traditional two-thirds rule. Van Buren's friends recognized that they likely would not be able to secure enough delegates to obtain the nomination. On the opening ballots Van Buren polled a majority but fell short of the two-thirds requirement. Over the next few ballots, his strength waned as Lewis Cass picked up Democrats who had abandoned the former president. After seven ballots, the convention recessed for the evening. It appeared as if Cass would win the nomination the next day.[24]

Throughout the evening, managers for Cass and Van Buren talked with the delegates at hotels and saloons in Baltimore. James K. Polk's friends also began meeting with delegates; the time had arrived to spring their plan. Gideon J. Pillow, a shrewd Tennessee political operative, had been urging delegates to commit to Polk as an excellent choice for vice president. However, with the convention about to nominate Cass, Pillow reversed this plan and argued that the former House Speaker should be brought forward as the presidential nominee. This appealed to the New York delegates, because it offered them an alternative to Cass. On the eighth ballot, New Hampshire gave its votes to Polk. Massachusetts, Tennessee, Alabama, and Louisiana joined New Hampshire, along with a scattering of delegates from other states. This remarkable shift created a stampede to Polk. On the next ballot, he won the unanimous nomination of the Democratic Party. After Silas Wright declined to be Polk's running mate, the convention selected George M. Dallas of Pennsylvania. Telegraph wires carried the news from Baltimore to Washington, and Democrats rejoiced. Whigs charged that their opponents had erred by nominating Polk. They suggested that he lacked the qualifications to be president by asking, "Who is James K. Polk?" The Whigs could hardly contain their euphoria when they learned of the opposing ticket. "I take it that no nomination more favorable to Mr. Clay could have been made, than that of Polk," Edward Everett laughed.[25] Willie P. Mangum bragged, "We will literally crush the ticket."[26]

While campaigning for the governorship of Tennessee in 1843, Whigs had charged Polk with being a supporter of a high protective tariff. Andrew Jackson informed an old friend that Polk "has always been in favor of a tariff for revenue to meet the wants of the government and economically administered, giving to our own country such incidental protection as that may afford."[27] During the 1843 gubernatorial campaign against James Jones, Polk wrote a public letter and said, "I am opposed to the tariff act of the late Congress" and "I am in favor of repealing that act, and restoring the compromise tariff act."[28] This statement could damage Polk's chances in the North. Robert J. Walker penned a note to the nominee the day after Polk won the nomination. "I write to you in haste to say that there is but one question which can by any possibility defeat your election," he wrote. "It is the tariff. We must have the vote of Pennsylvania in order to succeed." Moreover, the Mississippi senator advised Polk to advocate a tariff that would supply the necessary requirements of the government and one that would "embrace all the great interests of the whole union." According to Walker, if Polk followed his advice and adopted Van Buren's doctrine on the tariff, he would ensure the vote of Pennsylvania and guarantee a victory for the Democratic Party.[29] The next day, Andrew Jackson's nephew, Andrew Jackson Donelson, warned Polk that the tariff would be used against him in Pennsylvania. Therefore, Donelson counseled that before he issued any public statement on the tariff, he should "deliberate carefully." The best advice that he could offer Polk was to look over Jackson's messages to see the ground that the Old Hero occupied and the language that he employed on the tariff.[30]

Meanwhile, John J. Hardin, an Illinois Whig representative, penned a letter to James Irvin, a Whig representative from Pennsylvania, which was published in the *National Intelligencer*. Hardin informed Irvin that both Democrats and Whigs alike had been asking the same question: "What are his [Polk's] opinions on the Tariff?" Hardin noted that Polk, always an opponent of a protective tariff, favored a "horizontal" tariff of 20 percent. This had been the type of tariff that the nullifiers in South Carolina championed. Hardin pointed to statements that Polk had made while campaigning for the governorship of Tennessee in 1841 and 1843 against Jones. The best evidence of Polk's hostility to the protective system could be seen by the actions of the South Carolina delegates to the Baltimore convention, Hardin suggested. Although Francis W. Pickens and Franklin Elmore, whom Hardin dubbed the "ministers plenipotentiary from South Carolina to Baltimore," attended the convention, they refused to participate. Acting merely as observers, they applauded Polk's nomination and pledged that they would work on behalf of the Democratic Party's candidate. "And it now only remains to be seen whether that large portion of the Democratic Party who believe in the policy and propriety of bestowing fair protection upon American industry, will consent to *be handed over* without notice or consultation to the support of a free-trade-horizontal-tariff advocate," Hardin concluded.[31]

More than anyone else, Pennsylvanians wanted to know where Polk stood on the tariff. Across the state, editors and orators praised the 1842 tariff. Whig leaders always made sure to call it the "Whig Tariff of 1842," while protectionist Democrats reminded Pennsylvanians about Buchanan's efforts on behalf of that tariff. "There is but one question, on which in some parts of our state that we are vulnerable," John K. Kane notified Polk, referring to the tariff. He urged Polk to issue a statement in the "language of Gen. Jackson" to aid the chances of the Democrats in the Keystone State.[32] Other Democrats in the state quickly took to the stump and announced that Polk favored a "*judicious tariff.*" They pledged to adhere to this line of argument, unless their presidential nominee issued a statement contradicting it.[33]

Polk could not hide from the tariff, for he needed Pennsylvania's votes. "Young Hickory," as many now called him, sent a letter to Kane in Philadelphia. The Kane letter assured Pennsylvania Democrats that their nominee could be trusted on the tariff. It reminded many readers of Jackson's Coleman letter of 1824. In fact, after he read Polk's letter, J. George Harris, editor of the *Nashville Union*, assured Donelson that the letter "was of the old Jackson stamp." "I am in favor of a tariff for revenue," Polk explained, "such a one as will yield a sufficient amount to the Treasury to defray the expenses of the Government economically administered." By a revenue tariff, Polk meant one that allowed for "moderate discriminating duties as would produce the amount of revenue needed, and at the same time afford "reasonable incidental protection to our home industry." Polk then added, "I am opposed to a tariff for protection *merely*, and not for revenue." The Tennessean next stated that he voted against the tariff of 1828 and for the tariffs of 1832 and 1833 while a member of the House. Polk never mentioned the tariff of 1842 anywhere in his letter. Pennsylvanians interpreted Polk's endorsement of a tariff that afforded "reasonable incidental protection" to mean that the tariff of 1842 would be safe under a Polk administration. Newspapers across Pennsylvania published the Kane letter. Pennsylvania Democrats boasted that they would carry their state by over twenty thousand votes in the fall since their candidate appeared to favor the tariff of 1842.[34]

After Polk mailed the letter to Kane, he and Pillow began to have second thoughts about its content. "There is in fact no necessity for its publication," Pillow hastily wrote to Kane and Henry Horn almost two weeks after the letter had been mailed.[35] But by the time Pillow's letter reached Pennsylvania, Polk's tariff letter had gone to the presses and had begun to accomplish its goal. In fact, Wilson McCandless, an influential Democrat from Pittsburgh, informed Polk that "it has satisfied our mechanics and operators that you are as good a Tariff man as Clay."[36] However, the Kane letter left many Pennsylvanians pondering Polk's position on the tariff. They asked Polk for a further and more refined clarification, yet he balked and decided to stand by his original statement. "For heaven's sake let our friend the colonel write nothing more on the subject of the Tariff," Buchanan cried. "His letter to Kane was discreet and we can get along with it very well."[37]

Whigs in Pennsylvania cried foul when they read the Kane letter. This letter seemed to be little more than an outright lie, according to them. "We find our opponents putting up a candidate for president who has fought protection from the start, voted against it on every occasion that he had a chance to, and travelled all over Tennessee last summer opposing and decrying the present tariff," Horace Greeley announced.[38] Whigs urged voters to look at the statements of southern editors praising Polk's adherence to free trade. But for the Democrats in the Keystone State, Polk's letter became a perfect tonic. They produced banners attesting to his support of the tariff of 1842. Democrats such as Buchanan, McCandless, Richard Brodhead, Pottsville Hughes, and Samuel W. Black crisscrossed the state avowing that "Polk was as much a Tariff man as Clay." One banner announced, "Polk and Dallas—a High Tariff and Protection." A more popular banner was, "Polk, Dallas, and the Tariff of 1842." When a crowd of Philadelphians marched in front of George M. Dallas's home, the vice presidential nominee opened his door and predicted, "If you elect us, boys, the Tariff of 1842 is safe."[39]

The most egregious stretching of the truth came from the pen of a Pennsylvanian who called himself "A Columbia County Man." This unidentified writer published a short pamphlet entitled *Clay and Polk: The Difference between Them on the Tariff Question*. The title of this pamphlet was misleading since the author insisted that the two men occupied the same ground on the tariff. Clay's position as Speaker had prevented him from voting on the tariffs of 1816 and 1824, so Clay and Polk could not be compared on these tariffs. Polk voted against the tariff of abominations in 1828, the writer noted, but Clay "often declared his strong disapprobation of that tariff and of the manner in which it was passed." Both men voted for the tariff of 1832, and both men approved the Compromise Tariff of 1833. "They voted alike on all the tariff acts which were passed while they were in Congress," the writer declared. Neither man voted on the tariff of 1842, therefore, they could not be compared. "You cannot but agree with me that *on one subject at least, Mr. Clay and Mr. Polk think alike, and that subject is the tariff*," the "Columbia County Man" declared, while more than likely smiling at this grand prevarication.[40] "With an audacity unparalleled," Nathan Sargent, a Mississippi Whig, cried, the Democrats "claim Mr. Polk as the friend of protection, and denounce Mr. Clay as opposed to it!"[41] One Whig pamphlet put the matter succinctly: "Mr. Polk has never cast a vote or delivered a speech in favor of the protective policy. He is a free trade man."[42] Over the course of the campaign Whigs worried that they would lose Pennsylvania as a result of the Democrats' falsehoods.[43]

Whigs outside of Pennsylvania also defended the tariff of 1842. Willis Green, a Kentucky Whig who had voted for it, argued that the tariff belonged to the people and not politicians. "It is emphatically their measure, for it is the bread and sustenance of life to the toiling millions," he assured his audience. The tariff of 1842 had restored prosperity to the country, according to Green. He pointed to customs figures from New York to make his point. Since the tariff of 1842 went into operation, seven million dollars' worth of extra revenue had flowed into New York customhouses. Other ports would also show an increase in revenue under the new tariff, he suggested. If Polk became president, then the tariff of 1842 would be repealed. This would hurt not only American manufacturers but also laborers. "Let no friend to protection listen to their honeyed words—they are false and hypocritical; and above all, let none rely on their [Democrats'] assertions, however boldly made, that James K. Polk is in favor of protection," Green concluded.[44]

While the Kane letter convinced Pennsylvania Democrats that Polk could be trusted on the tariff, it weakened him in some areas of the South. Younger southerners worried about Polk's stance on the tariff. The price of cotton had once again begun to decline, forcing planters to sell land and slaves. Furthermore, diminishing returns on cotton meant that southern planters had to use more cotton to purchase manufactured goods, a strategy that pushed many into debt. The younger South Carolinians, like their fathers before them, blamed the tariff. They demanded action, but older leaders restrained them. This later generation of Palmetto State residents realized that they had sacrificed their personal and economic advancement to the political ambitions of Calhoun for too long. At Bluffton, Robert Rhett decided to act and increased the stakes. He wowed his audience of several hundred with the old idea of nullification. His listeners began raising their glasses and giving toasts, which called for an end to the federal union. They promoted a call for a convention to secede, much like they had in the summer of 1832. "The convention of 1776 formed our glorious Union," one South Carolinian proclaimed. "The Convention of 1845 would, if it could, lay in ruins the glorious temple of Union and Liberty, bequeathed to us by our patriot fathers."[45]

Calhoun had nothing to do with what came to be called the Bluffton Movement, because it represented a challenge to his control of the state. Rhett viewed Calhoun as too conservative and therefore wanted to end his dominance. Calhoun worried that Rhett's actions might jeopardize Polk's election. If Clay won the presidency, Calhoun reasoned, Texas would not be annexed. Surprisingly, Calhoun, who had fought against the tariff since 1828, viewed the annexation of Texas as more important than the reduction of the tariff. Calhoun also saw in the Bluffton Movement a threat to his plan to extricate Virginia from the intrigues of New York. If Calhoun could separate the Old Dominion from the Empire State, then perhaps Virginia would take the lead in a southern, free-trade, limited government movement. Calhoun prevailed on the Bluffton organizers to curtail their activities, and this allowed him to retain his grip on Palmetto State politics. Political leaders outside of South Carolina viewed the Bluffton Movement as yet another example of the state's residents using the threat of disunion to extract concessions from the rest of the union. "As if the danger to law, order, and regular government are not enough, the S. Carolinians are stepping forward and proclaiming in advance, that unless the presidential election terminates according to their wishes the Union must be dissolved," David Campbell groused.[46]

Tennessee Democrats invited fellow partisans from across the nation to attend a meeting in Nashville. The attendees discussed the Texas and tariff issues. Those Democrats unable to attend wrote letters to the committee chairmen affirming their support for tariff reduction. Francis W. Pickens, one of Calhoun's lieutenants, missed the Nashville meeting but met with Polk's advisors after it had concluded. He notified Calhoun, "Polk is entirely untrammeled and is determined if elected to do all he can to reform the Government and the 1st thing is to reduce the Tariff of 1842 to a revenue measure entirely and upon the principles of the compromise act."[47] Nullifiers, such as Pickens, kept their jubilation to themselves. If northern Democrats had observed who supported Polk in the South, they might have had reservations going into the fall election.[48]

Clay, as in his 1824 presidential campaign, had nowhere to go on the issue since almost everyone knew of his support for American manufacturers. Rather than avoid the issue, Clay declared his support for a protective tariff in speeches he made in the South. His friends, however, sought to remind audiences of Clay's authorship of the compromise tariff. "If ever there was a measure that originated in the most anxious desire to do that which, under all circumstances, was best for the country, and if a public man ever acted upon pure and disinterested motives, this was the measure and this was the man," one Clay campaign biography boasted.[49] Clay supporters charged over and over again that Polk supported free-trade ideals and speculated that if he became president, Calhoun would become the master spirit of his administration. Clay's position on the tariff and his opposition to the annexation of Texas hurt him grievously in the South. Since Polk emerged as an ardent champion of Texas annexation, this gave him maneuvering room on the tariff, since he had little to worry about in the Deep South. Southerners would stay with him, because he had unequivocally endorsed the annexation of Texas. Clay did not have that luxury.[50]

Unlike Polk, Clay wrote multiple letters on the tariff. He lauded the 1842 tariff at seemingly every opportunity. "I am of opinion that the operation of the tariff of 1842 has been eminently salutary; that I am decidedly opposed to its repeal; that I should regard its repeal as a great National calamity; and that I am unaware of the necessity of any modification of it," he wrote.[51] Clay believed that the fate of the protective policy hinged on Pennsylvania. "If the Key stone of the Federal Arch should give way," he lamented, "the whole policy of protection might be prostrated."[52]

During the campaign, Daniel Webster delivered a series of speeches designed not to praise Clay but rather to oppose Polk's candidacy. Webster urged antislavery Whigs to remain with the party, because their departure would ensure Polk's election. If the Tennessean became president, Webster warned, he would lower the tariff. Webster and other Whigs developed new defenses for the tariff and tied them to democracy. For example, Whigs rejected the notion that the tariff assisted only capitalists and manufacturers. "The principle of protection is for the benefit of all classes, and more especially for the laborer," Webster declared in New York, "whether it be in wood, brass, or iron, the weaver, shoemaker, tailor, everybody who lives by the exercise of his own industry." Subsequently at Pepperell, Massachusetts, Webster clarified that the tariff protected the "free white labor of the country." His statement could be interpreted as an extension of Clay's 1824 home-market argument. The concept of the tariff protecting "free white labor of the country" also appealed to the nativists who had emerged. Nativists, who could be found in many urban areas in the North, wanted to bar the further entry of foreigners into the country. They focused most of their energy on the Irish because of their Catholic faith. A high tariff, Whig orators such as Webster argued, protected American laborers, because it kept their wages at a high level. The free-trade doctrines of Polk and the Democracy, however, would reduce the wages of American workers, because foreign products would land at American ports and drive down the prices of goods manufactured domestically. This would force manufacturers to scuttle their businesses, and when this took place, workers would be unemployed.[53]

Polk bested Clay that fall. He carried Pennsylvania by six thousand votes and swept the Deep South, reversing gains that the Whigs had made in the past decade. "The slaveholders of the South and the Abolitionists of the North have gone equally against us," Philip Hone observed from New York City. "Free trade and protection have voted for Polk and Dallas."[54] The Whigs had no shortage of scapegoats for their losses in 1844. Indeed, they blamed abolitionists, nativists, and immigrants. But more sanguine Whigs pointed to Clay's poor handling of the Texas issue, while others maintained that the tariff had defeated them. According to some Whigs, Polk's treachery with the Kane letter had tricked the Pennsylvanians. Still others insisted that Clay should have equivocated on the tariff in the South, just as Polk had done in the North. Arthur Campbell wondered why had Clay lost in most of the South. "The tariff question," he conceded. "Everyone knows [it] has always been an uphill business in many of the states." Campbell argued that Clay should have refrained from endorsing a high tariff in the South and clarified his position on Texas instead.[55]

Just a few days after Polk learned of his victory, his mouthpiece, the *Nashville Union*, carried an editorial on his administration's prospects. "We rejoice in the result because we see in it a willingness on the part of the people to submit the existing system of tariff taxation to such modification as may be agreed upon by their own representative in Congress," the *Nashville Union* averred.[56] Whigs, however, shuddered at the prospects of Polk's initiatives as president. "What is to happen?" Thomas Corwin asked after the election. "What will the *charlatans* do now? Will they repeal the Tariff and wage war on Mexico?"[57] John Pendleton Kennedy even believed that Polk's election would result in disunion and civil war.[58]

But in his inaugural, Polk hedged on the tariff. He endorsed a revenue tariff that offered "incidental protection to our home interests."[59] "The ground taken in the inaugural is nothing but a repetition of Jackson's judicious Tariff, in different language," Calhoun sneered.[60] The largest part of Polk's address pertained to Texas and the western frontier. Herein was the blueprint for manifest destiny. The question of expansion into the frontier would one day overshadow all other political topics. Work remained to be done on the economic issues of the day, and Polk focused his attention on them shortly after he took the oath of office.[61]

16

"Mr. Polk's political death warrant is sealed"

O N DECEMBER 2, 1845, President James K. Polk forwarded his first annual message to Congress. Its tone and rhetoric reminded some Americans of Andrew Jackson's 1832 veto of the bill to recharter the Second Bank. Polk advocated American expansion in both the Northwest and the Southwest. If Great Britain or Mexico stood in the way of America's Manifest Destiny, he hinted that war would be the alternative. After rattling his saber, Polk turned to domestic issues. His opening statement left little doubt what he wanted Congress to do regarding the tariff: "The attention of Congress is invited to the importance of making suitable modifications and reductions of the rates imposed by our present tariff laws." Polk explained how a revenue tariff should function. He contended that when Congress raised duties on an article, the revenue coming into the government should likewise increase. However, if Congress increased a duty and the revenue now decreased, then that duty acted solely to protect a manufacturer. The president next asked congressmen to look at the Tariff of 1842. When they examined that tariff, they would see that the rates under that tariff were inconsistent with the principles that he had just articulated. Polk was only partially correct in this assertion. In 1843, the first year of the tariff of 1842, customs receipts plummeted to $7 million. But in 1844 and 1845, customs receipts had nearly tripled. Polk contended that most of the 1842 tariff's high rates fell on the poorer classes. While the "wealthy manufacturer" received increased profits by this tariff, it did not increase the wages of American laborers. "It [the tariff of 1842] imposes heavy and unjust burdens on the farmer, the planter, the commercial man, and those of all other pursuits except the capitalist who has made his investments in manufactures," the president asserted. Warming to the task, Polk then borrowed from Jackson's 1832 bank veto message by noting, "the government in theory knows no distinction of persons or classes, and should not bestow upon some favors and privileges which all others may not enjoy." Polk reminded Americans that the tariff of 1842 had passed by two votes in the House and one vote in the Senate. "Peculiar circumstances existing at the time," Polk declared, contributed to its approval more than anything else.[1]

Whigs found themselves in a difficult position after Polk announced his intention to lower the tariff. Few admitted that the tariff of 1842 constituted a perfect tariff. Defending a flawed bill seemed problematic for many Whig leaders. The safest strategy appeared to be to let the Democrats point out the flaws in the tariff and make their own proposal. This would allow Whigs to attack an imperfect bill. Whigs could also expose their rivals for not understanding the intricacies of commercial legislation. "For a man to say he is for Free Trade, or a Judicious Tariff is too indefinite," James Graham observed. "But when you call on men to propose some specific rate of duty, and make them show whether they are for cash duties, for specific or ad valorem duties, or minimums, or horizontal, or discriminatory duties, then they begin to expose their ignorance, and they get into deep water."[2] A few Whigs even wanted to let the Democrats pass their own tariff and then watch the country burn, thinking that they could use a failed tariff in the next election cycle.

Meanwhile, some Whigs championed the labor argument. Repeal the tariff, they charged, and thousands of workers would lose their employment. The 1842 tariff had flaws, Whigs admitted, but it offered aid to American laborers. However, one Democratic sheet assailed this argument. "If the government will protect the manufacturer the manufacturer will give employment to the laborer. What else is this, but a little more cunningly expressed, than the idea, 'Let Government take care of the rich, and the rich will take care of the poor.' "[3] Trickle-down economics apparently had no charms for Democrats in the nineteenth century. As soon as some Whigs read Polk's message, they began suggesting that a reduction of the tariff would lead to hard times and a panic.[4]

After Polk's message arrived in Congress, Secretary of the Treasury Robert J. Walker submitted a detailed report on the tariff. His document defended the agrarian vision of Thomas Jefferson and argued that the government needed only enough revenue to meet its expenses. Any extra would lead to fighting among politicians for the residual income. Free trade by the United States, Walker argued, would prompt other nations to abandon their restrictive policies as well. In this meticulously researched report, Walker had solicited information from customs collectors. His queries provided him with proof that high and protective duties lowered revenue. He wanted to abolish the minimum principle, and he believed that the tariff should have a sliding scale of duties. Walker's report recommended a series of classes or schedules for imported goods. At over eight hundred pages, the report listed all the proposed reductions in the tariff, which would lead to increased revenue, Walker argued. "Whilst it is impossible to adopt any horizontal scale of duties, or even any arbitrary maximum, experience proves that, as a general rule, a duty of 20 per cent ad valorem will yield the largest revenue," Walker noted. The secretary alleged that Polk's victory in 1844 demonstrated that a majority of Americans disapproved of protective tariffs and wanted a downward revision of the tariff.[5]

Whigs retorted that the recent election did not represent a referendum on the tariff, since Polk had deceived the people of the North with his Kane letter. The president's bait and switch on the tariff prompted one Pennsylvanian to predict, "So far as Pennsylvania is concerned Mr. Polk's political death warrant is sealed."[6] Walker's questions had alerted protectionists to his intentions. Since these reductions would benefit British manufacturers at the expense of American producers, they branded the new secretary "Sir Robert." It did not help Walker much when the House of Lords ordered copies of his report to be printed. According to William Graham, it would cause "quite a sensation on both sides of the water."[7]

James I. McKay introduced what became known as the "Walker tariff," or the "McKay tariff" on April 14. Democrats tended to call the bill the "McKay tariff," while Whigs insisted on calling it the "Walker tariff" to remind the people that it had been produced by the Polk administration and not Congress. With the assistance of customhouse collectors, Walker collaborated with McKay in drafting the new tariff bill. It adhered to all of Polk's recommendations. While Democrats stressed that the average rate on duties would be 20 percent, the items that manufacturers cared most about—iron, woolens, wool, paper, and glass—received a rate of 30 percent while cotton fabrics were taxed at a rate of 25 percent. The bill proposed to lower duties to about 20 percent, and the proposal eliminated the hated minimums. This tariff reduction allowed Democrats to argue that the Walker tariff reduced taxes on the American people. "The burdens of taxation, should be shifted off the shoulders of the poor, who had long borne an undue and exorbitant proportion of them, and should be put upon the wealth of the country," Andrew Johnson, a Tennessee Democrat announced.[8] As Walker had recommended, the proposed tariff included a series of schedules that ranged from 100 percent to 5 percent. Salt was placed in the 20 percent category. Cotton goods now had a tax rate of 25 percent. Walker placated Pennsylvania by placing iron in the 30 percent bracket. Yet Pennsylvanians voiced their displeasure and assailed the bill. Under the tariff of 1842, iron had a duty of over 160 percent, thus the reduction to 30 percent represented a drastic drop. Coal was slashed over 100 percent. The Pennsylvania legislature instructed its senators to work against the Walker tariff. From Ashland, Clay wrote to a Pennsylvania Whig, "I wish you would give my respects to some of our Democratic friends in the Pennsylvania delegation, and ask them whether they *now* think the President is a better tariff man than I am."[9]

For almost two months, the bill languished as McKay waited to bring it forward. Western Democrats wanted bills on public lands and internal improvements acted on before they would consent to lowering the tariff. These Democrats remained in a state of rage after Polk compromised with the British over the boundary of Oregon. The agreement over Oregon blocked northwestern expansion, while it presumably maintained cordial feelings between British textile manufacturers and southern planters. "I may forgive these southern gentlemen for this one offence about Oregon, that is as far as I can go," a western Democrat observed. "*But if they desert me upon the tariff, you may hang me if I ever trust them again.*"[10] Most western Democrats grumbled that the president had cheated them. Polk had urged Congress to declare war against Mexico in order to acquire more territory in the Southwest, yet he compromised in the Northwest. Would these disgruntled Democrats look for revenge over the tariff? When news arrived that the British ministry had repealed the Corn Laws, Democrats pressed the tariff in earnest. Exactly why Democrats now moved remains a mystery. Their decision to press forward was perhaps the result of a quid pro quo agreement with the British government. On June 15, McKay mustered the votes to bring the tariff to the floor.[11]

Just before the Democrats commenced the debate on their new tariff, manufacturers staged a public fair in Washington. They constructed a six-thousand-dollar building to display the products of American industry. For two weeks Americans could pay twelve and a half cents to examine goods manufactured in the United States. Manufacturers from New England, Pennsylvania, New York, New Jersey, Maryland, Delaware, and Virginia provided goods for the fair. "As American citizens, knowing no distinction between East and West, and North and South, but feeling convinced that the interest of the *whole* is most closely connected with the subject of *Domestic Industry*," a Whig editor boasted, "we rejoice in this Fair as having afforded the most gratifying testimony that a common ground is about to be established."[12] Another Whig sheet assured its readers, "It was a proud spectacle to see congregated into one structure, the products of all the useful arts, adapted to every department of life—suited to the necessities of the poor and the luxuries of the rich, embracing the results of genius, and skill, and industry, and all the work of *American* hands."[13] Horace Greeley, who had become the leading economic nationalist in the country after Hezekiah Niles retired in 1836, declared, "It will here be seen that the march of improvement in manufactures was never so rapid nor its results so gratifying as it has been under this tariff."[14]

Polk and his wife, Sarah Childress Polk, along with Robert J. Walker and Secretary of War William Marcy attended the fair together. The president left unimpressed. "The manufacturers have spent many thousands of dollars in getting up this fair," Polk confided to his diary, "with a view no doubt to operate upon members of Congress to prevent a reduction of the present rates of duty imposed by the oppressive protective tariff act of 1842." The president even accused the manufacturers of trying to deceive the public about the prices of their goods. He believed that they lied to convince the American people that "high duties make low goods."[15] For Polk, the lavish expense of the fair proved that manufacturers no longer required any assistance from the government. Hence, the fair increased the president's determination to ensure that Congress lowered the tariff.

Few observers anticipated trouble with the tariff in the House, since the Democrats had a comfortable majority in that chamber. However, sessions in the House lasted between eight and nine hours with each speaker limited to an hour. "It is not a new subject, the same arguments have been repeated over and over again in this Capitol at different periods for the last thirty years," Democrat Stephen Strong of New York scoffed.[16] Democrats defended the Walker tariff because it represented, they insisted, a significant improvement over the 1842 tariff. They regarded the Walker tariff as a revenue tariff that still offered modest protection. Lucien B. Chase, a Tennessee Democrat, reminded the House that free traders could have lowered the tariff shortly after the Compromise of 1833 went into effect, yet they abided by the compromise. Thus, protectionists had received over a decade's worth of extra protection; free traders had ample justification for lowering the tariff in 1846, he declared.[17]

Meanwhile, Whigs attacked the proposed tariff reduction on the basis that the 1842 tariff had restored economic prosperity in the country. The balance of trade had shifted in favor of the United States, and the country had an excess supply of specie. Furthermore, why should the country alter the revenue when it had just declared war against Mexico, they asked. George Rathbun, a New York Democrat, joined this Whig line of argument by reminding the House that when America went to war in 1812, Congress doubled the tariff. Now, in 1846, the House curiously wanted to slash tariff rates. Other Whigs charged that Walker's tariff scheme sacrificed protection to the free-trade opinions of the South Carolina nullifiers. If Congress approved this proposal, it would ruin the country, they maintained.[18]

Pennsylvania Democrats and Whigs found common ground in their denunciations of the Walker tariff. Both had been duped by Polk's 1844 Kane letter, which they now branded a fraud. Andrew Stewart, a Whig, avowed that this tariff battle was really a struggle between the North and the South. He charged that protectionism worked in the North, and that this made that region prosperous, while the South languished. In the first Congress, Stewart observed, the Carolinas and Virginia combined had only twenty members in the House. A half century later, these three states had a mere thirty, while New York and Pennsylvania, states that favored protectionism, had thirty-four and twenty-four members, respectively. "Judge the tree by its fruits," Stewart laughed. Even with "labor without wages" the South had been surpassed by the northern economy. Take the slaves out of the field and put them to work in blast furnaces, and the South would be just as successful as the North, he argued.[19]

Democratic and Whig newspaper editors carried on the debate with just as much passion. A common refrain among Whig and northern editors opposed to the Walker tariff was that it made no sense to tinker with the revenue after the country had declared war. Their nastiest assault became a sectional one. The president and treasury secretary cared nothing about the people of the North, many northern editors claimed. "The destruction of the Tariff is required for the benefit and protection of slave labor," the *Albany Evening Journal* concluded.[20] "Here the white man feels that he must be, in the prime of manhood, reduced to the reward of slave labor," the *United States Gazette* declared.[21] Other attacks against the Walker tariff involved a presumed deal between southern and western Democrats. The latter would sacrifice the tariff, as long as southern Democrats helped them with a bill that provided for the graduation of western land prices.[22]

As the House prepared to vote on the final passage of the new tariff, Jacob Brinkerhoff, an Ohio Democrat, secured the floor and announced that Ohio's thirteen Democrats had decided to vote against the bill. In an address filled with Jacksonian rhetoric, Brinkerhoff blasted the Polk administration. He announced that he and the other Ohio Democrats would vote for the bill only if tea and coffee were placed on the free list. Since these men potentially could defeat the bill, Polk, Walker, and McKay relented.[23]

After appeasing Brinkerhoff, House Democrats pushed the Walker tariff through by a vote of 114 to 95. Once supporters in the gallery knew the verdict, they cheered loudly. Robert J. Walker and Thomas Ritchie, editor of the *Washington Union*, congratulated each other on the House floor. "Mr. Walker and Mr. Ritchie were present," a New York correspondent reported. "Their eyes danced merrily, and joy was reflected on their faces from their grateful hearts." When Walker reached McKay's desk, the secretary shook his hand and said, "We've got it through." Walker pronounced this so loud that one witness claimed that a deaf man could have heard it. Ritchie approached McKay and congratulated him as well. The New York writer

Table 16.1. House vote, 1846

	Democrats		Whigs		Nativists		Total	
	For	Against	For	Against	For	Against	For	Against
New England	9	0	0	19	0	0	9	19
Middle	18	18	0	23	0	6	18	47
South	54	0	1	12	0	0	55	12
West	32	0	0	17	0	0	32	17
Total	113	18	1	71	0	6	114	95

Source: *House Journal*, 29th Cong., 1st Sess., 3 July 1846, 1029–30.

ended his account by characterizing the departure of McKay, Ritchie, and Walker thus: "The three distinguished Southern gentlemen withdrew from the hall, all feeling like Mr. Clay when he walked the Boulevard in Paris, after hearing of the battle of New Orleans—a foot higher!"[24]

Mississippi congressman Jefferson Davis notified his constituents that "an analysis of the votes upon this bill will show that its main strength was derived from the agricultural and exporting states."[25] Every southern and western state gave a majority vote for the tariff of 1846. House members from Alabama, Arkansas, Florida, Illinois, Michigan, Mississippi, Missouri, and Texas unanimously favored the Walker tariff.[26]

Remarkably, of the 114 aforementioned House votes, all but one of them came from Democrats. Henry W. Hilliard of Alabama cast the only Whig vote for the bill. Fifteen of the Democratic negative votes came from Pennsylvania and New York. Pennsylvania Democrats, who had earlier assured their followers that Polk would protect their interests, cast eleven negative votes and only one positive vote. While these Democrats cried betrayal, other Democrats believed that Pennsylvania had gotten what it deserved. "I do not grieve that this new bill has been passed without the aid of Pennsylvania," a Connecticut Democrat admitted. "I think she is exceedingly selfish on this subject."[27] David Wilmot was the only Pennsylvanian who agreed with the administration that the tariff should be lowered. Across Pennsylvania, editors assailed Wilmot. One harshly predicted, "His name as his deed will stink in the nostrils of every true hearted Pennsylvanian forever."[28] The *Nashville Union*, however, praised both Wilmot's speech in favor of the new tariff and his vote. "We wish there were a few more democrats in Pennsylvania, and we trust there will be before the next Presidential contest," the paper declared. The editor had forgotten the old adage—be careful what you wish for. Wilmot would soon become a scourge for southern Democrats.[29]

There was no time to lose in the Senate. The pending adjournment meant that the Senate would have only a month to deal with the tariff. To hasten the process, southern Democrats broke precedent and opted not to send the bill to any Senate committee. The bill should have gone to the Finance Committee. However, Mississippi Democrat Jesse Speight had departed the capital, leaving the committee evenly divided between Whigs and Democrats. This division would prevent the committee from reporting the bill. Whigs tried to refer the bill to the Finance Committee but failed.[30]

Once the measure arrived in the Senate, Democrats agreed to let the Whigs do all the talking. Dixon H. Lewis, a four-hundred-pound Alabamian, whom John Quincy Adams called "twenty score of flesh," defended the new tariff and argued that the American people preferred percentage duties, because these duties concealed nothing.[31] With a tariff of duties based on the value of the good, the people would know how much they were being taxed for a good. Lewis turned the tables on Whigs who charged that these duties encouraged frauds. Suppose a good is valued at one hundred dollars and had been assessed a duty of 20 percent, Lewis told the Senate. The importer had to pay twenty dollars. But suppose the foreigner valued his good at only ninety-five dollars. Thus, he now owed the customhouse nineteen dollars instead of twenty. For Lewis, this did not represent a major fraud. By undervaluing their goods, foreigners would only gain a few dollars, Lewis argued. Furthermore, specific duties required an army of men at the customhouses. The Walker tariff would allow the country to save money because it would no longer require numerous men at each customhouse. It would also free up the courts from having to hear cases where specific duties had led to conflicts between the merchant and the customhouse official. Lewis's final argument involved the revenue. The Alabamian charged that this new tariff would actually increase the revenue. Lewis believed this would happen because of an increase in the population of America, the admission of Texas, and the relaxation of the British tariff laws. After Lewis made his address, protectionists such as Daniel Webster and Simon Cameron challenged his figures. The friends of the tariff of 1842 would not be defeated without a fight.[32]

Petitions began arriving in the Senate as soon as the House passed the Walker tariff. Most of these came from Pennsylvania manufacturers who believed that the pending tariff would destroy their businesses. "Memorials are pouring in upon the Senate against the passage of the bill from every direction, and if the final vote can be delayed and the Senate influenced by public opinion, the bill may yet be defeated," one editor contended.[33] After Simon Cameron presented more petitions on July 23, Ambrose Sevier, an Arkansas Democrat, had seen enough. Sevier called these Pennsylvania petitions a "mere joke." They were nothing more than a "funeral dirge" of the manufacturers "at the taking away of the bounty we have allowed them for a few years past." Sevier then queried, "Was there any man who could read, and who did read for the last twenty years, who did not know that James K. Polk was a free trade man? Not one—and Pennsylvania tomorrow, notwithstanding all these petitions and all this fuss about the Tariff, would vote the Democratic ticket again."[34] Pennsylvania had put Polk into the executive mansion, and now they were about to pay for it.

Across the Keystone State, people gathered to pass resolutions and compose memorials. At these gatherings, Whigs and Democrats put aside partisan feelings to defend the tariff of 1842. Pennsylvanians warned that if McKay's tariff passed, it would ruin weavers, spinners, shoemakers, tailors, glass blowers, machinists, iron-workers, and even children in factories. Pennsylvanians comforted themselves with the belief that in the event of a tie vote, Vice President George M. Dallas would not forget from which state he hailed. "There is a whirlwind abroad in our state, that is gathering strength in every inch of its march, that will sweep all into oblivion who shall attempt for a moment to resist its force," one Pennsylvanian predicted."[35]

To force the bill through the Senate, Polk began exerting pressure on unde-clared senators. He believed that "capitalists" and "monopolists" conspired to defeat the bill. The president viewed this as undemocratic, because the people expected him to lower the tariff. Polk spent many nights worrying if the foes of democracy might bribe a senator. Hopkins L. Turney, a Democratic senator from Tennessee, confirmed these fears when he arrived at the executive mansion and told Polk that he had been offered a bribe to vote against the tariff. The "monopolists'" actions only strengthened Polk's resolve to lower the tariff.[36]

The president also fretted about defections among his fellow Democrats. He first tried to convince Democratic senator John Niles of Connecticut to vote for the bill. But Niles parried all of Polk's overtures. In the Senate, he spoke in opposition to the tariff and the administration. "No administration before ever assumed the responsibility of hazarding its popularity on a tariff bill," Niles claimed. This is not what the people of the North had endorsed in the 1844 election, Niles contended. The Connecticut Democrat ended his address with a warning to his congressional colleagues: "Let me say to my northern friends, that the time is coming, and now is, when we must take care of ourselves, when we must look after our own interests and our own principles."[37] Niles's speech revealed that the Democratic Party still had divisions that lingered after the 1844 campaign. When one Alabama Democrat read Niles's speech, he asked: "Has old Niles gone crazy again?"[38]

Polk next worried about disgruntled Illinois senator James Semple. Semple had wanted a position in the army, which Polk could not grant. On July 15, Polk's pri-vate secretary, J. Knox Walker, informed him that Semple had been absent from the Senate that day. The rumor winding its way around Washington was that Semple had packed his trunks and planned to leave the capital. His likely departure threat-ened the passage of the tariff. Immediately, Polk dispatched J. Knox Walker, Cave Johnson, Stephen A. Douglas, Robert Smith, and others to find Semple. Whoever found Semple had instructions to bring him to the executive mansion for a con-ference with the president. Orlando Ficklin, an Illinois Democrat, located Semple about an hour before his train was scheduled to depart for Illinois. Fortunately for Polk, Ficklin prevailed on Semple to meet with the president. When Semple arrived at the executive mansion, Polk appealed to his patriotism. After an hour's discus-sion, the Illinois senator agreed to stay in Washington and vote for the bill.[39]

With Temple's vote assured, Polk reevaluated the Walker tariff's prospects in the Senate. Twenty-eight Democrats would favor the bill for sure. All twenty-five Whigs would oppose it, as would three Democrats. This left Senator William Haywood, a North Carolina Democrat and a personal friend of the president who had attended the University of North Carolina, with him, as the swing vote. Haywood had been instructed by the North Carolina state legislature to oppose the bill. He called on

Polk and notified him that he could not support the bill unless the Senate added an amendment. Haywood wanted to move the date that the new tariff would go into operation from December 1, 1846, to March 4, 1847. Polk, however, feared that this delay might give the bill's opponents a second chance to defeat it. The president begged his friend to support the tariff reduction. Haywood responded, "I would rather die than vote for it." Polk retorted by telling Haywood that the Walker tariff was the "most important domestic measure" of his administration.[40] Haywood left White House uncommitted. On July 25, while Webster spoke in opposition to the tariff in the Senate, Haywood got out of his seat and handed a note to the vice president. He then walked out of the chamber as the previously quiet galleries began to chatter and spectators wondered what Haywood's note said. Secretary of the Navy George Bancroft saw the note and hastily wrote to the president, "Senator Haywood resigned this morning to the great consternation of the Capitol."[41]

Word of Haywood's resignation spread throughout the capital and the nation. The passage of the Walker tariff, it appeared, was now in jeopardy. "The news received this morning has astonished us all," a New York free trader cried. "We were defeated in a quarter least expected, by the hand of a Southern Democrat."[42] Polk charged that Haywood resigned as a result of misplaced ambition. Since his overtures to extend the date of operation had been rejected, Haywood decided to oppose the bill. Finding himself with few friends, he finally decided to resign, Polk believed. Whigs in North Carolina approved his course, but Democrats castigated his action.[43]

The tariff's fate now rested on the shoulders of Whig senator Spencer Jarnagin of Tennessee, who had been instructed by his state legislature to vote for the bill. Jarnagin vacillated and looked for a way out. Polk met with Jarnagin and reminded him of his instructions. With Jarnagin contemplating resigning his seat, many began to suspect that the outcome of the tariff vote might reside with the vice president. Democrats had placed Dallas on the ticket in 1844 in order to carry Pennsylvania. Now, they wondered if he would place allegiance to his home state ahead of his party. "If the responsibility falls upon George M. Dallas of giving the casting vote, he will immortalize his name or make a John Tyler of himself," a constituent warned Alabama congressman George S. Houston.[44]

The administration found itself in a difficult position with Niles's defection, Haywood's resignation, the mercurial maneuvers of Jarnagin, and questions surrounding the intentions of Dallas. Daniel Webster had prepared a compromise tariff and planned to present it in the Senate. His proposal would reduce the tariff of 1842 but gradually over five years. Webster calculated he could count on all the Whigs, as well as Niles and the two Pennsylvania senators. It appears that Webster prevailed on Jarnagin to support his compromise tariff as well; doing so would ensure its passage. However, just as Webster prepared to present it, John M. Clayton, a Delaware Whig, offered a motion to refer the House bill to the Senate Finance Committee, with instructions to add amendments providing increased protection to manufactured items at the expense of raw materials. According to Senate rules, Clayton's motion took precedence over Webster's. Since this motion favored protectionism, the Whigs supported it, and it passed. Whigs inside the capital district and throughout the country sighed with relief. The tariff would be lowered, but the pending amendments would soften the blow. Democrats complained that all their hard work had been in vain.[45]

Clayton had blundered. The timing of his motion prompted the Senate to adjourn for the day. The adjournment presented Polk with a delay to save his version of the tariff. He needed to have a meeting with Jarnagin. Webster and other Whigs scoured Washington that evening looking for Jarnagin. At ten o'clock, they learned that they were too late. Jarnagin had been to the executive mansion, where Polk and Tennessee senator Hopkins L. Turney had convinced Jarnagin to obey his instructions. When Webster found Jarnagin, he informed him that he had changed his mind and would not vote for his five-year reduction plan. On July 28, Dixon Lewis, chairman of the Finance Committee, asked that the committee be relieved of its instructions. The Senate voted to dismiss the committee by a vote of twenty-eight to twenty-seven, with Jarnagin's vote providing the difference. His switch made Webster's compromise proposal a moot point. If Clayton had not offered his motion, then it is probable that Webster's compromise would have been adopted by the Senate. The delay gave Polk and the Democrats the opportunity to persuade Jarnagin, and they took advantage of it.[46]

On the motion to engross the bill and read it a third time, the Senate divided evenly—twenty-seven to twenty-seven. Being pulled in different directions by his friends, Jarnagin abstained. He chose this course in order to ensnare the vice president. Now the fate of the Walker tariff rested in the hands of a Pennsylvanian. Dallas asked the indulgence of the Senate and made a few remarks that he had prepared. He interpreted Polk's election and the margin of victory in the House (nineteen votes) as proof that the people wanted lower import duties. The vice president regarded this bill as better than the tariff of 1842. Dallas told the Senate that on his election to the vice presidency, he became an agent and representative of every American and not the people of Pennsylvania. Because of these principles, and since there was no constitutional objection to the bill, Dallas voted in the affirmative and saved the bill. "I would rather be that man now, than the first crowned head in all Europe," one observer commented in praise of Dallas.[47]

A few minutes later, the Senate voted on the passage of the bill. This time, Jarnagin participated and his affirmative vote allowed the tariff to pass by a twenty-eight to twenty-seven margin. The Senate endorsed the Walker tariff on an almost straight party-line vote. Twenty-seven Democrats voted for the measure, and only four opposed it. On the Whig side, Jarnagin became the only Whig to approve the new tariff, while the other twenty-three opposed it.

When news reached Pennsylvania that Dallas had saved the "British bill," angry mobs burned the vice president in effigy. Polk, they roared, had deceived them and forced a Pennsylvanian to do his bidding. Whigs enjoyed the problems that Polk's duplicity had caused the Democrats. After all, they had warned them about Polk and his true intentions toward the tariff during the presidential campaign. "Pennsylvania, who will feel the crushing effects of the blow more severely than any other state in the Union, elected Polk," the *Buffalo Commercial Advertiser* declared. "She also secured the annexation of Texas, whose two Senators, made the tie on the en-

Table 16.2. Senate vote, 1846

	Democrats		Whigs		Total	
	For	Against	For	Against	For	Against
New England	2	2	0	8	2	10
Middle	2	2	0	6	2	8
South	15	0	1	5	16	5
West	8	0	0	4	8	4
Total	27	4	1	23	28	27

Source: *Senate Journal*, 29th Cong., 1st Sess., 28 July 1846, 454.

grossment of the bill, and a Pennsylvanian, Vice President Dallas, gave the casting vote, that ensured the passage."[48]

Other foes of the Walker tariff argued that democracy had succumbed to the wishes of a political party. The tariff of 1842 had been repealed "against the convictions of nine tenths of the intelligent and well informed men in the free states," a northern editor claimed. "It is a blow at northern labor which will fall with tremendous force upon the whole free labor of the North."[49] Democrat Gideon Welles cried that northern Democrats had caved to the demands of the South: "Walker is the master spirit in all that relates to this matter, and the president I apprehend, and all the members of the cabinet have not only given in to him but maintain and support him." Welles then added, "Members, in both houses, have surrendered their honest convictions, and been coaxed or driven into this measure."[50] In his diary, Philip Hone observed, "The tariff of 1842 is destroyed, the industry of the country laid at the feet of foreign competition, and national prosperity sacrificed to party discipline."[51] Even the administration's own newspaper, the *Washington Union*, suggested that party had trumped democracy. "Memorials, petitions, the press, the panic—all came up to aid the great talents which belong to the Whig party," the paper crowed. In the end, the voice of the people mattered little. Other Democrats said that democracy triumphed because the tariff had passed Congress, in spite of the efforts of lobbyists and corrupt manufacturers who had come to Washington to bribe senators and representatives.[52]

For Polk, passage of the tariff represented a crowning victory for his administration. He used a special pen to affix his signature to the Walker tariff. This pen had been given to him by a Virginia Democrat named Elizabeth H. Curtis. According to her, on the day the Whigs nominated Clay for the presidency, an eagle flew over her plantation, and a quill from the bird fell to the ground. Because her husband supported Henry Clay and the Whig Party, Elizabeth Curtis relished Polk's victory. She presented the quill to him as a gift. Polk made a pen out of the quill, and he used it to sign his first message to Congress, the resolution that admitted Texas into the union, the Walker tariff, and a proclamation announcing the ratification of the Treaty of Guadalupe Hidalgo, which concluded the Mexican War.[53]

The Walker tariff was just one of Polk's 1846 legislative successes. Congress also passed a warehouse bill. Under its provisions, merchants could store imported goods in a warehouse for an extended period of time. A merchant could wait until the value of a certain good dropped and then he would bring it out of the warehouse and pay a diminished duty. Before the ink dried on Polk's signature on the Walker tariff, Congress passed a bill that created the Independent Treasury System. The Independent Treasury, or Constitutional Treasury, as Polk called it, divorced the federal government from the banking system. It resolved the question of national bank until the Federal Reserve Act of 1913. As a result of these accomplishments, Democrats in Congress had reason to be ecstatic. "Texas has been annexed and is now represented on this floor. Oregon has been settled, and settled without blood," James Bowlin, a Missouri Democrat, said in the House. "The independent treasury, one of the reforms demanded by the people, is destined to become law. The tariff reform, one of the greatest acts of the age, and destined to lift millions of unnecessary and unjust burdens from the people, has also in its turn triumphed before this house."[54]

The normally stoic Polk engaged in some self-congratulating as the session neared its conclusion. "During the Session however most of the great measures of this Government prevailed. Among them the act to modify the tariff of 1842, the ware-house bill, and the establishment of a Constitutional Treasury became laws," he informed Louis McLane.[55] The low rates of the Walker tariff initiated a period of economic growth and development. In particular, the low duty on iron encouraged railroad building throughout the nation. The Walker tariff also commenced a trend of low tariffs that would not end until 1861. The road to a tariff solely for revenue purposes had been bumpy, but it had finally been accomplished.[56]

Commenting on the passage of the Walker tariff, a Midwestern correspondent proclaimed, "The simultaneous triumph of free trade in the United States and Great Britain, whose citizens and subjects comprehend one sixth of the human race, is the greatest event of our age."[57] Polk's success, however, came at a terrible price for the nation. Northerners believed that Polk only sought to aid the South. Polk had lowered the tariff, bestowed patronage on his southern friends, and then vetoed a bill that would have given federal funds to improve harbors along the Great Lakes. More and more northern Democrats cried betrayal as a result of Polk's actions. "The time has come, when the northern Democracy should make a stand," Gideon Wells wrote. "Everything has taken a southern shape and been controlled by southern caprice for years. The Northern states are treated as provinces to the South."[58] Shortly after Congress enacted Polk's legislative agenda, David Wilmot, the only Pennsylvanian to support the Walker tariff, stunned southern Democrats by offering an amendment to an appropriations bill. He proposed to exclude slavery from any territory captured in the Mexican War. The Wilmot Proviso and the question over slavery in the territories acquired from Mexico now came to the forefront of American politics.[59]

After Congress adjourned, Whigs divided on the best strategy to attack the Democrats. Clay wanted to continue to fight battles over economic issues. "As to the Tariff of 1846, I think our true policy is to go for its repeal, and the restoration of the Tariff of 1842, and nothing else than the repeal of the one and the restoration of the other," Clay informed a friend.[60] John Davis of Massachusetts predicted big Whig victories in the upcoming years. "The policy of the administration is enough to excite public alarm without Coon skins, hard cider, log cabins, or even a song or a hurrah," he opined. "The war is daily becoming unpopular and the revenue act meets with condemnation every where."[61] Other Whigs realized that the old economic arguments no longer resonated with the people. By the end of 1847, the Whig predictions of an economic collapse had failed to come to fruition. The American economy began a period of sustained growth that would last a decade. Commodity prices increased, and at long last the economy emerged from the Panic of 1837. The discovery of gold in California in 1848 lessened the need for paper bank notes in the country. Democrats touted their success and the booming economy that they had unleashed. At the same time, the Whigs' fortunes declined as they had predicted an economic collapse and then this did not occur.[62]

Although the economy prospered, northern Democrats had little to show for their support of Polk. Young Hickory had done nothing to assist their region. He reduced the tariff. His river and harbors bill veto injured northerners. The unpopularity of "Mr. Polk's War," his political agenda, and quarrels at the state level resulted in defeats for northern Democrats in the midterm elections of 1846. Local issues, according to Polk, contributed to defeats in New York and Pennsylvania in 1846. A Georgia Democrat would not let these recent Whig victories taper his enthusiasm for Polk or his policies, however. "I do not believe that Genl. Washington or Genl. Jackson in his prime, could have directed the ship of state with more ability," John H. Lumpkin wrote. "I am amazed when I see what was accomplished at the last session and can never censure the president for any of those disastrous results."[63] Northern Democrats, angry with their president, searched for a new issue to bring them victory. They realized that opposition to the further extension of slavery might work. While southern Democrats publicly charged northern Democrats with betraying them on the tariff, northern Democrats privately complained that their southern colleagues had betrayed them. Polk's nomination, they contended, revealed to northern Democrats that the "Slave Power" controlled their party.[64]

Buoyed by the victories in the fall of 1846, the Whigs prepared to roll back the gains made by the Democrats. "The Locos are in deep trouble about how to raise more Revenue," James Graham observed. "Low taxes and expensive Wars don't coincide. . . . To fill empty Treasuries out of the people's pockets is not a very popular vocation. They must raise the Tariff; but it will be a bitter pill just after this very Congress reduced it. There is no escape for them."[65] The Walker tariff, passed by the narrowest of margins, would remain unaltered until 1857. It turned out to have the longest life of any of the antebellum tariffs.[66]

17

"Even the tariff is not a question on which opposite political parties are united in taking opposite sides"

"OLD ISSUES ARE GRADUALLY passing away, and new issues engross the public attention," Millard Fillmore observed in 1848.[1] The tariff, along with the other economic issues that had galvanized voters since 1816, receded in importance at the end of the 1840s and throughout the early 1850s. Whig politicians and editors continued to talk about the tariff, but the issue no longer resonated with voters. When Congress debated a bill to organize territorial governments in Kansas and Nebraska in 1853, Charles Sumner announced, "the bank, sub-treasury, the distribution of the public lands, are each and all obsolete issues. Even the tariff is not a question on which opposite political parties are united in taking opposite sides."[2] In 1856, just before the voters went to the polls, William H. Seward asked, "What shall I discourse upon?" He then answered his own question. "The contest of the American Colonies with Great Britain, and the characters of the Whigs and Tories? No, these are themes for the Fourth of July. The adoption of the Constitution, and the disputes between Federalists and Republicans? No; let them sleep. The Tariff, National Bank, and Internal Improvements? No; they are past and gone."[3]

The tariff failed to attract much attention owing to an economic boom that commenced at the end of the 1840s and discussions over slavery in the areas taken from Mexico. As the economy enjoyed its first period of sustained growth since Andrew Jackson's administration, the Whigs, who had predicted a downturn in the economy because of the Walker tariff, now realized that they had played the role of a false prophet. The Whigs sidestepped this blunder by nominating military hero Zachary Taylor for president in 1848. They refrained from adopting an official platform. Taylor was a political novice who announced that he knew "nothing about the constitutionality of a bank or the expediency of a tariff for protection." This prompted one Democrat to sneer, "it seems to me that the Genl might know something about these vital measures as one of them has been under discussion for fifty-five years and the other for twenty-three."[4] Thurlow Weed, a Whig editor, had some of his fears assuaged on the tariff after he met Joseph P. Taylor, the Whig nominee's brother. Weed came away from this meeting with knowledge that Zachary Taylor refused to wear a coat unless it had been made from American cloth, nor would he allow a button to be on his coat that had been imported. Other Whigs became satisfied with Taylor after he published his Allison letter in April 1848. "I am a Whig, but not an ultra Whig," Taylor announced in a letter to J. S. Allison. "Upon the subject of the tariff," Taylor continued, "the will of the people, as expressed through their representatives in Congress, ought to be respected and carried out by the Executive."[5] Whigs interpreted this to mean that if elected, Taylor would defer to Congress on the tariff. He would not follow the example of John Tyler.[6]

Unlike the Whigs, the Democrats adopted a platform in 1848, one that sounded antitariff but one that could still be used to keep tariff-supporting northern Democrats committed to the party. The plank read, "That justice and sound policy forbid the federal Government to foster one branch of industry to the detriment of another, or to cherish the interests of one portion to the injury of another portion of our common country."[7] When Willie P. Mangum read this plank, it reminded him of the trickery that Democrats had used in 1844 over the tariff.[8]

Instead of economic issues, the 1848 campaign revolved around the question of slavery in the newly acquired territories. When the Democratic Party refused to endorse the Wilmot Proviso, some disgruntled northern members bolted the party, met in Buffalo, New York, and nominated Martin Van Buren as the candidate of the newly formed Free Soil Party. Van Buren siphoned off votes from both candidates on election day. However, the strong showing by the Free Soil ticket hurt Democratic nominee Lewis Cass more than Taylor and delivered New York, and thus the presidency, to the Whigs. Only in Pennsylvania did the tariff receive attention in 1848. Whigs attacked the Walker tariff and declared that Taylor would return the tariff to a protective level. They also reminded Pennsylvania voters that Cass had voted for the despised Walker tariff. Taylor's running mate, Millard Fillmore, had been the author of the tariff of 1842, which remained popular in the Keystone State. Taylor carried Pennsylvania by almost fourteen thousand votes, or almost 4 percentage points, and the state's twenty-six electoral votes helped to give Taylor the presidency.[9]

The Thirty-First Congress that assembled in Washington City in December 1849 had 114 confirmed Democrats in the House, while the Whigs had 106. A small group of Free Soilers held the balance of power. For nineteen days, the House engaged in a battle over the speakership. Shouts of disunion became common on the House floor. "I have long feared this question of slavery was to be the rock upon which the Union was to be wrecked," David Outlaw noted to his wife during a tense moment.[10] After a motion to dispense with tradition and elect the Speaker based on a plurality instead of a majority vote, Howell Cobb, a Democrat from Georgia, won the post. This battle frayed nerves and tested party allegiances across sectional lines. It also consumed much of the House's time.[11]

When Taylor finally sent his message to Congress, he wrote that the deficit produced by the Mexican War necessitated a new tariff. Taylor informed Congress that he desired a tariff that would offer "encouragement" to American industries. He announced his support for a tariff with specific duties. "It is now clearly evident that the tariff of 1846 will at least be modified during the next session of Congress, possibly a radical change will be attempted, and possibly the friends of protection will be satisfied with a change of the *ad valorem* to specific duties," a Kentucky Whig editor wrote.[12]

Taylor's message was the opening salvo for the Whigs in what they expected to be a lengthy battle over the tariff reminiscent of the ones of 1824, 1828, 1842, and 1846. Following Taylor's message, Secretary of the Treasury William M. Meredith submitted his annual report on the nation's finances. Meredith was a Pennsylvania attorney who had never participated in a tariff debate. His report, however, became a major document in the pending debate. Whereas Robert J. Walker had made an elaborate argument in favor of free trade in 1846, Meredith made the case for protectionism. Over the course of a thousand pages of arguments, tables, and statistics, he recommended that the country abandon the free-trade doctrines of the Walker tariff and readopt a protective tariff.

The report represented a classic Whig document, but Meredith also crafted it to alleviate sectional animosities. It endorsed Henry Clay's old argument about the tariff creating a home market. Both the North and the South benefitted from a protective tariff, he maintained. If Congress increased the tariff on cotton cloths, the treasury secretary announced, southern farmers would send their crop to northern mills. Also, the farmer would reap higher profits since many looms had begun operating in the South. On average, southern cotton farmers sent about sixty million dollars' worth of cotton to Great Britain. For Meredith, this was ludicrous. If American manufacturers turned southern cotton into cloth, it would allow the United States to export over $250 million worth of cotton textiles annually. "When we shall spin it ourselves, make our own iron, and manufacture our other staples," Meredith declared, "we shall have transferred to this country the great centers of wealth, commerce, civilization, and political as well as moral and intellectual power."[13] Nothing ever became of Meredith's Whig alternative to the Walker tariff, however. No sooner had the treasury secretary produced his elaborate report than the people of California applied for admission into the union. The tariff, the key issue in American politics since the 1820s, was pushed aside so congressmen could debate whether California should enter the union as a free state and what concessions southerners might be able to extract to allow its admission.[14]

As the debate over California raged, some Whigs still hoped to bring a new tariff bill before Congress. "It cannot but be highly gratifying to those who look to the Whig party to carry forward the government upon the true principles of the Fathers of the Republic, to restore a protective tariff, to revive the hopes and give a cheering prospect to the industry of the country," a Whig paper declared.[15] But California dominated the calendar. Spring turned into summer with no end in sight. The sudden death of Taylor in July of gastroenteritis increased the optimism for a new tariff among Whigs, however, because it elevated Millard Fillmore, author of the tariff of 1842, to the presidency. Many Whigs had wanted to put Abbott Lawrence, a wealthy cotton manufacturer from Boston, on the ticket, but the antislavery Whigs blocked his nomination. They announced that they would not allow "King Cotton both ends of the ticket."[16]

In September, Congress approved a series of bills that became known as the Compromise of 1850. California entered the union as a free state, the Texas boundary with New Mexico was settled, a government for the territory of Utah was established, a new fugitive slave law was enacted, and a law abolishing the slave trade in Washington, DC, became law. Some suspected that Clay, the father of the compromise measures, had a tariff increase "snugly stored in the boot of the omnibus to smuggle it through," but the tariff was omitted.[17] Fillmore signed all these measures as soon as they arrived on his desk. With the crisis settled, however, congressional Whigs sought to introduce a new tariff bill. On September 14, Robert Toombs, the Ways and Means Committee chairman, presented a report declaring that the committee deemed it "inexpedient" to debate the tariff. Samuel Finley Vinton, an Ohio Whig, moved to amend the report so as to bring forward a new tariff. However, by a vote of ninety-three to ninety-six, the House refused to adopt Vinton's amendment. Every southern Whig except for Thomas Clingman voted in favor of the amendment. Four Pennsylvania Democrats voted against it. Almost every western Democrat voted no, prompting a Pennsylvania observer to write, "we shall see how many railroad grants they get for this day's work."[18] An abolitionist editor, who suspected that some northern Whigs had voted for the fugitive slave law in return for southern support for a slight modification of the tariff, rejoiced when the movement to modify the tariff failed. "The Judases have lost the reward of their treason," he noted.[19]

When Congress returned in December, Clay, whose strength had been sapped by consumption, moved to bring forward a new tariff. He announced that the "apparent calmness upon the surface of public affairs" might make a revision of the tariff possible. He pointed to the extinguishment of numerous iron furnaces in Pennsylvania and the scuttling of looms in New England as a reason why Congress should investigate a modification of the tariff. Unfortunately for Clay, he did not have either the energy or the political support to make tariff reform a major issue. Since the country had been on the brink of disunion just four months earlier, congressmen did not want to revisit the divisive issue of the tariff.[20]

In his first annual message, Fillmore pressed forward with his desire to increase the tariff. He recommended that Congress return to specific duties. "Specific duties are equal and uniform in all ports and at all times, and offer a strong inducement to the importer to bring the best article, as he pays no more duty upon that than upon one of inferior quality," the president declared.[21] Fillmore also wanted to increase the scale of duties. The Walker tariff had levied higher duties on the raw materials necessary for manufactured items than on the finished product. The president contended that a higher duty should be levied on the finished product rather than on the raw material. Democrats, who no doubt sensed the division within the Whig ranks, would not allow the Walker tariff to be repealed and give their rivals a desperately needed political victory. Anger over the compromise and bitterness over patronage continued to thin Whig ranks. In the Thirty-Second Congress, the Democrats had an even firmer grip on the House, outnumbering the Whigs by nearly forty seats in the House and eleven in the Senate. The Free Soil contingent had shrunk, making them irrelevant. Fillmore called for a tariff modification in his other two annual messages, but the large Democratic majorities laughed at his suggestions.[22]

The Whigs' inability to modify the Walker tariff frustrated the new president. Fillmore urged Congress to change the tariff, hoping that a battle over the tariff, even a failed one, might help to bring together the discordant wings of his party. More than the Democrats, the Whig Party had been hurt politically by the Compromise of 1850. In the North, Whigs remained hopelessly divided into Cotton and Conscience Whigs. In Fillmore's home state of New York, the party had split into a faction of Silver Greys that supported Fillmore and a coalition that championed Fillmore's longtime enemy William H. Seward. Southern Whigs could not win elections at home if they remained tied to their antislavery compatriots in the North. These splits over slavery had put the Whig Party on the path to destruction.[23]

When the Whigs convened in Baltimore for their nominating convention in 1852, Fillmore's biggest problem became his secretary of state, Daniel Webster, who still harbored presidential aspirations in spite of his failing health. A small group of New Englanders clung to Webster after a series of ballots. Had they abandoned him in favor of Fillmore, then the incumbent president would have gotten the nomination. But after fifty-three ballots, enough of Fillmore's supporters shifted to Winfield Scott, giving him the nomination.[24]

The Whigs also mishandled the tariff at their convention. They had long been in favor of the repeal of the Walker tariff, but they included a tepid plank on the tariff. It seemed as if Whigs had adopted a position in support of revenue tariff because the plank read: "Revenue sufficient for the expenses of an economical administration of the Government in time of peace ought to be derived from a duty on imports, and not from direct taxation; and in laying such duties, sound policy requires a just discrimination, whereby suitable encouragement may be afforded to American industry, equally to all classes, and to all parts of the country." Little difference existed between the Whigs and Democrats in their tariff planks.[25] But as Michael F. Holt has demonstrated, the tariff plank that newspapers published was not the one they intended. Whigs had sought to include an additional sentence affirming their support for a tariff with specific duties. This change was approved by the platform committee and included in the official journal, but it was then omitted when newspapers published the actual platform. Its effect would have been marginal. Few newspapers commented on the issue, and few political leaders noticed it on the stump.[26]

The Whigs suffered their biggest defeat yet in 1852. Scott carried only four states—Vermont, Massachusetts, Kentucky, and Tennessee. Franklin Pierce became the new president. As southerners hoped, Pierce proved to be malleable. He embraced the southern position on slavery's expansion and also on the tariff. In 1853, Secretary of the Treasury James Guthrie sent out a circular to customhouse officials asking them for their opinions on a potential reduction of the tariff. He wanted to know which articles could be admitted duty free. This would ease the burden on the customs collectors. Guthrie recommended to Congress that medicines, clothing dyes, fruits, and spices be admitted duty free. He estimated that the admission of these items without a duty would reduce the revenue by four million dollars. This reduction would, according to a Boston paper, remove the temptation of members of Congress to engage in reckless spending with the revenue. In his first message to

Congress, Pierce echoed Guthrie's statements. The president informed the nation that the tariff no longer was a matter of "grave controversy." Pierce claimed that the Walker tariff had exceeded expectations and that it should be lowered since the nation had revenue in excess of nearly fifteen million dollars.[27] Congress did not act, on his recommendation. The next year, Pierce said tariffs for revenue instead of for protection "may now be regarded as the settled policy of the country."[28] The Democrats' ascendency, the success of their economic system, the fortuitous discovery of gold in California, and an annual surplus of about fifteen million dollars allowed Pierce to make this statement. In 1855, he even announced, "I am fully persuaded that it would be difficult to devise a system superior to that by which the fiscal business of the Government is now conducted."[29] He continued to call for reductions in the tariff, but Congress would not respond until his final months in office.[30]

The prospects for a tariff increase dwindled as the Whig Party faded into oblivion. Some Whigs abandoned politics and contented themselves with practicing law or aiding the railroad industry. Some southern Whigs joined the Democratic Party. Northern Whigs who wanted to remain active in politics found themselves with options. William H. Seward and Thurlow Weed tried to hold onto the Whig Party, but most northern Whigs abandoned the party. Some joined the Know Nothing or American Party. This organization wanted to modify the naturalization laws in order to prevent more immigrants from coming to America. Know Nothing lodges appeared all throughout the country in 1854, but the majority were in the North. After the House had deadlocked over the choice of a Speaker in 1855, the Know Nothings put one of their own, former Democrat Nathaniel P. Banks, into the speakership. Banks's victory was disappointing for many Know Nothings because they had wanted to place a former Whig into the post. More than likely this would lead to a new tariff bill coming to the floor. When the Know Nothings assembled to draft a platform in 1856, they avoided the tariff. Whig leaders had discussed how a tariff protected American labor back in the 1840s, but the Know Nothings failed to make this connection. Perhaps this had been done to avoid alienating former Democrats who had joined the party. The Know Nothings' twelfth plank, which called for the respect of all laws that respected slavery, angered many northern members. The convention, which met in early 1855, nominated former president Fillmore, a strong tariff man. Fillmore carried only Maryland in the 1856 election and fared better in the South than in the North.[31]

The poor showing of the Know Nothings in 1856 can be attributed to the rise of a second group that positioned itself to become the rival party of the Democrats. After the Kansas Nebraska Act of 1854, more and more northerners joined the Republican Party. Like the Know Nothing Party, the infant Republican Party avoided the tariff issue in 1856. Its presidential candidate, John C. Frémont, ran on a platform that called for the nonextension of slavery into the territories. Frémont carried every free state except California, Illinois, Indiana, New Jersey, and Pennsylvania, but the sixty electoral votes of those five states ensured the victory of the Democratic Party's nominee, James Buchanan. Republicans knew that if they could hold their states in 1860 and pick up thirty-seven more electoral votes, then a Republican would become president. Winning Pennsylvania and either Illinois or

Indiana became the easiest route to that goal. These three states bordered ones that permitted slavery, however, so antislavery radicalism could work as a detriment. "The next Republican candidate for president must, to be successful, carry Pennsylvania, Indiana and Illinois; he must reside in one of those states," an Indiana paper announced.[32] Large numbers of Know Nothing members who had supported Fillmore resided in these states. A different appeal had to be made to swing voters to the Republican column in these states.[33]

Southern Democrats likewise worried over Frémont's strong showing and what it portended for the future. "Looking ahead four years, I have serious fears that the black Republicans will succeed in the Presidential struggle," North Carolina Democrat William W. Holden noted. "The indications are that Mr. Seward will almost surely carry New York, Pennsylvania, and Ohio; and the lesser free states, with one or two exceptions, must follow in such a train. God defend and preserve the republic!"[34] At a ceremony celebrating the completion of the Charleston and Memphis Railroad, Charleston mayor William Porcher Miles called for southern unity to protect the region from northern attacks. He read a poem (a parody of a speech in *The Merchant of Venice*), and in his poem he included the tariff as a grievance that the South had against the North.

> Many a time and oft,
> Even in the Capitol, you have rated me,
> And ta'en my money by your grinding tariffs,
> Still have I borne it with a patient shrug,
> For sufferance is the badge of all the South,
> You call me ruffian, robber, cut-throat, dog,
> And spit upon my social policy—
> And all for use of that which is mine own.[35]

While few discussed the tariff in 1856, it reappeared in Congress in early 1857. Guthrie estimated that the federal government would soon have a surplus of over forty million dollars. He urged Congress to modify the tariff. One observer noted, "the subject creates far less anxiety and excitement than it did at a former period, and other and more serious causes of discordance and disunion have come into operation."[36] Several House members presented plans to reduce the tariff. William Boyce of South Carolina advocated George McDuffie's old idea of a horizontal tariff of 20 percent. Lewis D. Campbell, chairman of the Ways and Means Committee, used parliamentary trickery to allow his bill to come forward. He proposed a measure where the annual revenue from the tariff would be reduced by ten million dollars. This would reduce the incoming revenue, but it would not be as drastic as other proposals, which would remove the little protection that manufacturers still enjoyed. "The democrats are getting ready to knife the great manufacturing States," one editor noted.[37] Muscoe R. H. Garnett of Virginia retorted that Buchanan's recent victory meant that the country had agreed to administer the government on Democratic principles, "and one of the first of these Democratic principles is free trade."[38]

Many observers expected that there would not be enough time to enact any modification of the tariff. Most of the attention of House members was on a committee that investigated alleged corruption. According to one individual, manufacturers were prepared to spend one hundred thousand dollars to buy votes that would reduce rates on raw materials. "They would succeed if the other side did bid higher," he contended.[39] Perhaps there was something to this since Campbell's bill admitted silks, chemicals, drugs, and dyes duty free.[40]

Campbell's bill kept the schedules of the Walker tariff and reduced rates. Woolen manufacturers, who had clamored for more protection on woolens, contented themselves with a reduced duty on raw wool. Pennsylvanians had wanted higher duties on iron, but surrendered this call in order to retain the current duty and not suffer another drop. All told, Campbell's tariff sought to reduce revenue by placing more items on the free list.[41]

Since Congress had not debated a tariff bill since 1846, this became the first tariff debate for many of the House members. The debate lacked some of the technical details of previous tariff battles, and a few members spent more time discussing slavery than the tariff. While the debate lacked the sophistication of the earlier encounters, it did have its humorous moments. When Garnett referred to Campbell as a "leader of the Republican party," the Ohioan retorted, "For the benefit of the Republican party, let me say that I am not recognized, I believe, as one of its leaders." Garnett now had Campbell on the hook and began reeling him in. "Since that party does not recognize him, he stands by himself; and let me warn him, to get, as quick as he can, out of the uncomfortable position in which he has placed himself, both in regard to his party relations and his tariff scheme." The galleries erupted in laughter. Garnett then declared, "the doors of the Democratic fold are still open to him; but he must first wash himself seven times in the waters of Jordan." Here again the audience howled with laughter demonstrating that they understood the biblical reference. But Campbell gave as good as he got. "If the gentlemen will go back to the principles of Washington and Jefferson and Madison—the great leaders of the Democracy in its purer days—I will go with him."[42]

Table 17.1. House vote, 1857

	Democrats		Opposition		American		Total	
	For	Against	For	Against	For	Against	For	Against
New England	1	0	9	0	17	0	27	0
Middle	5	4	34	4	7	0	46	8
South	1	40	0	0	6	5	7	45
West	3	9	22	20	5	2	30	31
Total	10	53	65	24	35	7	110	84

Source: *House Journal*, 34th Cong., 3rd Sess., 20 Feb. 1857, 503–4.
Note: "Opposition" includes men calling themselves the opposition, Whigs, and Republicans.

The bill passed the House by a vote of 110 to 84 on February 20. The voting pattern suggests that House members saw the bill as a protective measure, because most of its support came from New England and the middle states. Every Pennsylvanian and New Englander supported it, while most southerners opposed it.[43]

The Senate, like it did with most tariffs, spent little time on the tariff. Shortly after the bill arrived, Finance Committee chairman Robert M. T. Hunter offered a substitute for the bill. He reduced most rates by either 25 or 20 percent. His substitute set the average rate at 20 percent. Woolen manufacturers applauded the bill because of a low rate on raw wool, which now paid a duty of 23 percent. Iron manufacturers, however, were angered when their item went from a rate of 30 percent to 24 percent. Senators approved Hunter's substitute by a vote of thirty-three to twelve, and then the Senate passed the measure without a recorded vote. The manufacturers who disapproved of the modifications perhaps could have scuttled the bill or filibustered it to death, but they no doubt realized that in addition to Buchanan's victory, the Democrats would now take control of the House. If they rejected these moderate reductions, then the incoming House would go much further.[44]

Shortly after Pierce signed the tariff of 1857 into law, the Panic of 1857 commenced. Though not as severe as the panics of 1819 and 1837, the Panic of 1857 hurt the North's economy much more than the South's. Unemployed workers filled the streets of northern cities hoping to find jobs. Midwestern farmers no longer had a market for their staples. In the North, the possibility of a European-style revolution haunted individuals. In the South, profits from cotton and tobacco exports declined, but no social upheavals occurred. Southern planters blamed unscrupulous northern financiers whose speculations on southern exports nearly ruined the nation. The panic proved the importance of southern staples to the commerce of not only America, but also the world, southern planters alleged. Horace Greeley, editor of the *New York Tribune*, blamed the tariff of 1857 for the economic downturn. Among the most vociferous proponents of economic nationalism, Greeley demanded that when Congress reconvened, it raise all duties. "We believe a protective tariff to be the true national remedy for our present commercial ills," Greeley declared. "Let it be decreed tomorrow that no foreign product that competes with a homemade one shall henceforth enter our ports without paying from forty to eighty percent duty and our banks would be all right within thirty days."[45] Even David Wilmot, the lone Pennsylvanian who had supported the Walker tariff, blamed the new tariff for the panic. Cries of protection had rung hollow during the prosperous decade since the Walker tariff, but the panic changed the sentiments of northerners. With textile workers, miners, shipbuilders, shoemakers, mechanics, ironworkers, and farmers clamoring for relief, Americans took a new look at an old issue.[46]

18

*"Free trade and slavery
are twin measures"*

FOLLOWING THEIR DEFEAT in the election of 1856, Republicans recognized that the party needed to broaden its appeal to win in 1860. They realized that the tariff could accomplish that goal. Republicans adopted a more nuanced stance on their tariff. Instead of discussing how the tariff protected American manufacturers, they now stressed how a tariff protected labor. The free-trade policies of the Democrats, Republicans charged, led to unemployment and a reduction in wages. At every opportunity, they linked southern demands for low tariffs and slavery. "Free trade and slavery are twin measures," roared one Republican editor.[1] By advocating protectionist doctrines, Republicans presented a clear alternative between themselves and their adversaries on an issue other than slavery. More importantly, free trade became synonymous with slavery since those became identified with the aristocracy of the South. But Republicans' advocacy of a tariff that protected American labor served other purposes. It allowed the new party to appeal to urban laborers who had tended to support the Democratic Party and also nativists who had supported Millard Fillmore in 1856.[2]

Republican editors and orators used certain terms to describe the kind of labor that a tariff would protect. A tariff protected American-born laborers from the pauper laborers in Europe. "It is simply a question involving the fair wages of our workmen, the independence of our farmers, and the prosperity of our manufacturers against the pauper workmen and the wealthy capitalists of Europe," according to Philadelphia's *North American*.[3] A tariff also protected free white labor, Republicans claimed. This ploy, with racist undertones, countered the arguments that the new party wanted to make the African slave the equal of the white man. "In the eyes of the Democracy, the laborer has no right to himself, no right to the proceeds of his labor, no right to aspire to the dignity of owning land, no right to aim at bettering his condition. He is a mud sill and he has no right but the right of being owned," one Pennsylvania newspaper announced.[4] Whereas James H. Hammond said, "cotton is king," James Campbell of Pennsylvania retorted, "In the whole land, iron is king."[5] When the Republicans coupled these arguments with a reminder that the proslavery and free-trade Democratic Party had squandered a Treasury surplus, the Republican Party had an issue to take to the American people in the 1860 elections. "The prosperity of American industry under the promptings of free labor is at war with the plans and purposes of the slavocracy," an editor declared.[6]

Many Republicans traced their origins to Clay's Whig Party. This has led some historians to argue that the Republican Party was nothing more than the Whig Party reincarnated. Yet many other Republicans traced their lineage back to the party of Andrew Jackson. "It is known that a very large minority of the Republican ranks is composed of persons who came out of the Democratic party when it was dominant in the federal administration, and in a majority of the states, because of its proslavery proclivities," a Republican sheet from upstate New York declared. Why, the editor asked rhetorically, did Democrats join the Republican Party? "It was 'the peculiar institution' and not the tariff or free trade that influenced them," he responded.[7] In a campaign against the slaveholding aristocracy of the South, the tariff became an issue that solidified the unification of old Democrats and Whigs into the Republican Party. By arguing that the tariff protected the worker and that the Democratic Party concerned itself only with the lot of the master class, Republicans outflanked their opponents. Influential Republicans such as Salmon P. Chase, Galusha Grow, John Hale, Hannibal Hamlin, Gideon Welles, and David Wilmot, who had been Democrats in the 1830s and 1840s before they joined the Republican Party, welcomed this appeal to equal rights. Instead of a national bank threatening the economic independence of Americans, Democratic converts to the Republican Party perceived the same threat from the concept of free trade. Though many of these men believed in low tariffs, they valued aiding the laborer against aristocratic monopolies.[8]

As nativists and disgruntled Democrats joined the Republican Party, those injured by the Panic of 1857 found little relief from the Buchanan administration. The new president urged retrenchment in federal spending and a new bankruptcy law. "The late disastrous monetary revulsion may have one good effect should it cause both the government and the people to return to the practice of a wise and judicious economy both in public and private expenditures," he said. The following year, the president mentioned the tariff in his annual message. He did not suggest an increase in duties. Rather, Buchanan urged Congress to implement specific duties instead on foreign goods.[9] Congress did not respond to his pleas. From 1858 until the spring of 1860, committees controlled by Democrats stymied all proposals to bring a tariff bill to the House floor. Democrats, influenced by Howell Cobb, Buchanan's treasury secretary, wanted to lower the tariff, not raise it. They believed that lower duties on imports would entice more foreign importations, thus driving down prices. Lower prices would increase consumption and allow the economy to return to its prepanic levels. Republicans charged that this policy would ruin the manufacturers and farmers who still languished because of the panic. The Democrats' inability to offer a viable response to the Panic of 1857, the violence in Kansas, and rampant corruption in the Buchanan administration allowed Republicans to take control of Congress in 1859. This meant that a protective tariff bill would more than likely be coming to the House floor.[10]

Not all Republicans agreed with the new direction of their party, however. Some began arguing that the party had broken from its antislavery moorings. In addition to a protective tariff, Republicans also called for federal aid to internal improvements, a homestead bill, and government support for a Pacific railroad. These issues could divide the party. The *Chicago Press and Tribune*, the leading Republican sheet in the Midwest, did not want to open this Pandora's box. "Start any one of these questions which may be raised by the incorporation of a high or low tariff, a system of internal improvements, or a metallic currency, in our creed, and a minority, large or small, now willing to cooperate with the body of the party in the further consecration of the territories to freedom, would find their ardor cooled and their action embarrassed by the indiscretion." The editor believed that the Republican Party should have a one-plank platform. This plank should declare: "Resolved, that we pledge ourselves to support the Constitution and laws of the United States and to use all constitutional and legal means to prevent the extension of human slavery into territories now free."[11] The *New York Evening Post*, the most vociferous free-trade journal in the land, concurred; it did not want to see the Republican Party distracted by what it called "nonessential issues." "The question of slavery is altogether too great and momentous to be thus prostituted to the selfish schemes of speculating capitalists and venal politicians, and narrow minded economical bigots," William Cullen Bryant wrote. Discussing the tariff was a waste of time. "The people of the United States have settled the question. After thirty years' struggle, in which the utmost was done that wealth and talent and eminent influence and political management could do to establish the protective system as the permanent policy of the country, the whole scheme was exploded, the party which upheld it was blotted out, and the political leaders who had bound their fortunes to that idea were consigned to private life or to the grave."[12]

Most Republicans recognized that their key to success had become the state of Pennsylvania. Pennsylvania had been a high-tariff bastion since 1820. The state had also been evenly divided between Democrats and Whigs during the Age of Jackson. However, both parties in Pennsylvania had championed a high tariff. This prompted Abraham Lincoln to refer to the tariff as the "peculiar interest" of Pennsylvania. A New England visitor to the federal capital who met a Pennsylvanian said that the man "thought of little beside the tariff."[13] Henry C. Carey lectured audiences throughout the Keystone State on the benefits of protection. Carey and his lieutenants convinced Republicans that they could carry Pennsylvania in 1860, and win the presidency, by embracing a protective tariff.[14]

As Republican presidential aspirants positioned themselves for the nominating convention in Chicago in 1860, editors throughout Pennsylvania suggested that only a high-tariff man could win the state's electoral votes. "Freedom and protection" are our watchwords, wrote one editor. "If the Chicago Convention will listen to the clearly expressed preferences of Pennsylvania, she will give the Republic a chief of which it shall never be ashamed."[15] A Philadelphia newspaper warned that if the Republicans nominated someone who could not be trusted on the tariff, then the "Charleston-Baltimore nominee will be elected, and we shall have a continuance of the Pierce and Buchanan system."[16] Philadelphia's *North American* minced no words: "We tell the convention, so soon to meet at Chicago, squarely, roundly, and in every other shape that means earnestness, that their candidates cannot carry the states of Pennsylvania and New Jersey unless they stand publicly on protective ground. . . . The candidate himself must be a known, avowed protectionist." This editor concluded with a dire warning. Should the convention disregard this advice, Pennsylvanians "will go back by tens of thousands or serve in a third party, which would be just as well for democracy. This state cannot be carried on an antislavery issue only. It is clear that the Chicago nominee, besides many other good principles, must, in any case, stand firmly by protection."[17]

When the House reconvened in December 1859, John Brown's raid at Harpers Ferry remained on the minds of members. Southerners warned that if the House elected a Republican speaker, then the South had the right to secede. The Republicans found themselves in a strong position at the onset. They had a plurality, but not a majority, of members. This forced members of the American Party and anti-Lecompton Democrats into the role of kingmaker. Republicans stood behind John Sherman of Ohio for the Speakership, but southern Democrats refused to allow his elevation. They contended that a House controlled by Sherman was equivalent to William H. Seward's election to the presidency. After eight weeks and forty-four ballots, the House chose Republican William Pennington of New Jersey as its Speaker. Only the second freshman congressman to secure the speakership, Pennington deferred to more experienced Republicans and followed the advice of Sherman in appointing committees. Southerners feared that the Republican leadership would "evade the Dred Scott decision" and disregard the fugitive slave law. "The House of Representatives is presided over by their uncompromising foe," the *Richmond Semi-weekly Examiner* warned Southerners, "and he [Pennington] has not been slow to show his hatred, nor has he bungled in the execution of his allotted task."[18] Republicans responded by suggesting that Pennington's election "is indeed a signal triumph over the Buchanan disunionists."[19]

On March 12, 1860, Justin S. Morrill of Vermont introduced a bill "to provide for the payment of outstanding treasury notes; to authorize a loan; to regulate and fix the duties on imports, and for other purposes." The Vermont Republican did not present his tariff bill as a measure of protection. He claimed that he had brought it forth solely for the purpose of raising revenue. His bill would end the loopholes by stopping the corrupt "systematic under valuations." "It will put new life into all branches of industry," Morrill declared, "and set the plow, the loom, and the anvil, at work throughout the whole length and breadth of the Republic." Morrill also said, "free trade abjures patriotism and boasts of cosmopolitism. It regards the labor of our own people with no more favor than that of the barbarian on the Danube or the coolly on the Ganges."[20]

Morrill's bill proposed to abandon the percentage schedules of the Walker and 1857 tariffs and replace them with specific duties. The percentage system, Morrill and other protectionists charged, encouraged corruption and prompted foreign manufacturers to dump their goods in America when prices waned. The Morrill tariff would also abolish the warehousing system, which had been in place since 1846. Specific duties and the end of the warehousing system gave the Morrill tariff much more protection.[21]

Most Republican papers lauded Morrill's proposed tariff. It reminded the American people of the Democratic Party's refusal to help American labor and industry. After perusing speeches made on the tariff in 1860, a correspondent for the

Table 18.1. House vote, 1860

	Republicans		Democrats		Opposition Party		Anti-Lecompton Democrats		American		Independent Democrats		Total	
	For	Against	For	Against	For	Against	For	Against	For	Against	For	Against	For	Against
New England	27	0	0	0	0	0	0	0	0	0	0	0	27	0
Middle	36	1	4	3	0	0	5	0	2	0	0	0	47	4
South	0	0	0	33	1	3	0	0	0	0	0	0	1	36
West	26	2	0	16	4	0	0	1	0	1	0	4	30	24
Total	89	3	4	52	5	3	5	1	2	1	0	4	105	64

Source: *House Journal*, 36th Cong., 1st Sess., 10 May 1860, 821–22.

Note: The Independent and Anti-Lecompton Democrats remained a part of the Democratic Party but embraced these labels to shield themselves from the unpopularity of President Buchanan's decision to force the fraudulent Lecompton Constitution through Congress.

Chicago Press and Tribune expressed his bewilderment at a discussion on the tariff. "It seemed strange to hear a speech upon any other topic beside slavery," he wrote. "Every auditor looked anxiously for the place where the Negro was to come in, but for once he was left entirely out of a speech in Congress."[22] The *New York Tribune* wrote that the bill "would open new and long closed mines; put furnaces into blast; reanimate long silent factories; and add immensely to the aggregate of our annual production. Hundreds of thousands now anxiously seeking work or vainly struggling for satisfactory wages would find new avenues to employment." Greeley then asked what stood in the way. "Nothing but the resolute will and supposed interest of 300,000 breeders and workers of slaves, who conceive that their profits will be diminished by a measure demanded by the interests and the voices of the great body of our eighteen millions of free laboring people."[23]

Republicans continued expounding on the theme of a tariff protecting labor. Henry Waldron of Michigan spoke of the dividing point between the Republican and Democratic parties. "On the one side is arrayed the Republican party, vindicating the dignity of free labor, and asserting the rights of toiling millions; while its antagonist is a false Democracy, reviling the laboring man as a slave, and prostituting itself to the interests and purposes of a purse proud oligarchy." "The great capital of the country is its labor, and, unemployed, it seeks investment in vain," Pennsylvania's Samuel S. Blair avowed. He then said that the "protected nation is rich, because the people are employed, and can therefore buy, while the nation whose laborers are idle is poor, and cannot buy from others." Another Pennsylvanian, John P. Verree, said, "the system of free trade ignores the dignity of labor." He then added that the issue of the protection of labor had resulted in the election of many members of the People's Party in Pennsylvania in 1858; "it is upon that principle," he concluded, "that we expect to carry the presidential candidate who may be nominated at Chicago." Even Garnett B. Adrain, an anti-Lecompton Democrat from New Jersey, advocated labor in his address. He said that Presidents Washington, Jefferson, Madison, Monroe, and Jackson "never turned their backs upon the American mechanic and laborer, and neglected the home industry of the country" because they knew that "it is the labor of the farmer that feeds us; that of the mechanic that gives us a house for shelter, and that of the manufacturer that clothes us."[24]

On May 10, the House voted on the tariff. As predicted by most observers, it passed with ease. Sixty-four congressmen opposed it while 105 supported it. Of the ninety-two Republicans present, all but three voted for the tariff. Conversely, only four of the fifty-six Democrats endorsed the tariff. Emerson Etheridge, a former Whig and member of the Opposition Party from Tennessee, was the only southerner to vote for the tariff. House Republicans had unified their party on an issue other than the expansion of slavery. All that remained was a public declaration of a protective tariff in their platform in their upcoming convention at Chicago. "Doubtless the passage of the bill through the popular branch of Congress would strengthen the hands of its friends," a newspaper correspondent informed his editor. "But I apprehend that the party will, at Chicago, adopt the measure, not because it is expedient, but because it is right."[25]

In Philadelphia, Pottsville, and Pittsburgh, Pennsylvania, artillery salvos greeted the news that the House had passed a new tariff bill. But most northerners realized that they had won a hollow victory. The Senate, controlled by Democrats, did not appear willing to increase the tariff. Southerners also prepared to halt passage of a homestead bill. Cheap western homesteads, they feared, would lead to more free states and more congressmen opposed to slavery. "We have not the faintest hope that either will be permitted to become law," cried one Midwestern editor.[26]

Other Republicans sensed an opportunity to make political capital out of the situation. If the Democrats blocked the tariff in the Senate, as most expected, Republicans reasoned that they could take the issue to the people in the upcoming elections. The *Pittsburgh Gazette* told its subscribers that "the Southern managers have not the shrewdness to see the advantage of tasking this question out of politics in the coming campaign, and they will accordingly defeat the bill, leaving the tariff to become a subject of agitation and a controlling question in the doubtful states."[27] The *New York Evening Post* complained that House Republicans, who knew little about the features of the tariff bill, voted for it just so they could use it as an issue in Pennsylvania.[28]

The fate of the tariff in the Senate fell into the hands of Robert M. T. Hunter of Virginia, chairman of the Senate Finance Committee. Hunter had hoped to gain the Democratic Party's presidential nomination in Charleston, but, according to Robert Toombs, he could never succeed because of his honesty. Never aligning with the southern fire-eaters, Hunter had been a Whig but joined the Democratic Party long before the Whig Party dissolved. In the 1840s, he had been a supporter of Calhoun. On June 15, Hunter moved to postpone consideration of the tariff until the next session of Congress. He argued that the tariff of 1857 had helped the country through the recent panic. The tariff that the House had passed, Hunter said, "is so complicated a piece of legislation that it would double your army of officials in order to execute it. It would open the doors to more fraud than any financial system devised here before. . . . It is in itself the most monstrous piece of legislation that I have ever seen." Hunter offered the postponement to remove the tariff question from the upcoming political contest. James Bayard, a Delaware Democrat, concurred with Hunter in wanting to remove the issue from politics. A Pennsylvanian cautioned Hunter about the importance of the tariff to his state. "Pennsylvania has on almost all occasions decided the presidential contest. She will decide the next," Henry S. Acker wrote to Hunter. He also told Hunter that the Morrill tariff could influence the fate of the Democratic Party. "I verily believe that it will defeat it for years to come, and may indeed result in influencing the destruction of our glorious union by elevating sectional discord." Acker recommended that a tariff modified by Hunter could help Democrats in Pennsylvania by as much as twenty thousand votes. If these votes were withheld from the Republican nominee then the Democrats might be able to hold onto the presidency.[29]

Both of Pennsylvania's senators responded to the charges of Hunter. William Bigler, a Democrat, claimed that the Morrill tariff would provide the government with ample revenue. He pleaded with his Democratic allies to help the people of Pennsylvania: "I do ask though, that my friends on this side, with whom I have acted in many a political contest where their peculiar institutions were involved,

Table 18.2. Senate vote to postpone, 1860

	Republicans		Democrats		Total	
	For	Against	For	Against	For	Against
New England	11	0	0	0	11	0
Middle	4	0	1	3	5	3
South	0	0	0	15	0	15
West	5	0	1	7	6	7
Total	20	0	2	25	22	25

Source: *Senate Journal*, 36th Cong., 1st Sess., 15 June 1860, 673. James Harlan of Indiana is listed as voting against the postponement in the *Congressional Globe*, but according to the *Senate Journal*, he did not cast a vote. He has not been included in this table.
Note: "For" votes indicate support for the Morrill tariff.

will consider favorably, if possible, the feelings and interests of my people."[30] Simon Cameron followed Bigler. He seized on his colleague's use of the "peculiar institution" and rephrased it in Republican ideology: "While you, gentlemen of the South, are protecting your peculiar institutions, you ought at least, not to forget that we of the North have a peculiar institution to protect and encourage—our free white labor." The bill before the Senate, he lectured, would end the system of false invoices. Without the system of corruption, the foreign manufacturer would no longer control the capital of the United States. He even tied the theme of corruption into the theme of labor at the end of his oration. "I hold that it is but fair, that our labor should be protected against custom-house frauds, and against the pauper labor of Europe," he said.[31]

The motion to postpone passed by a vote of twenty-five to twenty-two. All the Republicans present voted against the postponement, and two Democrats, Bigler of Pennsylvania and Milton S. Latham of California, joined them. Republican papers blamed the old southern Whigs—Thomas L. Clingman, Robert M. T. Hunter, James A. Pearce, and Robert Toombs—for the bill's defeat. "The party lash has subdued them thoroughly, and they calmly sacrifice everything, even the convictions of a lifetime, because the interests of slavery require it," a Republican charged.[32]

On May 16, while the debate on the tariff raged in Washington, Republican delegates gathered in Chicago, Illinois, to craft a platform for the national party and nominate a candidate for the presidency. The platform committee completed its work in little time. With the recent passage of the Morrill Tariff in the House and its expected defeat in the Senate, Republicans included a tariff resolution in their platform. However, only seventy-seven words of the platform (or 6.6 percent) addressed the tariff. "While providing revenue for the support of the general government by duties upon imports, sound policy requires such an adjustment of these imports as to encourage the development of the industrial interests of the whole country," the twelfth resolution stated. Nowhere in the entire platform did the committee use the word "tariff." But when the committee announced the twelfth plank, the convention hall erupted into thunderous applause. "At first it was scattered," reported an Indianan.

> But it grew thicker and came heavier, till at last the sense of the matter seemed to get fully into everybody's head, and then broke out into the wildest, fiercest hurrah that I ever heard. Hats, handkerchiefs, and parasols were waving in wild disorder, as if the tornado were whirling them about in the building. It was a scene of enthusiasm such as I never saw before, and may never see again.[33]

Republicans crafted this plank to cater to the ex-Democrats and free-trade elements in their party. A vigorous stand on protection could jeopardize the fragile coalition. In spite of the wild cheers in Chicago at the announcement of the tariff plank, some Republicans derived another meaning from the cryptic language. "We have read the resolution several times over, and cannot find in it a single word in favor of raising the duties on imported goods, nor the slightest mention of the doctrine of protection," the *New York Evening Post* claimed.[34]

The Republicans then turned their attention to selecting a nominee. William H. Seward entered the canvass as the leading contender for the nomination. In addition to the perception of Seward being radical, rumors abounded that he could not be trusted on the tariff. Seward's managers countered these rumors by saying that they would "spend oceans of money" to carry Pennsylvania. In spite of this, Murat Halstead, a veteran political observer, reported that the Republican candidates for the governorship of Pennsylvania and Indiana suggested that they would end their candidacies if Seward led the Republican ticket. Because of these threats, Republican delegates began to look elsewhere for a nominee.[35]

Instead of Seward, the Republicans nominated Abraham Lincoln, a man who proudly called himself a "Henry Clay Whig." Immediately after news of Lincoln's nomination reached the telegraph offices, reports emerged of Lincoln being "an old line Whig" and friendly to a tariff. Pennsylvanians, especially, rejoiced at the news. "Mr. Lincoln is a tariff man and stands on tariff platform," one editor wrote.[36] Another said: "Mr. Lincoln was, throughout, a consistent and devoted Whig, well known for his firm and unwavering fidelity to Henry Clay, and the great policy of protection to American industry."[37] "There is no sounder tariff man in the country than Abraham Lincoln," a Harrisburg sheet told the people of central Pennsylvania.[38] Even the *Reading Journal*, a Democratic sheet in Pennsylvania, referred to Lincoln as "a Henry Clay Whig, and the devoted personal friend of that great statesman, he is the advocate of protection to American industry."[39]

Republicans continued stressing how the tariff protected labor in the months leading up to the presidential election. They focused most of their energy on Pennsylvania. Democrat James Buchanan had carried the state by twenty-seven thousand votes in 1856. Then in the gubernatorial election of 1857, Democrat William F. Packer humbled Republican David Wilmot by over forty thousand votes. Economic relief and not antislavery rhetoric had come to define the political contours of Pennsylvania after the Panic of 1857. The Republicans grasped this idea and routed

the Democrats in the midterm elections of 1858. In the Pennsylvania gubernato-
rial election, which took place in October 1860, the Republican candidate, Andrew
Curtin, won by over thirty thousand votes. Coupled with Republican victories in
Ohio and Indiana, observers believed that this ensured Lincoln the presidency.
Curtin visited Boston's Faneuil hall a week before the November election day to encourage Republican voters. "I come here from a state which has recently declared at
the ballot box for freedom and protection of her labor," he declared.[40] As others did,
Curtin reminded his audience that a Democratically controlled Senate had rejected
the prayers of laborers with contempt.[41]

Lincoln won the presidency by obtaining every free-state electoral vote except
three of New Jersey's. He won Pennsylvania by almost ninety thousand votes over
the fusion ticket of his opponents. Howell Cobb of Georgia believed that the tariff
had little effect on voters, however. "With the exception of a few dull speeches in
favor of a protective tariff, the whole canvas was conducted by the most bitter and
malignant appeals to the anti-slavery sentiment of the North," he wrote."[42]

The second session of the Thirty-Sixth Congress commenced on December 3,
1860. On December 20, as church bells in Charleston announced South Carolina's
secession from the union, Robert M. T. Hunter asked the Senate once again to postpone consideration of the House tariff bill until March 4, 1861. If agreed to, this
parliamentary gambit would kill the tariff bill. In what can be called the first clash
of the Civil War, northerners refused to acquiesce. "There is still a majority against
us," James Simmons mused early in the session. "But I trust there will not be a great
deal longer."[43] Between December 1860 and February 1861, nine southern Democratic senators who had voted for the postponement of the tariff bill the previous
session withdrew when their states seceded. As the remaining southern senators
tried to bully Morrill into dropping his bill in order to keep the southern states
from seceding, Morrill, a former Whig, refused to be intimidated. He remembered
Jackson's stance against the nullifiers. "One blast from Old Hickory at this time
would be worth more than an army with banners," he wrote.[44]

Republicans now stressed the revenue aspects of Morrill's bill. If Congress refused to modify the tariff, they asserted, it would bankrupt the Treasury. The remaining Democrats criticized what they referred to as a "radical bill" with "monstrous duties." Republicans, they charged, planned to destroy the country in order
to carry out the principles of the Chicago platform. Stephen A. Douglas objected to
the bill because it would "irritate" other states to the point of separating. Thomas
L. Clingman of North Carolina did not blame tariffs or corruption for the financial
woes of the country. "The credit of this country fell on the seventh day of November, when it was understood that Lincoln and Hamlin were elected," he proclaimed.
The country did not need a tariff, according to Clingman; it needed the Republican
administration to resign even before it came into office. The sharpest attack on the
bill came at the very end from Joseph Lane of Oregon. "It is an unfair bill, a bill got
up for the protection of certain interests," he said. More importantly, in his opinion,
the architects had brought forward a bill that "is not calculated to give peace, but
to widen the breach." Republicans, Lane continued, "mean coercion, they mean to
enforce the federal laws, they mean to collect the revenue, they intend to carry on

a policy that will inaugurate in this country a civil war, a war that will drench these states with blood." His fear was that Lincoln might do the same things that Jackson had promised to do to South Carolina during the nullification crisis.[45]

When oratory failed, Democrats tried to emasculate the bill by amending it. By the end of debate, the Senate had added 156 amendments to the House bill. Sherman, who helped guide the bill through the House the previous session, said that the amendments "did not materially affect the general principles upon which the bill was founded." An amendment proposed by Seward, however, did alter the bill. Hoping to appease the merchants of New York City, he sought to increase the period of time that goods could be stored in warehouses. Instead of ninety days, Seward's amendment allowed for goods to be held in warehouses for three years. His amendment passed by a vote of twenty-six to nineteen. Seven Republicans voted for the crucial amendment. Only one Democrat, Bigler from Pennsylvania, who had voted with the Republicans throughout the tariff debate, opposed it.[46]

The Senate passed the Morrill tariff on February 20 by a vote of twenty-five to fourteen. All the negative votes came from Democrats. Bigler was the only Democrat to vote for the tariff. Half of the negative votes came from senators whose states would secede before long, and three negative votes came from the border states of Kentucky, Maryland, and Missouri. The only northerners to vote against the tariff were Democrats Stephen A. Douglas of Illinois and Henry M. Rice of Minnesota.[47]

House members grumbled over the amendments with which the Senate had saddled them. Morrill urged his colleagues to take the bill as it was. Pennsylvanians James T. Hale and Thaddeus Stevens reiterated these sentiments. "I am obliged to swallow this bill just as it is, or I know it will not be swallowed at all," Stevens groused. He also vented his displeasure at the Senate's amendment to the warehousing system. Stevens said this provision no longer made the bill a protective measure. Sherman responded that the tariff would yield enough revenue to meet expenditures and that when the next Congress convened, members could "remedy all defects and deficiencies of this bill." House Democrats increased their rhetoric. Virginia's Roger Pryor perceived a conspiracy in the tariff bill: "I declare that this tariff is the result of a compact between the abolitionists of New England and the protectionists of Pennsylvania, whereby the protectionists of Pennsylvania agreed to vote for an abolitionist for the presidency in consideration of an engagement that the abolitionists would concede a bounty to iron."[48]

The House concurred with all the Senate's amendments except for a duty on tea and coffee. The Senate yielded on this amendment and sent the bill to the president. "This is a democratic bill and was not acceptable to the Republicans; but it was thought best to pass it and put a stop to the augmentation of the national debt," an Oregon Republican complained.[49] The final hurdle remained securing the president's approval. "Old Buck will not dare to veto the bill, so we may consider it as law," an Ohio sheet reported.[50] Amid little fanfare, the departing president signed the Morrill tariff bill on March 2, 1861.

Buchanan signed the bill on a Saturday night. Few newspapers issued Sunday editions at this time. The advent of the telegraph should have made the enactment of the tariff the lead story, but on Monday, March 4, 1861, Lincoln took the oath

Table 18.3. Senate vote, 1861

	Republicans		Democrats		Total	
	For	Against	For	Against	For	Against
New England	10	0	0	0	10	0
Middle	4	0	1	1	5	1
South	0	0	0	7	0	7
West	10	0	0	6	10	6
Total	24	0	1	14	25	14

Source: *Senate Journal*, 36th Cong., 2nd Sess., 20 Feb. 1861, 275.

of office. Most newspapers filled their columns with speculations about what the new president would say. Would there be coercion of the seceded states, or would Lincoln continue Buchanan's acquiescence? Even in Pennsylvania, no cannons heralded the final passage of the tariff.[51]

The Morrill tariff ended more than ten years' worth of low tariffs. Iron and woolen manufacturers obtained the protection they had been craving since 1846. Northern protectionists had won a major victory, but they had secured their victory only as a result of the secession of the South. Had southern senators remained in Washington, senate Republicans could not have passed the tariff in 1861 because the Democrats would have had a majority in the Senate and a friendly vice president to break a tie. Furthermore, had secession not occurred, Democrats would still have had a five-vote majority in the Senate of the Thirty-Seventh Congress. This fact contradicts the claim that the tariff caused the Civil War. "There is but one way in which peace can be restored here," Charles Sumner wrote after the battle of Bull Run. "And that is by removal of slavery. This is the cause and origin of the rebellion; and nothing else. The Morrill tariff has had nothing to do with it."[52] "The war, whatever its nominal issues, whether federal sovereignty or states' rights, free trade or the Morrill tariff, the Republican constitution or the birthplace of the president, is really a war for and against slavery," announced the *London Spectator*, a British paper.[53]

As he prepared to leave the White House in 1837, Andrew Jackson delivered a farewell address. Jackson reminded the people how Washington, in his farewell, had still regarded the government under the Constitution as an "experiment." But in 1837, according to Jackson, "the trial has been made." A republican form of government had endured and prospered after the War of 1812. It survived threats of disunion in 1820, 1833, and 1850. Democracy had prevailed, so much so that over 80 percent of eligible voters voted in 1860. But as Congress wrestled with the Morrill tariff, the chords of union began to be severed. Many of the men who had battled alongside and against Jackson convened in Washington for a peace conference in February 1861. Dubbed the "Old Gentlemen's Conference," the old Whigs and Democrats could not find a solution.[54]

What had started on December 20 in South Carolina continued into the winter and spring of 1861. When eleven southern states seceded, none of them listed the tariff as a reason for their departure from the union. Instead, they referred to the victory of a "sectional party" and "recent developments in Federal affairs." The tariff did not cause the Civil War. It did, however, bring countless Americans into the political process. And with this newly discovered sense of democracy, some of the people urged their state leaders to secede, while others wanted their leaders to maintain the union at all costs. Abraham Lincoln referred to the war as a "people's contest" in July 1861. The democracy that the tariff installed in America, sadly, helped to bring about the Civil War, but it also helped to preserve the union.

William Lowndes. From *Life and Times of William Lowndes of South Carolina, 1782-1822,* by Harriott H. Ravenel (New York: Houghton, Mifflin, 1901)

John Tod. Courtesy of Bedford County, Pennsylvania, Commissioners.

Hon. Silas Wright of NY.
Brady-Handy Photograph
Collection, Library of Congress Prints and Photographs
Division, Washington, DC.

John Quincy Adams, oil on canvas
by Chester Harding (ca. 1827–1828).
Courtesy of the Redwood Library
and Athenaeum, Newport, Rhode
Island.

Hon. Gulian Crommelin Verplanck of NY. Brady-Handy Photograph Collection, Library of Congress Prints and Photographs Division, Washington, DC.

Henry Clay. A. Gibert del.
from a daguerreotype by Philip
Haas; lith. and published by
Philip Haas (Washington, DC,
ca. 1844). Library of Congress
Prints and Photographs Division, Washington, DC.

Millard Fillmore. Engrav-
ing by John Chester
Buttre, *N.E. Historical and
Genealogical Register* vol. 31
(1877). Library of Congress
Prints and Photographs
Division, Washington, DC.

James I. McKay, Representative from North Carolina. From *Life on Stone* by Charles Frederich (Baltimore: Lith. pr. by E. Weber & Co., 1840). Library of Congress Prints and Photographs Division, Washington, DC.

Robert M. T. Hunter, produced by Matthew Brady's studio between 1844–1860. Daguerreotype collection, Library of Congress Prints and Photographs Division, Washington, DC.

Justin S. Morrill, Representative from Vermont. Julian Vannerson, photographer. Illustration in *McClees Gallery of Photographic Portraits of the Senators, Representatives & Delegates of the Thirty-Fifth Congress* (Washington: McClees & Beck, 1859). Library of Congress Prints and Photographs Division, Washington, DC.

James K. Polk, from *Life on Stone* by Charles Fenderich (Baltimore: Lith. pr. by E. Weber & Co., 1840). Library of Congress Prints and Photographs Division, Washington, DC.

Martin Van Buren. Lithograph by Daniel Dickinson, ca. 1844.
Library of Congress Prints and Photographs Division, Washington, DC.

Daniel Webster (ca. 1831). Library of Congress Prints and Photographs Division, Washington, DC.

Andrew Jackson, oil on canvas by Auguste Jean Jaques Hervieu (ca. 1830). Courtesy of the Redwood Library and Athenaeum, Newport, Rhode Island.

James Buchanan, painted by Jacob Eichholz (1830); engraved by J. Sartain (ca. 1840). Library of Congress Prints and Photographs Division, Washington, DC.

John Tyler, from *Life on Stone* by Charles Fenderich (Baltimore: Lith. pr. by E. Weber & Co., 1840). Library of Congress Prints and Photographs Division, Washington, DC.

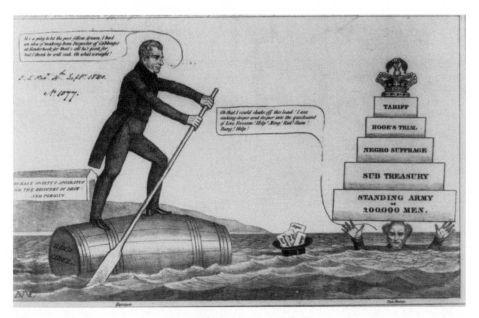

Matty's Perilous Situation Up Salt River. Published by J. Childs, 1840. Library of Congress Prints and Photographs Division, Washington, DC.

George McDuffie, oil on canvas by Charles Bird King. Courtesy of the Redwood Library and Athenaeum, Newport, Rhode Island.

John C. Calhoun, the sometime friend and longtime foe of protective tariffs. Calhoun's hand rests on a document that reads "Free Trade" in this 1845 likeness. Courtesy of the South Caroliniana Library, University of South Carolina, Columbia, SC.

Abbreviations

AFP	Adams Family Papers, Massachusetts Historical Society
AJP	Andrew Jackson Papers, Library of Congress
CAJ	*Correspondence of Andrew Jackson*, John S. Bassett, ed.
CFP	Campbell Family Papers, Duke University
CHP	Charles Hammond Papers, Ohio Historical Society
CJKP	*Correspondence of James K. Polk*, Herbert Weaver et al., eds.
CLC	*Circular Letters of Congressmen to Their Constituents, 1789–1829*, Noble E. Cunningham, ed.
CMPP	*A Compilation of the Messages and Papers of the Presidents, 1789–1902*, James D. Richardson, ed.
EEP	Edward Everett Papers, Massachusetts Historical Society
HGOP	Harrison Gray Otis Papers, Massachusetts Historical Society
MJQA	*Memoirs of John Quincy Adams*, Charles Francis Adams, ed.
JBP	James Buchanan Papers, Historical Society of Pennsylvania
JDP	John Davis Papers, American Antiquarian Society
JKPP	James K. Polk Papers, Library of Congress
MFP	Millard Fillmore Papers, State University of New York–Oswego
MVBP	Martin Van Buren Papers, Library of Congress
NPTP	Nathaniel P. Tallmadge Papers, Wisconsin Historical Society
PAJ	*The Papers of Andrew Jackson*, Sam B. Smith et al., eds.
PDWC	*The Papers of Daniel Webster*, Charles M. Wiltse et al., eds. (Correspondence)
PDWSFW	*The Papers of Daniel Webster*, Charles M. Wiltse et al., eds., (Speeches and Formal Writings)
PHC	*The Papers of Henry Clay*, James Hopkins et al., eds.
PJCC	*The Papers of John C. Calhoun*, Robert L. Meriwether et al., eds.
PWAG	*The Papers of William A. Graham*, J. G. de Roulhac Hamilton et al., eds.
PWPM	*The Papers of Willie Persons Mangum*, Henry T. Shanks, ed.
WFP	Winthrop Family Papers, Massachusetts Historical Society

Notes

INTRODUCTION

1. *Congressional Globe*, 34th Cong., 3rd Sess., appendix, 180.
2. *Congressional Globe*, 36th Cong., 1st Sess., 1928.
3. Robin L. Einhorn, *American Taxation, American Slavery* (Chicago: University of Chicago Press, 2006), 157–99.
4. Thomas Jefferson to Henry Baldwin, 15 Feb. 1821, Henry Baldwin Papers, Allegheny College; Lauchlin Bethune to the Freemen and Voters of Moore, Montgomery, Anson, Richmond, Robeson, and Cumberland, 20 June 1831, Edmund Deberry Papers, Southern Historical Collection—University of North Carolina.
5. Abraham Lincoln, "Speech at a Republican Banquet, Chicago, Illinois," Roy P. Basler (ed.), *The Collected Works of Abraham Lincoln* (8 vols., New Brunswick, NJ: Rutgers University Press, 1953–1955), II, 385.
6. Daniel Walker Howe, *What Hath God Wrought: The Transformation of America, 1815–1848* (New York: Oxford University Press, 2007); Walter A. McDougal, *The Throes of Democracy: The American Civil War Era* (New York: Harper Collins, 2008); Sean Wilentz, *The Rise of American Democracy: Jefferson to Lincoln* (New York: W. W. Norton, 2005); Daniel Peart, *Era of Experimentation: American Political Practices in the Early Republic* (Charlottesville: University of Virginia Press, 2014).
7. Mathew Carey, *The Crisis: A Solemn Appeal* (Philadelphia, 1823), vi–vii.
8. James Madison to Tench Coxe, 24 June 1789, William M. E. Rachal et al. (eds.), *The Papers of James Madison* (15 vols., Chicago: University of Chicago Press, 1962–1983), XII, 257.
9. Act of 4 July 1789, ch. 2, I *Stat.* 24.
10. Alexander Hamilton, "Final Version of the Report on the Subject of Manufactures," Harold C. Syrett, et al. (eds.), *The Papers of Alexander Hamilton* (27 vols., New York: Columbia University Press, 1961–1987), X, 298–304; Ron Chernow, *Alexander Hamilton* (New York: Penguin, 2004), 374–79; Alfred E. Eckes, *Opening America's Market: U.S. Foreign Trade Policy since 1776* (Chapel Hill: University of North Carolina Press, 1995), 16.
11. Thomas Jefferson to Dupont de Nemours, 18 Jan. 1802, Andrew A. Lipscomb (ed.), *The Writings of Thomas Jefferson* (20 vols., New York, 1903–1904), 344.
12. Victor S. Clark, *History of American Manufactures in the United States* (3 vols., Washington, DC: McGraw Hill, 1929), I, 263–70.
13. *Annals of Congress*, 13th Cong., 2nd Sess., 1959; John F. Marszalek, *The Petticoat Affair: Manners, Mutiny, and Sex in Andrew Jackson's White House* (Baton Rouge: Louisiana State University Press, 1997), 170–73.

CHAPTER 1

1. *Niles' Weekly Register* (Baltimore) 11 (22 Feb. 1817), 428; Winfield Scott to James Monroe, 24 Oct. 1814, National Archives, Record Group 45.

2. Maxine Berg, *The Age of Manufactures: Industry, Innovation, and Work in Britain, 1700–1820* (London: Fontana, 1985); Eric J. Evans, *The Forging of the Modern State: Early Industrial Britain, 1783–1870* (New York: Longman, 1983); Eric Pawson, *The Early Industrial Revolution: Britain in the Eighteenth Century* (New York: Barnes and Noble Books, 1979).

3. The best statement of the transition from an agrarian to a capitalist economy remains Charles Sellers, *The Market Revolution: Jacksonian America, 1815–1846* (New York: Oxford University Press, 1991). Additional information can be found in Daniel Walker Howe, *What Hath God Wrought: The Transformation of America, 1815–1848* (New York: Oxford University Press, 2007). On the American economy, see Douglas C. North, *The Economic Growth of the United States, 1790–1860* (Englewood Cliffs, NJ: Prentice Hall, 1961); Stuart Bruchey, *The Roots of American Economic Growth, 1607–1861: An Essay in Social Causation* (New York: Harper and Row, 1965); Diane Lindstrom, "American Economic Growth before 1840: New Evidence and New Directions," *Journal of Economic History* 39 (March 1979), 289–301.

4. *Senate Executive Journal*, 13th Cong., 3rd Sess., 15 Feb. 1815.

5. *Annals of Congress*, 13th Cong., 3rd Sess., 1186.

6. Madison, "Seventh Annual Message," CMPP, I, 567; Daniel Walker Howe, *What Hath God Wrought*, 80–86.

7. *Kentucky Gazette* (Lexington), 12 Feb. 1816.

8. George Washington Logan to Thomas Jefferson, 21 Oct. 1815, Thomas Jefferson Papers, Library of Congress; Thomas R. Gold to Gideon Granger, 19 Dec. 1815, Gideon and Francis Granger Papers, Library of Congress; *American State Papers: Finance* (5 vols., Washington, DC, 1832), III, 32–35, 52–54, 56; C. Edward Skeen, *1816: America Rising* (Lexington: University Press of Kentucky, 2003), 35.

9. Daniel Tompkins to Peter B. Porter, 6 Jan. 1816, Peter B. Porter Papers, Buffalo and Erie County Historical Society; George Rogers Taylor, *The Transportation Revolution, 1815–1860* (New York: Rinehart, 1951), 3–14.

10. Thomas Jefferson to Benjamin Austin, 9 Jan. 1816, Andrew A. Lipscomb (ed.), *The Writings of Thomas Jefferson* (20 vols., Washington, DC, 1903–1904), XIII, 391.

11. Act of 9 Feb. 1816, ch. 14, 3, *Stat.* 254.

12. *American State Papers: Finance*, III, 89–90.

13. Raymond Walters, *Alexander James Dallas, Lawyer, Politician, Financier, 1795–1817* (Philadelphia: University of Pennsylvania Press, 1943), 208.

14. Steven Watts, *The Republic Reborn: War and the Making of Liberal America, 1790–1820* (Baltimore: Johns Hopkins University Press, 1987), 298–316.

15. *Annals of Congress*, 14th Cong., 1st Sess., 962–66.

16. Donald R. Kennon and Rebecca M. Rogers, *The Committee on Ways and Means* (Washington, DC, 1989), 83–86.

17. Timothy Pickering to George Cabot, 14 Dec. 1815, Timothy Pickering Papers, Massachusetts Historical Society; Carl J. Vipperman, *William Lowndes and the Transition of Southern Politics, 1782–1822* (Chapel Hill: University of North Carolina Press, 1989), 126–31; Walters, *Alexander James Dallas*, 209.

18. Merrill D. Peterson, *The Great Triumvirate: Webster, Clay, and Calhoun* (New York: Oxford University Press, 1987), 6–18.

19. Clay, "Motion to Amend the Tariff Bill," PHC, I, 178–79; *Annals of Congress*, 14th Cong., 1st Sess., 1237–38.

20. *Annals of Congress*, 14th Cong., 1st Sess., 1243, 1247.

21. *Annals of Congress*, 14th Cong., 1st Sess., 1284.

22. Benjamin Ruggles to Charles Hammond, 27 Jan. 1816, CHP; Richard E. Ellis, *The Jeffersonian Crisis: Courts and Politics in the Young Republic* (New York: Oxford University Press, 1971), 104–7; Norman K. Risjord, *The Old Republicans: Southern Conservatism in the Age of Jefferson* (New York: Columbia University Press, 1965), 42; Aaron S. Crawford, "John Randolph of Roanoke and the Politics of Doom: Slavery, Sectionalism, and Self-Deception, 1773–1821" (PhD diss., University of Tennessee, 2012), 175–221.

23. Richard K. Cralle, "Memorandum," 4 Dec. 1831, PJCC, XI, 523; Charles M. Wiltse, *John C. Calhoun: Nationalist* (Indianapolis: Bobbs and Merrill, 1944), 120; Gerald M. Capers, *John C. Calhoun—Opportunist: A Reappraisal* (Gainesville: University of Florida Press, 1960), 45; Peterson, *Great Triumvirate*, 18–27.

24. Daniel Feller (ed.), *Retrospect of Western Travel* (Armonk, NY: M. E. Sharpe, 2000, reprint of 1838 ed.), 47.

25. Calhoun, "First Speech on the Military Academies Bill," PJCC, I, 288.

26. Calhoun, "Speech on the Revenue Bill," PJCC, I, 321.

27. Calhoun, "Speech on the Revenue Bill," PJCC, 348–50, 355; Wiltse, *John C. Calhoun: Nationalist*, 121–22.

28. *Life of John C. Calhoun, Presenting a Condensed History of Political Events from 1811 to 1843*, 19–21.

29. John Randolph to James M. Garnett, 2 Feb. 1816, John Randolph Papers, University of Virginia.

30. Charles Carroll to Robert G. Harper, 23 Feb. 1816, Robert Goodloe Harper Family Papers, Maryland Historical Society; *Annals of Congress*, 14th Cong., 1st Sess., 1350–52.

31. Norris W. Preyer, "Southern Support for the Tariff of 1816—a Reappraisal," *Journal of Southern History* 25 (Aug. 1959), 306–22; Mark Bils, "Tariff Protection and Production in the Early US Cotton Textile Industry," *Journal of Economic History* 44 (Dec. 1984), 1033–45.

32. David Waldstreicher, *In the Midst of Perpetual Fetes: The Making of American Nationalism, 1776–1820* (Chapel Hill: University of North Carolina Press, 1997), 294–348; Brian Balogh, *A Government Out of Sight: The Mystery of National Authority in Nineteenth-Century America* (New York: Cambridge University Press, 2009), 112–50.

33. Webster, "Second Speech on the Tariff," James W. McIntyre (ed.), *The Writings and Speeches of Daniel Webster* (18 vols., Boston: Little and Brown, 1903), V, 229; Wiltse, *John C. Calhoun: Nationalist*, 124; Peterson, *Great Triumvirate*, 72; Robert V. Remini, *Daniel Webster: The Man and His Time* (New York: W. W. Norton, 1997), 138–39; Robert F. Dalzell, *Enterprising Elite: The Boston Associates and the World They Made* (Cambridge, MA: Harvard University Press, 1987), 36.

34. *Maryland Gazette*, 29 Feb. 1816.

35. Richard Caton to Robert G. Harper, 22 Feb. 1816, Robert Goodloe Harper Family Papers, Maryland Historical Society; James H. Broussard, *The Southern Federalists, 1800–1816* (Baton Rouge: Louisiana State University Press, 1978), 186–87.

36. If Kentucky is included as a southern state in 1816, this gives six more favorable votes and one more negative one. With Kentucky included, southern support for the tariff of 1816 increases to 40 percent. However, if Tennessee is considered a western state and omitted along with Kentucky, then southern support for the tariff of 1816 falls to 31 percent.

37. *Annals of Congress*, 14th Cong., 1st Sess., 326, 331, 334; James Madison to William Eustis, 12 May 1816, William C. Rives (ed.), *Letters and Other Writings of James Madison* (4 vols., Philadelphia: J. B. Lippincott, 1865), III, 4.

38. *Annals of Congress*, 14th Cong., 1st Sess., 1261; Daniel Webster to Samuel Ayer Bradley, 21 April 1816, PDWC, I, 197.

39. *Merchants' Magazine and Commercial Review*, 1 May 1861, 578.

40. Paul A. David, "Learning by Doing and Tariff Protection: A Reconsideration of the Case of the Ante-bellum United States Cotton Textile Industry," *Journal of Economic History* 30 (Sept. 1970), 521–601.

41. Henry Clay to Unknown, 24 March 1816, PHC, II, 181; *Letters from the Hon. Abbott Lawrence to the Hon. William C. Rives of Virginia* (Boston, 1846), 25; Edward Stanwood, *American Tariff Controversies of the Nineteenth Century* (2 vols., Boston: Houghton Mifflin, 1903), I, 154–57; C. Skeen, *1816*, 63–64; Sellers, *Market Revolution*, 75; Frank W. Taussig, *The Tariff History of the United States* (New York: G. P. Putnam's Sons, 1888), 68–69.

42. *American State Papers: Finance*, IV, 466; Davis Rich Dewey, *A Financial History of the United States* (New York, 1918), 168–69.

43. *Richmond Enquirer*, 4 May 1816.

44. Nathaniel Macon to Joseph H. Nicholson, 12 Feb. 1816; Joseph H. Nicholson Papers, Library of Congress; Hugh Nelson to Joseph C. Cabell, 7 March 1816, Joseph C. Cabell Family Papers, University of Virginia; Davie (?) to William Gaston, 7 April 1816, William Gaston Papers, Southern Historical Collection—University of North Carolina; Skeen, *1816*, 211–31.

45. James Madison to D. Lynch, 27 June 1817, Gailard Hunt (ed.), *The Writings of James Madison* (9 vols., New York: G. P. Putnam's Sons, 1900–1910), VIII, 392–93; *Niles' Weekly Register* (Baltimore) 11 (25 Jan. 1817), 366–68; Shaw Livermore, *The Twilight of Federalism: The Disintegration of the Federalist Party, 1815–1830* (Princeton, NJ: Princeton University Press, 1962), 64–65; Paul K. Conkin, *Prophets of Prosperity: America's First Political Economists* (Bloomington: Indiana University Press, 1980), 177–78.

46. CLC, II, 978–79.

47. CLC, II, 996.

48. "The New Tariff," *Maryland Gazette and Political Intelligencer*, 22 Aug. 1816.

49. *Kentucky Gazette* (Lexington), 8 July 1816.

50. *Brief Remarks on the Proposed New Tariff* (New York, 1816), 4, 5, 10–14.

51. Calhoun to Alexander J. Dallas, 15 June 1816, PJCC, I, 361.

52. Montfort Stokes to James Iredell, 26 Jan. 1817, James Iredell Papers, Duke University; Skeen, *1816*, 77–95; George M. Blakey, "Rendezvous with Republicanism: John Pope vs. Henry Clay in 1816," *Indiana Magazine of History* 62 (1966), 233–50.

53. Murray N. Rothbard, *The Panic of 1819: Reactions and Policies* (New York: Columbia University Press, 1962), 9–17; North, *Economic Growth of the United States*, 75–77, 233–44; George Dangerfield, *The Awakening of American Nationalism, 1815–1828* (New York: Harper and Row, 1965), 72–89; Samuel Rezneck, "The Depression of 1819–1822: A Social History," *American Historical Review* 39 (Oct. 1933), 28–47; Sellers, *Market Revolution*, 103–36.

54. C. A. Trimble to William Allen Trimble, 1 June 1819, William Allen Trimble Papers, Ohio Historical Society.

55. *Lexington Public Advertiser*, 10 May 1820.

56. Charles Tait to Thomas W. Cobb, 29 Feb. 1820, John Williams Walker Papers, Alabama Department of Archives and History, Sellers, *Market Revolution*, 137–71; Bray Hammond,

Banks and Politics in America: From the Revolution to the Civil War (Princeton, NJ: Princeton University Press, 1957), 279–85.

57. *Niles' Weekly Register* (Baltimore) 16 (12 June 1819), 264–65.

58. Lyman Beecher, *The Means of National Prosperity: A Sermon Delivered at Litchfield, Connecticut, on the Day of Thanksgiving, December 2, 1819* (New York, 1820), 10, 13, 14.

59. Monroe, "Third Annual Message," CMPP, II, 6.

CHAPTER 2

1. John Adams to Thomas Jefferson, 23 Nov. 1819, Lester Jesse Cappon (ed.), *The Adams-Jefferson Letters: The Complete Correspondence between Thomas Jefferson and Abigail and John Adams* (2 vols., Chapel Hill: University of North Carolina Press, 1959), II, 548.

2. Thomas Jefferson to John Adams, 10 Dec. 1819, Cappon (ed.), *Adams-Jefferson Letters*, II, 548–49.

3. MJQA, IV, 495, 498.

4. George Dangerfield, *The Era of Good Feelings* (New York: Harcourt Brace, 1952), 95–121, 175–216; Harry Ammon, *James Monroe: The Quest for National Identity* (New York: McGraw Hill, 1971), 366–95.

5. Mathew Carey, *Addresses of the Philadelphia Society for the Promotion of National Industry* (Philadelphia, 1820); *A Memorial of a Convention of the Friends of National Industry Assembled in the City of New York* (Washington, DC, 1819); *Philadelphia Citizens Friendly to American Manufactures* (Philadelphia, 1819); *The Memorial of the Merchants and Others Interested in Commerce, in Salem and Its Vicinity* (Salem, MA, 1820); William Plumer to William Plumer Jr., 1 May 1820, William Plumer Papers, New Hampshire Historical Society; Murray N. Rothbard, *The Panic of 1819: Reactions and Policies* (New York: Columbia University Press, 1962), 1–24; George Dangerfield, *The Awakening of American Nationalism, 1815–1828* (New York: Harper and Row, 1965), 72–96; Charles Sellers, *The Market Revolution: Jacksonian America, 1815–1846* (New York: Oxford University Press, 1991), 131–39, 161–71.

6. On the Missouri Crisis, the standard remains Glover Moore, *The Missouri Controversy, 1819–1821* (Lexington: University of Kentucky Press, 1953). See also Robert P. Forbes, *The Missouri Crisis and Its Aftermath: Slavery and the Meaning of America* (Chapel Hill: University of North Carolina Press, 2007); John R. Van Atta, *Wolf by the Ears: The Missouri Crisis, 1819–1821* (Baltimore: Johns Hopkins University Press, 2015); Dangerfield, *Awakening of American Nationalism*, 97–140; William W. Freehling, *The Road to Disunion: Secessionists at Bay, 1776–1854* (New York: Oxford University Press, 1990), 144–61; Matthew Mason, *Slavery and Politics in the Early American Republic* (Chapel Hill: University of North Carolina Press, 2006), 177–212.

7. *Agricultural Intelligencer and Mechanic Register*, 28 Jan. 1820.

8. Charles S. Sydnor, *The Development of Southern Sectionalism, 1819–1848* (Baton Rouge: Louisiana State University Press, 1948), 104–33; John McCardell, *The Idea of a Southern Nation: Southern Nationalists and Southern Nationalism, 1830–1860* (New York: W. W. Norton, 1979), 23–25; Norman K. Risjord, *The Old Republicans: Southern Conservatism in the Age of Jefferson* (New York: Columbia University Press, 1965), 175–85; Susan Dunn, *Dominion of Memories: Jefferson, Madison, and the Decline of Virginia* (New York: Basic Books, 2007); Ammon, *James Monroe*, 515–28.

9. *Pendleton Messenger*, 9 Feb. 1820; Henry Clay to John J. Crittenden, 29 Jan. 1820, PHC, II, 769; Richard Peters to Rufus King, 29 Feb. 1820, Charles R. King (ed.), *The Life and*

Correspondence of Rufus King (New York: G. P. Putnam's Sons, 1894–1900, 6 vols.), VI, 287; Moore, *Missouri Controversy*, 91.

10. Charles Hammond to John C. Wright, 2 Feb. 1820, CHP.

11. William A. Trimble to C. A. Trimble, 2 March 1820, William Allen Trimble Papers, Ohio Historical Society.

12. *Annals of Congress*, 16th Cong., 1st Sess., 1586–87; Moore, *Missouri Controversy*, 88–89, 101–2; Forbes, *Missouri Compromise and Its Aftermath*, 69–120; Robert V. Remini, *Henry Clay: Statesman for the Union* (New York: W. W. Norton, 1991), 182–84.

13. Charles Tait to John Williams Walker, 20 May 1820, John Williams Walker Papers, Alabama Department of Archives and History.

14. Rufus King to Christopher Gore, 9 April 1820, King (ed.), *Life and Correspondence of Rufus King*, VI, 329; Hugh C. Bailey, *John Williams Walker: A Study in the Political, Social, and Cultural Life of the Old South* (Tuscaloosa: University of Alabama Press, 1964), 108–23.

15. Benjamin Ruggles to Charles Hammond, 11 Dec. 1819, CHP.

16. *New York Commercial Advertiser*, 10 April 1820.

17. *Philadelphia Aurora*, quoted in *Providence Patriot*, 10 April 1820.

18. *Centinel of Freedom*, 26 Sept. 1820.

19. William J. Cooper Jr., *Liberty and Slavery: Southern Politics to 1860* (New York: Alfred A. Knopf, 1983), 138–42; Risjord, *Old Republicans*, 216–18; Richard H. Brown, "The Missouri Crisis, Slavery, and the Politics of Jacksonianism," *South Atlantic Quarterly* 65 (Winter 1966), 55–72; Moore, *Missouri Controversy*, 320–32.

20. *Annals of Congress*, 16th Cong., 1st Sess., 704, 706–7, 708–10.

21. Daniel Webster to Henry Baldwin, 15 Feb. 1820, PDWC, I, 270; Baldwin to Webster, 15 Feb. 1820, PDWC, I, 270; *Pittsburgh Gazette*, 8 May 1820.

22. Rufus King to J. A. King and Charles King, 20 Feb. 1820, King (ed.), *Life and Correspondence of Rufus King*, VI, 278–79.

23. Moore, *Missouri Controversy*, 95; Shaw Livermore, *The Twilight of Federalism: The Disintegration of the Federalist Party, 1815–1830* (Princeton, NJ: Princeton University Press, 1962), 91–93; Leonard L. Richards, *The Slave Power: The Free North and Southern Domination, 1780–1860* (Baton Rouge: Louisiana State University Press, 2000); 84–86.

24. *Annals of Congress*, 15th Cong., 1st Sess., 1740–43; William Plumer Jr., to William Plumer, 7, 10, 11 April 1820, Everett S. Brown (ed.), *The Missouri Compromises and Presidential Politics, 1820–1825* (St. Louis: Missouri Historical Society, 1926), 17–18, 48–50; *Lexington Public Advertiser*, 10 May 1820; M. Flavia Taylor, "The Political and Civic Career of Henry Baldwin, 1799–1830," *Western Pennsylvania Historical Magazine* 24 (March 1941), 37–50.

25. *Annals of Congress*, 16th Cong., 1st Sess., 1663–69; *Niles' Weekly Register* (Baltimore) 18 (29 April 1820), 164–65; "Revision of the Tariff," *Charleston Courier*, 29 April 1820; "A Citizen," *Old and New Tariffs Compared with Observations on the Effect of High Duties on Revenue and Consumption* (Boston, 1820).

26. *Annals of Congress*, 16th Cong., 1st Sess., 1672.

27. William Plumer Jr. to William Plumer, 14 April 1820, William Plumer Papers, New Hampshire Historical Society; *Annals of Congress*, 16th Cong., 1st Sess., 1837–45; 1846–49; *American State Papers: Finance*, III, 522–25.

28. *Annals of Congress*, 16th Cong., 1st Sess., 1917–19, 1921–23, 1926, 1931–32, 1937, 1939, 1946–47.

29. *National Intelligencer* (Washington, DC), 23 March 1820.

30. *New York Evening Post*, 28 April 1820.

31. *Freeman's Journal*, 1 May 1820.

32. "The New Tariff," *Massachusetts Spy*, 3 May 1820.

33. Dangerfield, *Era of Good Feelings*, 98–104.

34. *Niles' Weekly Register* (Baltimore) 18 (1 April 1820), 81; *Annals of Congress*, 16th Cong., 1st Sess., 924, 1985.

35. *Annals of Congress*, 16th Cong., 1st Sess., 2000–2001, 2005, 2007.

36. *Annals of Congress*, 16th Cong., 1st Sess., 2015–16.

37. Clay, "Speech on the Tariff," PHC, II, 827, 833, 835–36, 838–39.

38. Clay, "Speech on the Tariff," PHC, II, 832, 836, 844.

39. Clay, "Speech on the Tariff," PHC, II, 844–45.

40. *New York Evening Post*, 29 April 1820.

41. *National Intelligencer* (Washington, DC), 28 April 1820.

42. William Plumer Jr. to William Plumer, 24 April 1820, William Plumer Papers, New Hampshire Historical Society.

43. Hezekiah Niles suspected that fifteen thousand American laborers lost their source of employment in the first half of 1819. See *Niles' Weekly Register* (Baltimore) 16 (19 June 1819), 274.

44. *Annals of Congress*, 16th Cong., 1st Sess., 2094, 2095, 2099, 2104, 2113, 2114; John A. Munroe, *Louis McLane: Federalist and Jacksonian* (New Brunswick, NJ: Rutgers University Press, 1973), 109.

45. *Annals of Congress*, 16th Cong., 1st Sess., 2116, 2120, 2126, 2128, 2130–31, 2135; Carl J. Vipperman, *William Lowndes and the Transition of Southern Politics, 1782–1822* (Chapel Hill: University of North Carolina Press, 1989), 201–32.

46. William Lowndes to Timothy Pickering, 14 April 1820, Timothy Pickering Papers, Massachusetts Historical Society; William Lowndes to Timothy Pickering, 12 May 1820, Timothy Pickering Papers, Massachusetts Historical Society.

47. *Annals of Congress*, 16th Cong., 1st Sess., 2150.

48. *Annals of Congress*, 16th Cong., 1st Sess., 2154–55; William Plumer Jr. to William Plumer, 28 April 1820, William Plumer Papers, New Hampshire Historical Society. On the final vote, the *Annals of Congress* lists that the vote passed by a vote of ninety-one to seventy-eight but lists only ninety names as being in favor of the bill's passage. The *House Journal* includes the name of Joseph S. Lyman, which the *Annals* omitted. See *House Journal* 16th Cong., 1st Sess., 29 April 1820, 467.

49. Edward Stanwood, *American Tariff Controversies of the Nineteenth Century* (2 vols., Boston: Houghton Mifflin, 1903), I, 190–91; Sydnor, *Development of Southern Sectionalism*, 143–44; Douglas R. Egerton, "Markets without a Market Revolution: Southern Planters and Capitalism," *Journal of the Early Republic* 16 (Summer 1996), 207–21.

50. Unknown to William Lowndes, 22 May 1820, William Lowndes Papers, Southern Historical Collection—University of North Carolina.

51. Joseph Dorfman, *The Economic Mind in American Civilization* (5 vols., New York: Viking Press, 1946–1959), I, 389; Daniel Peart, "Looking beyond Parties and Elections: The Making of United States Tariff Policy in the Early 1820s," *Journal of the Early Republic* 33 (Spring 2013), 87–108.

52. *Annals of Congress*, 16th Cong., 1st Sess., 373, 488, 605, 647, 650.

53. Harrison Gray Otis to Sally Foster Otis, 23 April 1820, HGOP.

54. Harrison Gray Otis to Sally Foster Otis, 2 May 1820, HGOP; Samuel Eliot Morison, *Harrison Gray Otis: The Urbane Federalist* (Boston: Houghton Mifflin, 1969), 420–32.

55. John Williams Walker to Unknown, 29 April 1820, John Williams Walker Papers, Alabama Department of Archives and History.

56. *Annals of Congress*, 16th Cong., 1st Sess., 656, 657, 660, 664–65.

57. *Annals of Congress*, 16th Cong., 1st Sess., 666, 667, 669–71.

58. *Annals of Congress*, 16th Cong., 1st Sess., 672.

59. *National Intelligencer* (Washington, DC), 9 May 1820.

60. *New York Evening Post*, 9 May 1820.

61. *Lexington Public Advertiser*, 17 May 1820.

62. *New York Evening Post*, 14 Aug. 1820.

63. "One of the People" [Churchill C. Cambreleng], *An Examination of the New Tariff Proposed by the Hon. Henry Baldwin* (New York, 1821), 93–94; Merrill D. Peterson (ed.), *Democracy, Liberty, and Property: The State Constitutional Conventions of the 1820s* (Indianapolis: Bobbs and Merrill, 1966); Sean Wilentz, *The Rise of American Democracy: From Jefferson to Lincoln* (New York: W. W. Norton, 2005), 183–202, 231–40; George P. Parkinson, "Antebellum State Constitution Making: Retention, Circumvention, Revision" (PhD diss., University of Wisconsin, 1972); Harold J. Counihan, "The North Carolina Constitutional Convention of 1835: A Study in Jacksonian Democracy," *North Carolina Historical Review* 46 (Autumn 1969), 335–64; Winbourne M. Drake, "The Mississippi Constitutional Convention of 1832," *Journal of Southern History* 23 (Aug. 1957), 354–70; Laura-Eve Moss, "Democracy, Citizenship, and Constitution Making in New York, 1777–1894" (PhD diss., University of Connecticut, 1999), 111–16.

64. James Pleasants to Joseph C. Cabell, 4 Feb. 1821, Joseph C. Cabell Family Papers, University of Virginia.

CHAPTER 3

1. Elisha Whittlesey to Charles Hammond, 17 Jan. 1824, CHP; John H. Eaton to Harrison Gray Otis, 23 March 1824, HGOP; Norman K. Risjord, *The Old Republicans: Southern Conservatism in the Age of Jefferson* (New York: Columbia University Press, 1965), 231–37; Daniel Peart, *Era of Experimentation: American Political Practices in the Early Republic* (Charlottesville: University of Virginia Press, 2014), 103.

2. *Niles' Weekly Register* (Baltimore) 18 (3 June 1820), 241.

3. *Niles' Weekly Register* (Baltimore) 25 (15 Nov. 1823), 161; William Plumer Jr. to William Plumer, 3 Dec. 1823, Everett S. Brown (ed.), *The Missouri Compromises and Presidential Politics, 1820–1825* (St. Louis: Missouri Historical Society, 1926), 83–84; *Argus of Western America* (Frankfort, KY), 31 Dec. 1823; Merrill D. Peterson, *The Great Triumvirate: Webster, Clay, and Calhoun* (New York: Oxford University Press, 1987), 122–23.

4. Henry Clay to Adam Beatty, 15 Feb. 1824, PHC, XI, 169.

5. There are no statewide studies of the antebellum period for either Missouri or Maine. For Missouri, useful information can be found in W. Stephen Belko, *The Invincible Duff Green: Whig of the West* (Columbia: University of Missouri Press, 2006), 47–74; William E. Foley, *The Genesis of Missouri: From Wilderness Outpost to Statehood* (Columbia: University of Missouri Press, 1989), 283–98. On Maine, information can be located in Ronald F. Banks, *Maine Becomes a State: The Movement to Separate Maine from Massachusetts, 1785–1820* (Middletown, CT: Wesleyan University Press, 1970); 184–207; Joyce Butler, "Rising Like a Phoenix: Commerce in Southern Maine, 1775–1830," Laura F. Sprague (ed.), *Agreeable Situations: Society, Commerce, and Art in Southern Maine, 1780–1830* (Boston: Northeastern University Press, 1987), 15–35.

6. James M. Garnett to John Randolph, 26 Dec. 1823, John Randolph Papers, University

of Virginia; Monroe, "Seventh Annual Message," CMPP, II, 215–16; Benjamin Ruggles to Charles Hammond, 1 Jan. 1824, CHP; *Annals of Congress*, 18th Cong., 1st Sess., 799; Harry Ammon, *James Monroe: The Quest for National Identity* (New York: McGraw Hill, 1971), 512, 540.

7. *National Intelligencer* (Washington, DC), 19 Oct. 1824; *Raleigh Register*, 25 June 1824.

8. *Annals of Congress*, 18th Cong., 1st Sess., 959–65, 1469. For a copy of Tod's proposed bill, see *Niles' Weekly Register* (Baltimore) 25 (17 Jan. 1824), 315–17.

9. *Annals of Congress*, 18th Cong., 1st Sess., 1471–73, 1476.

10. *Annals of Congress*, 18th Cong., 1st Sess., 1526–27.

11. *Annals of Congress*, 18th Cong., 1st Sess., 1552.

12. *Annals of Congress*, 18th Cong., 1st Sess., 1632; John C. Wright to Charles Hammond, 6 April 1824, CHP; James Hamilton to Charles K. Gardner, 17 April 1824, James Hamilton Papers, University of South Carolina; Edmund Pendleton to Robert S. Garnett, 27 Feb. 1824, Letter to Robert S. Garnett, University of Virginia; James F. Hopkins, *A History of the Hemp Industry in Kentucky* (Lexington: University of Kentucky Press, 1998), 112–50.

13. Interview of Thomas Jefferson by Samuel Whitcomb, Massachusetts Historical Society.

14. James Hamilton to Charles K. Gardner, 27 April 1824, James Hamilton Papers, University of South Carolina.

15. John Campbell to James Campbell, 9 April 1824, CFP.

16. *Annals of Congress*, 18th Cong., 1st Sess., 1702; *Newport Mercury*, 13 March 1824; James Huston, "Virtue Besieged: Virtue, Equality, and the General Welfare in the Tariff Debates of the 1820s," *Journal of the Early Republic* 14 (Winter 1994), 523–48.

17. Richard Leech to John Tod, 9 March 1824, John Tod Papers, Pennsylvania Historical and Museum Commission.

18. Nathaniel Macon to Bolling Hall, 1 March 1824, Bolling Hall Family Papers, Alabama Department of Archives and History.

19. "The Tariff," *Raleigh Register*, 30 March 1824.

20. *Annals of Congress*, 18th Cong., 1st Sess., 1916, 1926, 1944.

21. *Annals of Congress*, 18th Cong., 1st Sess., 1918–19.

22. Clay, "Speech on Tariff," PHC, III, 701–2; Robert V. Remini, *Henry Clay: Statesman for the Union* (New York: W. W. Norton, 1991), 228–32.

23. Clay, "Speech on Tariff," PHC, III, 719–20.

24. Daniel Peart, "Looking Beyond Parties and Elections: The Making of United States Tariff Policy in the Early 1820s," *Journal of the Early Republic* 33 (Spring 2013), 87–108.

25. Clay, "Speech on Tariff," PHC, III, 692–93, 723–26; Maurice G. Baxter, *Henry Clay and the American System* (Lexington: University of Kentucky Press, 1995), 26–27; Huston, "Virtue Besieged," 523–47.

26. *Annals of Congress*, 18th Cong., 1st Sess., 2005, 2010, 2025.

27. Daniel Webster to Ezekiel Webster, 14 March 1824, Daniel Webster Papers, Dartmouth College; Webster to Jeremiah Mason, 19 April 1824, PDWC, I, 357; Robert V. Remini, *Daniel Webster: The Man and His Time* (New York: W. W. Norton, 1997), 221–23; Richard C. Edwards, "Economic Sophistication in Nineteenth Century Congressional Tariff Debates," *Journal of Economic History* 30 (Dec. 1970), 802–38.

28. Webster, "The Tariff," PDWSFW, I, 123, 132, 143–44, 150.

29. *Annals of Congress*, 18th Cong., 1st Sess., 2149.

30. *Annals of Congress*, 18th Cong., 1st Sess., 2180, 2185.

31. *Annals of Congress*, 18th Cong., 1st Sess., 2206–8.

32. *Annals of Congress*, 18th Cong., 1st Sess., 2219, 2234; *National Intelligencer* (Washington, DC), 17 April 1824; John C. Wright to Charles Hammond, 6, 9 April 1824, CHP; James

Hamilton to Charles K. Gardner, 17 April 1824, James Hamilton Papers, University of South Carolina.

33.   Louis McLane to Kitty McLane, 18 April 1822, Louis McLane Papers, Library of Congress.

34.   *Annals of Congress*, 18th Cong., 1st Sess., 2404, 2420, 2421, 2425; Joseph Cumming, "The Cumming-McDuffie Duels," *Georgia Historical Quarterly* 44 (March 1960), 18–40.

35.   *Boston Courier*, 24 April 1824.

36.   *Pittsburgh Gazette*, 30 April 1824.

37.   *Illinois Gazette*, 22 May 1824; *Niles' Weekly Register* (Baltimore) 26 (24 April 1824), 113; Daniel Webster to James William Paige, 13 March 1824, Paige Papers, Massachusetts Historical Society.

38.   *Niles' Weekly Register* (Baltimore) 26 (24 April 1824), 113–14.

39.   *Annals of Congress*, 18th Cong., 1st Sess., 173; "The Tariff," *Boston Daily Advertiser*, quoted in *Charleston Courier*, 1 May 1824.

40.   "The Tariff," *New York Statesman*, quoted in *Albany Argus*, 7 May 1824.

41.   *Annals of Congress*, 18th Cong., 1st Sess., 614; John C. Wright to Charles Hammond, 8 March 1824, CHP; Elijah H. Mills to Harrison Gray Otis, 16 April 1824, HGOP; William Plumer Jr. to Levi Woodbury, 1 May 1824, Levi Woodbury Family Papers, Library of Congress; Timothy Phelps to John Tod, 7 May 1824, John Tod Papers, Pennsylvania Historical and Museum Commission; Martin Van Buren to Stephen Van Rensselear, 6 May 1824, Kohns Collection, New York Public Library.

42.   *Annals of Congress*, 18th Cong., 1st Sess., 622.

43.   *Annals of Congress*, 18th Cong., 1st Sess., 693, 698, 700.

44.   Charles Hammond to John C. Wright, 3 May 1824, CHP; Robert V. Remini, *Martin Van Buren and the Making of the Democratic Party* (New York: Columbia University Press, 1959), 53–55.

45.   George McDuffie to Virgil Maxcy, 14 May 1824, Galloway-Maxcy-Markoe Papers, Library of Congress.

CHAPTER 4

1.   *National Intelligencer* (Washington, DC), 23 July 1824.

2.   Donald J. Ratcliffe, *The One-Party Presidential Contest: Adams, Jackson, and 1824's Five-Horse Race* (Lawrence: University Press of Kansas, 2015), 25–134.

3.   Hezekiah Niles to Henry Baldwin, 29 March 1824, Henry Baldwin Papers, Allegheny College; Robert V. Remini, *Andrew Jackson and the Course of American Freedom, 1822–1832* (New York: Harper and Row, 1981), 49–51, 65; Charles Sellers, "Jackson Men with Feet of Clay," *American Historical Review* 62 (Apr. 1957), 537–51; Kim T. Phillips, "The Pennsylvania Origins of the Jackson Movement," *Political Science Quarterly* 91 (Fall 1976), 489–508.

4.   Romulus Saunders to Bartlett Yancey, 30 March 1824, A. R. Newsome (ed.), "Letters of Romulus M. Saunders to Bartlett Yancey, 1821–1828," *North Carolina Historical Review* 8 (Oct. 1931), 445.

5.   Charles Hammond to John C. Wright, 9 April 1824, CHP; Andrew Jackson to Littleton H. Coleman, 26 April 1824, PAJ, IV, 398–400; Mark R. Cheathem, *Andrew Jackson: Southerner* (Baton Rouge: Louisiana State University Press, 2013), 102; Joseph G. Tregle, *Louisiana in the Age of Jackson: A Clash of Cultures and Personalities* (Baton Rouge: Louisiana State University Press, 1999), 158.

6. John C. Fitzpatrick (ed.), *The Autobiography of Martin Van Buren* (Washington, DC, 1920), 240.

7. *National Intelligencer* (Washington, DC), 30 March 1824; Daniel Peart, *Era of Experimentation: American Political Practices in the Early Republic* (Charlottesville: University of Virginia Press, 2014), 131–32.

8. Thomas Hart Benton to Unknown, 22 March 1824, Gooch Family Papers, University of Virginia; Clay, "Speech on Tariff," PHC, IV, 726; Remini, *Andrew Jackson and the Course of American Freedom*, 69–70; *National Intelligencer* (Washington, DC), 4 May 1824.

9. William Plumer Jr. to William Plumer, 8 March 1824, Brown (ed.), *Missouri Compromises and Presidential Politics*, 105–6; Gershom Flagg to Artemas Flagg, 25 Jan. 1824, Solon J. Buck (ed.), *Pioneer Letters of Gershom Flagg* (Springfield: Illinois State Journal Co., 1912), 38–39; Marie B. Hecht, *John Quincy Adams: A Personal History of an Independent Man* (New York: Macmillan, 1972), 273–345; Thomas M. Coens, "The Formation of the Jackson Party, 1822–1825" (PhD diss., Harvard University, 2004), 61–63.

10. Joseph Gibbs to Louis McLane, 25 July 1824, Louis McLane Papers, Library of Congress.

11. *Richmond Whig* and *Troy Sentinel*, quoted in *Pittsburgh Mercury*, 25 June 1824.

12. John Quincy Adams to Robert Walsh, 1 March 1824, AFP.

13. "Coming Out!," *Chillicothe Supporter and Scioto Gazette*, 15 July 1824; MJQA, VI, 275, 343–44, 353.

14. A. Perry to John Tod, 2 March 1824, John Tod Papers, Pennsylvania Historical and Museum Commission.

15. *Pittsburgh Gazette*, 2 July 1824.

16. "The Tariff," *Albany Argus*, 2 March 1824; *Albany Argus*, 26 March 1824.

17. *American State Papers: Finance*, IV, 9; Norman K. Risjord, *The Old Republicans: Southern Conservatism in the Age of Jefferson* (New York: Columbia University Press, 1965), 228–55; Chase C. Mooney, *William H. Crawford, 1772–1834* (Lexington: University of Kentucky Press, 1974), 152–53, 161.

18. Elijah H. Mills to Harrison Gray Otis, 28 Feb. 1824, HGOP; Nathaniel Macon to Bolling Hall, 10 Feb. 1824, Bolling Hall Papers, Alabama Department of Archives and History; Robert Y. Hayne to Bolling Hall, 17 Aug. 1824, Bolling Hall Papers, Alabama Department of Archives and History; John Borckenborough to John Randolph, 18 Feb. 1824, John Randolph Papers, University of Virginia; E. Wayne Cutler, "William H. Crawford: A Contextual Biography" (PhD diss., University of Texas–Austin, 1971), 157–94.

19. Christopher Vandeventer to Unknown, 10 July 1823, Galloway-Maxcy-Markoe Families Papers, Library of Congress; R. B. Vance to Samuel F. Patterson, 25 Feb. 1824, Jones and Patterson Family Papers, Southern Historical Collection—University of North Carolina; John M. Belohlavek, *George Mifflin Dallas: Jacksonian Politician* (University Park: Pennsylvania State University Press, 1977), 19–22; C. Edward Skeen, "Calhoun, Crawford, and the Politics of Retrenchment," *South Carolina Historical Magazine* 73 (July 1972), 141–55; Roger J. Spiller, "John C. Calhoun as Secretary of War, 1817–1825" (PhD diss., Louisiana State University, 1977).

20. "A Citizen of New York," *Measures, Not Men: Illustrated by Some Remarks upon the Public Conduct and Character of John C. Calhoun* (New York, 1823), 26.

21. "The Tariff," *Washington Republican and Congressional Examiner*, 13 May 1824.

22. Henry Clay to George W. Featherstonhaugh, 10 Oct. 1824, PHC, XI, 181; MJQA, VI, 432.

23. John Randolph to James M. Garnett, 1 Nov. 1823, John Randolph Papers, University of Virginia.

24. Henry Clay to Francis T. Brooke, 29 Feb. 1824, PHC, III, 667.

25. "Our Country . . . Home Industry" (1824), Prints and Photographs Division, Library of Congress.

26. "The Presidency," *Argus of Western America* (Frankfort, KY), 14 April 1824; Henry Clay to Francis T. Brooke, 22 Jan. 1824, PHC, III, 603; Henry Clay to Peter B. Porter, 31 Jan. 1824, PHC, III, 630: Clay to Richard Bache, 17 Feb. 1824, PHC, III, 645; Clay to Charles Hammond, 22 Feb. 1824, PHC, III, 654; Clay to Amos Kendall, 18 March 1824, PHC, III, 674; Clay to George W. Featherstonhaugh, 26 May 1824, PHC, III, XI, 176; Robert V. Remini, *Henry Clay: Statesman for the Union* (New York: W. W. Norton, 1991), 234–50; Donald J. Ratcliffe, "The Role of Voters and Issues in Party Formation: Ohio, 1824," *Journal of American History* 49 (March 1973), 847–70.

27. *Louisville Public Advertiser*, 2 Feb. 1825; Remini, *Andrew Jackson and the Course of American Freedom*, 81–83; Ratcliffe, *One-Party Presidential Contest*, 201–28.

28. Christopher Vandeventer to Virgil Maxcy, 24 Aug. 1823, Galloway-Maxcy-Markoe Families Papers, Library of Congress; Samuel Ingham to William Gaston, 24 April 1824, William Gaston Papers, Southern Historical Collection—University of North Carolina; Remini, *Henry Clay*, 253–55.

29. MJQA, VI, 451; Daniel Feller, *The Public Lands in Jacksonian Politics* (Madison: University of Wisconsin Press, 1984), 63.

30. Amos Kendall to Henry Clay, 21 Jan. 1825, PHC, V, 35; Clay to Francis R. Brooke, 28 Jan. 1825, PHC, V, 45–46, Clay to Francis P. Blair, 29 Jan. 1825, PHC, V, 47; G. A. Worth to Ethan Allen Brown, 16 Feb. 1825, Ethan Allen Brown Papers, Ohio Historical Society.

31. John C. Wright to Charles Hammond, 22 Jan. 1825, CHP.

32. Jackson to William B. Lewis, 14 Feb. 1825, PAJ, VI, 29–30.

33. William R. King to Bolling Hall, 17 May 1824, Bolling Hall Family Papers, Alabama Department of Archives and History; CLC, III, 1240–41, 1244–45, 1256, 1283–84; *National Gazette and Literary Messenger*, 31 March 1824; Jonathan J. Pincus, *Pressure Groups and Politics in Antebellum Tariffs* (New York: Columbia University Press, 1977), 139–68.

34. Nathaniel Macon to Samuel P. Carson, 9 Feb. 1833, Charles H. Ambler (ed.), "Nathaniel Macon Correspondence," *John P. Branch Historical Papers* (1909), 92; Stephen J. Barry, "Nathaniel Macon: The Prophet of Pure Republicanism, 1758–1837" (PhD diss., University at Buffalo, 1996), 239–41.

35. *Annals of Congress*, 18th Cong., 1st Sess., 2203.

CHAPTER 5

1. *Pennsylvania Intelligencer*, 13 July 1824.

2. *Albany Argus*, 14 March 1827; Mark Bils, "Tariff Protection in the Early US Cotton Textile Industry," *Journal of Economic History* 44 (Dec. 1984), 1033–45; James L. Huston, "Virtue Besieged: Virtue, Equality, and the General Welfare in the Tariff Debates of the 1820s," *Journal of the Early Republic* 14 (Winter 1994), 523–47; Robert Zevin, *The Growth of Manufacturing in Early Nineteenth Century New England* (New York: Arno, 1975). The best source on the manufacturing of woolen fabrics in the United Sates is Arthur H. Cole, *The American Wool Manufacture* (2 vols., Cambridge, MA: Harvard University Press, 1926), I, 59–244.

3. For the events of 1826 commemorating America's independence, see Andrew Burstein, *America's Jubilee: A Generation Remembers the Revolution after Fifty Years of Independence* (New York: Alfred A. Knopf, 2001).

4. Felix Grundy to Henry Baldwin, 28 March 1826, Henry Baldwin Papers, Allegheny College.

5. Adams, "First Annual Message," CMPP, II, 316; George Dangerfield, *The Awakening of American Nationalism, 1815–1828* (New York: Harper and Row, 1965), 231–41; Mary W. M. Hargreaves, *The Presidency of John Quincy Adams* (Lawrence: University Press of Kansas, 1985), 165–68.

6. James K. Polk to William H. Polk, 22 March 1826, privately held, copy at the James K. Polk Project, University of Tennessee.

7. James Buchanan to John Reynolds, 9 Jan. 1827, James Buchanan Correspondence, Dickinson College.

8. Robert Harris to James K. Polk, 27 Feb. 1828, CJKP, I, 156; *Knoxville Enquirer*, 28 Feb. 1827; Donald B. Cole, *Vindicating Andrew Jackson: The 1828 Election and the Rise of the Two-Party System* (Lawrence: University Press of Kansas, 2009), 34–54. The Adams men felt confident about their chances too. See George Robertson to Thomas Ewing, 20 Oct. 1827, Thomas Ewing Papers, Notre Dame University; John Bailey to John Brazer Davis, 3 Jan. 1827, "Letters to John Brazer Davis," *Massachusetts Historical Society Proceedings* 59 (1916), 195.

9. Charles S. Sydnor, *The Development of Southern Sectionalism, 1819–1848* (Baton Rouge: Louisiana State University Press, 1948), 177–88; Richard E. Ellis, *Aggressive Nationalism: McCulloch v. Maryland and the Foundation of Federal Authority in the Young Republic* (New York: Oxford University, 2007), 111–91.

10. Herman V. Ames (ed.), *State Documents on Federal Relations: The States and the United States* (Philadelphia, 1906), 140.

11. William Smith to Stephen D. Miller, 13 Jan. 1827 [1828], Chestnut-Manning-Miller Papers, South Carolina Historical Society; John C. Calhoun to Andrew Jackson, 4 June 1826, PJCC, X, 110–11; William W. Freehling, *Prelude to Civil War: The Nullification Controversy in South Carolina, 1816–1836* (New York: Harper and Row, 1966), 91–121; Caroline P. Smith, "South Carolina 'Radical': The Political Career of William Smith to 1826" (MA thesis, Auburn University, 1971), 185–228.

12. *Niles' Weekly Register* 32 (21 April 1827), 138–39.

13. John Y. Mason to William Brodnax, 4 March 1827, John Y. Mason Papers, Library of Virginia; James Madison to Joseph Cabell, 18 March 1827, William C. Rives (ed.), *Letters and Other Writings of James Madison* (4 vols., Philadelphia: J. B. Lippincott, 1865), III, 570–74; entry of 15 Feb. 1828, Henry R. Storrs Diary, Buffalo and Erie County Historical Society; Dice R. Anderson, *William Branch Giles: A Study in the Politics of Virginia and the Nation from 1790 to 1830* (Gloucester, MA: Peter Smith 1965 reprint of 1915 ed.), 219–20; Richard E. Ellis, "The Persistence of Antifederalism after 1789," Richard Beeman et al. (eds.), *Beyond Confederation: Origins of the Constitution and American National Identity* (Chapel Hill: University of North Carolina Press, 1987), 295–314.

14. Adams, "Second Annual Message," CMPP, II, 357.

15. Edward Stanwood, *American Tariff Controversies in the Nineteenth Century* (2 vols., Boston: Houghton Mifflin, 1903), I, 253.

16. *Register of Debates in Congress, 1825–1837 (Washington, DC, 1825–1837)*, 19th Cong., 2nd Sess., 732–33.

17. *Register of Debates*, 19th Cong., 2nd Sess., 1073–74; *Reports of the Secretary of the Treasury of the United States* (7 vols., Washington, DC, 1837), II, 353–54.

18. *Register of Debates*, 19th Cong., 2nd Sess., 1094.

19. *Register of Debates*, 19th Cong., 2nd Sess., 749, 1010–11, 1099; Daniel Webster to William Plumer Jr., 11 Feb. 1827, PDWC, II, 156; *Eastern Argus*, 20 Feb. 1827; Philip S. Klein, *Pennsylvania Politics, 1817–1832: A Game without Rules* (Philadelphia: Historical Society

of Pennsylvania, 1940), 241; Kim T. Phillips, "The Pennsylvania Origins of the Jackson Movement," *Political Science Quarterly* 91 (Fall 1976), 489–508.

20. *Harrisburg Chronicle*, 18 June 1827; *New York Spectator*, 20 Feb. 1827.

21. Calhoun to Bartlett Yancey, 13 Feb. 1827, PJCC, X, 263.

22. Van Buren to Thomas W. Olcott, 11 Feb. 1827, Thomas W. Olcott Papers, Columbia University.

23. Calhoun to Andrew Jackson, 25 Feb. 1827, PJCC, X, 267; Martin Gabriel Mead to Martin Van Buren, 13 Feb. 1827, MVBP; *Rochester Telegraph*, quoted in *National Journal* (Washington, DC), 25 May 1827.

24. Daniel Webster to William Coleman, 23 Feb. 1827, PDWC, II, 161–62.

25. Nancy Scott (ed.), *A Memoir of Hugh Lawson White* (Philadelphia: J. B. Lippincott, 1856), 76.

26. Lance Banning, *The Jeffersonian Persuasion: Evolution of a Party Ideology* (Ithaca, NY: Cornell University Press, 1978), 204–5; John Ashworth, *"Agrarians" and "Aristocrats": Party Political Ideology in the United States, 1837–1846* (London: Cambridge University Press, 1983), 7–51.

27. Martin Van Buren to Thomas Ritchie, 13 Jan. 1827, MVBP; Martin Van Buren to William H. Crawford, 15 Feb. 1828, William H. Crawford Papers, Library of Congress; *Albany Argus*, 3 Aug. 1827; entry of 5 April 1828, Henry R. Storrs Diary, Buffalo and Erie County Historical Society; Dangerfield, *Awakening of American Nationalism*, 278; John Niven, *Martin Van Buren: The Romantic Age of American Politics* (New York: Oxford University Press, 1983), 182–85; Joseph H. Harrison, "Martin Van Buren and His Southern Supporters," *Journal of Southern History* 22 (Nov. 1956), 438–58.

28. Duff Green to Russell Jarvis, 23 Feb. 1828, Duff Green Papers, Library of Congress; Martin Van Buren to William H. Crawford, 15 Feb. 1828, MVBP.

CHAPTER 6

1. *Niles' Weekly Register* (Baltimore) 32 (16 June 1827), 259, 264; *Niles' Weekly Register* (Baltimore) 32 (28 July 1827), 363–64; *Albany Argus*, 7 July 1827.

2. *Niles' Weekly Register* (Baltimore) 33 (8 Sept. 1827), 28–31; Dumas Malone, *The Public Life of Thomas Cooper, 1783–1839* (New Haven, CT: Yale University Press, 1926), 307–16.

3. William W. Freehling, *Prelude to Civil War: The Nullification Controversy in South Carolina, 1816–1836* (New York: Harper and Row, 1966), 126–33.

4. "Brutus" [Robert J. Turnbull], *The Crisis* (Charleston, SC, 1827), 24, 50, 54, 75–79, 89, 112, 140–41.

5. "Brutus" [Robert J. Turnbull], *Crisis*, 27, 44, 89, 111, 115–16.

6. "Brutus" [Robert J. Turnbull], *Crisis*, 64, 124–25, 133–34; Douglas R. Egerton, " 'Its Origin Is Not a Little Curious': A New Look at the American Colonization Society," *Journal of the Early Republic* 5 (Winter 1985), 463–80.

7. *Harrisburg Chronicle*, 9 July 1827; *Oracle of Dauphin*, 14 July 1827; James Buchanan to Duff Green, 11 July 1827, JBP; Amos Kendall to Henry Baldwin, 15 July 1827, Henry Baldwin Papers, Allegheny College; *Richmond Enquirer*, 10 July 1827; *United States Telegraph* (Washington, DC), 9 July 1827; Malcolm Rogers Eiselen, *The Rise of Pennsylvania Protectionism* (Philadelphia: Porcupine, 1974 reprint of 1932 ed.), 74–75; Philip S. Klein, *Pennsylvania Politics, 1817–1832: A Game without Rules* (Philadelphia: Pennsylvania Historical Society, 1940), 241–43.

8. *New Hampshire Patriot*, 28 May 1827; *Richmond Enquirer*, 10 July 1827; John A. Munroe,

Louis McLane: Federalist and Jacksonian (New Brunswick, NJ: Rutgers University Press, 1973), 216–17.

9. *Troy Budget and City Advertiser* and *Rochester Daily Advertiser*, both quoted in *Albany Argus*, 9 July 1827.

10. William L. Marcy to Martin Van Buren, 25 June 1827, MVBP.

11. John C. Fitzpatrick (ed.), *The Autobiography of Martin Van Buren* (Washington, DC, 1920), 169; Martin Van Buren, *Speech of the Hon. Martin Van Buren Delivered at the Capitol in the City of Albany, before the Albany County Meeting* (Albany, NY, 1827), 2–5, 8, 14–16.

12. Fitzpatrick (ed.), *Autobiography of Martin Van Buren*, 171.

13. *Pittsburgh Mercury*, 17 July 1827; *Richmond Enquirer*, 27 July, 7 Aug. 1827; Clay, "Toast at Uniontown Public Dinner," PHC, VI, 687; Clay, "Toast and Response at Pittsburgh Public Dinner," PHC, VI, 700–703.

14. *Harrisburg Chronicle*, 15 June 1827; *United States Gazette* (Philadelphia), 9, 20 June, 17 July 1827, *Boston Courier*, 2 July 1827; *Oracle of Dauphin*, 9, 23, 30 June 1827; *Pennsylvania Intelligencer*, 5, 19, 26 June 1827; *Ohio State Journal*, 19 July 1827. For the speeches of Everett and Lawrence, see *United States Gazette* (Philadelphia), 13, 15, June 1827.

15. *Times and Hartford Advertiser*, 6 Aug. 1827, *Niles' Weekly Register* (Baltimore) 32 (11 Aug. 1827), 388–90.

16. *Niles' Weekly Register* (Baltimore) 32 (11 Aug. 1827), 395–96; *Connecticut Courant*, 3 Aug. 1827.

17. On the reform movements, see Ronald G. Walters, *American Reformers, 1815–1860* (New York: Hill and Wang, 1978); Steven Mintz, *Moralists and Modernizers: America's Pre-Civil War Reformers* (Baltimore: Johns Hopkins University Press, 1995).

18. *Niles' Weekly Register* (Baltimore) 33 (13 Oct. 1827), 100–11.

19. *Niles' Weekly Register* (Baltimore) 32 (4 Aug. 1827), 371; *Niles' Weekly Register* (Baltimore) 33 (29 Sept. 1827), 65; John L. Larson, *Internal Improvement: National Public Works and the Promise of Popular Government in the Early United States* (Chapel Hill: University of North Carolina Press, 2001), 141–44.

20. Calhoun to Littleton W. Tazewell, 25 Aug. 1827, PJCC, X, 300–301; Calhoun to James E. Colhoun, 26 Aug. 1827, PJCC, X, 304.

CHAPTER 7

1. For the interpretation that the bill was framed to be defeated, see Edward Stanwood, *American Tariff Controversies in the Nineteenth Century* (2 vols., Boston: Houghton Mifflin, 1903), I, 256–60; Malcolm Rogers Eiselen, *The Rise of Pennsylvania Protectionism* (Philadelphia: Porcupine, 1974 reprint of 1932 ed.), 82–83; George Dangerfield, *The Era of Good Feelings* (New York: Harcourt Brace, 1952), 405–6; Charles S. Sydnor, *The Development of Southern Sectionalism, 1819–1848* (Baton Rouge: Louisiana State University Press, 1948), 186–87; Charles M. Wiltse, *John C. Calhoun: Nationalist, 1782–1828* (Indianapolis: Bobbs and Merrill, 1944), 368–69.

2. John C. Calhoun, "Speech on the Bill to Reduce the Duties on Certain Imports," PJCC, XIII, 457–60. Six years later, however, in a campaign biography of Calhoun, the author, perhaps Calhoun, used more restrained language. "The bill passed the House by a small majority, a large portion of the New England members voting against it; but when it came to the Senate, where the relative strength of the Southern and New England States is much greater than in the House, it was ascertained that the bill could not pass unless it was modified so as to be acceptable to the senators from New England favourable

to the administration. It was so modified by the votes of the Senators opposed to the administration from the Middle and Western States, contrary to the expectations of the South; for the bill, as modified, received the votes of the New England senators in favour of the administration, which, added to those in favour of General Jackson from New York, New Jersey, Pennsylvania, and the Northwest, made a majority. It passed, accordingly, and became a law; but under such circumstances as not only to deprive the administration of the advantage from the scheme, but to turn it directly against them." *Life of John C. Calhoun, Presenting a Condensed History of Political Events from 1811 to 1843* (New York, 1843), 48–49.

3. *Congressional Globe*, 28th Cong., 1st Sess., appendix 747.

4. For the interpretation that Van Buren wanted the bill to pass, see Robert V. Remini, "Martin Van Buren and the Tariff of Abominations," *American Historical Review* 68 (July 1958), 903–17; Robert V. Remini, *Martin Van Buren and the Making of the Democratic Party* (New York: Columbia University Press, 1959), 170–85; Robert V. Remini, *The Election of Andrew Jackson* (New York: J. B. Lippincott, 1963), 171–80; George Dangerfield, *The Awakening of American Nationalism, 1815–1828* (New York: Harper and Row, 1965), 281–82; John Niven, *Martin Van Buren: The Romantic Age of American Politics* (New York: Oxford University Press, 1983), 194–99; Donald B. Cole, *Martin Van Buren and the American Political System* (Princeton, NJ: Princeton University Press, 1984), 162–69; Daniel Walker Howe, *What Hath God Wrought: The Transformation of America, 1815–1848* (New York: Oxford University Press, 2007), 270–75.

5. John Tyler to Curtis (?), 16 Dec. 1827, John Tyler Papers, Library of Congress; Francis F. Wayland, *Andrew Stevenson: Democrat and Diplomat, 1785–1857* (Philadelphia: University of Pennsylvania Press, 1949), 74–78.

6. James Hamilton to Stephen D. Miller, 18 Dec. 1827, James Hamilton Papers, University of South Carolina; John C. Wright to Charles Hammond, 6 Dec. 1827, CHP; William Van Dusen to Gideon Welles, 7 Dec. 1827, Gideon Welles Papers, Library of Congress; Silas Wright to A. C. Flagg, 13 Dec. 1827, A. C. Flagg Papers, New York Public Library; *Albany Argus*, 6, 10 Dec. 1827; "The New Speaker," *Richmond Enquirer*, 13 Dec. 1827.

7. *Register of Debates in Congress, 1825–1837 (Washington, DC, 1825–1837)*, 20th Cong., 1st Sess., 866.

8. *Register of Debates*, 20th Cong., 1st Sess., 1870.

9. "Congress," *Vermont Watchman and State Gazette*, 15 Jan. 1828. The petitions and memorials concerning the tariff can be found in *American State Papers: Finance*, V.

10. *American State Papers: Finance*, V, 722, 727, 848–49,

11. *American State Papers: Finance*, V, 761, 885–86; *National Journal* (Washington, DC), 17 March 1828.

12. *Register of Debates*, 20th Cong., 1st Sess., 2000; MJQA, VII, 369; *National Journal* (Washington, DC), 7 April 1828; Stanwood, *American Tariff Controversies in the Nineteenth Century*, I, 274.

13. "The Tariff," *Norwich (CT) Courier*, 12 March 1828.

14. "Editor's Correspondence," *Boston Courier*, 10 March 1828.

15. "Pennsylvania," *Scioto Gazette* (Chillicothe, Ohio), 27 March 1828; Thomas Ritchie to Martin Van Buren, 11 March 1828, MVBP; Silas Wright to A. C. Flagg, 21 March 1828, A. C. Flagg Papers, New York Public Library; *Register of Debates*, 20th Cong., 1st Sess., 1925; entry of 15 Feb. 1828, Henry R. Storrs Diary, Buffalo and Erie County Historical Society.

16. Charles Hammond to John C. Wright, 16 Dec. 1827, CHP.

17. A. Sterling to Gideon Welles, 18 Jan. 1828, Gideon Welles Papers, Library of Congress; entry of 27 Dec. 1828, Henry R. Storrs Diary, Buffalo and Erie County Historical

Society; James Tallmadge to John Taylor, 18 Dec. 1827, John W. Taylor Papers, New York Historical Society; Ambrose Spencer to John W. Taylor, 12 Jan. 1828, John W. Taylor Papers, New York Historical Society; Peter B. Porter to Henry Clay, 22 Nov. 1827, PHC, VI, 1304; Clay to Allen Trimble, 27 Dec. 1827, PHC, VI, 1384–85; MJQA, VII, 361, 365; "The President's Message," *Albany Argus*, 10 Dec. 1827; "The Tariff," *New Hampshire Patriot*, 14 Jan. 1828; "Mr. Adams and the Tariff," *Vermont Patriot and State Gazette*, 31 Dec. 1827; *Richmond Enquirer*, 13 Dec. 1827; *Knoxville Register*, 2 Jan. 1828.

18. *American State Papers: Finance*, V, 634–40; Daniel Feller, *The Public Lands in Jacksonian Politics* (Madison: University of Wisconsin Press, 1984), 91–95; William N. Chambers, *Old Bullion Benton: Senator from the New West, 1782–1858* (Boston: Little, Brown, 1956), 138–39.

19. *Register of Debates*, 20th Cong., 1st Sess., 862, 864, 872, 878; Edward Livingston, "Letter to the Constituents" (Draft), 1828 (?), Edward Livingston Papers, Princeton University. For previous congressional inquiries, see Arthur M. Schlesinger Jr. (ed.), *Congress Investigates: A Documented History* (New York: Chelsea House, 5 vols., 1975), I, 3–588.

20. *Register of Debates*, 20th Cong., 1st Sess., 885.

21. *Register of Debates*, 20th Cong., 1st Sess., 864, 889–90; "Congress," *New York Spectator*, 8 Jan. 1828; *Niles' Weekly Register* (Baltimore) 33 (12 Jan. 1828), 318; Orange Merwin to Gideon Welles, 12 Jan. 1828, Gideon Welles Papers, Library of Congress.

22. *American State Papers: Finance* V, 779–83, 792–832; *United States Telegraph* (Washington, DC), 5 Feb. 1828.

23. *American State Papers: Finance* V, 1039–40.

24. Stanwood, *American Tariff Controversies in the Nineteenth Century*, I, 272.

25. James Buchanan to Thomas Elder, 13 Feb. 1828, James Buchanan Correspondence, Dickinson College.

26. David Barker to Daniel Hoit, 22 Feb. 1828, Daniel Hoit Papers, Duke University.

27. Willis Alston to Willie P. Mangum, 16 March 1828, PWPM, I, 324.

28. "The Tariff Bill," *Ohio State Journal*, 24 April 1828.

29. John Bailey to John B. Davis, 8 March 1828, W. C. Ford (ed.), "Letters to John Brazer Davis," *Massachusetts Historical Society Proceedings* 49 (1916), 210. See also John Bailey to John B. Davis, 10 May 1828, Ford (ed.), "Letters to John Brazer Davis," 212.

30. William B. Fordney to James Buchanan, 15 April 1828, JBP.

31. Henry Clay to John J. Crittenden, 14 Feb. 1828, PHC, VII, 95.

32. Eliza C. Harrison (ed.), *Philadelphia Merchant: The Diary of Thomas P. Cope* (South Bend, IN: Gateway Editions, 1978), 272.

33. "The Tariff," *Scioto Gazette* (Chillicothe, Ohio), 27 March 1828.

34. *Norwich (CT) Courier*, 9 April 1828; "The Tariff," *Eastern Argus*, 12 Feb. 1828; *Christian Intelligencer and Eastern Chronicle* 2 (30 May 1828), 37; "The Proposed Bill for Altering the Tariff," *Boston Courier*, 14 Feb. 1828; "Editor's Correspondence," *Boston Courier*, 29 Feb. 1828; *Eastern Argus*, 11 April 1828.

35. *Register of Debates*, 20th Cong., 1st Sess., 2091.

36. "The Tariff," *United States Telegraph* (Washington, DC), 2 Feb. 1828 "The Tariff," *United States Telegraph* (Washington, DC), 5 Feb. 1828; "The Administration vs. The Tariff," *Argus of Western America* (Frankfort, KY), 21 April 1828; "The Tariff," *Trenton Emporium*, 19 April 1828; John A. Garraty, *Silas Wright* (New York: Columbia University Press, 1949), 56–59; David S. Reynolds, *Waking Giant: America in the Age of Jackson* (New York: Harper, 2008), 73–74.

37. *Register of Debates*, 20th Cong., 1st Sess., 1729.

38. *Register of Debates*, 20th Cong., 1st Sess., 1858, 1866; "From a Correspondent," *Boston Courier*, 17 March 1828; Garraty, *Silas Wright*, 57–61.

39. *Register of Debates*, 20th Cong., 1st Sess., 1998, 2001, 2009–10, 2355.

40. *Niles' Weekly Register* (Baltimore) 33 (19 Jan. 1828), 330.

41. Hezekiah Niles to John W. Taylor, 14 Feb. 1828, John W. Taylor Papers, New York Historical Society.

42. *Register of Debates*, 20th Cong., 1st Sess., 2040.

43. *National Journal* (Washington, DC), 28 March 1828.

44. *New York Evening Post*, 31 March 1828.

45. Augustine B. Shepperd to Bartlett Yancey, 17 April 1828, "Letters to Bartlett Yancey," *James Sprunt Historical Publications* 10 (1911), 74.

46. Entry of 9 April, Henry R. Storrs Diary, Buffalo and Erie County Historical Society.

47. Henry Clay to Peter B. Porter, 1 March 1828, PHC, VII, 136.

48. Henry Clay to Peter B. Porter, 2 April 1828, PHC, VII, 212.

49. *Register of Debates*, 20th Cong., 1st Sess., 2289–90.

50. *Register of Debates*, 20th Cong., 1st Sess., 2342.

51. E. I. DuPont to Richard Drummond, 14 April 1828, E. I. DuPont Papers, Hagley Library and Museum.

52. Entry of 15 April 1828, Henry R. Storrs Diary, Buffalo and Erie County Historical Society.

53. *Pittsburgh Mercury*, 22 April 1828.

54. *Register of Debates*, 20th Cong., 1st Sess., 2348–49; CLC, III, 1419; Clay to Porter, 12 April 1828, PHC, VII, 225; William Creighton to Charles Hammond, 16 April 1828, CHP; Timothy Pickering to John Randolph, 12 April 1828, John Randolph Papers, University of Virginia; P. T. O. to John Quincy Adams, 17 April 1828, AFP.

55. *Register of Debates*, 20th Cong., 1st Sess., 2390, 2403.

56. *Register of Debates*, 20th Cong., 1st Sess., 2444, 2468.

57. *Register of Debates*, 20th Cong., 1st Sess., 2471–72; Silas Wright to A. C. Flagg, 22 April 1828, A. C. Flagg Papers, New York Public Library.

58. *National Intelligencer* (Washington, DC), 23 April 1828.

59. During the presidential campaign, the Adams forces tried to win votes by arguing that the Jacksonians opposed a protective tariff. See "A Citizen," *Considerations Which Demand the Attention of Farmers, Mechanics, and Friends of the American System* (New York, 1828), 10–13.

60. Many of the speeches on the tariff in the Senate, including Smith's, went unrecorded. Daniel Webster attributed the term "a bill of abominations" to Smith in his address. See John Pancake, *Samuel Smith and the Politics of Business, 1752–1839* (Tuscaloosa: University of Alabama Press, 1972), 178.

61. John Tyler to H. Curtis, 1 May 1828, John Tyler Papers, Library of Congress.

62. John C. Calhoun to James Colhoun, 4 May 1828, PJCC, X, 383.

63. *Pendleton Messenger*, 30 May 1832; *Senate Journal*, 20th Cong., 1st Sess., 5 May 1828, 356–60; Robert V. Remini, *Martin Van Buren and the Making of the Democratic Party*, 170–85.

64. Daniel Webster to James Paige, 12 May 1828, PDWC, II, 345.

65. Abbott Lawrence to Daniel Webster, 7 May 1828, PDWC, II, 343.

66. Thomas Lord and Company to Daniel Webster, 29 April 1828, PDWC, II, 338–39; Samuel H. Babcock to Daniel Webster, 7 May 1828, PDWC, II, 341; Joseph T. Buckingham to Daniel Webster, 7 May 1828, PDWC, II, 342; Abbot Lawrence to Daniel Webster, 7 May 1828, PDWC, II, 342; Livermore and Dunn to Daniel Webster, 29 April 1828, Daniel Webster Papers, New Hampshire Historical Society; Tiffany, Sayles, and Hitchcock

to Daniel Webster, 29 April 1828, Daniel Webster Papers, New Hampshire Historical Society; Livermore and Dunn to Daniel Webster, 29 April 1828, Daniel Webster Papers, New Hampshire Historical Society; Edward Everett to Unknown, 9 May 1828, EEP.

67. James W. McIntyre (ed.), *The Writings and Speeches of Daniel Webster* (18 vols., Boston: Little and Brown, 1903), V, 238; *Register of Debates*, 20th Cong., 1st Sess., 786.

68. Daniel Webster, "Dinner at Faneuil Hall," McIntyre (ed.), *Writings and Speeches of Daniel Webster*, II, 15; entry of 12 May 1828, Diary of Henry R. Storrs, Buffalo and Erie County Historical Society; *Register of Debates*, 20th Cong., 1st Sess., 786; Alfred E. Eckes, *Opening America's Market: U.S. Foreign Trade Policy since 1776* (Chapel Hill: University of North Carolina Press, 1995), 23.

69. John Quincy Adams to Charles Francis Adams, 28 May 1828, AFP; Louisa Catherine Adams to ABA, 18 May 1828, AFP.

CHAPTER 8

1. *Niles' Weekly Register* (Baltimore) 34 (26 July 1828), 351–53.

2. James Hamilton to Martin Van Buren, 31 July 1828, MVBP; John C. Calhoun to James E. Colhoun, 4 May 1828, PJCC, X, 382; Calhoun to Andrew Jackson, 10 July 1828, PJCC, X, 396; Erika Jean Pribanic-Smith, "Sowing the Seeds of Disunion: South Carolina's Partisan Newspapers and the Nullification Crisis, 1828–1832" (PhD diss., University of Alabama, 2010), 29–43.

3. Andrew Jackson to George Washington Campbell, 14 Feb. 1828, PAJ, VI, 416–17.

4. John H. Eaton to Andrew Jackson, 4 March 1828, PAJ, VI, 428, 430.

5. Andrew Jackson to James Ray, 28 Feb. 1828, Stanley F. Horn Collection, Vanderbilt University; William B. Lewis to Ira Davis, 26 June 1828, AJP; *Niles' Weekly Register* (Baltimore) 33 (23 Feb. 1828), 439, *Niles' Weekly Register* (Baltimore) 34 (3 May 1828), 158.

6. James K. Polk to Andrew Jackson, 13 April 1828, CJKP, I, 176; "Jackson—the Tariff," *Argus of Western America* (Frankfort, KY), 23 April 1828.

7. "Gen. Jackson and the Tariff," *Cincinnati Gazette*, quoted in *National Journal* (Washington, DC), 23 April 1828.

8. *Connecticut Courant*, 27 May 1828.

9. Entry of 26 April 1828, Henry R. Storrs Diary, Buffalo and Erie County Historical Society.

10. "The Present Administration," *Ohio State Journal*, 6 March 1828.

11. *Charleston Mercury*, 7 July 1828.

12. *Edgefield Hive*, quoted in *Charleston Mercury*, 8 July 1828.

13. *Niles' Weekly Register* (Baltimore) 35 (20 Sept. 1828), 58–64; John C. Calhoun to Micah Sterling, 29 June 1828, PJCC, X, 391; Calhoun to John McLean, 10 July 1828; PJCC, X, 398; Calhoun to Bartlett Yancey, 16 July 1828, PJCC, X, 401; Calhoun to Samuel Smith, 28 July 1828, PJCC, X, 404.

14. Robert Y. Hayne to Andrew Jackson, 3 Sept. 1828, CAJ, III, 432–35.

15. Andrew Jackson to James Hamilton Jr., 29 June 1828, PAJ, VI, 476.

16. John Forsyth to Bolling Hall, 15 Sept. 1828, Bolling Hall Family Papers, Alabama Department of Archives and History.

17. Hines Holt to Bolling Hall, 20 June 1828, Bolling Hall Family Papers, Alabama Department of Archives and History.

18. *Niles' Weekly Register* (Baltimore) 34 (26 July 1828), 354; Charles S. Sydnor, *The Development of Southern Sectionalism, 1819–1848* (Baton Rouge: Louisiana State University Press, 1948), 187–89.

19. Martin Van Buren to Churchill C. Cambreleng, 8 Sept. 1828, MVBP.

20. Donald B. Cole, *Martin Van Buren and the American Political System* (Princeton, NJ: Princeton University Press, 1984), 167–69; John Niven, *Martin Van Buren: The Romantic Age of American Politics* (New York: Oxford University Press, 1983), 198–200.

21. Levi Woodbury to Martin Van Buren, 1 July 1828, MVBP; Unknown to Peter B. Porter, 20 July 1828, Peter B. Porter Papers, Buffalo and Erie County Historical Society; Stephen Pleasanton to James Buchanan, 6 Aug. 1828, James Buchanan and Harriet Lane Johnston Papers, Library of Congress; Hines Holt to Bolling Hall, 30 Aug. 1828, Bolling Hall Family Papers, Alabama Department of Archives and History; William Plumer Jr. to Henry Clay, 26 July 1828, PHC, VII, 403; Samuel Smith to Calhoun, 5 July 1828, PJCC, X, 393–94; Duff Green to Calhoun, 23 Sept. 1828, PJCC, X, 422–23; Calhoun to Martin Van Buren, 28 Sept. 1828, PJCC, X, 425.

22. *Harrisburg Chronicle*, 7 July 1828.

23. *Niles' Weekly Register* (Baltimore) 34 (Sept. 20 1828), 294; Duff Green to John C. Calhoun, 23 Sept. 1828, PJCC, X, 422; *Harrisburg Chronicle*, 21 July 1828; *Newport Mercury*, 19 July 1828.

24. Donald B. Cole, *Vindicating Andrew Jackson: The 1828 Election and the Rise of the Two-Party System* (Lawrence: University Press of Kansas, 2009), 179–203; Lynn H. Parsons, *The Birth of Modern Politics: Andrew Jackson, John Quincy Adams, and the Election of 1828* (New York: Oxford University Press, 2009), 180–83.

25. "The Prospect before Us," *Charleston Mercury*, 29 May 1828.

26. "Why Is the South Opposed to the Tariff," *Illinois Gazette* (Shawnee-town), 29 March 1828; James M. Banner, "The Problem of South Carolina," Stanley Elkins and Eric McKitrick (eds.), *The Hofstadter Aegis: A Memorial* (New York: Alfred A. Knopf, 1974), 60–93.

27. Andrew Jackson, "Fourth Annual Message," CMPP, II, 597; John L. Larson, *Internal Improvement: National Public Works and the Promise of Popular Government in the Early United States* (Chapel Hill: University of North Carolina Press, 2001), 161–80.

28. CLC, III, 471.

29. Calhoun to William C. Preston, 6 Nov. 1828, PJCC, X, 431, Calhoun to Preston, 21 Nov. 1828, PJCC, X, 433–34; Wiltse, *John C. Calhoun: Nationalist*, 372–73; William W. Freehling, *Prelude to Civil War: The Nullification Controversy in South Carolina, 1816–1836* (New York: Harper and Row, 1966), 143–44.

30. Gerald M. Capers, "A Reconsideration of John C. Calhoun's Transition from Nationalism to Nullification," *Journal of Southern History* 14 (Feb. 1948), 34–48.

31. Calhoun here considers any slaveholding state as southern.

32. Calhoun, "Exposition Reported by the Special Committee," PJCC, X, 457, 459, 461, 463; Lacy K. Ford, "Republican Ideology in a Slave Society: The Political Economy of John C. Calhoun," *Journal of Southern History* 54 (August 1988), 405–24.

33. James Hamilton Jr. to Andrew Jackson, 15 Nov. 1828, AJP; Francis Baylies to Timothy Pickering, 5 Jan. 1829, Timothy Pickering Papers, Massachusetts Historical Society; Robert Hubbard to Linaus Bolling, 8 Dec. 1828, Correspondence of Robert T. Hubbard, University of Virginia; John C. Wright to Charles Hammond, 12 Dec. 1828, CHP; Duff Green to Ninian Edwards, 23 Dec. 1828, Duff Green Papers, Library of Congress; J. M. Knell to J. G. M. Ramsey, 29 Dec. 1828, Ramsey Family Papers, University of Tennessee; David R. Williams to Stephen D. Miller, 5 Jan. 1829, David R. Williams Papers, University of South Carolina; William Elliott to Mrs. Elliott, 29 Nov. 1828, Elliott and Gonzales Family Papers, Southern Historical Collection—University of North Carolina; Richard E. Ellis, "The Market Revolution and the Transformation of American Politics, 1801–

1837," Melvyn Stokes and Stephen Conway (eds.), *The Market Revolution in America: Social, Political, and Religious Expressions, 1800–1880* (Charlottesville: University of Virginia Press, 1996), 149–76.

CHAPTER 9

1. *Columbia Telescope*, 10 July 1829.
2. James Madison to Frederick List, 3 Feb. 1829, William C. Rives (ed.), *Letters and Other Writings of James Madison* (4 vols., Philadelphia: J. B. Lippincott, 1865), IV, 13.
3. John Tipton to James B. Slaughter, 27 March 1832, Nellie R. Robertson et al. (eds.), *The John Tipton Papers* (3 vols., Indianapolis: Indiana Historical Bureau, 1942), II, 563.
4. *Harrisburg Chronicle*, 2 July 1832.
5. *Register of Debates in Congress, 1825–1837 (Washington, DC, 1825–1837)*, 22nd Cong., 1st Sess., 606; MJQA, VIII, 460; John C. Calhoun to Francis W. Pickens, 2 March 1832, PJCC, XI, 558.
6. James Madison to Richard Rush, 17 Jan. 1829, Rives (ed.), *Letters and Other Writings of James Madison*, IV, 6.
7. Andrew Jackson, "Inaugural Address," CMPP, II, 437.
8. Richard E. Ellis, *The Union at Risk: Jacksonian Democracy, States' Rights, and the Nullification Crisis* (New York: Oxford University Press, 1987), 41–45; Mark R. Cheathem, *Andrew Jackson: Southerner* (Baton Rouge: Louisiana State University Press, 2013), 134.
9. William Smith to David R. Evans, 8 Jan. 1829, William Smith Papers, University of South Carolina.
10. William Cullen Bryant to Gulian C. Verplanck, 27 Feb. 1829, William Cullen Bryant II (ed.), *The Letters of William Cullen Bryant* (6 vols., New York: Fordham University Press, 1975–1981), I, 277.
11. Charles M. Wiltse, *John C. Calhoun: Nullifier, 1829–1839* (Indianapolis: Bobbs and Merrill, 1949), 19–25; Richard B. Latner, *The Presidency of Andrew Jackson: White House Politics, 1829–1837* (Athens: University of Georgia Press, 1979), 37–41.
12. "Dinner to the Hon. Henry Baldwin," *National Intelligencer* (Washington, DC), 28 Jan. 1830.
13. *New York Daily Advertiser*, quoted in *United States Telegraph* (Washington, DC), 14 Jan. 1830; Philip S. Klein, *Pennsylvania Politics, 1817–1832: A Game without Rules* (Philadelphia: Pennsylvania Historical Society, 1940), 298–301; M. Flavia Taylor, "The Political and Civic Career of Henry Baldwin, 1799–1830," *Western Pennsylvania Historical Magazine*, 14 (March 1941), 37–50; Robert D. Ilisevich, "Henry Baldwin and Andrew Jackson: A Political Relationship in Trust?," *Pennsylvania Magazine of History and Biography* 120 (Jan./April 1996), 37–60; Caroline P. Smith, "Jacksonian Conservative: The Later Years of William Smith" (PhD diss., Auburn University, 1977), 143–44.
14. *Register of Debates*, 20th Cong., 1st Sess., 24.
15. "Webster vs. Hayne," *Boston Courier*, 4 Feb. 1830.
16. Herman Belz (ed.), *The Webster-Hayne Debate on the Nature of the Union: Selected Documents* (Indianapolis: Liberty Fund, 2000), 11.
17. Belz (ed.), *Webster-Hayne Debate on the Nature of the Union*, 42; Nathan Sargent, *Public Men and Events: From the Commencement of Mr. Monroe's Administration, in 1817, to the Close of Mr. Fillmore's Administration, in 1853* (2 vols., Philadelphia: J. B. Lippincott, 1875), I, 172; Peter Parish, "Daniel Webster, New England, and the West," *Journal of American History* 54 (Dec. 1967), 524–49.
18. Belz (ed.), *Webster-Hayne Debate on the Nature of the Union*, 109, 112–13.

19. Belz (ed.), *Webster-Hayne Debate on the Nature of the Union*, 126, 128; John Davis to Eliza Davis, 26 Jan. 1830, JDP; Joseph Vance to Charles Hammond, 29 Jan. 1830, CHP; Daniel Feller, *The Public Lands in Jacksonian Politics* (Madison: University of Wisconsin Press, 1984), 111–19; Merrill D. Peterson, *The Great Triumvirate: Webster, Clay, and Calhoun* (New York: Oxford University Press, 1987), 171–78; Theodore Jervey, *Robert Y. Hayne and His Times* (New York: Macmillan, 1909), 227–67; William N. Chambers, *Old Bullion: Senator from the New West, 1782–1858* (Boston: Little, Brown, 1956), 160–67; Harlow W. Shiedly, "The Webster-Hayne Debate: Recasting New England's Sectionalism," *New England Quarterly* 67 (March 1964), 5–29.

20. Belz (ed.), *Webster-Hayne Debate on the Nature of the Union*, 333.

21. William H. Crawford to Daniel Webster, 17 Sept. 1830; William H. Crawford Letter, University of South Carolina. For a recent retelling of the great debate, see John R. Van Atta, *Securing the West: Politics, Public Lands, and the Fate of the Old Republic, 1785–1850* (Baltimore: Johns Hopkins University Press, 2014), 139–69.

22. James Madison to Edward Everett, Aug. 1830 (?), Rives (ed.), *Letters and Other Writings of James Madison*, IV, 95–106; Drew R. McCoy, *The Last of the Fathers: James Madison and the Republican Legacy* (New York: Cambridge University Press, 1989), 119–62; Lacy K. Ford, "Inventing the Concurrent Majority: Madison, Calhoun, and the Problem of Majoritarianism in American Political Thought," *Journal of Southern History* 60 (Feb. 1994), 19–58; William K. Bolt, "Founding Father and Rebellious Son: James Madison, John C. Calhoun, and the Use of Precedents," *American Nineteenth Century History* 5 (Fall 2004), 1–27.

23. *Register of Debates*, 21st Congress, 1st Sess., 698.

24. Robert Y. Hayne to Martin Van Buren, 12 Oct. 1830, MVBP; Henry Lee to Andrew Jackson, 29 Aug. 1830, PAJ, VIII, 512–13; *Register of Debates*, 21st Cong., 1st Sess., 698–99; Jackson, "Veto Message," CMPP, II, 492–93; John L. Larson, *Internal Improvement: National Public Works and the Promise of Popular Government in the Early United States* (Chapel Hill: University of North Carolina Press, 2001), 183–84; Robert V. Remini, *Andrew Jackson and the Course of American Freedom, 1822–1832* (New York: Harper and Row, 1981), 251–55; Songho Ha, *The Rise and Fall of the American System: Nationalism and the Development of the American Economy, 1790–1837* (London: Pickering and Chatto, 2009), 116–17; Carlton Jackson, "The Internal Improvement Vetoes of Andrew Jackson," *Tennessee Historical Quarterly* 25 (Fall 1966), 261–79.

25. Jackson, "Second Annual Message," CMPP, II, 523.

26. "Mr. McDuffie's Speech," *Charleston Mercury*, 25 May 1831; James Hamilton Jr. to James H. Hammond, 21 May 1831, "Letters on the Nullification Movement in South Carolina, 1830–1835," *American Historical Review* 6 (July 1901), 746; William W. Freehling, *Prelude to Civil War: The Nullification Controversy in South Carolina, 1816–1836* (New York: Harper and Row, 1966), 195.

27. John C. Calhoun to Frederick Symmes, 26 July 1831, PJCC, XI, 430–31.

28. *New Hampshire Sentinel*, 26 Aug. 1831.

29. "The Crisis," *National Intelligencer* (Washington, DC), 27 Aug. 1831; "Mr. Calhoun's Opinion's," *Newbern Spectator*, quoted in *National Intelligencer* (Washington, DC), 1 Sept. 1831.

30. John Quincy Adams to Henry Clay, 7 Sept. 1831, PHC, VIII, 397; William Gaston to Robert Donaldson, 3 Sept. 1831, William Gaston Papers, Southern Historical Collection—University of North Carolina; *Richmond Enquirer*, 2 Sept. 1831; J. G. Swift to Henry A. S. Dearborn, 6 Aug. 1832, Henry A. S. Dearborn Papers, Duke University.

31. William C. Preston to Unknown, 25 March 1831, William C. Preston Papers, University

of South Carolina; Unknown to George C. Mackay, 9 Oct. 1830, Mackay Family Papers, University of South Carolina; Joshua Reynolds to William May Wightman, 30 Oct. 1830, William May Wightman Papers, University of South Carolina; Robert Y. Hayne, *An Oration Delivered in the Independent or Congregational Church, Charleston before the States Rights and Free Trade Party* (Charleston, SC, 1831); James Hamilton, *The Introductory Address of Governor Hamilton at the First Meeting of the Charleston States Rights and Free Trade Association* (Charleston, SC, 1831); William R. Taylor, *Cavalier and Yankee: The Old South and American National Character* (New York: G. Braziller, 1957), 263–64.

32.   Ellis, *Union at Risk*, 102–40; J. Mills Thornton, *Politics and Power in a Slave Society: Alabama, 1800–1860* (Baton Rouge: Louisiana State University Press, 1978), 26–34; Paul H. Bergeron, "Tennessee's Response to the Nullification Crisis," *Journal of Southern History* 39 (Feb. 1973), 23–44; Lucie Bridgforth, "Mississippi's Response to Nullification, 1833," *Journal of Mississippi History* 45 (Feb. 1983), 1–21; E. Merton Coulter, "The Nullification Movement in Georgia," *Georgia Historical Quarterly* 5 (March 1921), 3–39.

33.   Entry of p. 22, New England Man's Travel Diary, Duke University; *Banner of the Constitution* 3 (18 July 1832), 255; Condy Raguet to Stephen D. Miller, 17 July 1830, Stephen D. Miller Papers, Duke University; Paul K. Conkin, *Prophets of Prosperity: America's First Political Economists* (Bloomington: Indiana University Press, 1980), 215–21; H. Arthur Scott Trask, "The Constitutional Republicans of Philadelphia, 1818–1848: Hard Money, Free Trade, and States' Rights" (PhD diss., University of South Carolina, 1998), 262–91.

34.   *H.R. Doc. No. 82*, 22nd Cong., 1st Sess. (1832); William Plumer to John Quincy Adams, 19 March 1832, AFP; Thomas W. Gilmer to P. P. Barbour, 4 Nov. 1831, Ambler Family Papers, University of Virginia; Stephen D. Elliott to William Elliott, 31 Aug. 1831, Elliott and Gonzales Family Papers, Southern Historical Collection—University of North Carolina; James Brown to Henry Clay, 2 Oct. 1831, PHC, VIII, 410; John C. Calhoun to Francis W. Pickens, 2 March 1832, PJCC, XI, 559; Joseph Dorfman, *The Economic Mind in American Civilization* (5 vols., New York: Viking, 1946–1959), II, 512–26; Trask, "Constitutional Republicans of Philadelphia," 306–13; William S. Belko, *The Triumph of the Antebellum Free Trade Movement* (Gainesville: University Press of Florida, 2012), 28–36, 107–34.

35.   *Niles' Weekly Register* (Baltimore) 41 (12 Nov. 1831), 206, 215; Mahlon Dickerson to Samuel J. Bayard, 29 Oct. 1831, Mahlon Dickerson Papers, New Jersey Historical Society. For a comparison between the two conventions, see *North American Review*, 34 (Jan. 1832), 178–98.

CHAPTER 10

1.   James Martin Jr. to Willie P. Mangum, 27 Dec. 1831, PWPM, I, 441.

2.   Daniel Webster to Henry Clay, 5 Oct. 1831, PDWC, III, 129.

3.   Andrew Jackson to Martin Van Buren, 14 Nov. 1831, CAJ, III, 374.

4.   Charles H. Ambler (ed.), *The Life and Diary of John Floyd: Governor of Virginia, Apostle of Secession, and the Father of the Oregon Country* (Richmond: Richmond Press, 1918), 171.

5.   *Albany Evening Journal*, 7 May 1832; Jackson, "Third Annual Message," CMPP, II, 556.

6.   *H.R. Doc. 3*, 22nd Cong., 1st Sess. (1831); *Jackson Southern Statesman*, 31 Dec. 1831; Walter Lowrie to Martin Van Buren, 27 Jan. 1832, MVBP.

7.   Henry Clay to Francis T. Brooke, 9 Dec. 1831, PHC, VIII, 429; Clay to Samuel L. Southard, 12 Dec. 1831, PHC, VIII, 431; Clay to Francis T. Brooke, 25 Dec. 1831, PHC,

VIII, 436–37; Robert V. Remini, *Henry Clay: Statesman for the Union* (New York: W. W. Norton, 1991), 373, 380–82.

8. MJQA, VIII, 439, 443–45; "Mr. Adams and the Tariff," *Richmond Enquirer*, 24 Jan. 1832; Samuel Flagg Bemis, *John Quincy Adams and the Union* (New York: Alfred A. Knopf, 1956), 243–46.

9. MJQA, VIII, 446; Joel R. Poinsett to Joseph Johnson, 25 Jan. 1832, Joel R. Poinsett Papers, Historical Society of Pennsylvania; Joel R. Poinsett to Joseph Johnson, 4 Feb. 1832, Joel R. Poinsett Papers, Historical Society of Pennsylvania; Richard G. Miller, "The Tariff of 1832: The Issue That Failed," *Filson Club History Quarterly* 49 (July 1975), 221–30.

10. *Register of Debates in Congress, 1825–1837 (Washington, DC, 1825–1837)*, 22nd Cong., 1st Sess., 66, 72–75.

11. *Register of Debates*, 22nd Cong., 1st Sess., 260, 266, 277.

12. *American Advocate*, 13 April 1832; Clayne L. Pope, *The Impact of the Antebellum Tariff on Income Distribution* (New York: Arno, 1975), 5–12.

13. *Register of Debates*, 22nd Cong., 1st Sess., 86, 94, 99.

14. George M. Dallas to Henry Gilpin, 3 April 1832, George M. Dallas Papers, Historical Society of Pennsylvania; James Madison to Henry Clay, 22 March 1832, Rives (ed.), *Letters and Other Writings of James Madison*, IV, 216–17; Samuel Smith to John Spear Smith, 11 Jan. 1832; Samuel Smith Papers, Library of Congress; William B. Lewis to Moses Dawson, 15 Feb. 1832, Moses Dawson Collection, Xavier University.

15. *Register of Debates*, 22nd Cong., 1st Sess., 659; John Quincy Adams to Louisa Catherine Adams, 5 April 1832, AFP.

16. Edward Everett to Alexander H. Everett, 18 March 1832, EEP; MJQA, VIII, 482; Malcolm Rogers Eiselen, *The Rise of Pennsylvania Protectionism* (Philadelphia: Porcupine, 1974 reprint of 1932 ed.), 108.

17. Willie P. Mangum to William Gaston, 19 Jan. 1832, PWPM, I, 455.

18. *H.R. Doc. No. 279*, 22nd Cong., 1st Sess. (1832); Robert C. Winthrop (ed.), *Memoir of the Hon. Nathan Appleton* (Boston: John Wilson and Son, 1861), 33–34; MJQA, VIII, 476; Andrew Jackson to Martin Van Buren, 6 Dec. 1831, CAJ, IV, 379; John Quincy Adams to Charles Francis Adams, 15 Dec. 1831, AFP.

19. *H.R. Doc. No. 222*, 22nd Cong., 1st Sess. (1832); "The Treasury Tariff Scheme," *National Intelligencer* (Washington, DC), 1 May 1832; "The New Tariff Examined," *Charleston Mercury*, 4 Aug. 1832.

20. William L. Marcy to Nathaniel P. Tallmadge, 30 April 1832, NPTP.

21. Francis Jones to Willie P. Magnum, 7 June 1832, PWPM, I, 551.

22. "The Tariff," *United States Telegraph* (Washington, DC), 5 May 1832; *Alexandria Gazette*, 15 June 1832; Henry Clay to Peter B. Porter, 3 May 1832, PHC, VIII, 505; "The 'Judicious Tariff,'" *Boston Courier*, 10 May 1832; John A. Munroe, *Louis McLane: Federalist and Jacksonian* (New Brunswick, NJ: Rutgers University Press, 1973), 344–48.

23. *Albany Evening Journal*, 8 June 1832; "The Project," *Richmond Enquirer*, 15 May 1832; "The Tariff," *Boston Courier*, 21 May 1832.

24. John Quincy Adams to Louisa Catherine Adams, 23 May 1832, AFP.

25. *Niles' Weekly Register* (Baltimore) 42 (16 June 1832), 281.

26. "Adjustment of the Tariff," *Albany Argus*, 28 May 1832; *New York Evening Post*, 29 May 1832; *Niles' Weekly Register* (Baltimore) 42 (9 June 1832), 274–78.

27. William Huntington (ed.), "Diary and Letters of Charles P. Huntington," *Massachusetts Historical Society Proceedings* 57 (Feb. 1924), 246.

28. John D. Macoll, "Representative John Quincy Adams's Compromise Tariff of 1832," *Capitol Studies* 1 (Fall 1972), 41–58.

29. Joseph Gales to Nicholas Biddle, 16 June 1832, Nicholas Biddle Papers, Library of Congress; Littleton W. Tazewell to John N. Tazewell, 22 June 1832, Tazewell Family Papers, Library of Virginia; John Quincy Adams to Louisa C. Adams, 5 April 1832, AFP.

30. Andrew Jackson to Sarah Yorke Jackson, 6 May 1832, Andre deCoppet Collection, Princeton University.

31. Edward Everett to Alexander H. Everett, 1 July 1832, EEP.

32. "The Van Buren Tariff Bill," *United States Telegraph* (Washington, DC), 4 July 1832; "Van Buren Tariff Bill," *United States Telegraph* (Washington, DC), 17 July 1832.

33. John Quincy Adams to Louisa C. Adams, 11 June 1832, AFP; Daniel Webster to Stephen White, 28 June 1832, PDWC, III, 181; *Cheraw Republican*, quoted in *New Orleans Bee*, 23 Aug. 1832; *Albany Evening Journal*, 3 July 1832.

34. Hezekiah Niles to Henry Clay, 4 July 1832, PHC, VIII, 549; John Quincy Adams to Louisa Catherine Adams, 19 July 1832, AFP; Mahlon Dickerson to Hezekiah Niles, 13 July 1832, Mahlon Dickerson Papers, New Jersey Historical Society; Harrison Gray Otis to Daniel Webster, July 1832 (?), HGOP; Daniel Webster to Nathan Hale, 7 July 1832, Daniel Webster Papers, Maryland Historical Society; "Evening Session," *United States Telegraph* (Washington, DC), 20 July 1832; "The Tariff," *National Intelligencer* (Washington, DC), 9 July 1832; "The Tariff," *Nashville Republican and State Gazette*, 18 July 1832.

35. James Tallmadge to Nathaniel P. Tallmadge, 6 Sept. 1832, NPTP.

36. John Quincy Adams to Louisa Catherine Adams, 19 July 1832, AFP.

37. "State of Parties on the Tariff," *Boston Advocate*, quoted in *Jamestown Journal*, 25 July 1832.

38. "The Tariff," *New Bedford Courier*, 3 July 1832.

39. "The Tariff," *National Intelligencer* (Washington, DC), 14 July 1832.

40. Henry Horn to James K. Polk, 7 Aug. 1832, CJKP, I, 490; "Celebration of the Fourth of July," *Harrisburg Chronicle*, 16 July 1832; *New York Evening Post*, 30 June 1832.

41. "The Winding Up," *Richmond Enquirer*, 17 July 1832; "Bank, Judiciary, Tariff," *National Intelligencer* (Washington, DC), 30 July 1832.

42. John L. Hunter to William Elliott, 4 Sept. 1832, Elliott and Gonzales Family Papers, Southern Historical Collection—University of North Carolina; "Address to the People of South Carolina," *Banner of the Constitution* 3 (8 Aug. 1832), 278. For a sampling of the resolutions passed against the tariff throughout South Carolina, see *Banner of the Constitution* 3 (19 Sept. 1832), 324.

43. H. H. Townes to George H. Townes, 2 Aug. 1832, Townes Family Papers, University of South Carolina.

44. "Nullification—Symptoms of War," *Connecticut Courant*, 14 Aug. 1832.

45. *Charleston Mercury*, 23 Aug. 1832.

46. *Charleston Mercury*, 5 Sept. 1832.

47. *Columbia Telescope*, 11 Sept. 1832.

48. *United States Telegraph* (Washington, DC), 21 July 1832.

49. John C. Calhoun to Virgil Maxcy, 8 Oct. 1832, PJCC, XI, 665; Calhoun to Elias D. Earle and Others, 18 Sept. 1832, PJCC, XI, 659; Timothy W. Johnson to W. H. C. Storrs, 17 Aug. 1832, Timothy Johnson Letter, University of South Carolina; Orlando H. Reed to Stephen D. Miller, 9 Aug. 1832, Chestnut-Manning-Miller Papers, South Carolina Historical Society; T. H. Thurman to William Gaston, 15 Sept. 1832, William Gaston Papers, Southern Historical Collection—University of North Carolina; William H. Crawford to Mahlon Dickerson, 6 Sept. 1832, Mahlon Dickerson Papers, New Jersey Historical Society; John M. Berrien et al. to Albert Gallatin, 9 Aug. 1832, Albert Gallatin Papers,

New York Historical Society; Andrew Jackson to Henry Toland, 12 Sept. 1832, Andrew Jackson Letter, Massachusetts Historical Society.

50. Mathew Carey to Joseph C. Cabell, 23 Aug. 1832, Joseph C. Cabell Family Papers, University of Virginia.

51. "Movements at Washington," *Richmond Enquirer*, 14 Jan. 1832.

52. *Connecticut Courant*, 12 June 1832.

53. "Misrepresentation Corrected," *Washington Globe*, 19 March 1832.

54. *Norwich (CT) Courier*, 16 Jan. 1833; *New York Evening Post*, 9 Jan. 1833.

55. *S. Doc. No. 165*, 22nd Cong., 1st Sess. (1832); *H.R. Doc. No. 84*, 20th Cong., 1st Sess. (1828); *H.R. Doc. No. 258*, 22nd Cong., 1st Sess. (1832); Ronald P. Formisano, *The Transformation of Political Culture: Massachusetts Parties, 1790s–1840s* (New York: Oxford University Press, 1983), 283–84.

56. *Yankee and Boston Literary Gazette*, 4 June 1828.

57. *S. Doc. No. 169*, 22nd Cong., 1st Sess. (1832); Susan-Mary Grant, *North over South: Northern Nationalism and American Identity in the Antebellum Era* (Lawrence: University Press of Kansas, 2000), 61–74; *States Papers on Nullification*, 101–30, 244–66, 285–86.

58. Joel Roberts Poinsett to Andrew Jackson, 29 Nov. 1832, CAJ, IV, 492.

59. Andrew Jackson to Henry Toland, 12 Sept. 1832, Andrew Jackson Letter, Massachusetts Historical Society; Martin Van Buren to Andrew Jackson, 25 July 1830, CAJ, IV, 166; Andrew Jackson to John Coffee, 17 July 1832, CAJ, IV, 462–63; Mark R. Cheathem, *Andrew Jackson: Southerner*, 138; Manisha Sinha, *The Counter-revolution of Slavery: Politics and Ideology in Antebellum South Carolina* (Chapel Hill: University of North Carolina Press, 2000), 33–61; Sean Wilentz, *Rise of American Democracy: Jefferson to Lincoln* (New York: W. W. Norton, 2005), 375–76; James B. Stewart, "'A Great Talking and Eating Machine': Patriarchy, Mobilization, and the Dynamics of Nullification in South Carolina," *Civil War History* 37 (Sept. 1981), 197–220.

60. Entries of 23 and 27 Nov. 1832, Samuel C. Jackson Diary, Southern Historical Collection—University of North Carolina; James L. Petigru to Hugh S. Legare, 29 Oct. 1832, James L. Petigru Papers, University of South Carolina; entry of 23 Aug. 1832, Benjamin F. Perry Papers, Southern Historical Collection—University of North Carolina; Cave Johnson to Unknown, 9 Dec. 1832, JKPP; William Gilmore Simms to James Lawson, 25 Nov. 1832, Mary C. Simms et al. (eds.), *The Letters of William Gilmore Simms* (6 vols., Columbia: University of South Carolina Press, 1952–1982), I, 46–47; William W. Freehling, *Prelude to Civil War: The Nullification Controversy in South Carolina, 1816–1836* (New York: Harper and Row, 1966), 252–53.

61. Joel R. Poinsett to Andrew Jackson, 16 Oct. 1832, CAJ, IV, 481; John Riley to William Royal, 13 Oct. 1832, William Royal Letter, Southern Historical Collection—University of North Carolina; Freehling, *Prelude to Civil War*, 252–59; Robert V. Remini, "Election of 1832," Arthur M. Schlesinger Jr. (ed.), *History of American Presidential Elections, 1789–1968* (4 vols., New York: Chelsea House, 1971), I, 495–516; *Niles' Weekly Register* (Baltimore) 43 (20 Oct. 1832), 125.

62. *Charleston Mercury*, 24, 26 Nov. 1832.

63. *State Papers on Nullification* (Boston: Dutton and Wentworth, 1834), 2–4, 10–13, 16, 21, 23, 28–31.

64. Andrew Jackson to Martin Van Buren, 23 Oct. 1832, MVBP.

65. *Greenville Mountaineer*, 1 Dec. 1832; George Hooper to Edward McGrady, 17 Dec. 1832, Joel R. Poinsett Papers, Historical Society of Pennsylvania; James Hamilton to Patrick Noble, 9 Oct. 1832, James Hamilton Papers, University of South Carolina; James L.

Petigru to Hugh S. Legare, 21 Dec. 1832, James L. Petigru Papers, University of South Carolina; R. M. Rutledge to Lieutenant Rutledge, 5 Oct. 1832, Rutledge Family Papers, University of South Carolina; R. M. Rutledge to Lieutenant Rutledge, 30 Jan. 1833, Rutledge Family Papers, University of South Carolina; entry of 1 Feb. 1833, Robert Raymond Reid Diary, Florida State Library; Freehling, *Prelude to Civil War*, 254–59.

66. Michael Hoffman to A. C. Flagg, 18 Dec. 1832, MVBP; Freehling, *Prelude to Civil War*, 264; Robert Tinkler, *James Hamilton of South Carolina* (Baton Rouge: Louisiana State University Press, 2004), 134–36; Wiltse, *John C. Calhoun: Nullifier*, 151.

CHAPTER 11

1. George M. Dallas to H. D. Gilpin, 1 Dec. 1832, George M. Dallas Papers, Historical Society of Pennsylvania.

2. Charles Jarvis to Leonard Jarvis, 4 Dec. 1832, Jarvis Family Papers, Maine Historical Society.

3. Thomas F. Jones to James F. Patterson, 24 Nov. 1832, Jones and Patterson Family Papers, Southern Historical Collection—University of North Carolina; *Morning Courier and New York Enquirer*, 11 Dec. 1832; "The Union," *Globe*, 29 Nov. 1832; William W. Freehling, *Prelude to Civil War: The Nullification Controversy in South Carolina, 1816–1836* (New York: Harper and Row, 1966), 272–73; Joseph H. Parks, *Felix Grundy: Champion of Democracy* (Baton Rouge: Louisiana State University Press, 1940), 201.

4. *Boston Courier*, 31 Dec. 1832.

5. *Norwich (CT) Courier*, 26 Dec. 1832.

6. Thomas A. Marshall to John Marshall, 4 Jan. 1833, Charles Hobson et al. (eds.), *The Papers of John Marshall* (12 vols., Chapel Hill: University of North Carolina Press, 1974–2006), XII, 254.

7. "The Tariff," *Connecticut Courant*, 11 Dec. 1832.

8. "The Tariff," *Richmond Enquirer*, 23 Nov. 1832.

9. Andrew Jackson, "Fourth Annual Message," CMPP, II, 597–98, 600; John A. Munroe, *Louis McLane: Federalist and Jacksonian* (New Brunswick, NJ: Rutgers University Press, 1973), 364–65.

10. Archibald Yell to James K. Polk, 16 Dec. 1832, CJKP, I, 577.

11. *Charleston Mercury*, 10 Dec. 1832.

12. *Morning Courier and New York Enquirer*, 11 Dec. 1832.

13. *Scioto Gazette* (Chillicothe, Ohio), 19 Dec. 1832.

14. MJQA, VIII, 503.

15. E. I. DuPont to William Kemble, 5 Dec. 1832, E. I. DuPont Papers, Hagley Library and Museum.

16. George Poindexter to ?, 4 Dec. 1832, printed in *Natchez Courier and Adams, Jefferson and Franklin Advertiser*, 8 Feb. 1833.

17. *Easton (PA) Sentinel*, 14 Dec. 1832; *New York Evening Post*, 5 Dec. 1832; *Hampshire Gazette*, 12 Dec. 1832; Colt to Nicholas Biddle, 8 Dec. 1832, Reginald C. McGrane (ed.), *The Correspondence of Nicholas Biddle* (Boston: Houghton Mifflin, 1919), 199; Richard E. Ellis, *The Union at Risk, Jacksonian Democracy, States' Rights, and the Nullification Crisis* (New York: Oxford University Press, 1987), 83.

18. Jackson, "Proclamation," CMPP, II, 645, 650.

19. Jackson, "Proclamation," CMPP, II, 648, 650; William B. Hatcher, "Edward Livingston's View of the Nature of the Union," *Louisiana Historical Quarterly* 24 (July 1941), 698–728; Ellis, *Union at Risk*, 89–91.

20. Harriett Weed (ed.), *Autobiography of Thurlow Weed* (Boston: Houghton Mifflin, 1884), 422.

21. Webster, "Speech on Nullification," James W. McIntyre (ed.), *Writings and Speeches of Daniel Webster* (18 vols., Boston: Little and Brown 1903), XIII, 41.

22. *Pennsylvania Reporter*, quoted in *Washington Globe*, 18 Dec. 1832; John Davis, "Journal from Worcester to Washington," 12–16, JDP; John Reynolds to James Buchanan, 18 Dec. 1832, JBP; Edward Everett to Alexander H. Everett, 11 Dec. 1832, EEP; Condy Raguet to Stephen D. Miller, 15 Dec. 1832, Chestnut-Manning-Miller Papers, South Carolina Historical Society; John Quincy Adams to William Ellis, 15 March 1833, AFP; *State Papers on Nullification* (Boston: Dutton and Wentworth, 1834), 112–30, Norman D. Brown, "Webster-Jackson Movement for a Constitution and Union Party in 1833," *Mid-America* 46 (July 1964), 147–71.

23. "President's Proclamation," *Mobile Commercial Register*, 24 Dec. 1832.

24. Isaac J. Thomas to James K. Polk, 24 Dec. 1832, CJKP, I, 588.

25. William J. Alexander to James K. Polk, 29 Dec. 1832, CJKP, I, 593.

26. John Tyler to Littleton W. Tazewell, 2 Feb. 1833, Tazewell Family Papers, Library of Virginia.

27. *Morning Courier and New York Enquirer*, 15 Dec. 1832.

28. John Patton to Littleton W. Tazewell, 18 Dec. 1832, Tazewell Family Papers, Library of Virginia; John Randolph to Peter Browne 21 Jan. 1833, John Randolph Papers, University of Virginia; Thomas McCulloch to David Campbell, 16 Dec. 1832, CFP; James H. Pettigrew to Ebenezer Pettigrew, 3 Feb. 1833, Ebenezer Pettigrew Papers, Duke University; Maunsel White to Andrew Jackson, 12 Jan. 1833, Stanley F. Horn Collection, Vanderbilt University.

29. "Andrew Jackson's Proclamation," *Charleston Mercury*, 17 Dec. 1832; James H. Hammond to Robert Y. Hayne, 20 Dec. 1832, "Letters on the Nullification Movement in South Carolina, 1830–1835," *American Historical Review* 6 (July 1901), 751.

30. *Niles' Weekly Register* (Baltimore) 43 (26 Jan. 1833), 361.

31. James L. Petigru to Hugh S. Legare, 21 Dec. 1832, James L. Petigru Papers, University of South Carolina; James Hamilton to William C. Preston, 28 Dec. 1832, James Hamilton Papers, University of South Carolina; entry of 13 Jan. 1833, Benjamin F. Perry Papers, Southern Historical Collection—University of North Carolina; Freehling, *Prelude to Civil War*, 267–68.

32. Alan Nevins (ed.), *The Diary of Philip Hone* (2 vols., New York: Dodd, Mead, 1927), I, 85.

33. *Albany Argus*, 27 Feb. 1833.

34. Henry Clay to Francis T. Brooke, 12 Dec. 1832, PHC, VIII, 603.

35. MJQA, VIII, 510.

36. Mahlon Dickerson to Martin Van Buren, 11 Jan. 1833, MVBP; Robert V. Remini, "Election of 1832," Arthur M. Schlesinger Jr. (ed.), *History of American Presidential Elections, 1789–1968* (4 vols., New York: Chelsea House, 1971), I, 495–516.

37. *State Papers on Nullification* (Boston: Dutton and Wentworth, 1834), 201.

38. *State Papers on Nullification* (Boston: Dutton and Wentworth, 1834), 222.

39. *State Papers on Nullification* (Boston: Dutton and Wentworth, 1834), 229.

40. *State Papers on Nullification* (Boston: Dutton and Wentworth, 1834), 274.

41. Charles H. Ambler (ed.), *The Life and Diary of John Floyd: Governor of Virginia, Apostle of Secession, and the Father of the Oregon Country* (Richmond: Richmond Press, 1918), 205–6.

42. "Nullification at Last," *Washington Globe*, 3 Jan. 1833.

43. Charles Jarvis to Leonard Jarvis, 7 Dec. 1832, Jarvis Family Papers, Maine Historical Society.

44. Cave Johnson to Unknown, 9 Dec. 1832, JKPP; E. I. DuPont to G. Smith, 13 Jan. 1833, E. I. DuPont Papers, Hagley Library and Museum; Robert Y. Hayne to William C. Preston, 7 Feb. 1833, Robert Young Hayne Papers, University of South Carolina; John W. Taylor to Unknown, Dec. 1832 (?), John W. Taylor Letter, University of South Carolina; James L. Pettigru to James Dellet, 1 Feb. 1833, James Dellet Family Papers, Alabama Department of Archives and History; *New Hampshire Patriot*, 10 Dec. 1832; Mark R. Cheathem, *Old Hickory's Nephew: The Political and Private Struggles of Andrew Jackson Donelson* (Baton Rouge: Louisiana State University Press, 2007), 95–96; Richard E. Ellis, *The Union at Risk*, 78.

45. Samuel Cram Jackson to Elizabeth R. Jackson, 25 Jan. 1833, Samuel Cram Jackson Letters, University of South Carolina.

46. *Charleston Mercury*, 17 Dec. 1832; Joan Carbody to Clarissa Rushbridge, 28 Jan. 1833, Rosina Mix Papers, Southern Historical Collection—University of North Carolina; James Hamilton to William C. Preston, 28 Dec. 1832, James Hamilton Papers, University of South Carolina; Laura Cole Smith to Unknown, 7 Jan. 1833, Brumby and Smith Family Papers, Southern Historical Collection—University of North Carolina.

CHAPTER 12

1. Martin Van Buren, *An Inquiry into the Origin and Nature of Political Parties in the United States* (New York: Hurd and Houghton, 1867), 322.

2. Gulian C. Verplanck, *A Letter to Col. William Drayton, of South Carolina, in Assertion of the Constitutional Power of Congress to Impose Protecting Duties* (New York, 1831), 2–3, 5.

3. *Richmond Enquirer*, 12 Jan. 1833; "State Rights," *Globe*, 2 Jan. 1833; *H.R. Doc. No. 14*, 22nd Cong., 2nd Sess. (1833); Robert W. July, *The Essential New Yorker: Gulian Crommelin Verplanck* (Durham, NC: Duke University Press, 1951), 152–54.

4. "The Tariff and the Meeting," *United States Gazette* (Philadelphia), 21 Jan. 1833; *Norwich (CT) Courier*, 30 Jan., 6 Feb. 1833; *Niles' Weekly Register* (Baltimore) 43 (2 Feb. 1833), 370; Richard E. Ellis, *The Union at Risk, Jacksonian Democracy, States' Rights, and the Nullification Crisis* (New York: Oxford University Press, 1987), 99–100.

5. *Morning Courier and New York Enquirer*, 14 Jan. 1833.

6. "The Tariff," *Richmond Enquirer*, 10 Jan. 1833.

7. MJQA, VIII, 517; Frederick Whittlesey to William H. Seward, 9 Jan. 1833, William R. Seward Papers, University of Rochester; John W. Taylor to Unknown, 25 Dec. 1832, John W. Taylor Letter, University of South Carolina; Silas Wright to Martin Van Buren, 13 Jan. 1833, MVBP; *Norwich (CT) Courier*, 16 Jan. 1833; John C. Calhoun to Bolling Hall, 12 Jan. 1833, PJCC, XII, 7.

8. *Register of Debates in Congress, 1825–1837* (Washington, DC, 1825–1837), 22nd Cong., 2nd Sess., 949.

9. *Register of Debates*, 22nd Cong., 2nd Sess., 1161.

10. *Register of Debates*, 22nd Cong., 2nd Sess., 973.

11. *Register of Debates*, 22nd Cong., 2nd Sess., 1023.

12. *Register of Debates*, 22nd Cong., 2nd Sess., 1095.

13. *Register of Debates*, 22nd Cong., 2nd Sess., 1164; July, *Essential New Yorker*, 156–63; Charles Sellers, *James K. Polk: Jacksonian, 1795–1843* (Princeton, NJ: Princeton University Press, 1957), 158–60.

14. *Morning Courier and New York Enquirer*, 14 Jan. 1833.

15.   John G. Watmough to Nicholas Biddle, 17 Jan. 1833, Nicholas Biddle Papers, Library of Congress; Stephen Pleasanton to James Buchanan, 30 Jan. 1833, JBP; P. C. Brooks to Edward Everett, 31 Jan. 1833, EEP; *National Intelligencer* (Washington, DC), 28 Jan. 1833; *Nashville Republican and State Gazette*, 18 Feb. 1833; *Albany Argus*, 7 Feb. 1833.

16.   Isaac Tompkins to Helene Charlotte Tompkins, 30 Jan. 1833, Isaac Tompkins Letters, Southern Historical Collection—University of North Carolina; William R. King to Martin Van Buren, 9 Jan. 1833, MVBP; George McDuffie to Unknown, 25 Jan. 1833, George McDuffie Papers, Duke University; Ellis, *Union at Risk*, 99–100; William W. Freehling, *Prelude to Civil War: The Nullification Controversy in South Carolina, 1816–1836* (New York: Harper and Row, 1966), 288.

17.   John Davis to Levi Lincoln, 16 Jan. 1833, JDP.

18.   Jackson, "Force Bill Message," CMPP, II, 624; Ellis, *Union at Risk*, 165–67.

19.   Calhoun, "Remarks on the President's Message on South Carolina," PJCC, XII, 14; Calhoun to James Hamilton Jr., 16 Jan. 1833, PJCC, XII, 16.

20.   *New Orleans Bee*, 26 Jan. 1833; Daniel Webster to Stephen White, 18 Jan. 1833, PDWC, III, 208.

21.   *Charleston Courier*, 12 Feb. 1833.

22.   *Knoxville Register*, 9 Jan. 1833.

23.   *Albany Evening Journal*, 4 Jan. 1833.

24.   "The Tariff," *New Hampshire Patriot*, 7 Jan. 1833.

25.   *New York Evening Post*, 22 Jan. 1833.

26.   John M. Clayton to E. I. DuPont, 13 Feb. 1833, E. I. DuPont Papers, Hagley Library and Museum; *Woodville (MS) Republican*, 12 Jan. 1833; Andrew Jackson to Joel R. Poinsett, 7 Feb. 1833, CAJ, V, 16.

27.   William Hammett to F. W. White, 4 Feb. 1833, William Hammett Papers, Virginia Historical Society.

28.   John Tyler to John Floyd, 16 Jan. 1833, John Tyler Papers, Library of Congress; Clay to Peter B. Porter, 29 Jan. 1833, PHC, VIII, 617; "Important from Washington," *Nashville Republican and State Gazette*, 11 March 1833.

29.   Robert Tinkler, *James Hamilton of South Carolina* (Baton Rouge: Louisiana State University Press, 2004), 141–42; James L. Petigru to Hugh S. Legare, 6 Feb. 1833, James L. Petigru Papers, University of South Carolina; "The Day of Grace Extended," *Scioto Gazette* (Chillicothe, Ohio), 13 Feb. 1833.

30.   Andrew Jackson to Felix Grundy, 13 Feb. 1833, Whitefoord Cole Papers, Tennessee State Library and Archives.

31.   Churchill C. Cambreleng to Martin Van Buren, 5 Feb. 1832, MVBP.

32.   Webster, "The Constitution Not a Compact," PDWSFW, I, 619; Charles W. March, *Reminiscences of Congress* (New York: Baker and Scribner, 1850), 198–200, 235; Mark R. Cheathem, *Andrew Jackson: Southerner* (Baton Rouge: Louisiana State University Press, 2013), 139; Robert V. Remini, *Daniel Webster: The Man and His Time* (New York: W. W. Norton, 1997), 377–82.

33.   John C. Calhoun to William C. Preston, 3 Feb. 1833, PJCC, XII, 37; A. T. C. to John Randolph, 21 Jan. 1833, John Randolph Papers, University of Virginia; Daniel Webster to Joseph Hopkinson, 3 Feb. 1833, Joseph Hopkinson Papers, Historical Society of Pennsylvania; Daniel Webster to Joseph Hopkinson, 9 Feb. 1833, PDWC, III, 213; "The Collection Bill," *Globe*, 2 March 1833; *Columbia Telescope*, 5 March 1833; Ellis, *Union at Risk*, 171–72; Norman D. Brown, "Webster-Jackson Movement for a Constitution and Union Party in 1833," *Mid-America* 46 (July 1964), 147–71; David F. Ericson, "The Nullification Crisis, American Republicanism, and the Force Bill Debate," *Journal of*

Southern History 61 (May 1995), 249-70; Raymond C. Dingledine Jr., "The Political Career of William Cabell Rives" (PhD diss., University of Virginia, 1947), 190-200.

34. Controversy remains as to who approached who with the compromise plan. Clay had met with manufacturers in Philadelphia before presenting his plan. He had also discussed some of his ideas with John Tyler. See John Tyler to John Floyd, 10 Jan. 1833, "Original Letters," *William and Mary Quarterly* 21 (July 1912), 8-10. For an excellent summary of who originated the Compromise of 1833, see Merrill D. Peterson, *Olive Branch and Sword: The Compromise of 1833* (Baton Rouge: Louisiana State University Press, 1982), 67-70.

35. *Register of Debates*, 22nd Cong., 2nd Sess., 462, 468; *Raleigh Register and North Carolina Gazette*, 22 Feb. 1833; Thomas Hart Benton to James McDowell, 13 Feb. [1833], James McDowell Papers, Southern Historical Collection—University of North Carolina; William R. King to John Gayle, 26 Feb. 1833, William R. King Papers, Alabama Department of History and Archives; Thomas Hart Benton, *Thirty Years' View; or, A History of the Working of the American Government for Thirty Years from 1820 to 1850* (2 vols., New York: D. Appleton, 1854-1856), I, 343; *United States Gazette* (Philadelphia), 13 Feb. 1833; David S. Heidler and Jeanne T. Heidler, *Henry Clay: The Essential American* (New York: Random House, 2010), 252-54.

36. Ben Perley Poore, *Perley's Reminiscences of Sixty Years in the National Metropolis* (2 vols., Philadelphia: Hubbard Brothers, 1886), I, 138.

37. Nathan Sargent, *Public Men and Events: From the Commencement of Mr. Monroe's Administration, in 1817, to the Close of Mr. Fillmore's Administration, in 1853* (2 vols., Philadelphia: J. B. Lippincott, 1875), II, 239; Benton, *Thirty Years' View*, I, 342-43; Calhoun, "Further Remarks on Clay's Amendment to the Compromise Tariff Bill," PJCC, XI, 99-100; "Mr. Clay's New Tariff Project," *Albany Argus*, 28 Feb. 1833; Richard A. Wire, "Young Senator Clayton and the Early Jackson Years," *Delaware History* 17 (1976), 104-26.

38. MJQA, VIII, 525.

39. *Niles' Weekly Register* (Baltimore) 43 (16 Feb. 18334), 401; George M. Bibb to John J. Crittenden, 5 April 1833, John J. Crittenden Papers, Library of Congress; John Quincy Adams to Charles Francis Adams, 13 March 1833, AFP; Daniel Webster to Nathan Appleton, 17 Feb. 1833, PDWC, III, 216; Webster to Appleton, 21 Feb. 1833, PDWC, III, 220; "Murder and Parricide," *Harrisburg Chronicle*, 14 Feb. 1833; *Woodville (MS) Republican*, 9 March 1833; Ellis, *Union at Risk*, 170.

40. *Globe*, 15 Feb. 1833; Benton, *Thirty Years' View*, II, 345.

41. MJQA, VIII, 527.

42. Mitchell King to John Gayle, 26 Feb. 1833, Mitchell King Papers, University of South Carolina; *National Intelligencer* (Washington, DC), 27 Feb. 1833; *United States Gazette* (Philadelphia), 27 Feb. 1833; "The Tariff Bill and Judiciary Bill," *Globe*, 27 Feb. 1833; Benton, *Thirty Years' View*, I, 311-13.

43. *United States Gazette* (Philadelphia), 1 March 1833.

44. *Albany Evening Journal*, 4 March 1833.

45. *Register of Debates*, 22nd Cong., 2nd Sess., 804, 807-9. "The Tariff and the Judiciary Bill," *Globe*, 27 Feb. 1833; Henry Clay to James Barbour, 2 March 1833, PHC, VIII, 629; John Randolph Clay to James Buchanan, 4 March 1833, JBP; John Connell to Nicholas Biddle, 1 March 1833, Nicholas Biddle Papers, Library of Congress; Peterson, *Olive Branch and Sword*, 81; Ellis, *Union at Risk*, 175-76. For a comparison of the votes on the tariff bill and the enforcing bill, see *Niles' Weekly Register* (Baltimore) 44 (16 March 1833), 44.

46. *Norwich (CT) Courier*, 13 March 1833; *Niles' Weekly Register* (Baltimore) 44 (2 March

1833), 1; *Niles' Weekly Register* (Baltimore) 44 (9 March 1833), 17; John M. Clayton to E. I. DuPont, 2 March 1833, E. I. DuPont Papers, Hagley Library and Museum; Churchill C. Cambreleng to Martin Van Buren, 5 Feb. 1832, MVBP; MJQA, VIII, 522; Robert V. Remini, *Andrew Jackson and the Course of American Democracy, 1833–1845* (New York: Harper and Row, 1984), 41–42.

47. *Columbia Telescope*, 12 March 1833; *New York Evening Post*, 4 March 1833; *Niles' Weekly Register* (Baltimore) 44 (16 March 1833), 33.

48. Joel R. Poinsett to Tyrell (?), 25 March 1833, Joel R. Poinsett Papers, Historical Society of Pennsylvania.

49. R. M. Rutledge to Lieutenant Rutledge, 9 March 1833, Rutledge Family Papers, University of South Carolina; Augustus Fitch to Andrew Jackson, 16 March 1833, Massachusetts Historical Society; entry of 30 March 30, Benjamin F. Perry Papers, Southern Historical Collection—University of North Carolina; Freehling, *Prelude to Civil War*, 295–97.

50. Wiltse, *John C. Calhoun: Nullifier*, 196–98; Freehling, *Prelude to Civil War*, 295–97.

51. "Nullification," *United States Telegraph* (Washington, DC), 9 March 1833.

52. *New Hampshire Patriot*, 11 March 1833.

53. "Important from Washington," *Nashville Republican and State Gazette*, 11 March 1833.

54. Newton Cannon to John McLean, 29 Jan. 1833, John McLean Papers, Library of Congress.

55. *Jackson Southern Statesman*, 6 April 1833; Ellis, *Union at Risk*, 180–82; Richard B. Latner, *The Presidency of Andrew Jackson: White House Politics, 1829–1837* (Athens: University of Georgia Press, 1979), 160–61; Major L. Wilson, "Andrew Jackson: The Great Compromiser," *Tennessee Historical Quarterly* 26 (Spring 1967), 64–78.

56. *Richmond Enquirer*, 2 March 1833.

CHAPTER 13

1. *Washington Globe*, 14 Jan. 1835.

2. Michael F. Holt, "The Democratic Party, 1828–1861," Arthur M. Schlesinger Jr. (ed.), *History of U.S. Political Parties* (4 vols., New York: Chelsea House, 1971), I, 497–536; Lynn Marshall, "The Strange Stillbirth of the Whig Party," *American Historical Review* 72 (Jan. 1967), 445–68; Charles Sellers, "Who Were the Southern Whigs?," *American Historical Review* 59 (Jan. 1954), 335–46; Thomas Brown, "Southern Whigs and the Politics of Statesmanship, 1833–1841," *Journal of Southern History* 46 (Aug. 1980), 361–80; Edwin A. Miles, "The Whig Party and the Menace of Caesar," *Tennessee Historical Quarterly* 27 (Winter 1968), 361–79.

3. *Niles' Weekly Register* (Baltimore) 12 (19 Nov. 1836), 189.

4. Joel H. Silbey, "The Election of 1836," Arthur M. Schlesinger Jr. (ed.), *History of American Presidential Elections, 1789–1968* (4 vols., New York: Chelsea House, 1971), I, 577–600; Richard P. McCormick, "Was There a Whig Strategy in 1836?," *Journal of the Early Republic* 4 (Spring 1984), 47–70.

5. "Why Is the Compromise Tariff Binding," *United States Telegraph* (Washington, DC), 26 Jan. 1837.

6. *H.R. Doc. No. 86*, 24th Cong., 2nd Sess. (1837).

7. Silas Wright to A. C. Flagg, 9 Jan. 1837, A. C. Flagg Papers, New York Public Library; Silas Wright to A. C. Flagg, 15 Jan. 1837, A. C. Flagg Papers, New York Public Library; Elam Tilden to Martin Van Buren, 2 Feb. 1837, MVBP.

8. John C. Calhoun, "Speech on the Bill to Reduce the Duties on Certain Imports," PJCC, XIII, 457.

9. Merrill D. Peterson, *The Great Triumvirate: Webster, Clay, and Calhoun* (New York: Oxford University Press, 1987), 269.

10. *Georgia Constitutionalist*, quoted in *Washington Globe*, 3 Feb. 1837.

11. "The Tariff," *United States Telegraph* (Washington, DC), 16 Jan. 1837.

12. *New Yorker* (New York City) 2 (4 Feb. 1837), 314.

13. "Reduction of the Tariff," *Raleigh Register and North Carolina Gazette*, 7 March 1837.

14. *Congressional Globe*, 24th Cong., 2nd Sess., 206.

15. Jessica M. Lepler, *The Many Panics of 1837: People, Politics, and the Creation of a Transatlantic Financial Crisis* (New York: Cambridge University Press, 2013), 123–56; Reginald C. McGrane, *The Panic of 1837: Some Financial Problems of the Jacksonian Era* (Chicago: University of Chicago Press, 1965 reprint of 1924 ed.), 145–76; Major L. Wilson, *The Presidency of Martin Van Buren* (Lawrence: University Press of Kansas, 1984), 196–97.

16. *Congressional Globe*, 27th Cong., 2nd Sess., appendix, 48.

17. Charles M. Snyder, *The Jacksonian Heritage: Pennsylvania Politics, 1833–1848* (Harrisburg: Pennsylvania Historical and Museum Commission, 1958), 183; Richard McCormick, *The Second American Party System: Party Formation in the Jacksonian Era* (Chapel Hill: University of North Carolina Press, 1966); Michael F. Holt, *The Rise and Fall of the American Whig Party: Jacksonian Politics and the Onset of the Civil War* (New York: Oxford University Press, 1999), 61–88, 108; Daniel Walker Howe, *The Political Culture of the American Whig Party* (Chicago: University of Chicago Press, 1979), 11–42, 96–122; Joel H. Silbey, *The Shrine of Party: Congressional Voting Behavior, 1841–1852* (Pittsburgh: University of Pittsburgh Press, 1967), 18–34; William R. Brock, *Parties and Political Conscience: American Dilemmas, 1840–1850* (Millwood, NY: KTO, 1979), 3–31; Marvin Meyers, *The Jacksonian Persuasion: Politics and Belief* (Stanford, CA: Stanford University Press, 1957), 33–56.

18. Henry A. Wise, *Seven Decades of the Union* (Philadelphia: J. B. Lippincott, 1881), 172.

19. Robert Seagar, *And Tyler Too: A Biography of John and Julia Gardiner Tyler* (New York: McGraw Hill, 1963), 130–35.

20. *Crisis Devoted to the Support of the Democratic Principles of Jefferson* 1 (9 May 1840), 77.

21. *Niles' Weekly Register* (Baltimore) 25 (22 Aug. 1840), 393–94.

22. Stephen B. Gardner to Jonathan Worth, 25 Feb. 1841, J. G. de Roulhac Hamilton (ed.), *The Correspondence of Jonathan Worth* (2 vols., Raleigh: Edwards and Broughton, 1909), I, 32.

23. Andrew Jackson to Martin Van Buren, 24 Nov. 1840, CAJ, VI, 83.

24. Robert Klein (ed.), "Memoirs of a Senator from Pennsylvania: Jonathan Roberts, 1771–1854," *Pennsylvania Magazine of History and Biography* 61 (Oct. 1937), 513.

25. Andrew Jackson to Francis P. Blair, 19 April 1841, AJP.

26. Robert W. Barnwell to Robert Barnwell Rhett, 15 May 1841, Barnwell (ed.), "Hamlet to Hotspur," 244; O. H. Smith, *Early Indiana Trials and Sketches: Reminiscences by Hon. O. H. Smith* (Cincinnati: Moore, Wilstach, Keys, 1858), 594; George Harrison to Harrison Gray Otis, 14 April 1841, HGOP; Timothy Barlow to Nathaniel P. Tallmadge, 15 April 1841, NPTP; MJQA, X, 443; Michael F. Holt, "The Election of 1840, Voter Mobilization, and the Emergence of the Second American Party System: A Reappraisal of Jacksonian Voting Behavior," William J. Cooper Jr. et al. (eds.), *A Master's Due: Essays in Honor of David Herbert Donald* (Baton Rouge: Louisiana State University Press, 1985), 16–58.

27. Andrew Jackson to Francis P. Blair, 19 April 1841, AJP.

28. William B. Campbell to David Campbell, 24 July 1842, CFP; John Ashworth, *"Agrarians"*

and "Aristocrats": Party Ideology in the United States, 1837–1846 (London: Cambridge University Press, 1983), 52–84.

29. John C. Calhoun to Andrew Pickens Calhoun, 3 April 1842, PJCC, XVI, 211; *Congressional Globe*, 27 Cong., 2nd Sess., 629; Thomas Ritchie to Charles Campbell, 6 April 1842, *John P. Branch Historical Papers of Randolph-Macon College* 3 (June 1911), 249; "Things of the Day," *Charleston Mercury*, 13 July 1842.

30. *Congressional Globe*, 26th Cong., 2nd Sess., appendix, 352.

31. *Congressional Globe*, 26th Cong., 2nd Sess., appendix, 356; "Manufactures in Tennessee— Revenue Duties," *Nashville Republican Banner*, 29 April 1842; Norman D. Brown, *Edward Stanly: Whiggery's Tarheel "Conqueror"* (Tuscaloosa: University of Alabama Press, 1974), 70–72.

32. William A. Graham to Charles Plummer Green, 18 July 1841, PWAG, II, 214.

33. *Buffalo Commercial Advertiser*, 19 March 1842; Paul H. Bergeron, *Antebellum Politics in Tennessee* (Lexington: University of Kentucky Press, 1982), 76; Thomas E. Jeffrey, *State Parties and National Politics: North Carolina* (Athens: University of Georgia Press, 1989), 137; Jonathan M. Atkins, *Parties, Politics, and the Sectional Conflict in Tennessee* (Knoxville: University of Tennessee Press, 1997), 116–25. See also *Niles' Weekly Register* (Baltimore) 12 (2 April 1842), 72; William J. Cooper Jr., *The South and the Politics of Slavery, 1828–1856* (Baton Rouge: Louisiana State University Press, 1978), 155–57.

34. J. George Harris to James K. Polk, 3 Sept. 1841, CJKP, V, 752; Daniel Webster to Isaac Chapman Bates and Rufus Choate, 25 Aug. 1841, PDWC, V, 148; Holt, *Rise and Fall of the American Whig Party*, 135–36, Maurice Baxter, *Henry Clay and the American System* (Lexington: University of Kentucky Press, 1995), 168–71; Wellington G. Raynor, *The Political and Sectional Influence of the Public Lands, 1828–1842* (Cambridge, MA: Riverside, 1914), 99–104.

35. *The Mississippian*, 17 Sept. 1841; Calhoun, "Speech on the Bill to Distribute the Proceeds of the Sales of Public Lands to the States," PJCC, XV, 734; Donald B. Cole and John J. McDonough (eds.), *Witness to the Young Republic: A Yankee's Journal, 1828–1870* (Hanover, NH: University Press of New England, 1989), 123–24.

36. Abbot Lawrence to Robert C. Winthrop, 15 Feb. 1842, WFP; Entry of 30 Aug. 1841, Gideon Welles Papers, Library of Congress; John C. Calhoun to Andrew Pickens Calhoun, 12 Sept. 1841, PJCC, XV, 771; Holt, *Rise and Fall of the American Whig Party*, 136; *Charleston Mercury*, 17 Sept. 1841; Alasdar Roberts, *America's First Great Depression: Economic Crisis and Political Disorder after the Panic of 1837* (Ithaca, NY: Cornell University Press, 2012), 50–65.

CHAPTER 14

1. Hopkins L. Turney to James K. Polk, 12 Aug. 1841, CJKP, V, 722.

2. Samuel Tilden to Nelson J. Waterbury, 11 Sept. 1841, John Bigelow (ed.), *Letters and Literary Memorials of Samuel J. Tilden* (2 vols., New York: Harper Brothers, 1908), I, 8.

3. Thomas Hart Benton, *Thirty Years' View; or, A History of the Working of the American Government for Thirty Years from 1820 to 1850* (2 vols., New York: D. Appleton, 1854–1856), II, 207; "Mr. Van Buren," *Ohio Statesman*, 29 Dec. 1840; "Democratic Van Buren Flag," *Jonesborough Whig*, 13 Jan. 1841.

4. "The Tariff," *Pennsylvania Telegraph* (Harrisburg), 6 July 1842; *Niles' Weekly Register* (Baltimore) 12 (25 June 1842), 263.

5. Tyler, "First Annual Message," CMPP, IV, 82.

6. Horace Greeley to Millard Fillmore, 11 Jan. 1842, MFP.

7. J. H. Clifford to Robert C. Winthrop, 22 Dec. 1841, WFP.

8. Abel P. Upshur to Nathaniel B. Tucker, 12 Jan. 1842, Lyon G. Tyler (ed.), *The Letters and Times of the Tylers* (3 vols., Richmond: Whittet and Sheperson, 1884–1896), II, 155.

9. James Buchan to R. Frazer, 22 Jan. 1842, JBP; Dan Monroe, *The Republican Vision of John Tyler* (College Station: Texas A&M University Press, 2003), 119–20.

10. Charles Hudson to John Davis, 22 Dec. 1841, JDP; *New York American*, quoted in *Vermont Watchman and State Journal*, 13 Dec. 1841.

11. Robert C. Winthrop to J. P. Davis, 22 Feb. 1842, WFP; James Hamilton to Duff Green, 17 March 1842, Duff Green Papers, Southern Historical Collection—University of North Carolina; M. G. Woodbury to Levi Woodbury, 26 March 1842, Levi Woodbury Family Papers, Library of Congress; Hugh Brickhead to Daniel Webster, 14 April 1842, Sang Collection, Brandeis University; *Buffalo Commercial Advertiser*, 5 April 1842.

12. *Congressional Globe*, 27th Cong., 2nd Sess., 287–88; Aaron V. Brown to Sarah C. Polk, 14 Jan. 1844, JKPP.

13. William C. Preston to Waddy Thompson, 23 March 1842, William C. Preston Papers, University of South Carolina; Benton, *Thirty Years' View*, II, 400–401; Nathan Sargent, *Public Men and Events: From the Commencement of Mr. Monroe's Administration, in 1817, to the Close of Mr. Fillmore's Administration, in 1853* (2 vols., Philadelphia: J. B. Lippincott, 1875), II, 160–61.

14. Abel P. Upshur to Nathaniel B. Tucker, 6 March 1842, Tyler (ed.), *Letters and Times of the Tylers*, II, 155.

15. Tyler, "Special Message," CMPP, IV, 108; Charles Hudson to John Davis, 30 March 1842, JDP; Norma L. Peterson, *The Presidencies of William Henry Harrison and John Tyler* (Lawrence: University Press of Kansas, 1989), 100.

16. Robert C. Winthrop to John Davis, 31 March 1842, JDP.

17. Hoffman Whitehouse to Willie P. Mangum, 28 May 1842, PWPM, III, 346.

18. "The Whigs and the Tariff—the Denouement," *Madisonian* (Washington, DC), 17 June 1842; *Plattsburgh Republican*, quoted in *Albany Argus*, 16 June 1842; J. Newton Dexter to Millard Fillmore, 5 April 1842, MFP.

19. *Congressional Globe*, 27th Cong., 2nd Sess., 616; Millard Fillmore to Millard Powers Fillmore, 12 April 1842, MFP; A. Davis to John Quincy Adams, 4 April 1842, AFP.

20. *Niles' National Register* (Baltimore) 12 (23 July 1842). James W. McCulloch's instructions to customs officials can be found in *Charleston Mercury*, 6 July 1842.

21. Millard Fillmore, "On the Tariff Bill of 1842," Frank H. Severance (ed.), *Millard Fillmore Papers* (2 vols., Buffalo, NY: Buffalo Historical Society, 1907), I, 206, 216.

22. Thomas Hart Benton to Martin Van Buren, 8 June 1842, MVBP. For a list of the duties in the "Provisional Tariff," see *Niles' National Register* 12 (Baltimore) (11 Jun. 1842), 225.

23. *Congressional Globe*, 27th Cong., 2nd Sess., 628.

24. *Congressional Globe*, 27th Cong., 2nd Sess., 636; Louisa Catherine Adams to Charles Francis Adams, 25 June 1842, AFP.

25. Silas Wright Jr. to John Niles, 18 April 1842, Gideon Welles Papers, Library of Congress; Aaron Vanderpeol to Levi Woodbury, 25 April 1842, Levi Woodbury Family Papers, Library of Congress; William B. Campbell to David Campbell, 22 June 1842, CFP.

26. Winfield Scott to Thaddeus Stevens, 2 Aug. 1842, Thaddeus Stevens Papers, Library of Congress.

27. "The Provisional Tariff Bill," *National Intelligencer* (Washington, DC), 27 June 1842.

28. Robert P. Letcher to John J. Crittenden, 21 June 1842, Chapman Coleman (ed.), *Life of John J. Crittenden: With Selections from His Correspondence and Speeches* (Philadelphia: J. B. Lippincott, 1871), 183.

29. *Louisville Daily Journal*, 23 June 1842; Joel H. Silbey, *The Shrine of Party: Congressional Voting Behavior, 1841–1852* (Pittsburgh: University of Pittsburgh Press, 1967), 55; William J. Cooper Jr., *The South and the Politics of Slavery, 1828–1856* (Baton Rouge: Louisiana State University Press, 1978), 155–57.

30. Millard Fillmore to Thurlow Weed, 28 June 1842, Thurlow Weed Papers, University of Rochester.

31. Tyler, "Veto Message," CMPP, IV, 182; John Tyler to Robert McCandlish, 10 July 1842, Tyler (ed.), *Letters and Times of the Tylers*, II, 173; William B. Campbell to David Campbell, 30 June 1842, CFP; Monroe, *Republican Vision of John Tyler*, 136–38; Robert Seagar, *And Tyler Too: A Biography of John and Julia Gardiner Tyler* (New York: McGraw Hill, 1963), 165–66.

32. Henry Clay to John J. Crittenden, 16 July 1842, PHC, IX, 735; Clay to John Quincy Adams, 24 July 1842, PHC, IX, 742; Clay to John M. Clayton, 8 Aug. 1842, PHC, IX, 753; John White to Robert P. Letcher, 11 July 1842, John Crittenden Papers, Library of Congress; John Pendleton Kennedy to P. C. Pendleton, 4 Aug. 1842, John P. Kennedy Papers, Maryland Historical Society; Richard A. Gantz, "Henry Clay and the Harvest of Bitter Fruit: The Struggle with John Tyler, 1841–1842" (PhD diss., Indiana University, 1986), 312–22.

33. John J. Crittenden to Henry Clay, 2 July 1842, PHC, IX, 722.

34. *Rochester Democrat*, quoted in *Buffalo Commercial Advertiser*, 9 July 1842.

35. A copy of the proceedings from this meeting, dated 11 Aug. 1842, was addressed to John Quincy Adams and can be found in the AFP.

36. Calhoun to James E. Colhoun, 18 Aug. 1842, PJCC, XVI, 392.

37. MJQA, XI, 204.

38. "The Great Tariff Bill," *National Intelligencer* (Washington, DC), 18 July 1842; *Niles' Weekly Register* (Baltimore) (20 Aug. 1842), 389; "The New Tariff," *Charleston Mercury*, 23 July 1842; Silbey, *The Shrine of Party*, 54.

39. Calhoun, "Speech before the Passage of the Tariff Bill," PJCC, XVI, 364.

40. Daniel Webster to John Tyler, 8 Aug. 1842, PDWC, V, 236; Aaron V. Brown to James K. Polk, 16 July 1842, JKPP; *Buffalo Commercial Advertiser*, 13 Aug. 1842; *Madisonian* (Washington, DC), 10 Aug. 1842.

41. Alan Nevins and Milton Halsey Thomas (eds.), *The Diary of George Templeton Strong* (4 vols., New York: Macmillan, 1952), I, 185; Aaron V. Brown to James K. Polk, 16 July 1842, JKPP; "The Veto," *Buffalo Commercial Advertiser*, 13 Aug. 1842; "The Fourth Veto," *Madisonian* (Washington, DC), 10 Aug. 1842.

42. "The Impeachment," *Albany Argus*, 18 July 1842; Samuel Flagg Bemis, *John Quincy Adams and the Union* (New York: Alfred A. Knopf, 1956), 441–42; Monroe, *Republican Vision of John Tyler*, 138–39; Peterson, *Presidencies of William Henry Harrison and John Tyler*, 104–6.

43. John Pendleton Kennedy to P. C. Pendleton, 9 Aug. 1842, John Pendleton Kennedy Papers, Maryland Historical Society.

44. Thurlow Weed to Nathaniel P. Tallmadge, 4 Aug. 1842, NPTP.

45. Millard Fillmore to John Ridgway et al., 6 Aug. 1842, MFP; Robert C. Winthrop to Unknown, 1 Aug. 1842, WFP; Nathaniel P. Tallmadge to John Tyler, 7 Aug. 1842, NPTP.

46. Gilbert Davis to Levi Woodbury, 5 July 1842, Levi Woodbury Family Papers, Library of Congress.

47. "What Will the Whigs Do?," *Charleston Mercury*, 18 Aug. 1842; John White to Henry Clay, 18 Aug. 1842, PHC, XI, 288; Willie P. Mangum to Priestly H. Mangum, 10 Aug. 1842, PWPM, III, 377; John Pendleton Kennedy to Unknown, 12 Aug. 1842, John

Pendleton Kennedy Papers, Maryland Historical Society; Robert McClellan to Martin Van Buren, 15 Aug. 1842, MVBP; John J. Crittenden to James Harlan, 16 Aug. 1842, John J. Crittenden Papers, Library of Congress; Michael F. Holt, *The Rise and Fall of the American Whig Party: Jacksonian Politics and the Onset of the Civil War* (New York: Oxford University Press, 1999), 148.

48. "The Tariff Question," *National Intelligencer* (Washington, DC), 23 Aug. 1842.

49. *Congressional Globe*, 27th Cong., 2nd Sess., 925.

50. Stanly's quote appeared in "Painfully Interesting," *Concord Patriot*, 1 Sept. 1842.

51. "House of Representatives," *Washington Globe*, 22 Aug. 1842; Leverett Saltonstall to Robert C. Winthrop, 23 Aug. 1842, WFP. These events can be followed in newspapers that had correspondents in the House that day. The best account can be found in *North American* (Philadelphia), 24 Aug. 1842. See MJQA, XI, 242–43. For an account that contends that Thomas Marshall of Kentucky initiated the tariff without distribution, see *Washington Globe*, 10 Sept. 1842.

52. "Senate," *Globe*, 27 Aug. 1842.

53. *Congressional Globe*, 27th Cong., 2nd Sess., 951; Martin Van Buren to Francis P. Blair, 12 Sept. 1842, Blair Family Papers, Library of Congress.

54. Cave Johnson to James K. Polk, 28 Aug. 1842, CJKP, VI, 104; R. Wallace to Martin Van Buren, 12 Sept. 1842, MVBP; H. M. Waterston to James K. Polk, 14 Sept. 1842, JKPP; John A. Garraty, *Silas Wright* (New York: Columbia University Press, 1949), 227.

55. Silas Wright to A. C. Flagg, 26 Aug. 1842, A. C. Flagg Papers, New York Public Library.

56. Aaron V. Brown to Peter Vroom, 24 Aug. 1842, Aaron V. Brown Letter, University of Tennessee.

57. "Adjournment of Congress—Passing and Signing of the Tariff Bill," *North American* (Philadelphia), 31 Aug. 1842; James H. Hammond to John C. Calhoun, 10 Sept. 1842, PJCC, XVI, 453–55; James Buchanan to Francis P. Blair, 24 Sept. 1842, Blair Family Papers, Library of Congress; Robert J. Walker to Martin Van Buren, 31 Aug. 1842, MVBP; Francis P. Blair to Martin Van Buren, 4 Sept. 1842, MVBP; Edward P. Crapol, *John Tyler: The Accidental President* (Chapel Hill: University of North Carolina Press, 2006), 106–7.

58. William M. Gwin to James K. Polk, 27 Aug. 1842, CJKP, VI, 100–101; Cave Johnson to James K. Polk, 28 Aug. 1842, CJKP, VI, 103; John Niven, *Martin Van Buren: The Romantic Age of American Politics* (New York: Oxford University Press, 1983), 503–4.

59. *Niles' Weekly Register* (Baltimore) 13 (5 Nov. 1842), 138–39; "The South and the Tariff," *Pennsylvania Telegraph* (Harrisburg), 10 Aug. 1842; "Defining Their Position," *Berkshire County Whig*, 6 Oct. 1842.

60. Act of August 29, 1842, ch. 270, 5 *Stat.* 566–67; Robert J. Rayback, *Millard Fillmore: Biography of a President* (Buffalo, NY: Buffalo Historical Society, 1959), 132–35. For a listing of the rates of the tariff of 1842 and how they compared with the previous tariffs, see *Niles' National Register* (Baltimore) 13 (17 Sept. 1842), 39.

61. *Niles' National Register* (Baltimore) 13 (19 Nov. 1842), 179.

62. Tyler, "Fourth Annual Message," CMPP, IV, 352.

63. *National Intelligencer* (Washington, DC), 1 Nov. 1843. Statistical figures derived from *DeBow's Review*, May 1858, 457.

64. Henry Clay to John M. Berrien, 4 Sept. 1842, PHC, IX, 762–63; Holt, *Rise and Fall of the American Whig Party*, 151–63; William Mills to Millard Fillmore, 1 Dec. 1842, MFP; *Richmond Enquirer*, 15 Sept. 1842. In 1842, Congress approved a bill changing the ratio for apportionment in the House to 70,680 to 1. This reduced the number of seats in the House to 223.

65.   "Senate," *Washington Globe*, 5 Aug. 1842; "The Tariff Question—a Full Broadside," *Nashville Union*, 2 Sept. 1842.

CHAPTER 15

1.   David Campbell to William B. Campbell, 20 June 1842, CFP; Robert Toombs to John M. Berrien, 28 Jan. 1844, John M. Berrien Papers, Southern Historical Collection—University of North Carolina.

2.   Cave Johnson to James K. Polk, 30 March 1844, CJKP, VII, 98. For a comparison of McKay's proposed tariff and the tariff of 1842, see *National Intelligencer* (Washington, DC), 15 March 1844.

3.   *Congressional Globe*, 28th Cong., 1st Sess., appendix, 689; Michael F. Holt, *The Rise and Fall of the American Whig Party: Jacksonian Politics and the Onset of the Civil War* (New York: Oxford University Press, 1999), 167.

4.   *Congressional Globe*, 28th Cong., 1st Sess., appendix, 658, 430; George McDuffie to John C. Calhoun, 10 March 1844, PJCC, XVII, 855–56.

5.   *New York Herald*, 26 April 1844; *National Intelligencer* (Washington, DC), 24 April 1844; *Charleston Mercury*, 27 April 1844; *Congressional Globe*, 28th Cong., 1st Sess., appendix, 741.

6.   Alexander H. Stephens to P. Shaw, 17 May 1844, Alexander Stephens Papers, Library of Congress.

7.   Cave Johnson to James K. Polk, 8 May 1844, CJKP, VII, 126; Robert B. Rhett to Robert M. T. Hunter, 30 Aug. 1844, Charles H. Ambler (ed.), "Correspondence of Robert M. T. Hunter, 1826–1876," *American Historical Association Annual Report for 1916* (2 vols., Washington, DC, 1918), II, 70–71.

8.   Willie P. Mangum to J. Watson Webb, 20 April 1844, PWPM, V, 476–77.

9.   *Congressional Globe*, 28th Cong., 1st Sess., 633; John Slidell to Martin Van Buren, 2 Feb. 1844, MVBP; George McDuffie to David J. McCord, 7 May 1844, George McDuffie Papers, University of South Carolina; John A. Garraty, *Silas Wright* (New York: Columbia University Press, 1949), 253–54.

10.   Henry Clay to Clay Club of Dauphin County, PA., 11 May 1844, PHC, X, 59.

11.   "The British Tariff Killed!," *Fayetteville Observer*, 15 May 1844.

12.   *Richmond Whig*, quoted in *Boston Daily Atlas*, 23 May 1844.

13.   William A. Graham, "Campaign Speech," PWAG, II, 511; R. Murchison to David S. Reid, 31 May 1844, David S. Reid Papers, North Carolina State Archives; Edward Stanwood, *American Tariff Controversies in the Nineteenth Century* (2 vols., Boston: Houghton Mifflin, 1903), II, 39.

14.   "Opinions of Mr. Van Buren on the Subject of a National Bank, Distribution of the Proceeds of the Public Lands, an Exchequer or Government Fiscal Agent, a Tariff, the Veto Power, and a National Convention," MVBP; John Niven, *Martin Van Buren: The Romantic Age of American Politics* (New York: Oxford University Press, 1983), 506–7.

15.   Andrew Jackson to Martin Van Buren, 21 April 1843, MVBP.

16.   Andrew Jackson to Martin Van Buren, 22 Sept. 1843, MVBP; Donald B. Cole, *Martin Van Buren and the American Political System* (Princeton, NJ: Princeton University Press, 1984), 389–90.

17.   James Buchanan to George C. Leiper, 22 May 1842, JBP; Robert P. Letcher to John J. Crittenden, 8 Dec. 1842, Chapman Coleman (ed.), *Life of John J. Crittenden: With Selections from His Correspondence and Speeches* (Philadelphia: J. B. Lippincott, 1871), 195.

18. "Gen. Lewis Cass," *Ohio Statesman*, 29 March 1843.

19. A. P. Stinson to Thomas G. Clemson, 8 July 1843, PJCC, XVII, 299.

20. John C. Calhoun, "The Address of Mr. Calhoun to His Political Friends and Supporters (First Version)," PJCC, XVII, 630; John C. Calhoun, "The Address of Mr. Calhoun to His Political Friends and Supporters (Published Version)," PJCC, XVII, 740; John C. Calhoun to Robert M. T. Hunter, 21 Feb. 1844, PJCC, XVII, 529; John C. Calhoun to Franklin H. Elmore, 16 Jan. 1844, PJCC, XVII, 711; Willard Carl Klunder, *Lewis Cass and the Politics of Moderation* (Kent, OH: Kent State University Press, 1996), 127–31.

21. *Congressional Globe*, 28th Cong., 1st Sess., appendix, 705.

22. James Buchanan to Mrs. Roosevelt, 13 May 1844, John B. Moore (ed.), *The Works of James Buchanan* (12 vols., Philadelphia: J. B. Lippincott, 1901–1911), VI, 2–3.

23. Thomas Ritchie to Howell Cobb, 6 May 1844, Charles H. Ambler (ed.), "Three Letters from Thomas Ritchie to Howell Cobb," *John P. Branch Historical Papers* 3 (June 1911), 355; Niven, *Martin Van Buren*, 526–29; William W. Freehling, *The Road to Disunion: Secessionists at Bay, 1776–1854* (New York: Oxford University Press, 1990), 428–29; Michael Morrison, "Martin Van Buren, the Democracy, and the Partisan Politics of Texas Annexation," *Journal of Southern History* 61 (Nov. 1995), 695–722.

24. Charles Sellers, "Election of 1844," Arthur M. Schlesinger Jr. (ed.), *History of American Presidential Elections* (4 vols., New York: Chelsea House, 1971), II, 747–75.

25. Edward Everett to John C. Winthrop, 18 June 1844, WFP.

26. Willie P. Mangum to Priestly H. Mangum, 29 May 1844, PWPM, IV, 128; Charles Sellers, *James K. Polk: Continentalist, 1843–1846* (Princeton, NJ: Princeton University Press, 1966), 69–98; Mark R. Cheathem, *Old Hickory's Nephew: The Political and Private Struggles of Andrew Jackson Donelson* (Baton Rouge: Louisiana State University Press, 2007), 161–64.

27. Jackson to Moses Dawson, 19 Oct. 1842, Moses Dawson Collection, Xavier University.

28. James K. Polk, *Answers of Ex-gov. Polk, to Two Series of Interrogatories Propounded to Him and Gov. Jones through the Presses of Memphis* (Memphis, 1843), 12–13.

29. Robert J. Walker to James K. Polk, 30 May 1844, CJKP, VII, 168.

30. Andrew J. Donelson to James K. Polk, 31 May 1844, CJKP, VII, 169.

31. John J. Hardin to James Irvin, 30 May 1844, printed in *National Intelligencer* (Washington, DC), 31 May 1844; Henry A. Muhlenberg to James K. Polk, 3 June 1844, CJKP, VII, 193–95.

32. John K. Kane to James K. Polk, 30 May 1844, JKPP.

33. Joseph Furnace to Aaron V. Brown, 31 May 1844, JKPP.

34. James K. Polk to John K. Kane, 19 June 1844, CJKP, VII, 267; J. George Harris to James K. Polk, 25 June 1844, CJKP, VII, 282; George M. Dallas to James K. Polk, 26 June 1844, CJKP, VII, 284.

35. Gideon J. Pillow to Henry Horn and John K. Kane, July 2 1844, John Kintzing Kane Papers, American Philosophical Society Library.

36. William McCandless to James K. Polk, 11 Aug. 1844, JKPP.

37. James Buchanan to Unknown, 6 Sept. 1844, JBP.

38. *New York Tribune*, 27 June 1844.

39. *New London Morning News*, 12 Aug. 1846; *North American* (Philadelphia), 26 Sept. 1844; William K. Bolt, "'A Tax in Some Other Form': James K. Polk and the Tariff Debates," *Journal of East Tennessee History* 87 (2015), 26–46.

40. "A Columbia County Man," *Clay and Polk: The Difference between Them on the Tariff Question* (Philadelphia, 1844), 4, 8.

41. Nathan Sargent to Willie P. Mangum, 21 Aug. 1844, PWPM, IV, 180.

42. *The Prospect before Us; or, Locofoco Impositions Exposed* (Washington, DC, 1844), 16–17.

43. Truman Smith to William B. Campbell, 18 Aug. 1844, CFP; James E. Harvey to Willie P. Mangum, 23 July 1844, PWPM, IV, 161; Nicholas Carroll to Willie P. Mangum, 7 Oct. 1844, PWPM, IV, 206.

44. Willis Green, *Address of the Hon. Willis Green of Kentucky, before the Alexandria (D.C.) Clay Club* (1844), 7, 11.

45. "The Recoil," *National Intelligencer* (Washington, DC), 22 Aug. 1844; James A. Seddon to Robert M. T. Hunter, 19 Aug. 1844, Ambler (ed.), "Correspondence of Robert M. T. Hunter," II, 68; William C. Davis, *Rhett: The Turbulent Life and Times of a Fire-Eater* (Columbia: University of South Carolina Press, 2001), 196–210; Charles M. Wiltse, *John C. Calhoun: Sectionalist, 1840–1850* (Indianapolis: Bobbs and Merrill, 1951), 188–93.

46. David Campbell to William C. Rives, 9 Aug. 1844, CFP; John C. Calhoun to Armistead Burt, 7 Aug. 1844, PJCC, XIX, 526; Calhoun to William D. Porter, 19 Aug. 1844, PJCC, XIX, 614; Calhoun to Francis Wharton, 17 Sept. 1844, PJCC, XIX, 806.

47. Francis W. Pickens to John C. Calhoun, 9 Sept. 1844, PJCC, XIX, 728.

48. George McDuffie to the Central Committee, 12 July 1844, Samuel Laughlin Papers, Tennessee Historical Society.

49. Nathan Sargent, *Life of Henry Clay* (Philadelphia, 1844), 30.

50. Aaron Vanderpeol to James K. Polk, 26 July 1844, JKPP; J. B. Clements to Polk, 2 Aug. 1844, JKPP; Seth Clover to James K. Polk, 5 Aug. 1844, JKPP; "An Irish Adopted Citizen," *Fifty Reasons Why Henry Clay Should Be Elected President* (Baltimore, 1844), 14–16; David S. Heidler and Jeanne T. Heidler, *Henry Clay: The Essential American* (New York: Random House, 2010), 384.

51. Henry Clay to Thomas C. Miller et al., 9 Sept. 1844, PHC, X, 110–11.

52. Henry Clay to Joseph Paxton, 19 Sept. 1844, PHC, X, 118–19; Clay to John M. Clayton, 22 Aug. 1844, PHC, X, 102; Clay to Joseph R. Ingersoll, 29 Aug. 1844, PHC, X, 106.

53. Webster, "Speech at Boston," James W. McIntyre (ed.), *The Writings and Speeches of Daniel Webster* (18 vols., Boston: Little and Brown, 1903), V, 264; Webster, "Speech in New York, McIntyre (ed.), *Writings and Speeches of Daniel Webster*, V, 274; Webster, "Speech at Pepperell," McIntyre (ed.), *Writings and Speeches of Daniel Webster*, V, 288.

54. Alan Nevins (ed.), *The Diary of Philip Hone* (2 vols., New York: Dodd, Mean, 1927), I, 719–20.

55. Arthur Campbell to Unknown, 17 Nov. 1844, CFP.

56. "The Result of the Great Contest," *Nashville Union*, 19 Nov. 1844.

57. Thomas Corwin to John J. Crittenden, 15 Nov. 1844, John J. Crittenden Papers, Library of Congress.

58. John Pendleton Kennedy to P. C. Pendleton, 17 Oct. 1844, John Pendleton Kennedy Papers, Maryland Historical Society.

59. James K. Polk, "Inaugural Address," CMPP, IV, 379.

60. John C. Calhoun to Robert M. T. Hunter, 26 March 1845, PJCC, XXI, 449.

61. Walter R. Borneman, *Polk: The Man Who Transformed the Presidency and America* (New York: Random House, 2008), 141–43.

CHAPTER 16

1. Polk, "First Annual Message," CMPP, IV, 398, 403–4.

2. James Graham to William Graham, 7 April 1846, PWAG, III, 114.

3. *Detroit Free Press*, 21 July 1846.

4. James Graham to William A. Graham, 4 Jan. 1846, PWAG, III, 91–92; *New York Tribune*, 23 July 1846.

5. *S. Doc. No.* 2, 29th Cong., 1st Sess. (1845), 5; James P. Shenton, *Robert J. Walker: A Politician from Jackson to Lincoln* (New York: Columbia University Press, 1961), 74–81.

6. James B. Sawyer to John C. Calhoun, 10 July 1846, PJCC, XXIII, 297.

7. William Graham to James W. Bryan, 23 Feb. 1846, PWAG, III, 107; Pittsburgh *Morning Chronicle*, 6, 9 Dec. 1845; Nathan Appleton, *What Is a Revenue Standard and a Review of Secretary Walker's Report on the Tariff* (Boston, 1846), 13–23.

8. Andrew Johnson, "Speech on the Tariff and Oregon," Leroy Graf et al. (eds.), *The Papers of Andrew Johnson* (16 vols., Knoxville: University of Tennessee Press, 1967–2000), I, 320.

9. Henry Clay to Andrew Stewart, 26 June 1846, Andrew Stewart, *The American System: Speeches Delivered on the Tariff Question, and Internal Improvements* (Philadelphia, 1872), 71; Frank W. Taussig *The Tariff History of the United States* (New York: G. P. Putnam's Sons, 1888), 114.

10. *Detroit Free Press*, 20 July 1846.

11. Milo Quafie (ed.), *Diary of James K. Polk* (4 vols., Chicago: A. C. McClurg, 1910), I, 470–71; James K. Polk to Louis McLane, 22 June 1846, CJKP, XI, 216–17; Cave Johnson to A. O. P. Nicholson, 26 April 1846, A. O. P. Nicholson Papers, New York Historical Society; Paul H. Bergeron, *The Presidency of James K. Polk* (Lawrence: University Press of Kansas, 1987), 132–35; Merrill D. Peterson, *The Great Triumvirate: Webster, Clay, and Calhoun* (New York: Oxford University Press, 1987), 421; Malcolm Rogers Eiselen, *The Rise of Pennsylvania Protectionism* (Philadelphia: Porcupine, 1974 reprint of 1932 ed.), 188.

12. "National Fair—Concluding Notice," *National Intelligencer* (Washington, DC), 5 June 1846.

13. "Washington Correspondence," *North American* (Philadelphia), 23 May 1846.

14. *New York Tribune*, 22 May 1846.

15. Quafie (ed.), *Diary of James K. Polk*, I, 421–22.

16. *Congressional Globe*, 29th Cong., 1st Sess., appendix, 762.

17. *Congressional Globe*, 29th Cong., 1st Sess., appendix, 760.

18. *Congressional Globe*, 29th Cong., 1st Sess., appendix, 772.

19. *Congressional Globe*, 29th Cong., 1st Sess., appendix, 937.

20. "Sub-treasury—Free Trade," *Albany Evening Journal*, 1 July 1846.

21. "Pennsylvania, the Tariff, and the Party," *United States Gazette* (Philadelphia), 21 July 1846.

22. *Congressional Globe*, 29th Cong., 1st Sess., appendix, 783.

23. "The New Tariff Passed," *New Hampshire Patriot*, 9 July 1846; William J. Hamersley to Gideon Welles, 4 July 1846, Gideon Welles Papers, Library of Congress.

24. "The Tariff—the Joy of the Members, and Mr. Walker and Mr. Ritchie," *New York Herald*, 5 July 1846.

25. Jefferson Davis, "To the People of Mississippi," Lynda L. Crist et al. (eds.), *The Papers of Jefferson Davis* (14 vols., Baton Rouge: Louisiana State University Press, 1971–2015), III, 3.

26. Charles S. Sydnor, *The Development of Southern Sectionalism, 1819–1848* (Baton Rouge: Louisiana State University Press, 1948), 326.

27. William J. Hamersley to Gideon Welles, 4 July 1846, Gideon Welles Papers, Library of Congress.

28. *Pennsylvania Telegraph* (Harrisburg), 8 July 1846.

29. *Nashville Union*, 14 July 1846; "Pennsylvania and the Tariff," *Pittsfield Sun*, 16 July 1846; Joel H. Silbey, *The Shrine of Party: Congressional Voting Behavior, 1841–1852* (Pittsburgh:

University of Pittsburgh Press, 1967), 71–72; Jonathan H. Earle, *Jacksonian Antislavery and the Politics of Free Soil, 1824–1854* (Chapel Hill: University of North Carolina Press, 2004), 130–31.

30. *Congressional Globe*, 29th Cong., 1st Sess., 1054.

31. MJQA, XII, 25.

32. *Congressional Globe*, 29th Cong., 1st Sess., appendix, 786–89.

33. *New Hampshire Sentinel*, 29 July 1846.

34. *Congressional Globe*, 29th Cong., 1st Sess., 1132.

35. *Niles' Weekly Register* 20 (Baltimore) (18 July 1846), 309; 324.

36. Quafie (ed.), *Diary of James K. Polk*, II, 26–28, 49; Charles Sellers, *James K. Polk: Continentalist, 1843–1846* (Princeton, NJ: Princeton University Press, 1966), 460–65.

37. *Congressional Globe*, 29th Cong., 1st Sess., appendix, 881–82.

38. M. C. Galloway to George S. Houston, 27 July 1846, George S. Houston Papers, Duke University.

39. Quafie (ed.), *Diary of James K. Polk*, II, 26–27; Stephen A. Douglas to John J. Hardin, 6 July 1846, Robert W. Johannsen (ed.), *The Letters of Stephen A. Douglas* (Urbana: University of Illinois Press, 1961), 140–41; *Washington Union*, 18 July 1846.

40. Quafie (ed.), *Diary of James K. Polk*, II, 43–45.

41. George Bancroft to James K. Polk, 25 July 1846, JKPP.

42. Charles C. Walden to John C. Calhoun, PJCC, XXXIII, 373.

43. James Graham to William A. Graham, 29 July 1846, PWAG, III, 135; *Albany Argus*, 28 July 1846; "Hon. William H. Haywood," *Mecklenburg Jeffersonian*, 11 Aug. 1842, copy held by the James K. Polk Project, University of Tennessee. For Haywood's explanation, see *New York Daily Tribune*, 20 Aug. 1846, and *Niles' National Register* (Baltimore) 20 (29 Aug. 1846), 410–15.

44. M. C. Galloway to George S. Houston, 27 July 1846, George S. Houston Papers, Duke University.

45. *Charleston Mercury*, 31 July 1846; Abbott Lawrence to John J. Crittenden, 24 July 1846, John J. Crittenden Papers, Library of Congress; William J. Hamersley to Gideon Welles, 28 July 1846, Gideon Welles Papers, Library of Congress; Peterson, *The Great Triumvirate*, 421–22.

46. Daniel Webster to Daniel Fletcher Webster, 29 July 1846, Daniel Webster Papers, New Hampshire Historical Society; Spencer A. Jarnagin to Daniel Webster, 28 July 1846, Daniel Webster Papers, New Hampshire Historical Society; Quafie (ed.), *Diary of James K. Polk*, II, 51–52; Sellers, *James K. Polk: Continentalist*, 466–67.

47. "The Senate of the United States," *Washington Union*, 28 July 1846; George M. Dallas, *The Casting Vote of Vice-president Dallas on the Tariff of 1846* (Philadelphia, 1846), 5–7; John M. Belohlavek, *George Mifflin Dallas: Jacksonian Politician* (University Park: Pennsylvania State University Press, 1977), 111–18.

48. *Buffalo Commercial Advertiser*, 30 July 1846; Charles M. Snyder, *The Jacksonian Heritage: Pennsylvania Politics, 1833–1848* (Harrisburg: Pennsylvania Historical and Museum Commission, 1958), 195–98.

49. "The Tariff," *Farmer's Cabinet*, 6 Aug. 1846.

50. Gideon Welles to Martin Van Buren, 28 July 1846, MVBP.

51. Alan Nevins (ed.), *The Diary of Philip Hone* (2 vols., New York: Dodd, Mean 1927), I, 769.

52. "The Revenue System Reformed," *Washington Union*, 29 July 1846.

53. "Memoranda Regarding Eagle's Quill Pen," James K. Polk Collection, Tennessee State Library and Archives.

54. *Congressional Globe*, 29th Cong., 1st Sess., 1062.

55. James K. Polk to Louis McLane, 13 Aug. 1846, CJKP, XI, 278.

56. *The Statistical History of the United States: Colonial Times to the Present* (Stanford, CT: Fairfield, 1965), 539.

57. "The Tariff Crisis of 1846," *Cincinnati Enquirer*, 4 Aug. 1846.

58. Gideon Welles to Martin Van Buren, 28 July 1846, MVBP.

59. *Remarks on President Polk's Veto of the River and Harbor Bill* (Washington, DC, 1846), 5; David M. Potter, *The Impending Crisis, 1848–1861* (New York: Harper and Row, 1976), 20–23; Eric Foner, "The Wilmot Proviso Revisited," *Journal of American History* 61 (Sept. 1969), 262–79.

60. Henry Clay to Henry White, 27 Nov. 1846, Calvin Colton (ed.), *The Works of Henry Clay: Comprising His Life, Correspondence, and Speeches* (10 vols., New York: G. P. Putnam's Sons, 1904), V, 538.

61. John Davis to Henry Clay, 13 Nov. 1846, PHC, X, 287.

62. Holt, *Rise and Fall of the American Whig Party*, 246; James L. Huston, *Calculating the Value of Union: Slavery, Property Rights, and the Economic Origins of the Civil War* (Chapel Hill: University of North Carolina Press, 2003), 154–57; William J. Cooper Jr., *Liberty and Slavery: Southern Politics to 1860* (New York: Alfred A. Knopf, 1983), 213–15.

63. John H. Lumpkin to Howell Cobb, 13 Nov. 1846, Ulrich B. Phillips (ed.), "Correspondence of Robert Toombs, Alexander H. Stephens, and Howell Cobb," *Annual Report of the American Historical Association for 1911* (Washington, DC, 1913), II, 87.

64. Calhoun, "Speech at a Meeting of Citizens of Charleston," PJCC, XXIV, 257; James K. Polk to Louis McLane, 9 Nov. 1846, CJKP, XI, 391; Wiltse, *John C. Calhoun: Sectionalist, 1840–1850* (Indianapolis: Bobbs and Merrill, 1951), 308–10; John H. Schroeder, *Mr. Polk's War: American Opposition and Dissent, 1846–1848* (Madison: University of Wisconsin Press, 1973), 57–62.

65. James Graham to William Graham, 10 Jan. 1847, PWAG, III, 172.

66. Eiselen, *Rise of Pennsylvania Protectionism*, 208–10.

CHAPTER 17

1. Millard Fillmore to John H. Bryant, 28 July 1848, Frank H. Severance (ed.), *Millard Fillmore Papers* (2 vols., Buffalo, NY: Buffalo Historical Society, 1907), II, 278–79.

2. *Congressional Globe*, 33rd Cong., 1st Sess., appendix, 269.

3. William H. Seward, "The Parties of the Day," Joel H. Silbey (ed.), *The American Party Battle: Election Campaign Pamphlets, 1828–1876* (2 vols., Cambridge, MA: Harvard University Press, 1999), II, 73.

4. Alfred Balch to James K. Polk, 3 Sept. 1847, JKPP; Michael F. Holt, *The Rise and Fall of the American Whig Party: Jacksonian Politics and the Onset of the Civil War* (New York: Oxford University Press, 1999), 309–10.

5. *Mississippi Free Trader and Natchez Gazette*, 29 April 1848.

6. Harriet Weed (ed.), *Life of Thurlow Weed* (Boston: Houghton Mifflin, 1884), 571; Holt, *Rise and Fall of the American Whig Party*, 309–10.

7. Donald Bruce Johnson et al. (eds.), *National Party Platforms, 1840–1956* (Urbana: University of Illinois Press, 1956), 10–11.

8. Willie P. Mangum, "Democratic Platform," PWPM, V, 669, 671.

9. Asa Biggs to James K. Polk, 27 Dec. 1848, Asa Biggs Papers, North Carolina State Archives, Willard C. Klunder, *Lewis Cass and the Politics of Moderation* (Kent, OH: Kent State University Press, 1996), 213–17; Jonathan H. Earle, *Jacksonian Antislavery and the Politics of Free Soil, 1824–1854* (Chapel Hill: University of North Carolina Press, 2004),

163–80; Joel H. Silbey, *Party over Section: The Rough and Ready Presidential Election of 1848* (Lawrence: University Press of Kansas, 2009), 114–15.

10. David Outlaw to Emily Outlaw, 10 Dec. 1849, David Outlaw Papers, Southern Historical Collection—University of North Carolina.

11. John C. Calhoun to Thomas G. Clemson, 8 Dec. 1849, PJCC, XXVII, 134; David Outlaw to Emily Outlaw, 13 Dec. 1849, David Outlaw Papers, Southern Historical Collection—University of North Carolina; Holt, *Rise and Fall of the American Whig Party*, 466–72.

12. *Louisville Journal*, quoted in *National Intelligencer* (Washington, DC), 9 Aug. 1849; K. Jack Bauer, *Zachary Taylor: Soldier, Planter, Statesman of the Old Southwest* (Baton Rouge: Louisiana State University Press, 1985), 269.

13. *H.R. Doc. No. 4*, 31st Cong., 1st Sess., 11.

14. Holt, *Rise and Fall of the American Whig Party*, 446–49, 473–74.

15. *Bangor Daily Whig and Courier*, 16 May 1850.

16. Weed (ed.), *Life of Thurlow Weed*, 578.

17. Francis P. Blair to Martin Van Buren, 30 Sept. 1850, MVBP.

18. "From Washington," *North American and US Gazette*, 16 Sept. 1850.

19. "Slavery and the Tariff," *Emancipator and Republican*, 19 Sept. 1850; *Congressional Globe*, 31st Cong., 1st Sess., 1812; "Tariff Bill Defeated," *Cleveland Herald*, 19 Sept. 1850; Henry Clay to F. R. Backus, 13 Sept. 1850, PHC, X, 811.

20. *Congressional Globe*, 31st Cong., 2nd Sess., 114.

21. Millard Fillmore, "First Annual Message," CMPP, V, 84.

22. Fillmore, "Second Annual Message," CMPP, V, 126; Fillmore, "Third Annual Message," CMPP, V, 169–70; Holt, *Rise and Fall of the American Whig Party*, 553–97, 619.

23. Robert J. Rayback, "The Silver Grey Revolt," *New York History* 30 (April 1949), 151–64; Harry J. Carman and Reinhard H. Luthin, "The Seward-Fillmore Feud and the Disruption of the Whig Party," *New York History* 24 (July 1943), 335–57.

24. Holt, *Rise and Fall of the American Whig Party*, 719–25.

25. Donald Bruce Johnson et al. (eds.), *National Party Platforms, 1840–1956* (Urbana: University of Illinois Press, 1956), 16–17, 20.

26. Johnson et al.(eds.), *National Party Platforms, 1840–1956*, 718. The *National Intelligencer* and *Fayetteville Observer* included the text of the Whig tariff plank. See "The Whig Platform," *National Intelligencer* (Washington, DC), 24 June 1852; "Whig National Convention," *Fayetteville Observer*, 24 June 1852.

27. Pierce, "First Annual Message," CMPP, V, 213.

28. Pierce, "Second Annual Message," CMPP, V, 285.

29. Pierce, "Third Annual Message," CMPP, V, 337–38.

30. *Boston Daily Atlas*, 6 Oct. 1853.

31. Holt, *Rise and Fall of the American Whig Party*, 962–63; Tyler Anbinder, *Nativism and Slavery: The Northern Know Nothings and the Politics of the 1850s* (New York: Oxford University Press, 1992), 167–87; William J. Evitts, *A Matter of Allegiances: Maryland from 1850 to 1861* (Baltimore: Johns Hopkins University Press, 1974), 99–100.

32. *Indianapolis Journal*, 25 Jan. 1859, copy in William H. Hanna to Abraham Lincoln, 26 Jan. 1859, Abraham Lincoln Papers, Library of Congress.

33. James L. Huston, *The Panic of 1857 and the Coming of the Civil War* (Baton Rouge: Louisiana State University Press, 1987), 28; William E. Gienapp, *The Origins of the Republican Party, 1852–1856* (New York: Oxford University Press, 1987), 109–10, 124–25, 143–46; David M. Potter, *The Impending Crisis, 1848–1861* (New York: Harper and Row, 1976), 255–65; Holt, *The Political Crisis of the 1850s* (New York: Wiley, 1978), 198–201;

Anbinder, *Nativism and Slavery*, 238–45; Arthur M. Lee, "The Development of an Economic Policy in the Early Republican Party" (PhD diss., Syracuse University, 1953).

34.   William W. Holden to John W. Ellis, 19 Jan. 1857, Noble J. Tolbert (ed.), *Papers of John J. Ellis* (2 vols., Raleigh, 1964), I, 162.

35.   *DeBow's Review*, 1 July 1857, 93.

36.   *Boston Recorder*, 1 Jan. 1857.

37.   *New Bedford Mercury*, 16 Jan. 1857.

38.   *Congressional Globe*, 34th Cong., 3rd Sess., appendix, 281; Edward Stanwood, *American Tariff Controversies in the Nineteenth Century* (2 vols., Boston: Houghton Mifflin, 1903), II, 98–101.

39.   "Bribery in Congress," *Boston Recorder*, 29 Jan. 1857.

40.   Mark W. Summers, *The Plundering Generation: Corruption and the Crisis of the Union, 1849–1861* (New York: Oxford University Press, 1987), 102.

41.   Malcolm Rogers Eiselen, *The Rise of Pennsylvania Protectionism* (Philadelphia: Porcupine, 1974 reprint of 1932 ed.), 238–39.

42.   *Congressional Globe*, 34th Cong., 3rd Sess., appendix, 280.

43.   Kenneth M. Stampp, *America in 1857: A Nation on the Brink* (New York: Oxford University Press, 1990), 21–22.

44.   Henry Harrison Simms, *Life of Robert M. T. Hunter: A Study in Sectionalism and Secession* (Richmond: William Byrd, 1935), 104–6; Stanwood, *American Tariff Controversies in the Nineteenth Century*, II, 103–8. "New Tariff," *Portland Weekly Advertiser*, 10 March 1857.

45.   *New York Tribune*, 2 October 1857, Huston, *Panic of 1857 and the Coming of the Civil War*, 50.

46.   Huston, *Panic of 1857 and the Coming of the Civil War*, 14–34; Jeter A. Isley, *Horace Greeley and the Republican Party, 1853–1861: A Study of the New York Tribune* (Princeton, NJ: Princeton University Press, 1947), 218–21; Michael F. Holt, *Forging a Majority: The Formation of the Republican Party in Pittsburgh, 1848–1860* (New Haven, CT: Yale University Press, 1969), 243; Eiselen, *Rise of Pennsylvania Protectionism*, 244–46; Benjamin J. Klebaner, "Poor Relief and Public Works during the Depression of 1857," *Historian* 22 (May 1960), 264–79.

CHAPTER 18

1.   *Pennsylvania Telegraph* (Harrisburg), 22 March 1860.

2.   Eric Foner, *Free Soil, Free Labor, Free Men: The Ideology of the Republican Party before the Civil War* (New York: Oxford University Press, 1970), 11–39.

3.   *North American* (Philadelphia), 15, 21 March, 23 May 1860.

4.   *Pittsburgh Gazette*, 11 June 1860.

5.   *Congressional Globe*, 36th Cong., 1st Sess., 1847, 1955.

6.   "The Tariff Measure," *Buffalo Morning Express*, 9 June 1860; Drew Gilpin Faust, *James Henry Hammond and the Old South: A Design for Mastery* (Baton Rouge: Louisiana State University Press, 1982), 346–47; William Dusinberre, *Civil War Issues in Philadelphia, 1856–1865* (Philadelphia: University of Pennsylvania Press, 1965), 78.

7.   "Slavery and Free Trade," *Buffalo Morning Express*, 29 May 1860.

8.   William B. Hesseltine, *Lincoln and the War Governors* (New York: Alfred A. Knopf, 1948), 7–8; Foner, *Free Soil, Free Labor, Free Men*, 149–85; Eiselen, *Rise of Pennsylvania Protectionism*, 255; Arthur M. Schlesinger Jr., *The Age of Jackson* (Boston: Little, Brown,

1945), 478; Frederick J. Blue, *Salmon P. Chase: A Life in Politics* (Kent, OH: Kent State University Press, 1987), 121–22.

9.   Buchanan, "First Annual Message," CMPP, V, 440, 461; Buchanan, "Second Annual Message," CMPP, V, 522.

10. Roy F. Nichols, *The Disruption of American Democracy* (New York: Macmillan, 1948), 236–45; Bruce W. Collins, "The Democrats' Loss of Pennsylvania in 1858," *Pennsylvania Magazine of History and Biography*, CIX (1985), 499–536; David E. Meerse, "The Northern Democratic Party and the Congressional Elections of 1858," *Civil War History* 19 (1973), 119–37; Samuel Rezneck, "The Influence of Depression upon American Opinion," *Journal of Economic History* 2 (May 1942), 1–23.

11. *Chicago Press and Tribune*, 2 May 1860.

12. "The Republicans Not Protectionists," *New York Evening Post*, 6 March 1860.

13. *Bangor Daily Whig and Courier*, 16 March 1860.

14. Abraham Lincoln, "Remarks at the Monongahela House," Roy P. Basler (ed.), *The Collected Works of Abraham Lincoln* (8 vols., New Brunswick, NJ: Rutgers University Press, 1953–1955), IV, 208; Arthur M. Lee, "Henry C. Carey and the Republican Tariff," *Pennsylvania Magazine of History* 81 (July 1951), 280–302; Philip S. Klein, *James Buchanan: A Biography* (University Park: Pennsylvania State University Press, 1962), 172–73.

15. *Pennsylvania Daily Telegraph*, 24 February 1860.

16. *Philadelphia Evening Bulletin*, 8 May 1860.

17. "Protection at Chicago," *North American* (Philadelphia), 30 March 1860; "Pennsylvania," *New York Tribune*, 11 June 1860.

18. Dwight L. Dumond (ed.), *Southern Editorials on Secession* (Gloucester, MA: Peter Smith, 1964 reprint of 1931 ed.), 36.

19. William Jenkins to Lawrence O'Bryan Branch, 9 Jan. 1860, Mrs. John L. O'Bryan Branch Papers, North Carolina State Archives; *Pennsylvania Daily Telegraph*, 3 February 1860; Richard F. Bensel, *Yankee Leviathan: The Origins of Central State Authority in America, 1859–1877* (New York: Cambridge University Press, 1990), 51–56; Ollinger Crenshaw, "The Speakership Contest of 1859–1860: John Sherman's Election a Cause of Disruption?," *Mississippi Valley Historical Review* 29 (Dec. 1942), 323–38.

20. *Congressional Globe*, 36th Cong., 1st Sess., 1832, 1834; J. McCulloch to Justin S. Morrill, 26 April 1860, Justin S. Morrill Papers, Library of Congress; Phillip W. Magness, "Morrill and the Missing Industries: Strategic Lobbying Behavior and the Tariff, 1858–1861," *Journal of the Early Republic* 29 (Summer 2009), 287–329; Randal Leigh Hoyer, "The Gentleman from Vermont: The Career of Justin S. Morrill in the United States House of Representatives" (Ph. D. diss., Michigan State University, 1974), 91–93.

21. *Congressional Globe*, 36th Cong., 1st Sess., 1833.

22. "Our Washington Letter," *Chicago Press and Tribune*, 28 April 1860.

23. "Tariff Revision," *New York Tribune*, 20 March 1860.

24. *Congressional Globe*, 36th Cong., 1st Sess., 1873, 1880–81, 1930–31; appendix, 409, 412; Dusinberre, *Civil War Issues in Philadelphia*, 77.

25. *Congressional Globe*, 36th Cong., 1st Sess., 2056; *North American* (Philadelphia), 24 May 1860; "From Washington," *Chicago Press and Tribune*, 16 May 1860; Philadelphia *Evening Bulletin*, 11 May 1860.

26. "Morrill's Bill Passed," *Chicago Press and Tribune*, 12 May 1860.

27. *Pittsburgh Gazette*, 7 May 1860.

28. "The New Tariff Bill," *New York Evening Post*, 30 May 1860.

29. Robert Toombs to Alexander H. Stephens, 20 April 1860, Ulrich B. Phillips (ed.),

"Correspondence of Robert Toombs, Alexander H. Stephens, and Howell Cobb," *Annual Report of the American Historical Association for 1911* (2 vols., Washington, DC, 1913), II, 467; *Congressional Globe*, 36th Cong., 1st Sess., 3010–13, 3185, 3187; A. G. Holmes to R. M. T. Hunter, 3 April 1860, Charles H. Ambler (ed.), "Correspondence of Robert M. T. Hunter," *Annual Report of the American Historical Association for 1916* (2 vols., Washington, DC, 1918) II, 312; Henry S. Acker to R. M. T. Hunter, 8 June 1860, Ambler (ed.), "Correspondence of Robert M. T. Hunter," 333.

30. *Congressional Globe*, 36th Cong., 1st Sess., 3017.

31. *Congressional Globe*, 36th Cong., 1st Sess., 3018–19; Mark W. Summers, *The Plundering Generation: Corruption and the Crisis of the Union, 1849–1861* (New York: Oxford University Press, 1987), 239–60.

32. "The Republicans and the Tariff," *Pittsburgh Gazette*, 19 June 1860; *Congressional Globe*, 36th Cong, 1st Sess., 3027.

33. "Glory over the Tariff," *Indianapolis Journal*, 19 May 1860; Harold Holzer and Norton Garfinkle, *A Just and Generous Nation: Abraham Lincoln and the Fight for American Opportunity* (New York: Basic Books, 2015), 49–51.

34. "Free Trade at Chicago," *New York Evening Post*, 18 May 1860; "The Republican Platform," *Burlington Free Press*, 19 May 1860; Donald Bruce Johnson et al. (eds.), *National Party Platforms, 1840–1956* (Urbana: University of Illinois Press, 1956), 31–33; Thomas J. McCormack (ed.), *Memoirs of Gustave Koerner, 1809–1896: Life Sketches Written at the Suggestion of His Children* (2 vols., Cedar Rapids, IA: Torch, 1909) II, 87–89. For other reactions to the announcement of the tariff plank, see *Pennsylvania Daily Telegraph*, 18 May 1860; *North American* (Philadelphia), 21 May 1860; *Chicago Press and Tribune*, 18 June 1860; *National Intelligencer* (Washington, DC), 23 May 1860.

35. "Pennsylvania and the Presidency," *New York Evening Post*, 15 March 1860; Paul M. Angle et al. (eds.), *Fire the Salute! Abe Lincoln Is Nominated: Murat Halstead Reports* (Kingsport: Kingsport Press, 1960), 33–34; Walter Stahr, *Seward: Lincoln's Indispensable Man* (New York: Simon and Schuster, 2012), 186–93; David M. Potter, *The Impending Crisis, 1848–1861* (New York: Harper and Row, 1976).

36. "The Chicago Nominees," *Philadelphia Evening Bulletin*, 21 May 1860.

37. "Lincoln and Hamlin," *North American* (Philadelphia), 19 May 1860.

38. "Lincoln and the Tariff," *Pennsylvania Daily Telegraph*, 6 June 1860.

39. *Reading Journal*, quoted in *Pittsburgh Gazette*, 22 May 1860; Abraham Lincoln to Edward Wallace, 12 May 1860, Abraham Lincoln Papers, Library of Congress; Reinhard H. Luthin, "Abraham Lincoln and the Tariff," *American Historical Review* 49 (July 1944), 609–29; Gabor S. Borit, "Old Wine into New Bottles: Abraham Lincoln and the Tariff Reconsidered," *Historian* 38 (Feb. 1966), 289–317.

40. *Boston Daily Advertiser*, 29 October 1860.

41. John Hickman to A. N. Swain, 24 Sept. 1860, Rugg Autograph Collection, Dartmouth University.

42. Howell Cobb to the People of Georgia, 6 Dec. 1860, Phillips (ed.), "Correspondence of Robert Toombs, Alexander H. Stephens, and Howell Cobb," 508; Henry Wilson to Justin S. Morrill, 25 Sept. 1860, Justin S. Morrill Papers, Library of Congress; James G. Blaine, *Twenty Years of Congress: From Lincoln to Garfield* (2 vols., Norwich, CT: Henry Bill, 1884–1886), I, 206; Eiselen, *Rise of Pennsylvania Protectionism*, 239–66; Potter, *Impending Crisis*, 430–47; William Belmont Parker, *The Life and Public Services of Justin Smith Morrill* (Boston: Houghton Mifflin, 1924), 107, 112; David H. Donald, *Lincoln* (New York: Simon and Schuster, 1996), 256; James M. McPherson, *Battle Cry of Freedom: The Civil War Era* (New York: Oxford University Press, 1988), 221–32.

43. *Congressional Globe*, 36th Cong., 2nd Sess., 154, 904.

44. Justin S. Morrill to Stephen Thomas, 23 Dec. 1860, Justin S. Morrill Papers, Library of Congress.

45. *Congressional Globe*, 36th Cong., 2nd Sess., 950, 1018, 1056, 1061; Aaron S. Crawford, "Patriot Slaveholder: Andrew Jackson and the Winter of Secession," *Journal of East Tennessee History* 82 (2010), 10–32.

46. *Congressional Globe*, 36th Cong., 2nd Sess., 950; Patrick J. Devine to William H. Seward, 25 Feb. 1861, William H. Seward Papers, University of Rochester; John Sherman, *John Sherman's Recollections of Forty Years in the House, Senate, and Cabinet: An Autobiography* (2 vols., Chicago: Werner, 1895), I, 187.

47. *Congressional Globe*, 36th Cong., 2nd Sess., 1065.

48. *Congressional Globe*, 36th Cong., 2nd Sess., 1187, 1196, 1190.

49. "The New Tariff Bill," *Oregonian*, 6 April 1861.

50. "The New Tariff," *Cleveland Plain Dealer*, 28 February 1861.

51. Act of 2 March 1861, ch. 68, 12 *Stat.* 178–98.

52. Charles Sumner to Martin F. Tupper, 11 Nov. 1861, Beverly Wilson Palmer (ed.), *The Selected Letters of Charles Sumner* (2 vols., Boston: Northeastern University Press, 1990), II, 82.

53. *London Spectator*, quoted in *New York Times*, 3 June 1861; *Pittsburgh Gazette*, 5, 7 March 1861.

54. Mark Tooley, *The Peace That Almost Was: The Forgotten Story of the 1861 Washington Peace Conference and the Final Attempt to Avert the Civil War* (Nashville: Nelson Books, 2015), 117–61; Robert Gray Gunderson, *Old Gentlemen's Convention: The Washington Peace Conference of 1861* (Madison: University of Wisconsin Press, 1961), 81–92.

Bibliography

MANUSCRIPTS

Alabama Department of
Archives and History
    James Dellet Family Papers
    Bolling Hall Family Papers
    William R. King Papers
    John Williams Walker Papers
Allegheny College
    Henry Baldwin Papers
American Antiquarian Society
    John Davis Papers
American Philosophical Society Library
    John Kintzing Kane Papers
Brandeis University
    Sang Collection
Buffalo and Erie County Historical Society
    Peter B. Porter Papers
    Henry R. Storrs Diary
Columbia University
    Thomas W. Olcott Papers
Dartmouth College
    Rugg Autograph Collection
    Daniel Webster Papers
Dickinson College
    James Buchanan Correspondence
Duke University
    Campbell Family Papers
    Henry A. S. Dearborn Papers
    Daniel Hoit Papers
    George S. Houston Papers
    James Iredell Papers
    George McDuffie Papers
    Stephen D. Miller Papers
    New England Man's Travel Diary
    Ebenezer Pettigrew Papers

Florida State Library
    Robert Raymond Reid Diary
Hagley Library and Museum
    E. I. DuPont Papers
Historical Society of Pennsylvania
    James Buchanan Papers
    George M. Dallas Papers
    Joseph Hopkinson Papers
    Joel R. Poinsett Papers
Library of Congress
    Nicholas Biddle Papers
    Blair Family Papers
    James Buchanan and Harriet Lane
        Johnston Papers
    William H. Crawford Papers
    John J. Crittenden Papers
    Galloway-Maxcy-Markoe Families
        Papers
    Gideon and Francis Granger Papers
    Duff Green Papers
    Andrew Jackson Papers
    Thomas Jefferson Papers
    Abraham Lincoln Papers
    Louis McLane Papers
    John McLean Papers
    Justin S. Morrill Papers
    Joseph H. Nicholson Papers
    William Plumer Papers
    James K. Polk Papers
    Samuel Smith Papers
    Alexander Stephens Papers
    Thaddeus Stevens Papers
    John Tyler Papers
    Martin Van Buren Papers
    Gideon Welles Papers
    Levi Woodbury Family Papers

Library of Virginia
    John Y. Mason Papers
    Tazewell Family Papers
Maine Historical Society
    Jarvis Family Papers
Maryland Historical Society
    Robert Goodloe Harper Family Papers
    John Pendleton Kennedy Papers
    Daniel Webster Papers
Massachusetts Historical Society
    Adams Family Papers
    Edward Everett Papers
    Andrew Jackson Letter
    Interview of Thomas Jefferson
        by Samuel Whitcomb
    Harrison Gray Otis Papers
    Paige Papers
    Timothy Pickering Papers
    Winthrop Family Papers
National Archives
    Record Group 45
New Hampshire Historical Society
    William Plumer Papers
    Daniel Webster Papers
New Jersey Historical Society
    Mahlon Dickerson Papers
New York Historical Society
    Albert Gallatin Papers
    A. O. P. Nicholson Papers
    John W. Taylor Papers
New York Public Library
    A. C. Flagg Papers
    Kohns Collection
North Carolina State Archives
    Asa Biggs Papers
    Mrs. John L. O'Bryan Branch Papers
    Edmund Deberry Papers
    David S. Reid Papers
Notre Dame University
    Thomas Ewing Papers
Ohio Historical Society
    Ethan Allen Brown Papers
    Charles Hammond Papers
    William Allen Trimble Papers
Pennsylvania Historical and
Museum Commission
    John Tod Papers
Princeton University

Andre deCoppet Collection
    Edward Livingston Papers
South Carolina Historical Society
    Chestnut-Miller-Manning Papers
Southern Historical Collection—
University of North Carolina
    John M. Berrien Papers
    Brumby and Smith Family Papers
    Edmund Deberry Papers
    William Gaston Papers
    Elliott and Gonzales Family Papers
    Duff Green Papers
    Samuel C. Jackson Diary
    Jones and Patterson Family Papers
    William Lowndes Papers
    James McDowell Papers
    Rosina Mix Papers
    David Outlaw Papers
    Benjamin F. Perry Papers
    William Royal Letter
    Isaac Tompkins Letters
State University of New York–Oswego
    Millard Fillmore Papers
Tennessee Historical Society
    Samuel Laughlin Papers
Tennessee State Library and Archives
    Whitefoord Cole Papers
    James K. Polk Collection
University of Rochester
    William H. Seward Papers
    Thurlow Weed Papers
University of South Carolina
    William H. Crawford Letter
    James Hamilton Papers
    Robert Young Hayne Papers
    Samuel Cram Jackson Papers
    Timothy Johnson Letter
    Mitchell King Papers
    Mackay Family Papers
    George McDuffie Papers
    James L. Petigru Papers
    William C. Preston Papers
    Rutledge Family Papers
    William Smith Papers
    John W. Taylor Letter
    Townes Family Papers
    William May Wightman Papers
    David R. Williams Papers

University of Tennessee
    Aaron V. Brown Letter
    Ramsey Family Papers
University of Virginia
    Ambler Family Papers
    Joseph C. Cabell Family Papers
    Letter to Robert S. Garnett
    Gooch Family Papers
    Correspondence of Robert T. Hubbard
    John Randolph Papers
Vanderbilt University
    Stanley F. Horn Collection
Virginia Historical Society
    William Hammett Papers
Wisconsin Historical Society
    Nathaniel P. Tallmadge Papers
Xavier University
    Moses Dawson Collection

NEWSPAPERS AND OTHER PERIODICALS

Agricultural Intelligencer and
    Mechanic Register
Albany Argus
Albany Evening Journal
Alexandria Gazette
American Advocate
Argus of Western America (Frankfort, KY)
Bangor Daily Whig and Courier
Banner of the Constitution
Berkshire County Whig
Boston Courier
Boston Daily Advertiser
Boston Daily Atlas
Boston Recorder
Buffalo Commercial Advertiser
Buffalo Morning Express
Burlington Free Press
Centinel of Freedom
Charleston Courier
Charleston Mercury
Chicago Press and Tribune
Chillicothe Supporter and Scioto Gazette
Christian Intelligencer and Eastern Chronicle
Cincinnati Enquirer
Cleveland Herald
Cleveland Plain Dealer

Columbia Telescope
Concord Patriot
Connecticut Courant
Crisis Devoted to the Support of the
    Democratic Principles of Jefferson
DeBow's Review
Detroit Free Press
Eastern Argus
Easton (PA) Sentinel
Emancipator and Republican
Farmer's Cabinet
Fayetteville Observer
Freeman's Journal
Greenville Mountaineer
Hampshire Gazette
Harrisburg Chronicle
Illinois Gazette (Shawnee-town)
Indianapolis Journal
Jackson Southern Statesman
Jamestown Journal
Jonesborough Whig
Kentucky Gazette (Lexington)
Knoxville Enquirer
Knoxville Register
Lexington Public Advertiser
Louisville Daily Journal
Louisville Public Advertiser
Madisonian (Washington, DC)
Maryland Gazette and Political Intelligencer
Massachusetts Spy
Mecklenburg Jeffersonian
Merchants' Magazine and Commercial Review
Mississippian
Mississippi Free Trader and Natchez Gazette
Mobile Commercial Register
Morning Courier and New York Enquirer
Nashville Republican Banner
Nashville Republican and State Gazette
Nashville Union
Natchez Courier and Adams, Jefferson
    and Franklin Advertiser
National Gazette and Literary Messenger
National Intelligencer (Washington, DC)
National Journal (Washington, DC)
New Bedford Courier
New Bedford Mercury
Newbern Spectator
New Hampshire Patriot

New Hampshire Sentinel
New London Morning News
New Orleans Bee
Newport Mercury
New Yorker
New York Commercial Advertiser
New York Daily Advertiser
New York Evening Post
New York Herald
New York Spectator
New York Tribune
Niles' National Register (Baltimore)
Niles' Weekly Register (Baltimore)
North American (Philadelphia)
North American and US Gazette
    (Philadelphia)
North American Review
Norwich (CT) Courier
Ohio State Journal
Ohio Statesman
Oracle of Dauphin
Oregonian
Pendleton Messenger
Pennsylvania Intelligencer
Pennsylvania Daily Telegraph
Pennsylvania Telegraph (Harrisburg)

Philadelphia Evening Bulletin
Pittsburgh Gazette
Pittsburgh Mercury
Pittsburgh Morning Chronicle
Pittsfield Sun
Portland Weekly Advertiser
Providence Patriot
Raleigh Register
Raleigh Register and North Carolina Gazette
Richmond Enquirer
Scioto Gazette (Chillicothe, Ohio)
Times and Hartford Advertiser
Trenton Emporium
United States Gazette (Philadelphia)
United States Telegraph (Washington, DC)
Vermont Patriot and State Gazette
Vermont Watchman and State Gazette
Vermont Watchman and State Journal
Washington Globe
Washington Republican and Congressional
    Examiner
Washington Union
Woodville (MS) Republican
Yankee and Boston Literary Gazette

PAMPHLETS

Appleton, Nathan. *What Is a Revenue Standard and a Review of Secretary Walker's Report on the Tariff* (Boston, 1846).
Brief Remarks on the Proposed New Tariff (New York, 1816).
"Brutus" [Robert J. Turnbull]. *The Crisis* (Charleston, SC, 1827).
Beecher, Lyman. *The Means of National Prosperity: A Sermon Delivered at Litchfield, Connecticut, on the Day of Thanksgiving, December 2, 1819* (New York, 1820).
Carey, Mathew. *Addresses of the Philadelphia Society for the Promotion of National Industry* (Philadelphia, 1820).
———. *The Crisis: A Solemn Appeal* (Philadelphia, 1823).
"A Citizen." *Considerations Which Demand the Attention of Farmers, Mechanics, and Friends of the American System* (New York, 1828).
"A Citizen." *Old and New Tariffs Compared with Observations on the Effect of High Duties on Revenue and Consumption* (Boston, 1820).
"A Citizen of New York." *Measures, Not Men: Illustrated by Some Remarks upon the Public Conduct and Character of John C. Calhoun* (New York, 1823).
"A Columbia County Man." *Clay and Polk: The Difference between Them on the Tariff Question* (Philadelphia, 1844).
Dallas, George M. *The Casting Vote of Vice-president Dallas on the Tariff of 1846* (Philadelphia, 1846).

Green, Willis. *Address of the Hon. Willis Green of Kentucky, before the Alexandria (D.C.) Clay Club* (1844).

Hamilton, James. *The Introductory Address of Governor Hamilton at the First Meeting of the Charleston States Rights and Free Trade Association* (Charleston, SC, 1831).

Hayne, Robert Y. *An Oration Delivered in the Independent or Congregational Church, Charleston before the States Rights and Free Trade Party* (Charleston, SC, 1831).

"An Irish Adopted Citizen." *Fifty Reasons Why Henry Clay Should Be Elected President* (Baltimore, 1844).

Letters from the Hon. Abbott Lawrence to the Hon. William C. Rives of Virginia (Boston, 1846).

Life of John C. Calhoun, Presenting a Condensed History of Political Events from 1811 to 1843 (New York, 1843).

A Memorial of a Convention of the Friends of National Industry Assembled in the City of New York (Washington, DC, 1819).

The Memorial of the Merchants and Others Interested in Commerce, in Salem and Its Vicinity (Salem, MA, 1820).

"One of the People" [Churchill C. Cambreleng]. *An Examination of the New Tariff Proposed by the Hon. Henry Baldwin* (New York, 1821).

Philadelphia Citizens Friendly to American Manufactures (Philadelphia, 1819).

Polk, James K. *Answers of Ex-gov. Polk, to Two Series of Interrogatories Propounded to Him and Gov. Jones through the Presses of Memphis* (Memphis, 1843).

The Prospect before Us; or, Locofoco Impositions Exposed (Washington, DC, 1844).

Remarks on President Polk's Veto of the River and Harbor Bill (Washington, DC, 1846).

Sargent, Nathan. *Life of Henry Clay* (Philadelphia, 1844).

Van Buren, Martin. *Speech of the Hon. Martin Van Buren Delivered at the Capitol in the City of Albany, before the Albany County Meeting* (Albany, NY, 1827).

Verplanck, Gulian C. *A Letter to Col. William Drayton, of South Carolina, in Assertion of the Constitutional Power of Congress to Impose Protecting Duties* (New York, 1831).

BOOKS, ARTICLES, ESSAYS, AND OTHER PUBLISHED SOURCES

Adams, Charles Francis, ed. *Memoirs of John Quincy Adams* (Philadelphia: J. B. Lippincott, 1874–1877), 12 vols.

Ames, Herman V., ed. *State Documents on Federal Relations: The States and the United States* (Philadelphia, 1906).

Ambler, Charles H., ed. "Correspondence of Robert M. T. Hunter, 1826–1876." *American Historical Association Annual Report for 1916* (Washington, DC, 1918), 2 vols.

———, ed. *The Life and Diary of John Floyd: Governor of Virginia, Apostle of Secession, and the Father of the Oregon Country* (Richmond: Richmond Press, 1918).

———, ed. "Nathaniel Macon Correspondence." *John P. Branch Historical Papers* (1909), 27–93.

———, ed. "Three Letters from Thomas Ritchie to Howell Cobb." *John P. Branch Historical Papers* 3 (June 1911), 354–57.

American State Papers: Finance (Washington, DC, 1832), 5 vols.

Ammon, Harry. *James Monroe: The Quest for National Identity* (New York: McGraw Hill, 1971).

Anbinder, Tyler. *Nativism and Slavery: The Northern Know Nothings and the Politics of the 1850s* (New York: Oxford University Press, 1992).

Anderson, Dice R. *William Branch Giles: A Study in the Politics of Virginia and the Nation from 1790 to 1830* (Gloucester, MA: Peter Smith, 1965 reprint of 1915 ed.).

Angle, Paul, et al., eds. *Fire the Salute! Abe Lincoln Is Nominated: Murat Halstead Reports* (Kingsport: Kingsport Press, 1960).

Annals of Congress (Washington, DC, 1834–1856), 42 vols.

Ashworth, John. *"Agrarians" and "Aristocrats": Party Ideology in the United States, 1837–1846* (London: Cambridge University Press, 1983).

Atkins, Jonathan M. *Parties, Politics, and the Sectional Conflict in Tennessee* (Knoxville: University of Tennessee Press, 1997).

Bailey, Hugh C. *John Williams Walker: A Study in the Political, Social, and Cultural Life of the Old South* (Tuscaloosa: University of Alabama Press, 1964).

Balogh, Brian. *A Government Out of Sight: The Mystery of National Authority in Nineteenth-Century America* (New York: Cambridge University Press, 2009).

Banks, Ronald F. *Maine Becomes a State: The Movement to Separate Maine from Massachusetts, 1785–1820* (Middletown, CT: Wesleyan University Press, 1970).

Banner, James M. "The Problem of South Carolina." In Stanley Elkins and Eric McKitrick, eds., *The Hofstadter Aegis: A Memorial* (New York: Alfred A. Knopf, 1974).

Banning, Lance. *The Jeffersonian Persuasion: Evolution of a Party Ideology* (Ithaca, NY: Cornell University Press, 1978).

Barnwell, John, ed. "Hamlet to Hotspur: Letters of Robert Woodward Barnwell to Robert Barnwell Rhett." *South Carolina Historical Magazine* 77 (Oct. 1976), 236–56.

Basler, Roy P., ed. *Collected Works of Abraham Lincoln* (New Brunswick, NJ: Rutgers University Press, 1953–1955), 8 vols.

Bassett, John S., ed. *Correspondence of Andrew Jackson* (Washington, DC: Carnegie Institution of Washington, 1926–1933), 7 vols.

Bauer, K. Jack. *Zachary Taylor: Soldier, Planter, Statesman of the Old Southwest* (Baton Rouge: Louisiana State University Press, 1985).

Baxter, Maurice G. *Henry Clay and the American System* (Lexington: University of Kentucky Press, 1995).

Belko, W. Stephen. *The Invincible Duff Green: Whig of the West* (Columbia: University of Missouri Press, 2006).

Belko, William S. *The Triumph of the Antebellum Free Trade Movement* (Gainesville: University Press of Florida, 2012).

Belohlavek, John M. *George Mifflin Dallas: Jacksonian Politician* (University Park: Pennsylvania State University Press, 1977).

Belz, Herman, ed. *The Webster-Hayne Debate on the Nature of the Union: Selected Documents* (Indianapolis: Liberty Fund, 2000).

Bemis, Samuel Flagg. *John Quincy Adams and the Union* (New York: Alfred A. Knopf, 1956).

Bensel, Richard F. *Yankee Leviathan: The Origins of Central State Authority in America, 1859–1877* (New York: Cambridge University Press, 1990).

Benton, Thomas Hart. *Thirty Years' View; or, A History of the Working of the American Government for Thirty Years from 1820 to 1850* (New York: D. Appleton, 1854–1856), 2 vols.

Berg, Maxine. *The Age of Manufactures: Industry, Innovation, and Work in Britain, 1700–1820* (London: Fontana, 1985).

Bergeron, Paul H. *Antebellum Politics in Tennessee* (Lexington: University of Kentucky Press, 1982).

———. *The Presidency of James K. Polk* (Lawrence: University Press of Kansas, 1987).

———. "Tennessee's Response to the Nullification Crisis." *Journal of Southern History* 39 (Feb. 1973), 23–44.

Bigelow, John, ed. *Letters and Literary Memorials of Samuel J. Tilden* (New York: Harper Brothers, 1908), 2 vols.

Bils, Mark. "Tariff Protection and Production in the Early US Cotton Textile Industry." *Journal of Economic History* 44 (Dec. 1984), 1033–45.

Blaine, James G. *Twenty Years of Congress: From Lincoln to Garfield* (Norwich, CT: Henry Bill 1884–1886), 2 vols.

Blakey, George M. "Rendezvous with Republicanism: John Pope vs. Henry Clay in 1816." *Indiana Magazine of History* 62 (1966), 233–50.

Bolt, William K. "Founding Father and Rebellious Son: James Madison, John C. Calhoun, and the Use of Precedents." *American Nineteenth Century History* 5 (Fall 2004), 1–27.

———. "'A Tax in Some Other Form': James K. Polk and the Tariff Debates." *Journal of East Tennessee History* 77 (2015), 26–46.

Borit, Gabor S. "Old Wine into New Bottles: Abraham Lincoln and the Tariff Reconsidered." *Historian* 38 (Feb. 1966), 289–317.

Blue, Frederick J. *Salmon P. Chase: A Life in Politics* (Kent, OH: Kent State University Press, 1987).

Borneman, Walter R. *Polk: The Man Who Transformed the Presidency and America* (New York: Random House, 2008).

Bridgforth, Lucie. "Mississippi's Response to Nullification, 1833." *Journal of Mississippi History* 45 (Feb. 1983), 1–21.

Brock, William R. *Parties and Political Conscience: American Dilemmas, 1840–1850* (Millwood, NY: KTO, 1979).

Broussard, James H. *The Southern Federalists, 1800–1816* (Baton Rouge: Louisiana State University Press, 1978).

Brown, Everett S., ed. *The Missouri Compromises and Presidential Politics, 1820–1825* (St. Louis: Missouri Historical Society, 1926).

Brown, Norman D. *Edward Stanly: Whiggery's Tarheel "Conqueror"* (Tuscaloosa: University of Alabama Press, 1974).

———. "Webster-Jackson Movement for a Constitution and Union Party in 1833." *Mid-America* 46 (July 1964), 147–71.

Brown, Richard H. "The Missouri Crisis, Slavery, and the Politics of Jacksonianism." *South Atlantic Quarterly* 65 (Winter 1966), 55–72.

Brown, Thomas. "Southern Whigs and the Politics of Statesmanship, 1833–1841." *Journal of Southern History* 46 (Aug. 1980), 361–80.

Bruchey, Stuart. *The Roots of American Economic Growth, 1607–1861: An Essay in Social Causation* (New York: Harper and Row, 1965).

Bryant, William Cullen, II, ed. *The Letters of William Cullen Bryant* (New York: Fordham University Press, 1975–1981), 6 vols.

Buck, Solon J., ed. *Pioneer Letters of Gershom Flagg* (Springfield: Illinois State Journal Co., 1912).

Burstein, Andrew. *America's Jubilee: A Generation Remembers the Revolution after Fifty Years of Independence* (New York: Alfred A. Knopf, 2001).

Butler, Joyce. "Rising Like a Phoenix: Commerce in Southern Maine, 1775–1830." In Laura F. Sprague, ed., *Agreeable Situations: Society, Commerce, and Art in Southern Maine, 1780–1830* (Boston: Northeastern University Press, 1987), 15–35.

Capers, Gerald M. *John C. Calhoun—Opportunist: A Reappraisal* (Gainesville: University of Florida Press, 1960).

———. "A Reconsideration of John C. Calhoun's Transition from Nationalism to Nullification." *Journal of Southern History* 14 (Feb. 1948), 34–48.

Cappon, Lester Jesse, ed. *The Adams-Jefferson Letters: The Complete Correspondence between*

Thomas Jefferson and Abigail and John Adams (Chapel Hill: University of North Carolina Press, 1959), 2 vols.

Carman, Harry J., and Reinhard H. Luthin. "The Seward-Fillmore Feud and the Disruption of the Whig Party." *New York History* 24 (July 1943), 335–57.

Chambers, William N. *Old Bullion Benton: Senator from the New West, 1782–1858* (Boston: Little, Brown, 1956).

Cheathem, Mark R. *Andrew Jackson: Southerner* (Baton Rouge: Louisiana State University Press, 2013).

———. *Old Hickory's Nephew: The Political and Private Struggles of Andrew Jackson Donelson* (Baton Rouge: Louisiana State University Press, 2007).

Chernow, Ron. *Alexander Hamilton* (New York: Penguin, 2004).

Clark, Victor S. *History of American Manufactures in the United States* (Washington, DC: McGraw Hill, 1929), 3 vols.

Cole, Arthur H. *The American Wool Manufacture* (Cambridge, MA: Harvard University Press, 1926), 2 vols.

Cole, Donald B. *Martin Van Buren and the American Political System* (Princeton, NJ: Princeton University Press, 1984).

———. *Vindicating Andrew Jackson: The 1828 Election and the Rise of the Two-Party System* (Lawrence: University Press of Kansas, 2009).

Cole, Donald B., and John J. McDonough, eds. *Witness to the Young Republic: A Yankee's Journal, 1828–1870* (Hanover, NH: University Press of New England, 1989).

Coleman, Chapman, ed. *Life of John J. Crittenden: With Selections from His Correspondence and Speeches* (Philadelphia: J. B. Lippincott, 1871).

Collins, Bruce W. "The Democrats' Loss of Pennsylvania in 1858." *Pennsylvania Magazine of History and Biography* 109 (1985), 499–536.

Colton, Calvin, ed. *The Works of Henry Clay: Comprising His Life, Correspondence, and Speeches* (New York: G. P. Putnam's Sons, 1904), 10 vols.

Congressional Globe (Washington, DC, 1834–1873), 44 vols.

Conkin, Paul K. *Prophets of Prosperity: America's First Political Economists* (Bloomington: Indiana University Press, 1980).

Cooper, William J., Jr. *Liberty and Slavery: Southern Politics to 1860* (New York: Alfred A. Knopf, 1983).

———. *The South and the Politics of Slavery, 1828–1856* (Baton Rouge: Louisiana State University Press, 1978).

Coulter, E. Merton. "The Nullification Movement in Georgia." *Georgia Historical Quarterly* 5 (March 1921), 3–39.

Counihan, Harold J. "The North Carolina Constitutional Convention of 1835." *North Carolina Historical Review* 46 (Autumn 1969), 335–64.

Crapol, Edward P. *John Tyler: The Accidental President* (Chapel Hill: University of North Carolina Press, 2006).

Crawford, Aaron S. "Patriot Slaveholder: Andrew Jackson and the Winter of Secession." *Journal of East Tennessee History* 82 (2010), 10–32.

Crenshaw, Ollinger. "The Speakership Contest of 1859–1860: John Sherman's Election a Cause of Disruption?" *Mississippi Valley Historical Review* 29 (Dec. 1942), 323–38.

Crist, Linda L., et al., eds. *The Papers of Jefferson Davis* (Baton Rouge: Louisiana State University Press, 1971–2015), 14 vols.

Cumming, Joseph. "The Cumming-McDuffie Duels." *Georgia Historical Quarterly* 44 (March 1960), 18–40.

Cunningham, Noble E., ed. *Circular Letters of Congressmen to Their Constituents, 1789–1829* (Chapel Hill: University of North Carolina Press, 1977), 3 vols.

Dalzell, Robert F. *Enterprising Elite: The Boston Associates and the World They Made* (Cambridge, MA: Harvard University Press, 1987).

Dangerfield, George. *The Awakening of American Nationalism, 1815–1828* (New York: Harper and Row, 1965).

———. *The Era of Good Feelings* (New York: Harcourt Brace, 1952).

David, Paul A. "Learning by Doing and Tariff Protection: A Reconsideration of the Case of the Ante-bellum United States Cotton Textile Industry." *Journal of Economic History* 30 (Sept. 1970), 521–601.

Davis, William C. *Rhett: The Turbulent Life and Times of a Fire-Eater* (Columbia: University of South Carolina Press, 2001).

Dewey, Davis Rich. *A Financial History of the United States* (New York, 1918).

Donald, David H. *Lincoln* (New York: Simon and Schuster, 1996).

Dorfman, Joseph. *The Economic Mind in American Civilization* (New York: Viking, 1946–1959), 5 vols.

Drake, Winbourne M. "The Mississippi Constitutional Convention of 1832." *Journal of Southern History* 23 (Aug. 1957), 354–70.

Dumond, Dwight L., ed. *Southern Editorials on Secession* (Gloucester, MA: Peter Smith, 1964 reprint of 1931 ed.).

Dunn, Susan. *Dominion of Memories: Jefferson, Madison, and the Decline of Virginia* (New York: Basic Books, 2007).

Dusinberre, William. *Civil War Issues in Philadelphia, 1856–1865* (Philadelphia: University of Pennsylvania Press, 1965).

Earle, Jonathan H. *Jacksonian Antislavery and the Politics of Free Soil, 1824–1854* (Chapel Hill: University of North Carolina Press, 2004).

Eckes, Alfred E. *Opening America's Market: U.S. Foreign Trade Policy since 1776* (Chapel Hill: University of North Carolina Press, 1995).

Edwards, Richard C. "Economic Sophistication in Nineteenth Century Congressional Tariff Debates." *Journal of Economic History* 30 (1970), 802–38.

Egerton, Douglas R. " 'Its Origin Is Not a Little Curious': A New Look at the American Colonization Society." *Journal of the Early Republic* 5 (Winter 1985), 463–80.

———. "Markets without a Market Revolution: Southern Planters and Capitalism." *Journal of the Early Republic* 16 (Summer 1996), 207–21.

Einhorn, Robin L. *American Taxation, American Slavery* (Chicago: University of Chicago Press, 2006).

Eiselen, Malcolm Rogers. *The Rise of Pennsylvania Protectionism* (Philadelphia: Porcupine, 1974 reprint of 1932 ed.).

Ellis, Richard E. *Aggressive Nationalism: McCulloch v. Maryland and the Foundation of Federal Authority in the Young Republic* (New York: Oxford University Press, 2007).

———. *The Jeffersonian Crisis: Courts and Politics in the Young Republic* (New York: Oxford University Press, 1971).

———. "The Market Revolution and the Transformation of American Politics, 1801–1837." In Melvyn Stokes and Stephen Conway, eds., *The Market Revolution in America: Social, Political, and Religious Expressions, 1800–1880* (Charlottesville: University of Virginia Press, 1996), 149–76.

———. "The Persistence of Antifederalism after 1789." In Richard Beeman et al., eds. *Beyond Confederation: Origins of the Constitution and American National Identity* (Chapel Hill: University of North Carolina Press, 1987), 295–314.

————. *The Union at Risk: Jacksonian Democracy, States' Rights, and the Nullification Crisis* (New York: Oxford University Press, 1987).

Ericson, David F. "The Nullification Crisis, American Republicanism, and the Force Bill Debate." *Journal of Southern History* 61 (May 1995), 249–70.

Evans, Eric J. *The Forging of the Modern State: Early Industrial Britain, 1783–1870* (New York: Longman, 1983).

Evitts, William J. *A Matter of Allegiances: Maryland from 1850 to 1861* (Baltimore: Johns Hopkins University Press, 1974).

Faust, Drew Gilpin. *James Henry Hammond and the Old South: A Design for Mastery* (Baton Rouge: Louisiana State University Press, 1982).

Feller, Daniel. *The Public Lands in Jacksonian Politics* (Madison: University of Wisconsin Press, 1984).

————, ed. *Retrospect of Western Travel* (Armonk, NY: M. E. Sharpe, 2000, reprint of 1838 ed.).

Fitzpatrick, John C., ed. *The Autobiography of Martin Van Buren* (Washington, DC, 1920).

Foley, William E. *The Genesis of Missouri: From Wilderness Outpost to Statehood* (Columbia: University of Missouri Press, 1989).

Foner, Eric. *Free Soil, Free Labor, Free Men: The Ideology of the Republican Party before the Civil War* (New York: Oxford University Press, 1970).

————. "The Wilmot Proviso Revisited." *Journal of American History* 61 (Sept. 1969), 262–79.

Forbes, Robert P. *The Missouri Crisis and Its Aftermath: Slavery and the Meaning of America* (Chapel Hill, 2007).

Ford, Lacy K. "Inventing the Concurrent Majority: Madison, Calhoun, and the Problem of Majoritarianism in American Political Thought." *Journal of Southern History* 60 (Feb. 1994), 19–58.

————. "Republican Ideology in a Slave Society: The Political Economy of John C. Calhoun." *Journal of Southern History* 54 (August 1988), 405–24.

Ford, W. C., ed. "Letters to John Brazer Davis," *Proceedings of the Massachusetts Historical Society* 49 (1916), 178–256.

Formisano, Ronald P. *The Transformation of Political Culture: Massachusetts Parties, 1790s–1840s* (New York: Oxford University Press, 1983).

Freehling, William W. *Prelude to Civil War: The Nullification Movement in South Carolina, 1816–1836* (New York: Harper and Row, 1966).

————. *The Road to Disunion: Secessionists at Bay, 1776–1854* (New York: Oxford University Press, 1990).

Garraty, John A. *Silas Wright* (New York: Columbia University Press, 1949).

Gienapp, William. *The Origins of the Republican Party, 1852–1856* (New York: Oxford University Press, 1987).

Graf, Leroy, et al., eds. *The Papers of Andrew Johnson* (Knoxville: University of Tennessee Press, 1967–2000), 16 vols.

Grant, Susan-Mary. *North over South: Northern Nationalism and American Identity in the Antebellum Era* (Lawrence: University Press of Kansas, 2000).

Gunderson, Robert Gray. *Old Gentlemen's Convention: The Washington Peace Conference of 1861* (Madison: University of Wisconsin Press, 1961).

Ha, Songho. *The Rise and Fall of the American System: Nationalism and the Development of the American Economy, 1790–1837* (London: Pickering and Chatto, 2009).

Hamilton, J. G. de Roulhac, ed. *The Correspondence of Jonathan Worth* (Raleigh: Edwards and Broughton, 1909), 2 vols.

Hamilton, J. G. de Roulhac, et al., eds. *The Papers of William A. Graham* (Raleigh: State Department of Archives and History, 1957–), 8 vols.

Hammond, Bray. *Banks and Politics in America: From the Revolution to the Civil War* (Princeton, NJ: Princeton University Press, 1957).

Hargreaves, Mary W. M. *The Presidency of John Quincy Adams* (Lawrence: University Press of Kansas, 1985).

Harrison, Eliza C., ed. *Philadelphia Merchant: The Diary of Thomas P. Cope* (South Bend, IN: Gateway Editions, 1978).

Harrison, Joseph H. "Martin Van Buren and His Southern Supporters." *Journal of Southern History* 22 (Nov. 1956), 438–58.

Hatcher, William B. "Edward Livingston's View of the Nature of the Union." *Louisiana Historical Quarterly* 24 (July 1941), 698–728.

Hecht, Marie B. *John Quincy Adams: A Personal History of an Independent Man* (New York: Macmillan, 1972).

Heidler, David S., and Jeanne T. Heidler, *Henry Clay: The Essential American* (New York: Random House, 2010).

Hesseltine, William B. *Lincoln and the War Governors* (New York: Alfred A. Knopf, 1948).

Historical Statistics of the United States, Colonial Times to 1970 (Washington, DC, 1975).

Hobson, Charles, et al., eds. *The Papers of John Marshall* (Chapel Hill: University of North Carolina Press, 1974–2006), 12 vols.

Holt, Michael F. "The Democratic Party, 1828–1861." In Arthur M. Schlesinger Jr., ed., *History of U.S. Political Parties, 1789–1968* (New York: Chelsea House, 1971), 4 vols. I, 497–536.

———. "The Election of 1840, Voter Mobilization, and the Emergence of the Second American Party System: A Reappraisal of Jacksonian Voting Behavior." In William J. Cooper Jr. et al., eds., *A Master's Due: Essays in Honor of David Herbert Donald* (Baton Rouge: Louisiana State University Press, 1985), 16–58.

———. *Forging a Majority: The Formation of the Republican Party in Pittsburgh, 1848–1860* (New Haven, CT: Yale University Press, 1969).

———. *The Political Crisis of the 1850s* (New York: Wiley, 1978).

———. *The Rise and Fall of the American Whig Party: Jacksonian Politics and the Onset of the Civil War* (New York: Oxford University Press, 1999).

Holzer, Harold, and Norton Garfinkle. *A Just and Generous Nation: Abraham Lincoln and the Fight for American Opportunity* (New York: Basic Books, 2015).

Hopkins, James, et al., eds. *The Papers of Henry Clay* (Lexington: University of Kentucky Press, 1959–1992), 11 vols.

Hopkins, James F. *A History of the Hemp Industry in Kentucky* (Lexington: University of Kentucky Press, 1998).

House Journal.

Howe, Daniel Walker. *The Political Culture of the American Whig Party* (Chicago: University of Chicago Press, 1978).

———. *What Hath God Wrought: The Transformation of America, 1815–1848* (New York Oxford University Press, 2007).

Hunt, Gaillard, ed. *The Writings of James Madison* (New York: G. P. Putnam's Sons, 1900–1910), 9 vols.

Huntington, William, ed. "Diary and Letters of Charles P. Huntington." *Massachusetts Historical Society Proceedings* 57 (Feb. 1924).

Huston, James L. *Calculating the Value of Union: Slavery, Property Rights, and the Economic Origins of the Civil War* (Chapel Hill: University of North Carolina Press, 2003).

————. *The Panic of 1857 and the Coming of the Civil War* (Baton Rouge: Louisiana State University Press, 1987).

————. "Virtue Besieged: Virtue, Equality, and the General Welfare in the Tariff Debates of the 1820s." *Journal of the Early Republic* 14 (Winter 1994), 523–47.

Ilisevich, Robert D. "Henry Baldwin and Andrew Jackson: A Political Relationship in Trust?" *Pennsylvania Magazine of History and Biography* 120 (Jan./April 1996), 37–60.

Isley, Jeter A. *Horace Greeley and the Republican Party, 1853–1861: A Study of the New York Tribune* (Princeton, NJ: Princeton University Press, 1947).

Jackson, Carlton. "The Internal Improvement Vetoes of Andrew Jackson." *Tennessee Historical Quarterly* 25 (Fall 1966), 261–79.

Jeffrey, Thomas E. *State Parties and National Politics: North Carolina* (Athens: University of Georgia Press, 1989).

Jervey, Theodore. *Robert Y. Hayne and His Times* (New York: Macmillan, 1909).

Johannsen, Robert W., ed. *The Letters of Stephen A. Douglas* (Urbana: University of Illinois Press, 1961).

Johnson, Donald Bruce, et al., eds. *National Party Platforms, 1840–1956* (Urbana: University of Illinois Press, 1956).

July, Robert W. *The Essential New Yorker: Gulian Crommelin Verplanck* (Durham, NC: Duke University Press, 1951).

Kennon, Donald R. and Rebecca M. Rogers. *The Committee on Ways and Means* (Washington, DC, 1989).

King, Charles R., ed. *The Life and Correspondence of Rufus King* (New York: G. P. Putnam's Sons, 1894–1900), 6 vols.

Klebaner, Benjamin J. "Poor Relief and Public Works during the Depression of 1857." *Historian* 22 (May 1960), 264–79.

Klein, Philip S. *James Buchanan: A Biography* (University Park: Pennsylvania State University Press, 1962).

————. *Pennsylvania Politics, 1817–1832: A Game without Rules* (Philadelphia: Pennsylvania Historical Society, 1940).

Klein, Robert, ed. "Memoirs of a Senator from Pennsylvania: Jonathan Roberts, 1771–1854." *Pennsylvania Magazine of History and Biography* 61 (Oct. 1937), 446–74.

Klunder, Willard Carl. *Lewis Cass and the Politics of Moderation* (Kent, OH: Kent State University Press, 1996).

Larson, John L. *Internal Improvement: National Public Works and the Promise of Popular Government in the Early United States* (Chapel Hill: University of North Carolina Press, 2001).

Latner, Richard B. *The Presidency of Andrew Jackson: White House Politics, 1829–1837* (Athens: University of Georgia Press, 1979).

Lee, Arthur M. "Henry C. Carey and the Republican Tariff." *Pennsylvania Magazine of History* 81 (July 1951), 280–302.

"Letters on the Nullification Movement in South Carolina, 1830–1835." *American Historical Review* 6 (July 1901), 736–65; 7 (Oct. 1901), 92–119.

"Letters to Bartlett Yancey." *James Sprunt Historical Publications* 10 (1911), 23–76.

"Letters to John Brazer Davis." *Massachusetts Historical Society Proceedings* 59 (1916), 195.

Lepler, Jessica M. *The Many Panics of 1837: People, Politics, and the Creation of a Transatlantic Financial Crisis* (New York: Cambridge University Press, 2013).

Lindstrom, Diane. "American Economic Growth before 1840: New Evidence and New Directions." *Journal of Economic History* 39 (March 1979), 289–301.

Lipscomb, Andrew A., ed. *The Writings of Thomas Jefferson* (New York, 1903–1904), 20 vols.

Livermore, Shaw. *The Twilight of Federalism: The Disintegration of the Federalist Party, 1815–1830* (Princeton, NJ: Princeton University Press, 1962).

Luthin, Reinhard H. "Abraham Lincoln and the Tariff." *American Historical Review* 49 (1944), 609–29.

Macoll, John D. "Representative John Quincy Adams's Compromise Tariff of 1832." *Capitol Studies* 1 (1972), 41–58.

Magness, Phillip W. "Morrill and the Missing Industries: Strategic Lobbying Behavior and the Tariff, 1858–1861." *Journal of the Early Republic* 29 (Summer 2009), 287–329.

Malone, Dumas. *The Public Life of Thomas Cooper, 1783–1839* (New Haven, CT: Yale University Press, 1926).

March, Charles W. *Reminiscences of Congress* (New York: Baker and Scribner, 1850).

Marshall, Lynn. "The Strange Stillbirth of the Whig Party." *American Historical Review* 72 (Jan. 1967), 445–68.

Marszalek, John F. *The Petticoat Affair: Manners, Mutiny, and Sex in Andrew Jackson's White House* (Baton Rouge: Louisiana State University Press, 1997).

Mason, Matthew. *Slavery and Politics in the Early American Republic* (Chapel Hill: University of North Carolina Press, 2006).

McCardell, John. *The Idea of a Southern Nation: Southern Nationalists and Southern Nationalism, 1830–1860* (New York: W. W. Norton, 1979).

McCormack, Thomas J., ed. *Memoirs of Gustave Koerner, 1809–1896: Life Sketches Written at the Suggestion of His Children* (Cedar Rapids, IA: Torch, 1909), 2 vols.

McCormick, Richard P. *The Second American Party System: Party Formation in the Jacksonian Era* (Chapel Hill: University of North Carolina Press, 1966).

———. "Was There a Whig Strategy in 1836?" *Journal of the Early Republic* 4 (Spring 1984), 47–70.

McCoy, Drew R. *The Last of the Fathers: James Madison and the Republican Legacy* (New York: Cambridge University Press, 1989).

McDougal, Walter A. *The Throes of Democracy: The American Civil War Era* (New York: Harper Collins, 2008).

McGrane, Reginald C., ed. *The Correspondence of Nicholas Biddle* (Boston: Houghton Mifflin, 1919).

———. *The Panic of 1837: Some Financial Problems of the Jacksonian Era* (Chicago: University of Chicago Press, 1965 reprint of 1924 ed.).

McIntyre, James W., ed. *The Writings and Speeches of Daniel Webster* (Boston: Little and Brown, 1903), 18 vols.

McPherson, James M. *Battle Cry of Freedom: The Civil War Era* (New York: Oxford University Press, 1988).

Meerse, David E. "The Northern Democratic Party and the Congressional Elections of 1858." *Civil War History* 19 (1973), 119–37.

Meriwether, Robert L., et al., eds. *The Papers of John C. Calhoun* (Columbia: University of South Carolina Press, 1959–2003), 28 vols.

Meyers, Marvin. *The Jacksonian Persuasion: Politics and Beliefs* (Stanford, CA: Stanford University Press, 1957).

Miles, Edwin A. "The Whig Party and the Menace of Caesar." *Tennessee Historical Quarterly* 27 (Winter 1968), 361–79.

Miller, Richard G. "The Tariff of 1832: The Issue That Failed." *Filson Club History Quarterly* 49 (July 1975), 221–30.

Mintz, Steven. *Moralists and Modernizers: America's Pre–Civil War Reformers* (Baltimore: Johns Hopkins University Press, 1995).

Monroe, Dan. *The Republican Vision of John Tyler* (College Station: Texas A&M University Press, 2003)

Mooney, Chase C. *William H. Crawford, 1772–1834* (Lexington: University of Kentucky Press, 1974).

Moore, Glover. *The Missouri Controversy, 1819–1821* (Lexington: University of Kentucky Press, 1953).

Moore, John B., ed. *The Works of James Buchanan* (Philadelphia: J. B. Lippincott, 1901–1911), 12 vols.

Morrison, Michael. "Martin Van Buren, the Democracy, and the Partisan Politics of Texas Annexation." *Journal of Southern History* 61 (Nov. 1995), 695–722.

Morison, Samuel Eliot. *Harrison Gray Otis: The Urbane Federalist* (Boston: Houghton Mifflin, 1969).

Munroe, John A. *Louis McLane: Federalist and Jacksonian* (New Brunswick, NJ: Rutgers University Press, 1973).

Newsome, A. R., ed. "Letters of Romulus M. Sanders to Bartlett Yancey, 1821–1828." *North Carolina Historical Review* 8 (Oct. 1931), 427–62.

Nevins, Alan, ed. *The Diary of Philip Hone* (New York: Dodd, Mean, 1927), 2 vols.

Nevins, Alan, and Milton Halsey Thomas, eds. *The Diary of George Templeton Strong* (New York: Macmillan, 1952), 4 vols.

Nichols, Roy F. *The Disruption of American Democracy* (New York: Macmillan, 1948).

Niven, John. *Martin Van Buren: The Romantic Age of American Politics* (New York: Oxford University Press, 1983).

North, Douglas C. *The Economic Growth of the United States, 1790–1860* (Englewood Cliffs, NJ: Prentice Hall, 1961).

"Original Letters." *William Mary Quarterly* 21 (July 1912), 1–11.

Palmer, Beverly Wilson, ed. *The Selected Letters of Charles Sumner* (Boston: Northeastern University Press, 1990), 2 vols.

Pancake, John. *Samuel Smith and the Politics of Business, 1752–1839* (Tuscaloosa: University of Alabama Press, 1972).

Parish, Peter. "Daniel Webster, New England, and the West." *Journal of American History* 54 (Dec. 1967), 524–49.

Parker, William Belmont. *The Life and Public Services of Justin Smith Morrill* (Boston: Houghton Mifflin, 1924).

Parks, Joseph H. *Felix Grundy: Champion of Democracy* (Baton Rouge: Louisiana State University Press, 1940).

Parsons, Lynn H. *The Birth of Modern Politics: Andrew Jackson, John Quincy Adams, and the Election of 1828* (New York: Oxford University Press, 2009).

Pawson, Eric. *The Early Industrial Revolution: Britain in the Eighteenth Century* (New York: Barnes and Noble Books, 1979).

Peart, Daniel. *Era of Experimentation: American Political Practices in the Early Republic* (Charlottesville: University of Virginia Press, 2014).

———. "Looking beyond Parties and Elections: The Making of United States Tariff Policy in the 1820s." *Journal of the Early Republic* 33 (Spring 2013), 87–108.

Peterson, Merrill D., ed. *Democracy, Liberty, and Property: The State Constitutional Conventions of the 1820s* (Indianapolis: Bobbs and Merrill, 1966).

———. *The Great Triumvirate: Webster, Clay, and Calhoun* (New York: Oxford University Press, 1987).

———. *Olive Branch and Sword: The Compromise of 1833* (Baton Rouge: Louisiana State University Press, 1982).

Peterson, Norma L. *The Presidencies of William Henry Harrison and John Tyler* (Lawrence: University Press of Kansas, 1989).

Phillips, Kim T. "The Pennsylvania Origins of the Jackson Movement." *Political Science Quarterly* 91 (Fall 1976), 489–508.

Phillips, Ulrich B., ed. "Correspondence of Robert Toombs, Alexander H. Stephens, and Howell Cobb." *Annual Report of the American Historical Association for 1911* (Washington, DC, 1913).

Pincus, Jonathan J. *Pressure Groups and Politics in Antebellum Tariffs* (New York: Columbia University Press, 1977).

Poore, Ben Perley. *Perley's Reminiscences of Sixty Years in the National Metropolis* (Philadelphia: Hubbard Brothers, 1886), 2 vols.

Pope, Clayne L. *The Impact of the Antebellum Tariff on Income Distribution* (New York: Arno, 1975).

Potter, David M. *The Impending Crisis, 1848–1861* (New York: Harper and Row, 1976).

Preyer, Norris W. "Southern Support for the Tariff of 1816—a Reappraisal." *Journal of Southern History* 25 (Aug. 1959), 306–22.

Quafie, Milo, ed. *Diary of James K. Polk* (Chicago: A. C. McClurg, 1910), 4 vols.

Rachal, William M. E., et al., eds. *The Papers of James Madison* (Chicago: University of Chicago Press, 1962–1983), 15 vols.

Ratcliffe, Donald J. *The One-Party Presidential Contest: Adams, Jackson, and 1824's Five-Horse Race* (Lawrence: University Press of Kansas, 2015).

———. "The Role of Voters and Issues in Party Formation: Ohio, 1824." *Journal of American History* 49 (March 1973), 847–70.

Rayback, Robert J. *Millard Fillmore: Biography of a President* (Buffalo, NY: Buffalo Historical Society, 1959).

———. "The Silver Grey Revolt." *New York History* 30 (April 1949), 151–64.

Raynor, Wellington G. *The Political and Sectional Influence of the Public Lands, 1828–1842* (Cambridge, MA: Riverside, 1914).

Register of Debates in Congress, 1825–1837 (Washington, DC, 1825–1837), 29 vols.

Remini, Robert V. *Andrew Jackson and the Course of American Freedom, 1822–1832* (New York: Harper and Row, 1981).

———. *Andrew Jackson and the Course of American Democracy, 1833–1845* (New York: Harper and Row, 1984).

———. *Daniel Webster: The Man and His Time* (New York: W. W. Norton, 1997).

———. *The Election of Andrew Jackson* (New York: J. B. Lippincott, 1963).

———. "Election of 1832." In Arthur M. Schlesinger Jr., ed., *History of American Presidential Elections, 1789–1968* (New York: Chelsea House, 1971), 495–516.

———. *Henry Clay: Statesman for the Union* (New York: W. W. Norton, 1991).

———. *Martin Van Buren and the Making of the Democratic Party* (New York: Columbia University Press, 1959).

———. "Martin Van Buren and the Tariff of Abominations." *American Historical Review* 68 (July 1958), 903–17.

Reports of the Secretary of the Treasury of the United States (Washington, DC, 1837), 7 vols.

Reynolds, David S. *Waking Giant: America in the Age of Jackson* (New York: Harper, 2008).

Rezneck, Samuel. "The Depression of 1819–1822: A Social History." *American Historical Review* 39 (Oct. 1933), 28–47.

———. "The Influence of Depression upon American Opinion." *Journal of Economic History* 2 (May 1942), 1–23.

Richards, Leonard L. *The Slave Power: The Free North and Southern Domination, 1780–1860* (Baton Rouge: Louisiana State University Press, 2000).

Richardson, James D., ed. *A Compilation of the Messages and Papers of the Presidents, 1789–1902* (Washington, DC: Government Printing Office, 1905), 10 vols.

Risjord, Norman K. *The Old Republicans: Southern Conservatism in the Age of Jefferson* (New York: Columbia University Press, 1965).

Rives, William C., ed. *Letters and Other Writings of James Madison* (Philadelphia: J. B. Lippincott, 1865), 4 vols.

Roberts, Alasdar. *America's First Great Depression: Economic Crisis and Political Disorder after the Panic of 1837* (Ithaca, NY: Cornell University Press, 2012).

Robertson, Nellie B., et al., eds. *The John Tipton Papers* (Indianapolis: Indiana Historical Bureau, 1942), 3 vols.

Rothbard, Murray N. *The Panic of 1819: Reactions and Policies* (New York: Columbia University Press, 1962).

Sargent, Nathan. *Public Men and Events: From the Commencement of Mr. Monroe's Administration, in 1817, to the Close of Mr. Fillmore's Administration, in 1853* (Philadelphia: J. B. Lippincott, 1875), 2 vols.

Schlesinger, Arthur M. Jr. *The Age of Jackson* (Boston: Little, Brown, 1945).

———, ed. *Congress Investigates: A Documented History* (New York: Chelsea House, 1975), 5 vols.

Schroeder, John H. *Mr. Polk's War: American Opposition and Dissent, 1846–1848* (Madison: University of Wisconsin Press, 1973).

Scott, Nancy, ed. *A Memoir of Hugh Lawson White* (Philadelphia: J. B. Lippincott, 1856).

Seagar, Robert. *And Tyler Too: A Biography of John and Julia Gardiner Tyler* (New York: McGraw Hill, 1963).

Sellers, Charles. "Election of 1844." In Arthur M. Schlesinger Jr., ed., *History of American Presidential Elections, 1789–1968* (New York: Chelsea House, 1971), 747–75.

———. "Jackson Men with Feet of Clay." *American Historical Review* 62 (April 1957), 537–51.

———. *James K. Polk: Continentalist, 1843–1846* (Princeton, NJ: Princeton University Press, 1966).

———. *James K. Polk: Jacksonian, 1795–1843* (Princeton, NJ: Princeton University Press, 1957).

———. *The Market Revolution: Jacksonian America, 1815–1846* (New York: Oxford University Press, 1991).

———. "Who Were the Southern Whigs?" *American Historical Review* 59 (Jan. 1954), 335–46.

Senate Executive Journal.

Senate Journal.

Severance, Frank H., ed. *Millard Fillmore Papers* (Buffalo, NY: Buffalo Historical Society, 1907), 2 vols.

Shanks, Henry T., ed. *The Papers of Willie Persons Mangum* (Raleigh, 1950–1956), 5 vols.

Shenton, James P. *Robert J. Walker: A Politician from Jackson to Lincoln* (New York: Columbia University Press, 1961).

Sherman, John. *John Sherman's Recollections of Forty Years in the House, Senate, and Cabinet: An Autobiography* (Chicago: Werner, 1895), 2 vols.

Shiedly, Harlow W. "The Webster-Hayne Debate: Recasting New England's Sectionalism." *New England Quarterly* 67 (March 1964), 5–29.

Silbey, Joel H., ed. *The American Party Battle: Election Campaign Pamphlets, 1828–1876* (Cambridge, MA: Harvard University Press, 1999), 2 vols.

———. "The Election of 1836." In Arthur M. Schlesinger Jr., ed., *History of American Presidential Elections, 1789–1968* (New York: Chelsea House, 1971), 4 vols., I, 577–600.

———. *Party over Section: The Rough and Ready Presidential Election of 1848* (Lawrence: University Press of Kansas, 2009).

———. *The Shrine of Party: Congressional Voting Behavior, 1841–1852* (Pittsburgh: University of Pittsburgh Press, 1967).

Simms, Henry Harrison. *Life of Robert M. T. Hunter: A Study in Sectionalism and Secession* (Richmond: William Byrd, 1935).

Simms, Mary C., et al., eds. *The Letters of William Gilmore Simms* (Columbia: University of South Carolina Press, 1952–1982), 6 vols.

Sinha, Manisha. *The Counter-revolution of Slavery: Politics and Ideology in Antebellum South Carolina* (Chapel Hill: University of North Carolina Press, 2000).

Skeen, C. Edward. "Calhoun, Crawford, and the Politics of Retrenchment." *South Carolina Historical Magazine* 73 (July 1972), 141–55.

———. *1816: America Rising* (Lexington: University of Kentucky Press, 2003).

Smith, O. H. *Early Indiana Trials and Sketches: Reminiscences by Hon. O. H. Smith* (Cincinnati: Moore, Wilstach, Keys, 1858).

Smith, Sam B., et al., eds. *The Papers of Andrew Jackson* (Knoxville: University of Tennessee Press, 1980–), 6 vols.

Snyder, Charles M. *The Jacksonian Heritage: Pennsylvania Politics, 1833–1848* (Harrisburg: Pennsylvania Historical and Museum Commission, 1958).

Stahr, Walter. *Seward: Lincoln's Indispensable Man* (New York: Simon and Schuster, 2012).

Stampp, Kenneth M. *America in 1857: A Nation on the Brink* (New York: Oxford University Press, 1990).

Stanwood, Edward. *American Tariff Controversies in the Nineteenth Century* (Boston: Houghton Mifflin, 1903), 2 vols.

State Papers on Nullification (Boston: Dutton and Wentworth, 1834).

The Statistical History of the United States: Colonial Times to the Present (Stanford, CT: Fairfield, 1965).

Statutes at Large, 1789–1875 (Washington, DC, 1845–1878), 18 vols.

Stewart, Andrew. *The American System: Speeches Delivered on the Tariff Question, and Internal Improvements* (Philadelphia, 1872).

Stewart, James B. " 'A Great Talking and Eating Machine': Patriarchy, Mobilization, and the Dynamics of Nullification in South Carolina." *Civil War History* 37 (Sept. 1981), 197–220.

Summers, Mark W. *The Plundering Generation: Corruption and the Crisis of the Union, 1849–1861* (New York: Oxford University Press, 1987).

Sydnor, Charles S. *The Development of Southern Sectionalism, 1819–1848* (Baton Rouge: Louisiana State University Press, 1948).

Syrett, Harold C., et al., eds. *The Papers of Alexander Hamilton* (New York: Columbia University Press, 1961–1987), 27 vols.

Taussig, Frank W. *The Tariff History of the United States* (New York: G. P. Putnam's Sons, 1888).

Taylor, George Rogers. *The Transportation Revolution, 1815–1860* (New York: Rinehart, 1951).

Taylor, M. Flavia. "The Political and Civic Career of Henry Baldwin, 1799–1830." *Western Pennsylvania Historical Magazine* 24 (March 1941), 37–50.

Taylor, William R. *Cavalier and Yankee: The Old South and American National Character* (New York: G. Braziller, 1957).

Thornton, J. Mills. *Politics and Power in a Slave Society: Alabama, 1800–1860* (Baton Rouge: Louisiana State University Press, 1978).

Tinkler, Robert. *James Hamilton of South Carolina* (Baton Rouge: Louisiana State University Press, 2004).

Tolbert, Noble J., ed. *Papers of John J. Ellis* (Raleigh, 1964), 2 vols.

Tooley, Mark. *The Peace That Almost Was: The Forgotten Story of the 1861 Washington Peace Conference and the Final Attempt to Avert the Civil War* (Nashville: Nelson Books, 2015).

Tregle, Joseph G. *Louisiana in the Age of Jackson: A Clash of Culture and Personalities* (Baton Rouge: Louisiana State University Press, 1999).

Tyler, Lyon G., ed. *The Letters and Times of the Tylers* (Richmond: Whittet and Sheperson, 1884–1896), 3 vols.

Van Atta, John R. *Securing the West: Politics, Public Lands, and the Fate of the Old Republic, 1785–1850* (Baltimore: Johns Hopkins University Press, 2014).

———. *Wolf by the Ears: The Missouri Crisis, 1819–1821* (Baltimore: Johns Hopkins University Press, 2015).

Van Buren, Martin. *An Inquiry into the Origin and Nature of Political Parties in the United States* (New York: Hurd and Houghton, 1867).

Vipperman, Carl J. *William Lowndes and the Transition of Southern Politics, 1782–1822* (Chapel Hill: University of North Carolina Press, 1989).

Waldstreicher, David. *In the Midst of Perpetual Fetes: The Making of American Nationalism, 1776–1820* (Chapel Hill: University of North Carolina Press, 1997).

Walters, Raymond. *Alexander James Dallas: Lawyer, Politician, Financier, 1759–1817* (Philadelphia: University of Pennsylvania Press, 1943).

Walters, Ronald G. *American Reformers, 1815–1860* (New York: Hill and Wang, 1978).

Watts, Steven. *The Republic Reborn: War and the Making of Liberal America, 1790–1820* (Baltimore: Johns Hopkins University Press, 1987).

Wayland, Francis W. *Andrew Stevenson: Democrat and Diplomat, 1785–1857* (Philadelphia: University of Pennsylvania Press, 1949).

Weaver, Herbert, Wayne Cutler, Tom Chaffin, and Michael David Cohen, eds. *Correspondence of James K. Polk.* 12 vols. (Nashville: Vanderbilt University Press, 1969–1989; Knoxville: University of Tennessee Press, 1993–). trace.tennessee.edu/utk_polk.

Weed, Harriet., ed. *Autobiography of Thurlow Weed* (Boston: Houghton Mifflin, 1884).

Wilentz, Sean. *The Rise of American Democracy: From Jefferson to Lincoln* (New York: W. W. Norton, 2005).

Wilson, Major L. "Andrew Jackson: The Great Compromiser." *Tennessee Historical Quarterly* 26 (Spring 1967), 64–78.

———. *The Presidency of Martin Van Buren* (Lawrence: University Press of Kansas, 1984).

Wiltse, Charles M. *John C. Calhoun: Nationalist, 1782–1828* (Indianapolis: Bobbs and Merrill, 1944).

———. *John C. Calhoun: Nullifier, 1829–1839* (Indianapolis: Bobbs and Merrill, 1949).

———. *John C. Calhoun: Sectionalist, 1840–1850* (Indianapolis: Bobbs and Merrill, 1951).

Wiltse, Charles M., et al., eds. *The Papers of Daniel Webster* (Hanover, NH: University Press of New England, 1974–1989), 15 vols.

Winthrop, Robert C., ed. *Memoir of the Hon. Nathan Appleton* (Boston: John Wilson and Son, 1861).

Wire, Richard A. "Young Senator Clayton and the Early Jackson Years." *Delaware History* 17 (1976), 104–26.

Wise, Henry A. *Seven Decades of the Union* (Philadelphia: J. B. Lippincott, 1881).

Zevin, Robert. *The Growth of Manufacturing in Early Nineteenth Century New England* (New York: Arno, 1975).

DISSERTATIONS AND THESES

Barry, Stephen J. "Nathaniel Macon: The Prophet of Pure Republicanism, 1758–1837." PhD diss., University at Buffalo, 1996.

Coens, Thomas M. "The Formation of the Jackson Party, 1822–1825." PhD diss., Harvard University, 2004.

Crawford, Aaron S. "John Randolph and the Politics of Doom: Slavery, Politics, and Self-Deception." PhD diss., University of Tennessee, 2012.

Cutler, E. Wayne. "William H. Crawford: A Contextual Biography." PhD diss., University of Texas–Austin, 1971.

Dingledine, Raymond C., Jr. "The Political Career of William Cabell Rives." PhD diss., University of Virginia, 1947.

Gantz, Richard A. "Henry Clay and the Harvest of Bitter Fruit: The Struggle with John Tyler, 1841–1842." PhD diss., Indiana University, 1986.

Hoyer, Randall Leigh. "The Gentleman from Vermont: The Career of Justin S. Morrill in the United States House of Representatives." PhD diss., Michigan State University, 1974.

Lee, Arthur M. "The Development of an Economic Policy in the Early Republican Party." PhD diss., Syracuse University, 1953.

Moss, Laura-Eve. "Democracy, Citizenship, and Constitution Making in New York, 1777–1894." PhD diss., University of Connecticut, 1999.

Parkinson, George P. "Antebellum State Constitution Making: Retention, Circumvention, Revision." PhD diss., University of Wisconsin, 1972.

Pribanic-Smith, Erika Jean. "Sowing the Seeds of Disunion: South Carolina's Partisan Newspapers and the Nullification Crisis, 1828–1832." PhD diss., University of Alabama, 2010.

Smith, Caroline P. "South Carolina 'Radical': The Political Career of William Smith to 1826." MA thesis, Auburn University, 1971.

———. "Jacksonian Conservative: The Later Years of William Smith, 1826–1840." PhD diss., Auburn University, 1977.

Spiller, Roger J. "John C. Calhoun as Secretary of War, 1817–1825." PhD diss., Louisiana State University, 1977.

Trask, H. Arthur Scott. "The Constitutional Republicans of Philadelphia, 1818–1848: Hard Money, Free Trade, and States' Rights." PhD diss., University of South Carolina, 1998.

Index

Numbers in **bold** refer to figures